The Cambridge Companion to Lévi-Strauss

Claude Lévi-Strauss is one of the major thinkers of the modern age. Regarded as a crucial figure in the development of structuralism, his writings are studied across a wide range of disciplines, including anthropology, philosophy and literary studies. *The Cambridge Companion to Lévi-Strauss* presents a major reassessment of his work and influence. The fifteen specially commissioned chapters in this volume engage with the controversies that have surrounded his ideas, explore the concealed influences that have shaped his thought and expose the obscuring clichés that have all too often been used by commentators and critics. The contributors are experts drawn from a number of fields, and demonstrate the durability and importance of Lévi-Strauss's work in contemporary thought. Written for students and researchers alike, these incisive, jargon-free essays will be essential reading for anybody who wishes to gain a deeper understanding of this important thinker.

BORIS WISEMAN is Senior Lecturer in the School of Modern Languages and Cultures, University of Durham.

The Cambridge Companion
to Lévi-Strauss

Edited by

Boris Wiseman

CAMBRIDGE
UNIVERSITY PRESS

CAMBRIDGE UNIVERSITY PRESS
Cambridge, New York, Melbourne, Madrid, Cape Town, Singapore, São Paulo, Delhi

Cambridge University Press
The Edinburgh Building, Cambridge CB2 8RU, UK

Published in the United States of America by Cambridge University Press, New York

www.cambridge.org
Information on this title: www.cambridge.org/9780521608671

© Cambridge University Press 2009

First published 2009

Printed in the United Kingdom at the University Press, Cambridge

A catalogue record for this publication is available from the British Library

Library of Congress Cataloging-in-Publication Data

The Cambridge companion to Lévi-Strauss / edited by Boris Wiseman.
    p.   cm.
    Includes bibliographical references and index.
    ISBN 978-0-521-84630-1 (hardback) – ISBN 978-0-521-60867-1 (pbk.)
1. Structural anthropology.   2. Lévi-Strauss, Claude–Philosophy.   3. Lévi-Strauss,
Claude–Criticism and interpretation.   I. Wiseman, Boris.   II. Title.
    GN362.C345 2009
    301.01–dc22

                                                                        2009009062

ISBN 978-0-521-84630-1 hardback
ISBN 978-0-521-60867-1 paperback

Contents

Figures

Contributors

PHILIPPE DESCOLA studied philosophy at the École normale supérieure of Saint-Cloud and ethnology at the École pratique des hautes études (VIe section), where he completed his PhD under the supervision of Claude Lévi-Strauss. After several years of ethnographic fieldwork in Amazonia, he was appointed to the École des hautes études en sciences sociales, first as a Maître de conférences then a Directeur d'études. He became Professor at the Collège de France in June 2000. Philippe Descola was awarded the silver medal of the Centre national de la recherche scientifique (CNRS) in 1996 for his anthropological work on the uses and knowledge of nature in tribal societies. He is the author of numerous articles and books, among them: *La Nature domestique*; *Les Lances du crépuscule*; *Par-delà nature et culture*.

WENDY DONIGER graduated from Radcliffe College and received her PhD from Harvard University and her DPhil from Oxford University. She is the Mircea Eliade Distinguished Service Professor of the History of Religions at the University of Chicago and the author of many books, most recently *The Bedtrick: Tales of Sex and Masquerade* and *The Woman Who Pretended to Be Who She Was*.

PETER GOW is Professor of Social Anthropology at the University of St Andrews. His major ethnographic research has been with the indigenous and other peoples of the Bajo Urubamba River in Peruvian Amazonia, resulting in two books, *Of Mixed Blood: Kinship and History in Peruvian Amazonia*, and *An Amazonian Myth and Its History*, aside from numerous articles. Along with ongoing research on Western Amazonia, he is engaged in a project applying Lévi-Strauss's analysis of myth and history to archival and other materials from the Southern Highlands of Scotland from the late seventeenth century onwards.

MICHAEL E. HARKIN is Professor and Chair of Anthropology at the University of Wyoming. He received his PhD in anthropology from the University of Chicago, and has conducted fieldwork in Canada, the US and France. He is author or editor of five books, including (with Marie Mauzé and Sergei Kan) *Coming to Shore: Northwest Coast Ethnology, Traditions and Visions*. He is editor of the journal *Ethnohistory*, and theme editor for cultural anthropology of the *Encyclopedia of Life Support Systems*, published by UNESCO.

MARCEL HÉNAFF has taught at the University of Copenhagen and at the Collège international de philosophie in Paris. He studied ethnology at the University of Abidjan, Ivory Coast. Since 1988 he has been a Professor at the University of California, San Diego. His publications include *Sade, the Invention of the Libertine Body*; *Claude Lévi-Strauss and the Making of Structural Anthropology*; *Public Space and Democracy* (co-edited with Tracy Strong); *The Price of Truth: Gift, Money, Philosophy* (forthcoming, Stanford University Press; orig. Seuil, 2002: Grand Prix de l'Academie Française); *La Ville qui vient* (City in the making). His main field of research is political philosophy and the anthropology of political institutions and religious practices.

CLAUDE IMBERT is Emerita Professor of Philosophy at the École normale supérieure, Ulm, where she currently coordinates a seminar on 'Art, Creation, Cognition'. She is a member of the European Academy of Sciences and has held posts as Associate Professor at UC Davis and The Johns Hopkins University. She is now Associate Professor at Fudan University (Shanghai). Her main publications are on logic (Greek, Port Royal, and mathematical twentieth-century Logic), and contemporary philosophy. Her most recent essays focus on Cavaillès, Merleau-Ponty, Wittgenstein and Lévi-Strauss, and on a new approach to the human sciences. She is currently writing a book on the relationship between contemporary French philosophy and anthropology, and the conditions of a second modernism. Selected publications include: *Maurice Merleau-Ponty*; *Pour une histoire de la logique*; *Phénoménologies et langues formulaires*.

CHRISTOPHER JOHNSON is Professor of French at the University of Nottingham, specialising in contemporary French thought and the philosophy of technology. He is the author of *System and Writing in the Philosophy of Jacques Derrida*; *Jacques Derrida: The Scene of Writing* and *Claude Lévi-Strauss: The Formative Years*. He is a member of the editorial board of *Paragraph: A Journal of Modern Critical Theory* and a founding member of the Science Technology Culture Research Group at Nottingham.

DENIS KAMBOUCHNER is Professor of Philosophy at the University Paris-I Panthéon Sorbonne. As a historian of early modern philosophy, he is the author of *L'Homme des passions. Commentaires sur Descartes* and *Les*

Méditations métaphysiques de Descartes, I. He has also published various studies on contemporary French thought (Lévi-Strauss, Derrida, Foucault, Bourdieu) and on the philosophy of culture and education, including his essay on 'La Culture', in *Notions de philosophie*.

FRÉDÉRIC KECK is Chargé de Recherches at the CNRS in Paris. He works as a member of the Groupe de Sociologie Politique et Morale, an interdisciplinary laboratory in the social sciences combining theoretical questions with empirical studies. Frédéric Keck has conducted research on the relations between philosophy and the social sciences in the French context (Comte, Lévy-Bruhl, Lévi-Strauss), has translated Paul Rabinow's *French DNA* into French, and is currently beginning a research project on food safety raising contemporary questions on a classical anthropological theme. He has published two books on Lévi-Strauss (2004, 2005) and one on Lévy-Bruhl (2008).

JEFFREY MEHLMAN, University Professor at Boston University, is a literary critic and a historian of ideas. Over a number of years, he has been writing an implicit history of speculative interpretation in France in the form of a series of readings of canonical literary works. His books include *A Structural Study of Autobiography*; *Revolution and Repetition*; *Cataract: A Study in Diderot*; *Legacies: Of Anti-Semitism in France*; *Walter Benjamin for Children: An Essay on His Radio Years*; *Genealogies of the Text* and *Émigré New York: French Intellectuals in Wartime Manhattan, 1940–1944*. In addition, Professor Mehlman's numerous translations, beginning with his collection *French Freud*, have played an important role in the naturalisation of French thought in English.

JEAN PETITOT is a mathematician specialising in dynamical modelling in structural and cognitive sciences. He is currently Director of the CREA (Centre de recherché en épistémologie appliqué) at the École polytechnique and Directeur d'études at the Centre d'analyse et de mathématiques sociales at the École des hautes études en sciences sociales in Paris. He is a member of the scientific committee of CNRS and of the executive committee of many international associations. He is also a member of the Editorial Board of the journals *Western Philosophy Series*, *Mathématiques et sciences humaines*, *Archives de philosophie*, *Intellectica*, *Semiotic Inquiry*, *Analise`*, *Biologica*, *Scripta Semiotica*, *VISIO*. He is the author of *Morphogenèse du Sens* (English translation, Peter Lang); *Les Catastrophes de la parole: de Roman Jakobson à René Thom*; *La Philosophie transcendantale et le problème de l'objectivité*; *Physique du sens*; *Morphologie et* *esthétique* and more than 250 papers. He is also the editor (with F. Varela, J.-M. Roy and B. Pachoud) of *Naturalizing Phenomenology: Issues in Contemporary Phenomenology and Cognitive Science*.

ABRAHAM ROSMAN received a PhD from Yale University. His first field-work was with the Kanuri of Bornu Province in Northern Nigeria. He conducted further research in Iran, Afghanistan, New Guinea and New Ireland. He has taught at Vassar College, Antioch College and Barnard College, Columbia University. He is now Professor Emeritus at Barnard College.

PAULA G. RUBEL has a PhD in anthropology from Columbia University. She carried out fieldwork with an émigré group of Kalmyk Mongols living in the United States. Her doctoral dissertation was published as *The Kalmyk Mongols: A Study of Continuity and Change*. She also did fieldwork in Iran, Afghanistan, New Guinea and New Ireland. She has taught at Hunter College and Barnard College, Columbia University where she is now Professor Emerita.

ERIC SCHWIMMER (born in Amsterdam, Netherlands, in 1923), now retired, became interested in the structuralism of Lévi-Strauss in 1962, when he was a journalist in New Zealand; he decided to become an anthropolo-gist after reading *La Pensée sauvage*. He subsequently did a PhD in anthropology at the University of British Columbia and taught at L'Université Laval, Québec. He has published work on the New Zealand Mâori, on the Orokaiva of Papua New Guinea and, since his retirement, on theoretical topics. The chapter in this volume is based on his researches into the canonical formula for the structural analysis of myth and the place of that formula in a possible future humanistic anthropology.

MARCELA COELHO DE SOUZA teaches anthropology at Brasília University, Brasília, Brazil. Her doctoral research focused on the social organisation and kinship systems of Jê-speaking Central Brazilian indigenous peoples (Museu Nacional of Rio de Janeiro, 2002). She is now carrying out long-term research among the Kisêdjê Indians of the Xingu, centred on experi-ments which involve relations of property and appropriations of (the notion of) culture and concern questions of 'intellectual property', 'traditional knowledge', 'intangible wealth' and 'cultural heritage'. She has published articles related to both these topics.

BORIS WISEMAN is a Senior Lecturer in the Department of French, University of Durham. In 2007 he was made an Inaugural Fellow of the Institute of Advanced Study, Durham University. His research is centrally concerned with various forms of interdisciplinary connections.

He has written extensively about structural anthropology and Lévi-Strauss's aesthetic thought. As part of an ongoing involvement with the International Rhetoric Culture project, he has published on the figure of chiasmus. More recently, his research has focused on qualia and sensory experience. Selected publications include: *Claude Lévi-Strauss and Structural Anthropology*; *Lévi-Strauss, Anthropology and Aesthetics*; *Chiasmus in the Drama of Life* (with Anthony Paul (eds.)), (Berghahn Books, forthcoming).

Introduction

Boris Wiseman

The chapters in this volume aim to demonstrate the continuing relevance and productiveness of Lévi-Strauss's writings for an understanding of the contemporary world. They are emphatically turned towards the *future* of Lévi-Strauss's ideas and theories, their future not only for anthropology, but also philosophy, aesthetics, literary criticism, politics and other areas still. Such an aim does not imply an unconditional acceptance of his ideas, of 'structuralism' or of any kind of orthodoxy. Far from ignoring the criticisms and controversies that have surrounded the dissemination of Lévi-Strauss's thought, these essays have made criticism, contestation and opposition central to the movement forward that they attempt. In *The Raw and the Cooked* (1964a; 1969d; 1970),[1] Lévi-Strauss traces a series of narrative inversions that show that a Bororo myth about the origin of rain-water (the 'reference myth' M1) is a transformation of a group of myths (M7–12) told by a neighbouring Gé population, about the origin of fire. Myths die out, we subsequently learn, when they cease to engender transformations or when they can only transform by becoming something else: a legend, a novelette or simply history. The same could be said about the works of any major thinker; they die out when they cease to engender transformations. The fundamental aim of the readings that follow is to partake in the transformational process, to reread and thereby reinvent the meaning of a series of texts that are far from having exhausted their generative potential, their ability to give rise to new variants that, like the myth-become-legend, break with the past and provide new points of departure. The condition of such transformations is attentiveness to the letter of Lévi-Strauss's texts, to their explicit and implicit fabric of meaning. The readings that follow do not simplify or reduce complex ideas to convenient sound bites. But neither do they unnecessarily obscure or mystify an author often deemed to be difficult. The aim of this volume is to move the debate forward by contributing to a better understanding of Lévi-Strauss's ideas, which it achieves through a kind of virtual interdisciplinary dialogue.

Lévi-Strauss, who has always been suspicious of fashions, once remarked that there were in France only three structuralists: Georges Dumézil, Émile Benvéniste and himself. I interpret this as a warning against the temptation to dissolve Lévi-Strauss's thinking in the homogenising cloud 'structuralism' (the fad, not the system of thought), and as an invitation to be attentive to the specificity and distinctiveness of his writings. In this spirit, the chapters in this volume (see below for a detailed presentation of them) provide a sharply focused re-examination of these writings, of the complex and multifaceted project perused by Lévi-Strauss, of its articulations, its development, its ambiguities and its place in the broader contexts that shaped it and that it has shaped. For, to understand Lévi-Strauss's works properly, one needs to read them with an eye for their connections to their many sources of inspiration – Rousseau, Wagner, Goethe, Proust, Jakobson, and Mauss and others are all discussed in what follows – and for the often secretive relationships those works entertain with one another. Each of his works should thereby take on a new meaning, just as a painting, with which one believes to be familiar, takes on a new meaning when seen as part of a major retrospective which places it side by side with earlier and later works by the same artist, and by other artists belonging to the same sphere of influence.

One may legitimately ask whether versions of 'structuralism', invented *a posteriori* by certain post-structuralist critics, have substituted themselves in the popular imagination at least, for the real thing. These caricatures sometimes present structural anthropology as a kind of quest for binary opposites or reproach it for its alleged formalism. It is seen, in such contexts, as a kind of decoding exercise, whereby signifiers are correlated on a one-to-one basis with their signifieds. In such contexts, post-structuralism is presented, in an equally caricatured way, as an exploration of the 'unstable effect of a never-ending process of signification' (Potts 1996: 19). (Classic post-structuralist readings of Lévi-Strauss's works, such as those by Derrida, are, of course, much more complex than this.) According to such a summary, one would have to label Lévi-Strauss a post-structuralist thinker, if such labels have any meaning. The whole point of the *Mythologiques* (1964a; 1966a; 1968; 1971a), for example, is to show that myths do not have meaning in themselves, but only in relation to each other, hence the need to analyse them in the course of their transformations. Suzanne Saïd (1993: 98) is right to point out that Lévi-Strauss's theory of primitive myth belongs in the allegorical tradition of mythical exegesis which originated in classical antiquity (Lévi-Strauss is a great admirer of Plutarch's writings on myth). However, one needs to qualify this view by adding that it resists assigning to myths a single or fixed coded meaning that predates, as it were, the myths themselves. Hence, Lévi-Strauss criticises Freud's readings of classical mythology, on the grounds that they always favour the psycho-sexual code. For Lévi-Strauss, a myth is not a code so much as a superimposition of multiple codes in which there is no original meaning, no founding or grounding 'signified'. His aim is not to crack the code of myth, in the manner of classical allegorical readings (e.g. in Book XX of the *Iliad* Apollo is fire, Poseidon, water, and the battle of the gods, a battle of the elements). Rather, it is a vast tracking exercise in which he follows, from one end of the American continent to the other, the 'logic' by which myths transform as they are adapted by successive indigenous groups to solve a series of local problems and paradoxes. Amerindian myths are not simply construed as *structures* but also as *forces* that require that the mythographer and his or her reader experience their generative potential and thereby undergo a process of personal transformation, a kind of partial conversion to a mytho-poetic mode of thinking.

More fundamentally still, to follow the development of Lévi-Strauss's thought is to follow one of the major stages in the 'decentring' of twentieth-century Western thought as it has come into contact, via anthropology, with other cultures and modes of thinking. These contacts are not new. However, the development of anthropology over the last century has profoundly modified what it means to experience a culture that is 'other'. Lévi-Strauss, as an anthropologist, has contributed to this new openness (which is not without its own problems and drawbacks, including ethical ones). For the anthropological critique of ethnocentrism – which has shown the constructed nature of our particular cultural point of view – is the condition of access to an understanding of cultural difference; it is what enables us to start to genuinely see and hear other cultures and hence be transformed by them. The value of the confrontation with otherness – or rather with others – is that it results in a modification of our own modes of perception and understanding. It can never result in a fixing of meanings, a simple decoding of signifieds. As Derrida remarks:

Ethnology could have been born as a science only at the moment when a de-centring had come about: at the moment when European culture – and, in consequence, the history of metaphysics and of its concepts – had been dislocated, driven from its locus, and forced to stop considering itself as the culture of reference. (2005: 251)

One might also have cited Foucault, here, who devoted part of the conclusion of *The Order of Things* (*Les Mots et les choses*) (1977) to a joint portrait of psychoanalysis and anthropology (it is clearly *structural* anthropology he has in mind), which he characterises in terms of their shared dislocated position within the field of the 'human sciences', a field in which they have no designated place but which they traverse in its totality, addressing all of its disciplines, modifying their methods, their aims and objectives and the connections between them.

It will already have become obvious from what precedes that it is inadequate to reduce structuralism to the application of a method of analysis. Structural linguistics does not provide Lévi-Strauss with a set of recipes for analysing social phenomena. Linguistics is a body of knowledge and concepts – and indeed metaphors – on which he draws and which he transforms to elaborate his own model of culture. This is apparent, for example, in his ideas about kinship systems, which he construes, by *analogy* with the structure of the phonological system of a language, as a network of differential relations between nuclear families, and one, furthermore, in which the relations are more important than the terms they relate.

Lévi-Strauss does indeed explain the relationship between the symbolic systems (e.g. kinship nomenclatures) that make up social reality and that reality itself in terms of a *langue/parole* distinction (the 'symbolic order' – to use the Lacanian phrase in a somewhat modified sense – he is in effect saying, has an unconscious origin).[2] However, not only is the 'symbolic order' that is realised by any given society always unfinished (1950a: 23; 1987a: 22), it never coincides exactly with its 'ideal', i.e. unconscious, template. There is a mismatch, he recognises as early as 1950, between the level of '*langue*' (the 'emic') and that of '*parole*' (the 'etic'). History, in particular, introduces extrinsic elements that distort or modify a society's underlying symbolic structures (1950a: 20–1; 1987a: 17–19). This is what happens when the social institutions invented by one population are reshaped or distorted as they come into contact with those invented by another, neighbouring population. Furthermore, the different kinds of symbolic systems constitutive of a given society transform at different paces and are thus always incommensurable (1950a: 20–1; 1987a: 17–19).

A close rereading of early essays such as the *Introduction to the Work of Marcel Mauss* (1950a; 1987a), 'The Sorcerer and His Magic' and 'The Effectiveness of Symbols' (both originally published in the 1940s (1949b; 1949c)) – essays that had a profound impact on Lacan, who refers to them in his seminal 'The Mirror Stage as Formative of the Function of the I' (1949) and 'The Function and Field of Speech and Language in Psychoanalysis' or 'Rome Discourse' (1953) – reveals a typically post-structuralist interest in what happens at the margins of the 'symbolic order'. In these essays, Lévi-Strauss is concerned with individuals – shamans, psychopaths, the physically and mentally ill – that the social group places at the borders of the 'symbolic order', requiring that they create symbolic syntheses out of what one might think of as the residues of dominant discourses, fragments that do not quite fit in any collective system of representation. What he calls the 'shamanistic complex' (1963a: 179; 1958a: 197) is an intricate social dynamic involving the shaman, his or her victims or patients, and the social group as a whole. It brings to light, at the very core of social interaction, a constant negotiation in the supply and demand of signifieds and signifiers. At one pole of social life, we have the suffering individual, for whom the experience of pain is made worse by a deficit of signifieds (his/her experiences mean something, but he/she does not know what). At the opposite pole, shamans are professional providers of signifiers (their chants, myths, magical tools, etc.), which they possess in *excess* and which they provide for their patients, along with a narrative that incorporates inchoate impressions into a story.

At a yet deeper level, these essays are concerned with an issue that, in recent years, has come to occupy the centre stage in social theory as well as literary studies – that of the body/sign interface. They bring to light the way in which the social is projected onto, and shapes, the corporeal. The ultimate signifier of the Amerindian medicine song analysed in 'The Effectiveness of Symbols' is the patient's own suffering body. What the shamanistic complex reveals is the inescapable fact that the complementarity of the psychic and the somatic is written into the very structure of the individual's relationship to the social group to which he/she belongs. This is what explains the 'efficacy' – therapeutic or otherwise – of the shaman's symbolic manipulations. And perhaps also those of the artist?

Lévi-Strauss's texts form a complex interrelated whole – but not a *closed* system – a constantly evolving, multifaceted project. They cannot be reduced to the exposition of a reproducible *method*. Their 'scientific' value lies elsewhere: in the reflexive movement, for example, whereby the efficacy of the concepts and models that he deploys is constantly appraised and evaluated, so that one is presented at once with a series of analyses and a kind of running commentary on them. Structural anthropology has indeed taken formalisation to a much further point than many other social theories. The elucidation of patterns of kinship exchange in his early works required collaboration with the mathematician A. Weil. Lévi-Strauss's study of the patterns of mythical transformations led him to formulate his famous canonical equation:

$$fx(a) : fy(b) :: fx(b) : fa^{-1}(y)$$

These formalisations are provisional attempts at describing a complex reality, not a representation of some fixed truth or final cause of the phenomena being studied. They are put forward in the spirit of something *tried out*. The canonical equation captures a formal pattern in the genesis of myths, a kind of double twist (see Maranda 2001: 4). It is essentially chiastic in structure and verifies an intuition that may well have been arrived at via other routes, namely the recurring importance, in creative mechanisms, of a certain kind of inversion, which rhetoricians also understood very well. It does not attempt to reduce mythical thought to a formula but simply to capture something of its creative dynamism. To demystify this four-term homology, whose structure is also intimately related to that of analogical thinking (it is a twisted version of A: B :: C: D), one need only remark that, in principle at least, it could be translated into a sound pattern and, for example, played on a piano. It is telling that if one is to follow Lévi-Strauss to the most abstract point of his formalism, one ends somewhere else, in music, aesthetics or poetics. I do not have the space to do so here, but it would be possible to trace the idea at the core of what Jakobson calls the poetic function – 'the projection of the principle of equivalence from the axis of selection to the axis of combination' (Jakobson 1960: 358) – to Lévi-Strauss's theorisation of classificatory systems in *The Savage Mind* (1966b) and his understanding of the structure of myth, in which narrative *sequences* are also determined by underlying non-sequential equivalences (nature = raw; culture = cooked).

One should substitute in place of the cliché of Lévi-Strauss as a kind of austere scientist, that of an explorer of boundaries. Lévi-Strauss famously described anthropologists as the astronomers of the social sciences (*Structural Anthropology*) (1963a) because they use the *distancing effect* that arises from the contact between the members of different cultures as a tool of understanding. The journey to the boundary does not, however, yield what one expects. For example, the attempt to use mathematics to grasp the structures of transformation in the genesis of myths leads to the discovery that there is already geometry and algebra contained in the images deployed by mythical thought. The relationship between the familiar and the unfamiliar, the close and the far is never a relationship of simple juxtaposition or even opposition, but rather a mutually constitutive dynamic tension which often leads to paradox and reversal. This may explain why Lévi-Strauss so often conceives of the self–other relationship in terms of the figure of chiasmus.[3] Finally, one must also see Lévi-Strauss as more than a scientist, as a writer, in the Barthesian sense. And indeed, the *Mythologiques* is arguably one of the twentieth-century texts that perhaps comes closest to fulfilling Barthes's ideal of the *texte scriptible* (writerly text): a collage of citations, with multiple entries, whose order of reading can be modified and which requires of the reader a perpetual work of assembly, and hence act of creation. With the *Mythologiques*, the analysing/reading subject is, as it were, internalised by mythical discourse, which ends up generating its own analyst/reader (Lévi-Strauss *follows* the paths of transformation dictated by the myths themselves). One might say about the analyst/reader of the *Mythologiques* what Apollinaire says about Autumn crocuses in the poem by the same name, to which Lévi-Strauss devotes a revealing essay in *The View from Afar* (1985a), namely that they are like 'mothers' daughters of their daughters'.

[***]

The chapters in this volume, all specially commissioned with the exception of that by Philippe Descola, are grouped together in four parts – 'Society and culture'; 'Myth and mind'; 'Language and alterity' and 'Literature and aesthetics' – which correspond to some of the key domains in which Lévi-Strauss has made major contributions to contemporary thought. The first part covers key epistemological issues in the anthropological study of other cultures and societies and explores, in more concrete terms, the nature of social organisation.

Society and culture

What is perhaps most striking about the opening chapter of this volume, by Sorbonne philosopher Denis Kambouchner, is its refusal to treat Lévi-Strauss's ideas as a finalised system of thought. Kambouchner reconstructs Lévi-Strauss's grappling with problems and searching for solutions. And in this particular instance, the searching for solutions has continued in the form of a dialogue, since Lévi-Strauss has responded to Kambouchner's chapter, adding his own final twist to the argument developed here (see below Lévi-Strauss's letter to the author). This argument is concerned with Lévi-Strauss's complex and ambivalent relationship to humanism. In the homage he pays to Rousseau in *Structural Anthropology II* (1976a), Lévi-Strauss stigmatises a 'corrupt' and 'narcissistic' humanism that is the flipside (mask) of a vast project of domination. However, at the same time, in other parts of his works, Lévi-Strauss suggests that humanism, in its oldest and most general forms, is by nature connected to the anthropological project of studying the diversity of human cultures. Kambouchner shows that structural anthropology, beyond this constitutive tension, despite its propensity to dissolve subjectivity in broader social structures, despite its rejection of any form of direct identification with the populations it studies, despite its negative (entropic) view of history, nevertheless may be seen to formulate a humanist ideal of sorts – one that provides a good basis for ecological thought, in a broad sense of the term.

Anthropologist Michael E. Harkin, who, like Lévi-Strauss, has worked on the Northwest Coast populations of North America (Heiltsuk, Nuu-chah-nulth), pursues some of the concerns raised by Kambouchner along a different axis – the diachronic axis. What interests Harkin is Lévi-Strauss's thinking about historical processes – how they are lived, imagined and theorised, at once by those involved in them and others. History is, of course, at the very heart of the question of how cultures relate to one another and think about one another. Not least of all because different societies conceptualise historical change in different ways (which is not to say that some societies somehow exist 'outside' of history). In this connection, Harkin complicates Lévi-Strauss's opposition between 'hot' and 'cold' societies by adding to it a third category – that of 'lukewarm' societies. He also raises the key question of the extent to which Lévi-Strauss's generalisations are shaped by the specific histories of the Amerindian societies that he studied, which are all post-colonial societies whose institutions and culture bear the mark of the European invasion. More fundamentally still, he tries to imagine, drawing in part on

Sahlins's own version of structuralism, a truly structuralist history, one that goes beyond showing how 'the historical becomes embedded in mythical structures' (this volume) to analyse how, at the level of a specific society, historical actions, i.e. praxis, are shaped by and in turn shape mythical thought (i.e. ideology). The chain of events that followed the invasion of the New World was in part a function of the 'cognitive habits', as Harkin puts it, of the various protagonists involved.

The next two chapters, the first by Abraham Rosman and Paula G. Rubel, the second by Marcela Coelho de Souza – all three experienced field workers – bring us to the interconnected domains of kinship and exchange, in which Lévi-Strauss made his first major contributions to anthropology. Lévi-Strauss's ideas about kinship may be seen as an elaboration of Marcel Mauss's theory of exchange, formulated in his seminal work *The Gift*. Mauss showed, crucially, that gift-giving was one of the forms taken by a broader and more elemental system of exchanges that is essential to the elaboration and maintenance of social order. He showed that much social life was regulated by a triple unspoken obligation: to give, to receive and to return. Exchange is one of the basic gestures whereby social integration occurs. Lévi-Strauss's original – and controversial – move was to argue that marriage itself takes the form of a gift exchange, an exchange of women between social groups. *The Elementary Structures of Kinship* (1949a; 1969a) thus disentangles the myriad marital rules and customs created by many non-European societies and brings to light the basic, elementary recurring patterns according to which marital exchange takes place. In formulating these new ideas, as Rosman and Rubel show very well, Lévi-Strauss brought about a major shift in anthropological thinking about kinship. One may think of this shift in terms of a move away from theories that see the vertical relations of filiations (e.g. mother–child) as being primordial in the constitution of kinship systems, towards one that treats the horizontal relations between groups (i.e. alliance) as foundational. The radical nature of a theory that denies that the nuclear family is the basic building block of kinship systems has perhaps not quite been measured to its full extent – including by gender theorists. Crucially, Lévi-Strauss's theory also extricates family relations from biology (a point explored by Marcela Coelho de Souza), giving them a new basis in systems of exchange, which are themselves ultimately mapped onto the circuits of verbal exchange – i.e. communication. Rosman and Rubel's chapter is at heart a defence of the validity of Lévi-Strauss's core intuitions and of their applicability in the field. It shows, with reference to a number of ethnographic examples, that structures of exchange of goods and services at *rites de passage* like pregnancy, marriage and funerals are identical to structures based on marriage rules, such as they were analysed by Lévi-Strauss.

Marcela Coelho de Souza's chapter addresses some crucial questions which, despite their technical appearance, go to the core of key issues pertaining to gender theory, the construction of identity, and the foundation of social life. Are families biological or cultural entities? Where does the realm of nature stop and that of culture start? Should one even pose these questions in binary terms and, if not, how should one reconfigure our model of kinship systems? Part of the answer lies in the way that Lévi-Strauss derives concrete kinship systems from mental structures and, more importantly, in his assimilation of these mental structures to structures of exchange. Self and Other, Marcela shows, are exchange partners, constituted as terms *connected* through their *differentiation* regarding a third party (the object of their exchange). Hence, the importance of the brother-in-law in structural models of kinship systems.

Myth and mind

Lévi-Strauss's works progressively move away from the study of relatively concrete social structures, among them kinship systems, towards that of more intangible symbolic systems, such as classificatory systems (including totemism) and myths. This development in the orientation of Lévi-Strauss's thinking goes hand in hand with an increased interest in the functioning of the mind, engaged in the production of symbolic systems of all kinds – i.e. with the mind engaged in creative processes. This explains, in part, the opening up of the relevance of Lévi-Strauss's writings to other fields, among them aesthetics and poetics. It is the issues thrown up by this phase in Lévi-Strauss's thinking that will be addressed in the next section of the Companion, 'Myth and mind'. More particularly, these chapters will generally be concerned with what Lévi-Strauss calls *pensée sauvage*, a 'wild' mode of thought at the heart of cultural creation, which is rooted in an exploration of our sensory environment, and which takes as its basis what structural anthropology calls 'concrete logic' or 'logic of sensible properties'. Unlike so-called 'domesticated' thinking, a utilitarian, i.e. instrumental, mode of thought that aims to act upon and change the world we live in and thereby serve as the motor of 'progress', 'wild' thinking is essentially a disinterested, classificatory mode of thought, whose primary ambition is a kind of symbolic totalisation of experience.

The chapter by Amazonian specialist Philippe Descola explores the contradictory meanings given by Lévi-Strauss to the contrastive opposition between 'nature' and 'culture' according to the various contexts in which he makes use of it: as a tool for the structural analysis of myths and folk classifications, as a philosophical foundation accounting for the origin of society or as an antinomy to be superseded in the edification of a (monist) theory of knowledge which refuses the traditional opposition between the mind and the objective world. Paradoxically, Lévi-Strauss has been seen as either an advocate of a materialist conception of the cognitive process (i.e. one that explains this process by the workings of neural mechanisms) or as an epitome of intellectual dualism (according to this view, culture, a product of the mind, imposes meaning on nature). Descola will show that these diverging interpretations stem from the contradiction between the emphasis Lévi-Strauss places on the 'natural' determinations of culture (the laws of the mind are not different from those that govern the physical world) and his method of analysis wherein 'nature' and 'culture' are treated as universal categories that can be detected everywhere as templates structuring symbolic thought (in spite of the growing ethnographic evidence that most non-modern peoples do not view their cosmologies as being divided between a natural world and a social world).

The major claim made by French philosopher Claude Imbert, in 'On anthropological knowledge', is that Lévi-Strauss has made significant progress towards articulating a different conception of our mental capacities. Three linked enigmas will serve as a guiding thread throughout this philosophical enquiry: that of the provenance of the mathematical structures that underpin kinship exchange (in societies that often do not possess a formalised mathematics), that of the nature of the symbolism at work in Caduveo body painting and that of the nature of the operation, initially uncovered by Mauss, that underpins exchange. Imbert will show that, in order to solve these enigmas, Lévi-Strauss will have to rethink experience itself, in particular free it of its Kantian premises. Doing so, she will show, involves understanding the conditions of possibility of an 'adherent' logic, as she usefully calls it. Much of Western philosophy, starting with the Greeks, was concerned with a logic that is essentially propositional. This is the logic of statements and arguments whose structures of inference, for example, have been formalised in various ways. Imbert shows that Lévi-Strauss rejoins a certain Wittgenstein on the terrain of the exploration of a logic that remains rebellious to propositional articulations, a logic of colours in the case of the latter, a (mytho-) logic of qualities, forms and temporal intervals for the former. One is not all that far, here, from Baudelaire's comment about painting that: 'in certain of its aspects the art of the colourist has an evident affinity with mathematics and music' (1965: 160). And indeed, Imbert's exploration of how 'qualities function as cognitive mediators' (this volume) provides ample material for a philosophy of art.

Philosopher and anthropologist Frédéric Keck's chapter, 'The limits of classification: Claude Lévi-Strauss and Mary Douglas', in many ways complements Imbert's discussion of *pensée sauvage*. 'Wild' thinking, as described by Lévi-Strauss in *The Savage Mind* (1966b), is essentially a classificatory form of thinking that aims to extend a net of ever proliferating categories over a reality which it thereby tries to 'grasp', albeit at the level of the symbol.

Keck's chapter is a reflection on what happens at the very limits of classificatory systems, the point where they encounter 'undecidable' or otherwise problematic elements. It compares the analyses of classificatory systems developed by Lévi-Strauss and Mary Douglas to reveal two contrasting conceptions of the boundaries of classification. To the analysis of risks, found in Douglas's works, Keck opposes an anthropology of the catastrophic, derived from Lévi-Strauss. Here, Keck's chapter also rejoins the reflection started by Harkin about temporality and history, since what is being integrated by classificatory systems, Keck shows, are essentially what we call 'events'.

Anthropologist Eric Schwimmer, in 'The local and the universal', explores a tension in Lévi-Strauss's works which underpins the whole of anthropology – that between the anthropologist's endeavour to understand a particular social group and the ambition to extrapolate from this understanding a form of knowledge that applies across cultures. While Lévi-Strauss always starts with local cultural phenomena – the specific sign systems that underpin a given society's kinship, ecology, history, myths, rites and the internal as well as external comparisons between these sign systems – his final objective is to explore basic universal structures. In early works, he describes these as 'mental', but as the enquiry progresses, the boundary between mental and corporeal structures loses its relevance, Schwimmer shows, and the structures finally elicited (notably in *Mythologiques*) include many orders, at once mental, material and corporeal. Schwimmer begins by surveying the potent resistance encountered by Lévi-Strauss's early theories and then goes on to retrace the exacting epistemological operations that necessarily underlie the attempt to reveal the universal existence of certain fundamental structures within human nature. In the process, he shows that the *Mythologiques*, whose chief operations and outcomes are not well understood by anthropologists or other scholars, reveal the general nature of the concrete, fundamental, mental–corporeal structures that form part of the armature of humankind's everyday strategies and operations. In doing so, he sketches out a series of connections that link Lévi-Strauss's thinking, through that of Durkheim, to some basic tenets of Spinoza's philosophy.

The chapter by Marcel Hénaff, whose research lies at the intersection of philosophy, cultural anthropology and political science, examines Lévi-Strauss's innovative use of the concept of symbolism. It treats the body of ideas relating to this concept as a coherent doctrine, but one that contains elements that are either obscure or remain to be developed and that it is necessary to submit to the test of critical enquiry. Hénaff distinguishes two approaches to the question of symbolism in Lévi-Strauss's works. The first is concerned with the symbolic origin of society, with symbolism as the basis of the construction of a social order. Hénaff shows that the key to the Lévi-Straussian concept of symbolism taken in this sense, is to be sought in the pact of reciprocity implied in the very etymology of the term symbol (in Greek '*sumballein*' = to put together). The second approach is concerned with symbolism as a specific mode of expression, different from that of the sign or the image, for example. Here, the key to the Lévi-Straussian concept of symbolism is to be found in the *operative* or *performative* value he assigns to the symbol. Having distinguished these two approaches to the theory of symbolism, the more difficult question Hénaff raises is, how do they fit together? A clue to the answer, we shall see, is to be found in the workings of a shamanistic cure. This chapter reinforces a key point made on a number of occasions throughout this volume, namely that, contrary to received wisdom, far from ushering the human subject into a world of abstract signs, structural anthropology is very much concerned with the materiality of signs, with the way in which symbolic systems take hold of us, including bodily.

Wendy Doniger, a specialist in the history of religions, in particular Hinduism, deals with a topic already touched upon by a number of contributors to this volume – Lévi-Strauss's theory of mythical thought. Doniger separates the theory of mythical analysis from its practice, rejecting the former and praising the latter. She argues that his classic essay, 'The Structural Study of Myth', provides an unusable technique that reduces its primary example, the myth of Oedipus, to nonsense. Yet, she also shows that his actual analyses, such as that of the myth of Asdiwal, not only yields interesting results but also grows out of a theoretical approach that is not difficult to extract from the applied methods. Doniger focuses, in particular, on his concept of *bricolage* – a form of conceptual DIY – which has borne fruit in many subsequent applied theories of literary analysis and in film studies. Doniger's chapter, which is attuned to what she takes to be core contradictions in Lévi-Strauss's thought – the oscillation between local and universal perspectives that is seen as a strength by Eric Schwimmer is presented, here, as a basic problem – is distinctive for the way in which it balances frank criticism with the attempt to find, in Lévi-Strauss's own thought, a means of getting beyond them.

Language and alterity

When the Spanish conquistadors first travelled to the New World, late in the fifteenth century, they were uncertain whether the 'savages' they encountered fully qualified as humans. Some thought that they were no more than beasts. As it turns out, the 'savages' were asking themselves a similar question about their invaders: are they men or are they gods? Each group was grappling, in its own way, with a question that is as philosophically and ethically problematic today as it was then – that of the nature of otherness. It is this question that the two chapters in the next part of this Companion will address, the first in relation to myth, the second in relation to language.

Anthropologist Peter Gow's chapter is perhaps best read in parallel with that of Michael Harkin, in as much as it is also concerned with the interconnections between myth and history. Gow's approach is innovative and should also be of interest to historians and to students of literature and narratology. His starting point is a curious myth told by Pedro Manuyama Fumachi, a resident of the town of Requena in Peruvian Amazonia. It tells the story of the origin of scabies and includes, as one of its central episodes, the story of an encounter with Jesus Christ. Instead of reading this myth simply as an instance of syncretism, Gow explores its openness to other narratives, such as Christian, and what this tells us about the cultural schemas shaping the mythmaker's world-view. One of the broader issues at stake in this discussion is how different cultures conceive of various kinds of dualism, from twins to the self–other relationship. This is of fundamental importance, he will show, for an understanding of different models of cultural belonging, identity and idigineity, an understanding which is crucial for any reading of colonial history – not least of all the history of the relations between Europe and the New World.

The chapter by Christopher Johnson, a counterpoint to the opening chapter in this volume by Denis Kambouchner, is concerned with a lacuna in Lévi-Strauss's thought, namely a certain blindness, in the elaboration of his model of cultural differentiation, to the specifically linguistic dimension of intercultural contact. Language, as is well known, is invoked by structural anthropology as model of culture and, as such, it is treated essentially in its universal dimensions. But what about languages, in the plural, asks Johnson? The question of the mediating presence of languages – i.e. the question of translation – is, he argues, a subliminal problematic in Lévi-Strauss's work. It may be found in the autobiographical scenes of *Tristes Tropiques* (1973c) and in the demonstrations of the *Mythologiques*. This problematic is one that, furthermore, threatens to undermine Lévi-Strauss's ideal of a democratic humanism rooted in a 'dialogue of cultures'.

Literature and aesthetics

The chapters in the final section of the Companion address a series of literary and aesthetic questions that are thrown up directly or indirectly by Lévi-Strauss's works. These chapters confirm, each in their own way, that the aesthetic questions that are treated by Lévi-Strauss in what may appear to be digressions (see, for example, the passage in Chapter 1 of *The Savage Mind* on a lace ruff painted by the seventeenth-century miniaturist François Clouet) are in fact central to any understanding of structural anthropology.

Lévi-Strauss is a distinctive thinker precisely because his theories are not confined by disciplinary boundaries. He has shown, on the contrary, that anthropological problems frequently lead to aesthetic ones and vice versa.

Literary critic and historian of ideas Jeffrey Mehlman examines the pride of place given to Wagner in the structural analysis of myth and explores the connections between Lévi-Strauss's tetralogy and its operatic antecedent (among them, that between leitmotif and mytheme). To what extent, he asks, is music a privileged medium of mythic analysis? He shows that Lévi-Strauss's fascination with the relationship between myth and music is a legacy of French Symbolism and to be understood in that context. We need to situate Lévi-Strauss's works between the minimalism of Mallarmé and the maximalism of Wagner. On the one hand, Mallarmé's legendary line: 'rien n'aura eu lieu que le lieu'; on the other, Lévi-Strauss's verdict on Wagner's 'Ring' in *The View from Afar* (1987b): 'Au total rien ne se sera passé.' One of the goals of Mehlman's reading of Lévi-Strauss is to place them in the context of the modernist myth of Wagner which, Mehlman argues, can be analysed in quasi-structuralist terms.

The chapter by Jean Petitot, a cognitive scientist and specialist in the philosophy of mathematics, is a vigorous defence of the continuing relevance of structural anthropology to contemporary aesthetic theory. His argument is developed at the intersection of mathematics, philosophy and the history of ideas. He argues convincingly that, beyond the well-known Saussurean and Jakobsonian sources of structuralism, the latter's genealogy is also rooted in Gestaltist conceptions about self-organising forms and morphodynamic thinking about the relationship of parts to a whole in natural organisms. It has perhaps not been sufficiently taken into account that, as Lévi-Strauss himself indicates (1991b: 113; 1988a: 159), key sources for the concept of structure, which is inseparable from that of transformation, are to be found in Goethe's botanical writings (*The Metamorphosis of Plants*, 1790), in D'Arcy Wentworth Thompson's *On Growth and Form* (1917) and in Albert Dürer's *Treatise on the Proportions of the Human Body* (1528). Reading Lévi-Strauss's essay on Nicholas Poussin's *Eliezer and Rebecca at the Well* (in *Look, Listen, Read* (1997)) in the light of this genealogy, Petitot reveals all that it has to offer to an understanding of the conditions of possibility of a purely visual, i.e. immanent, pictorial 'language'.

In as much as it is centrally concerned with the relations between the sensible and the intelligible, my own chapter in this volume approaches some of the key themes broached by Petitot, although from a very different vantage point. It traces the development of Lévi-Strauss's works around the gradual excavation of the logic of sensible qualities already evoked, in this Companion, by Claude Imbert, Frédéric Keck and others. My own concern is with the way in which structural anthropology imbricates the mind and the sensory environment, in its theory of cultural production. Mind and world cannot be thought of in terms of a simple juxtaposition, as the nature/culture dichotomy suggests, and even less as standing in opposition to one another. Lévi-Strauss is well aware of this, even if certain statements may seem to suggest the contrary. As I try to show, he develops a complex theory of cultural creation that places at its heart the dynamic interaction of mental categories and the sensorium. Exploring this theory furthermore provides the opportunity to revisit the question of Lévi-Strauss's relationship to Rousseau and to explore, via some Proustian connections and the art of mnemonics, an insufficiently addressed question – that of the status of the *Mythologiques* as a text.

NOTES

1. A bibliography of works by Lévi-Strauss may be found at the end of this volume. Reference lists, pertaining to other works cited, appear at the end of each chapter.
2. Much has been written about the concept of the unconscious in Lévi-Strauss's thought. Suffice to say, here, that it is not a collective unconscious in a Jungian or Durkheimian sense. It is construed more as the product of a dynamic interaction between self and other, as the outcome of the translation processes which this interaction requires. Like structures, which are relations between systems, it is knowable only through the analysis of transformation.
3. For a more detailed theorisation of the connections between anthropology and chiasmus, see volume I of the Studies in Rhetoric and Culture series to be published by Berghahn Books from 2008: *Culture and Rhetoric*, Strecker and Tyler (eds.) and, in the same series, *Chiasmus in the Drama of Life*, Wiseman and Paul (eds.).

REFERENCES

Baudelaire, C. 1965. *Art in Paris: 1845–1862: Salons and Exhibitions Reviewed by Charles Baudelaire*. Translated by Jonathan Mayne. London: Phaidon Press.
Derrida, J. 2005. *Writing and Difference*. Translated by Alan Bass. London: Routledge Classics.
Jakobson, R. 1960. 'Linguistics and Poetics', in T. A. Sesoek (ed.), *Style in Language*. Cambridge, MA: MIT Press, pp. 350–77.
Maranda, P. (ed.) 2001. *The Double Twist: From Ethnography to Morphodynamics*. Toronto: University of Toronto Press.
Potts, A. 1996. 'Sign', in Robert S. Nelson and Richard Shiff (eds.), *Critical Terms for Art History*. Chicago: University of Chicago Press, pp. 17–30.
Saïd, S. 1993. *Approches de la mythologie grecque*. Paris: Nathan.

Part I

Society and culture

1   Lévi-Strauss and the question of humanism

followed by a letter from Claude Lévi-Strauss

Denis Kambouchner

1

Were we to distinguish the themes purposely adopted as part of a theoretical undertaking from those imposed by an era, then undoubtedly for Lévi-Strauss 'the question of humanism' belongs to the second category. A systematic history of the 'humanist' theme in twentieth-century Europe and notably in post-war France should one day be written. It could not remain a pure history of words and ideas, but would necessarily overflow into social and political history and would encompass what one could call the competition between ecclesiastical forms (church, political parties, intellectual chapels) associated, in the same period, with an exceptionally important and manifest 'ideological' demand. This is as Michel Foucault somewhat bluntly stated in a 1981 interview:

> One cannot imagine into what a moralistic pond of humanist sermons we were plunged in the post-war period. Everyone was a humanist. Camus, Sartre, Garaudy [the official philosopher of the Communist Party] were all humanists. Stalin was a humanist too . . . This does not compromise humanism, but simply allows us to understand that at that time I could no longer think in the terms of that category. (Foucault 2001: 1485–6)

In the aftermath of the Second World War, in a country where the main political parties believed that they bore a message, and where the 'intellectuals' themselves spoke in the name of all, the restoration of a certain confidence in the future of humanity had seemed a priority, just as the reconstruction of cities and economies had been from the outset. Hence, the recurrence of the question which was asked, in various ways, to whoever intended to make a contribution to intellectual life: 'As for man, what do you make of man?' The question was, of course, asked of Sartre, who replied just after the war with the opuscule: *Existentialism and Humanism* (1946; 1948) and, later and in more substantial manner in his *Critique of Dialectical Reason* (1960). The question was also asked of Lévi-Strauss, especially after the reception of the acclaimed *Tristes Tropiques* (1955a; 1973c). This had obviously been made inevitable by the proposal of a discipline called 'structural anthropology' itself and, in *The Elementary Structures of Kinship* (1949a; 1969a), Lévi-Strauss had already advanced a response to the question. The Lévi-Straussian position, as formulated in the early fifties in *Race and History* (1952a; cf. 1978b: 323–63), was simply given more explicit articulation – albeit each time with new inflections – in a number of texts over the following twenty years. Outstanding among these are the last part of *Tristes Tropiques*, entitled 'The Return' (1973c: 373–415); the 1956 note on 'The Three Humanisms' (1978b: 271–4); the 1962 conference on 'Jean-Jacques Rousseau, Founder of the Sciences of Man' (1978b: 33–44); the last chapter of *The Savage Mind*, 'History and Dialectic' (1966b: 245–69); the last page of *The Origin of Table Manners* (1978c: 507–8); the 'Finale' of *The Naked Man* (1981: 625–95), and the 1971 conference on 'Race and Culture' (1985d: 3–24).

Lévi-Strauss's answer to the 'question of humanism', as it arises from the majority of these texts, is of a respectable complexity; it is, however, fairly easy to sketch out, and is also, in its double dimension, fairly well known. It is, in fact, entirely based on the distinction between two forms of humanism: the first praises a certain human essence or liberty, separated from nature, and which is always in danger of being confused with a certain model of the Western man; the other, also present in Western culture without being specific to it, is on the contrary, one of curiosity, interest and respect for the foreign and the distant. The first tries 'to put man out of question' by giving him 'a transcendental retreat' (1978b: 38); the second, inseparable from a 'technique of estrangement' (1978b: 272), proclaims that 'nothing human can be strange to man' (1978b: 274) while 'reintegrate[ing] man in nature' (1981: 687: cf. 1966b: 247). The former, of which Sartrian existentialism could be regarded as a caricature, can be traced back partly to the Cartesian *Cogito* (1978b: 36–8). The other found its herald and founder in Jean-Jacques Rousseau, whose thinking emphasised our identification with all living beings. The former is par excellence cultivated by philosophers, while to the latter belongs to the human sciences, of which Rousseau is considered the founder.

This explains the surprising polarity concerning humanism displayed by two chapters of *Structural Anthropology II* (1978b). On the one hand, humanism is denounced in chapter 2 ('Jean-Jacques Rousseau, Founder of the Sciences of Man') as 'unable to establish the exercise of virtue among men' and, furthermore, as 'corrupted at birth, by taking self-interest as its principle and its notion' (1978b: 41). This 'Cartesian' humanism pertains to a philosophy that, 'imprisoned by the hypothetical evidences of the self . . . believes that [it] proceeds directly from a man's interiority to the exteriority of the world, without seeing that societies, civilisations – in other words, worlds of men – place themselves between these two extremes' (1978b: 36). On the other hand, chapter 15 details the progressive extension of a humanism, which finds its ultimate and 'most general' form in the science of ethnology

(1978b: 271), which displays an interest in comparing cultures, with all the real humility and distance from oneself that this presupposes.

Even then one must add that this second humanism – the only authentic one – has taken three successive forms: the first in the late Middle Ages and the Renaissance when scholars, rediscovering Graeco-Roman antiquity, implemented 'the first form of ethnology' in order to study it (1978b: 272); the second, in the eighteenth and nineteenth centuries, broached the great civilisations of China and India; the third, in the twentieth century, 'concern[ed] itself today with those last still disregarded civilisations – the so-called primitive societies' (1978b: 272), with all the new problems of method and principles these objects could raise. In its first two forms, this humanism would have been indissociable from the pursuit of determined interests (in the first, education; in the second, commerce). In its third form alone does this humanism seem to be based purely on an interest in humanity, or on 'the reconciliation of man and nature'? As it is the sole 'democratic' form of humanism (following an aristocratic form and a bourgeois form), it is the only one which is 'doubly universal' (1978b: 274).

2

Is it necessary, then, to expand further on the 'question of humanism'? Does the clear exposition of this double standpoint not constitute a sufficient reply, liberating us from an inescapable obligation?

On the contrary, it is precisely here that numerous questions arise. First of all, the very structure of Lévi-Strauss's approach presents difficulties. For example, if it is necessary to distinguish two forms of humanism – the one legitimate and fruitful, the other false and pernicious – why was this distinction never explicitly presented, either in the text on 'Rousseau as founder of the sciences of man' or in any other work? Further, how can we explain why it seems that, in all of Lévi-Strauss's work, only the note on 'The Three Humanisms', written in reply to an enquiry, directly expresses ethnology's claim to be the only complete form of humanism – whereas more or less everywhere else humanism is seen as no more than a case of 'concealed mysticism' (1981: 645–6)?

However, if we are to take this apparent *hapax legomenon* seriously, then there arise questions of definition, and therefore also questions of consistency – all of which the 1956 note seems to have wilfully ignored:

(1) According to the terms of this note, 'generalised humanism' would not only be that which 'proclaims that nothing human can be strange to man', but also that which works towards 'the reconciliation of man and nature'. How then can this reconciliation be apprehended? Lévi-Strauss wrote elsewhere that structural anthropology 'reintegrates man in nature' instead of extracting

him from it, as the philosophers did. Is this not taking the risk of dissolving the human into something which is not him? In fact, *The Savage Mind* speaks of 'ventur[ing] to undertake the resolution of the human into the non-human' (1966b: 246). What can this 'humanism' possibly mean, then, if its principal project consists not at all in exalting the specificities and potentialities of the human, but rather in putting the forms and the works of humanity back into the heart of a wider and more anonymous order?

(2) Humanism in its usual sense cannot be turned exclusively towards the past: it implies a certain faith in the future of humanity. But Lévi-Strauss has offered elsewhere a strikingly pessimistic view of history. On the last page of *The Naked Man* (1981), and therefore of *Mythologiques*, Lévi-Strauss writes that his own tetralogy, which was finished a century after Wagner's and 'in harsher times', 'foresees the twilight of man, after that of the gods which was supposed to ensure the advent of a happy and liberated humanity' (1981: 693). Fifteen years before this, the end of *Tristes Tropiques* held a similar stance: the power acquired by man was explained by the fact that the great determinisms of the physical universe no longer appeared as 'fearsome foreigners', and that henceforth they 'use[d] thought itself as an intermediary medium and are [now] colonizing us on behalf of a silent world of which we have become the agents' (1973c: 391). Correlatively, within a great process of entropy which coincides with the dynamics of civilisation, 'the . . . rainbow of human cultures' will in time vanish 'into the void created by our frenzy' (1973c: 414). Strictly speaking, can we find in these conditions an alternative and a programme for the future, one that bases its own thinking on 'the indefinable grandeur of man's beginnings', and recognises 'the immense riches accumulated by the human race on either side of the narrow furrow on which they [the zealots of progress] keep their eyes fixed' (1973c: 393)?

(3) On first approach, the ethnological humanism of the note of 1956 (in Lévi-Strauss 1978b: 271) bears a certain bias, already embodied in various earlier forms, but presented here at greater length. However, a second reading reveals that this ultimate form can emerge only from criticism of its forebears. In proclaiming that 'nothing human can be strange to man', ethnology founds 'a democratic humanism in opposition to those preceding it and created from privileged civilisations for the privileged classes' (1978b: 274). 'Always this side of traditional humanism or even going beyond it', it therefore 'surpasses it' 'in every way' (1978b: 273). If we consider things more closely, it takes very little consequently for *all* humanism of Western tradition to share the defects of 'Cartesian' humanism; in which case ethno-logical humanism, far from inscribing itself within this tradition, draws rather on inspirations or dispositions which are alien to the West. This is confirmed by a passage of 'Race and Culture', in which Lévi-Strauss defends

the 'vast systems of rites and beliefs' of so-called primitive peoples, systems which we often consider as 'ridiculous superstitions' (1987b: 14).

> A plant may be viewed as a respectable being, which one does not pick without a legitimate motive . . . the idea that human beings, animals, and plants share a common stock of life, so that any human abuse of any species, is tantamount to lowering the life expectancies of human beings themselves. All these beliefs may be naïve, yet they are highly effective testimonies to a wisely conceived humanism, which does not center on man but which gives him a reasonable place within nature, rather then letting him make himself its master and plunderer without regard for even the most obvious needs and interests of later generations. (1987b: 14)

By gathering together all the themes that have just been discussed, this text seems to suggest that the ethnologist's humanism – 'seeking its inspiration in the midst of the most humble and despised societies' (1978b: 274) – differs not at all, in essence or intent, from the philosophically structured 'humanism' of the 'primitives'. But, on the other hand, these 'primitives' are busy defending their own culture, and therefore their ecosystem, against all sorts of aggressions, perpetuating wherever possible 'those old particularisms, which had the honour of creating the aesthetic and spiritual values that make life worthwhile' (1987b: 23). Can the words 'humanism' and 'particularism' go together? Does the temptation to draw them together not ultimately confirm that Lévi-Strauss's use of the notion of humanism is subject to unbearable tensions and paradoxes?

In their most general sense, these questions are not new. They all emerged, for one reason or another, during the controversies that sprang up during the fifties and sixties: in the argument with Roger Caillois, the attacks conducted by communists and friends of Georges Gurvitch, and the sparring with Sartre and the *Temps modernes* group about the *Critique of Dialectical Reason.* Amid the various criticisms that arose, which centred less on the problem of cultural relativism than did those of the following decades, one can pick out two or three fundamental recurring objections: that the excavation of structures and laws of structure in the cultures under scrutiny substituted 'a philosophy of constraints' in place of a 'philosophy of liberty' (Lefebvre 1971); that instead of a philosophy of 'praxis' which could answer the questions of contemporary man, Lévi-Strauss, beyond formal analysis, offers only a nostalgic primitivism, turned exclusively towards the fusion of the human with nature, thus signalling his hostility to an intellectual tradition which had nurtured him nonetheless.

The great tensions inherent in Lévi-Strauss's use of the notion of humanism cannot reasonably be denied. However, it is one thing to note them and quite another to subject them to superficial interpretation, hastily concluding that they are incoherent or inconsequential. The theoretical oeuvre, the style and the construction of Lévi-Strauss's work, bear enough signs of exceptional skill for one to abstain from treating the author – as has often been done, especially in France – as a simple ideologist or a rather shallow thinker. Lévi-Strauss displeases on occasion: for example, when he praises 'the old particularisms . . . that make life worthwhile', or when, in a text that is fairly critical of cubism and Picasso ('Apropos of a Retrospective' in 1978b: 276–81), he condemns the sudden fad of contemporary 'false taste' to which, under the criteria of authenticity, a psychopath's 'sense of beauty and truth' (1978b: 279) would be far preferable (he is referring here to the male character in William Wyler's film *The Collector*). However, the proximity of the reference to Rousseau enables us to interpret these occasions as calculated provocations, numerous examples of which can be found in the works of classical authors. As far as the latter are concerned, we do not have the bad taste to suppose that these provocations were upheld *to the bitter end*. Therefore, the least we can do is to admit that the paradoxes linked to Lévi-Strauss's 'humanism' cannot have escaped him, and that he might have added a dose of wit to his distinctive and *non-standard* use of what had become a trite and largely hackneyed notion.

All the fundamental questions we have tried to enumerate here call for clarification – in other words, for a change in the way we look at them, by the end of which Lévi-Strauss's position should have had restored to it all its subtle and fascinating singularity. Three seemingly negative theses provide a starting point; namely: (1) Structural anthropology is not naturalism. (2) The entropic theory of civilisation is not nihilism. (3) The eulogy of 'untamed thinking' (*pensée sauvage*) is not a primitivism. The first theme will be discussed here at length, the second two more briefly.

3

Structural anthropology is not naturalism

The beginning of autumn 1961 found Lévi-Strauss writing *The Savage Mind*'s last chapter, 'History and Dialectic', which was conceived as a philosophical reply to Sartre, whose *Critique of Dialectical Reason*, introduced by *The Problem of Method*, had been published the year before (it was translated into English in 1963). Sartre's work intended, in relation to new developments in the human sciences, not only to save but also to impose the rights of a specifically philosophical analysis, characterised as dialectic and motivated from start to finish by a concern for the human as such. Thus, one could read in the 'Conclusion' of *The Problem of Method*:

Existentialism poses to itself the question of its fundamental relations with those disciplines which are grouped under the general heading of *anthropology*. And – although its field of application is theoretically larger – existentialism is anthropology too, insofar as anthropology seeks to give itself a foundation. (Sartre 1963: 168)

Indeed, added Sartre, in an argument of a Husserlian or Heideggerian style:

The sciences of man *do not question themselves* about man; they study the development and the relation of human facts, and man appears as a signifying milieu (determinable by significations) in which particular facts are constituted (such as the structures of a society, or a group, the evolution of institutions, etc.) . . . But to the degree that anthropology, at a certain point in its development perceives that it is denying man (by the systematic rejection of anthropomorphism) or that it takes him (as the ethnologist does at every moment), it implicitly demands to know what is the *being* of human reality. (Sartre 1963: 168–9)

To the degree that human reality 'makes itself' at each instant (Sartre 1963: 170), this knowledge cannot be direct; it consists rather of a 'rational and comprehensive *non-knowledge*' (Sartre 1963: 174), concerning a being which 'defines itself by his project' and 'perpetually goes beyond the condition which is made for him' (Sartre 1963: 150). This knowledge is provided by philosophy alone.

When writing in *The Savage Mind* that 'the ultimate goal of the human sciences [is] not to constitute, but to dissolve man' (1966b: 247), Lévi-Strauss was taking a view completely opposite to such theses: in reality, anthropology is no more driven to 'deny' man than it is to 'presuppose' him. By definition, it is concerned with man and with man's works; but this is precisely not in order to enclose them within a certain notion of humanity – not even a 'dialectical' notion. On the contrary, wrote Lévi-Strauss:

The pre-eminent value of anthropology is that it represents the first step in a procedure which involves others. Ethnographic analysis tries to arrive at invariants beyond the empirical diversity of human societies . . . However, it would not be enough to reabsorb particular humanities into a general one. This first enterprise opens the way for others . . . which are incumbent on the exact natural sciences: the reintegration of culture in nature and finally of life within the whole of its physico-chemical conditions. (1966b: 247)

And he added as a footnote:

The opposition between nature and culture to which I attached much importance at one time (notably in *The Elementary Structures of Kinship* [1949a; 1969a], chap. I and II) now seems to be of primarily methodological importance. (1969a: 247)

This page has been much discussed: almost thirty years afterwards, Lévi-Strauss was still specifying its meaning and intentions (1998a: 70). In this connection, several points need to be brought to attention:

(1) If we are to take the project of an anthropological science seriously, the first problem posed should not be that of its aim, but that of its method. With

regard to this, Lévi-Strauss has meditated, more than anyone, Rousseau's words in *On the Origin of Language* (chap. 8): 'When one wants to study men, one must look around oneself; but to study man, one must first learn to look into the distance: one must first see differences in order to discover characteristics' (cf. 1978b: 35). This means first of all that in no way can the human sciences begin with the examination of the very subject who sets out to develop them. To do so would amount to taking the premise *I am a human* as the basis of the conclusion *humanity is me*. On the contrary, the human being that is the object of the human sciences is *everything but me*. He is the world – or, rather, the worlds – of men, with everything they hold: a multitude of worlds, which can in some measure come to constitute one's own world only after a very long process of dispossession of oneself. 'To attain acceptance of oneself in others (the goal assigned to human knowledge by the ethnologist), one must first deny the self in oneself' (1978b: 36); in return for this, the *Confessions*, to which without doubt the ethnologist is dedicated (1966b: 250; 1978b: 38–9) will escape sterility. By contrast, 'he who begins by steeping himself in the allegedly self-evident truths of introspection never emerges from them' (1966b: 249). In this respect, through his discipline in which 'the questioner, the question and the questioned are one' (Sartre 1963: 174), Sartre loses himself even more than had Descartes: Descartes's Cogito 'made it possible to attain universality, but conditionally on remaining psychological and individual' (1966b: 249). But Sartre 'socialises the Cogito' (Sartre 1966: 249); as an outcome of his method, 'each subject's group and period now takes the place of timeless consciousness'. Hence, in staying faithful to existentialism, this 'self-admiring activity which allows contemporary man, rather gullibly, to commune with himself in ecstatic contemplation of his own being', contemporary philosophy 'cuts itself off from a scientific knowledge which it despises, as well as from human reality, whose historical perspectives and anthropological dimensions it disregards, in order to arrange a closed and private little world for itself' (1981: 640).

The origin of the sciences of man, which cannot be found in *the experience of the self*, generally cannot, in fact, be found in any *lived experience* but only in collections of facts formed through ethnographic observation. Therefore, subjective phenomena are not ignored at all, but are necessarily put second (see 1981: 627–30). As for naming these facts 'human', or according to them as a subject 'man', this is a 'blank' operation which will add absolutely nothing to our understanding of them.

(2) The formulas of *The Savage Mind*, which situate human science from a standpoint of 'the resolution of the human into the non-human' (1966b:

246), were 'intentionally brutal' (1966b: 247; 1998a: 70) Their provocative nature does not, however, preclude our finding a consistent meaning in them, if we consider jointly three conditions:

(a) It is not a question of making a dogmatic reduction of social and symbolic facts, or individual and collective events, to a nature defined by a determined type of relations and causality. Lévi-Strauss was quick to make this clear: not only is it essential here that 'the phenomena subjected to reduction must not be impoverished' (1966b: 247), but the very process of reduction widens and complicates the reality at which one arrives:

the level taken as superior must, through the reduction, be expected to communicate retroactively some of its richness to the inferior level to which it will have been assimilated. Scientific explanation consists not in moving from the complex to the simple but in the replacement of a less intelligible complexity by one which is more so. (1966b: 248)

In short, scientific explanation consists in a process of analytically integrating the various levels of facts or phenomena. In no way is it a preliminary decision about the real nature of the phenomena studied.

(b) 'The reintegration of culture in nature and finally of life within the whole of its physico-chemical conditions': these words fixed a horizon – that of a great scientific unification to which Kant had already accorded the status of 'regulating idea' in the work of reason. In other words, this reintegration constituted neither a short-term programme nor even a currently conceivable possibility. Undertakings aiming *directly* to reintegrate culture into nature, such as the sociobiology of E. O. Wilson, are to be condemned for their simplicity, their contradictions, their 'overwhelming pretension', and their incapability of reflecting upon the formal properties of culture or justifying their differences of content (1987b: 29–36). In reality, the gap which separates social anthropology and biology remains at the moment 'so enormous that a sound method prompts one to judge it unsurpassable' (1998a: 70; my translation). But in the same way that all progress towards a physico-chemical explanation of life would be valuable – however far off this outcome appears – so also, any analysis that reveals ordering laws in a complex totality of cultural phenomena would represent progress in coming to know an *enlarged nature*, in which the phenomena thus analysed would find their legitimate place. In as much as it discovers these laws and uncovers structures, ethnology cannot fail to inscribe itself in proximity to sciences such as botany, zoology, ethology, crystallography, chemistry or molecular biology (see 1981: 691–2): just like these sciences, ethnology helps to transform our view of the universe by enriching it with new forms, presenting a high degree of stability and surprising complexity.

(c) To a certain extent, it is irrevelant whether or not we regard the universe of structures and laws which are unearthed as 'natural', or whether we prefer the *transcendental place* in which the studied phenomena are reinserted. Going against the 'sociobiologists', Lévi-Strauss underlines the fact that to the extent that culture 'stems from neither genetics nor rational thought', culture is 'neither natural nor artificial' – and this 'even if the demarcation line between nature and culture seems more tenuous and sinuous today than we once fancied' (1987b: 34). In the same way, what is expressed through myths is not only a power of forming and differentiating complex structures but, as we are told in *The Naked Man*, a 'great anonymous voice whose utterance comes from the beginning of time and the depths of the mind' (1981: 640). We may well, then, vary the approaches: the only requirement here is to avoid the traps of an ever more dogmatic dualism, which would have not only the consequence, but also the secret wish, of preventing any serious research. How can one *define* the human in its exteriority to nature, or determine a principle appropriate to all culture, without risking the *petitio principii*, or transforming the analysis into a mere construct, or seeking for each theoretical development the confirmation of a dogmatic hypothesis? With regard to this, even though Lévi-Strauss distinguishes himself from the intellectual universe, the intentions and the rhetoric of Heidegger, he did, in a way, criticise the humanism of philosophers for succumbing to a certain determination of the essence of man (Heidegger 1946). However, for Lévi-Strauss, the problem did not lie in the fact that this essence remained unquestioned: Sartre, when writing that 'man defines himself by his project' (1963: 150), justifies it at length. The problem was only that, in relation to the analysis of the phenomena pertaining to culture, this determination is always simplistic and parasitic. The philosopher who claims to know what makes us human and what defines culture is in reality venturing beyond what he/she actually knows. On this same point, the attitude of structural anthropology is not that of negation, but of a suspension of judgement: structural anthropology is not based on a doctrine but rather, to us an expression of which Lévi-Strauss is fond, on a form of *agnosticism*.

(3) Does *The Savage Mind* (1966b) envisage the resolution of *all* humanity into the 'non-human'? The nature of these categories, both imposing and vague, makes any reply problematic. One cannot, however, fail to appeal here to the difference of register between the structures or ordering laws unearthed by ethnological analysis – structures and laws which are essentially unconscious – and the discourse, reflections and explicit pre-occupations of the members of the societies studied. As regards whether

structural anthropology believed it could explain the former category of facts as precisely as the established social and symbolic forms, the answer is: certainly not. And to say that these structures *command* or *define* the afore-mentioned discourse and reflections, as well as a number of these agents' facts and gestures, does not mean that they entirely *explain* them. As Philippe Descola wrote:

The viewpoint held by Lévi-Strauss, is that of the astronomer, forced by the distance of the objects he studies to extract only their essential characteristics, and not that of the physiologist, who tries to understand the mechanisms according to which the structural regularities which are isolated take a concrete form for the individuals of one society or another. (2005: 143; my translation)

Indeed, Lévi-Strauss himself underlined this:

Gurvitch's error, like that of most opponents of anthropology – and they exist – stems from the fact that he regards the goal of our discipline as the acquisition of a complete knowledge of the societies we study. The disparity between such an ambition and the resources which are available to us is so great that we might be called charlatans, and with good reason. (1963a: 328)

And later:

Do we not turn our backs on this human nature, when, in order to extract our invariants, we replace experiential data with models upon which we perform abstract operations, as the algebraist does with equations? We have sometimes been reproached for this. The objection carries little weight with the expert, who knows with what fastidious fidelity to concrete reality he pays for the liberty of skimming over it for a few brief moments. (1978b: 24)

Concerns, therefore, have often been raised too hastily: the ethnologists are the first to acknowledge that there is and always will be a 'non-reduced' humanity. A work such as *Tristes Tropiques* (1973c) attests to this. And we cannot conclude from the fact that this 'non-reduced' humanity is not raised to the rank of a theoretical object (which, by definition, is impossible, except if theory is reduced to vain rhetoric) that it is ignored as such and not respected. The rule adopted by Lévi-Strauss, which is more Cartesian than he probably had thought, happens in this respect to be recalled in *The Naked Man*: 'The . . . primary duty as thinkers . . . is to explain what can be explained, and to reserve judgement for the time being on the rest' (1981: 686–7). Moreover, what is true concerning *Tristes Tropiques* is, to a certain degree, also true of all other works: 'none of these works is lacking in feeling' (1981: 667).

4

The entropic theory of civilisation is not nihilism

In his 1952 essay on *Race and History,* written at the request of UNESCO (1952a), Lévi-Strauss presented his famous theory of the 'coalition of cultures'. According to this still-famous theory, the springboard for the development of any collective order, in any chosen path of innovation (and not only in that chosen by Western societies), is found less inside a given culture than in its dynamic relationship with others – to such an extent that 'the exclusive fatality, the unique fault which can afflict a human group and prevent it from completely fulfilling its nature, is to be alone' (1978b: 356). From the 'coalition' of several cultures (a word that suggests a long-term relationship and not just an accidental encounter) ensures a 'complex totality of inventions of all orders' which are shared by all the cultures involved, and which define a *civilisation* (1978b: 355). But the positive or productive aspect of these coalitions has its reverse side: the progressive homogenisation of the cultures involved, and the consequent weakening of the 'contrasting features' which influence the dynamics under scrutiny. Hence, 'a strange paradox' (1978b: 358–9) culminating with the unavoidable advent of a 'world civilisation': the greater the sharing, the weaker the prospect of a gain – so much so that a civilisation in which all others had merged would make no progress at all in any direction.

Regarding this growing entropy, the author of *Race and History* (1952a) advised international institutions to watch over cultural diversity, though at the same time warning that:

It will not be enough to favour local traditions and to allow some respite to times gone by. It is the fact of diversity which must be saved, not the historical content given to it by each era (and which no era could perpetuate beyond itself). We must listen to the wheat growing, encourage secret potentialities, awaken all the vocations to live together that history holds in reserve. (1978b: 362)

However, the question remains of knowing whether these formulas – the most clearly 'humanist' in the sense used here – will find an equivalent in later texts. And we cannot fail to compare this text with the end of *Race and Culture* (1987), which is in many respects symmetrical with it:

[T]he road we are taking today is so fraught with tension that racial hatreds offer but a meager image of *the regime of exacerbated intolerance that might be established tomorrow*, without even having to use ethnic differences as a pretext. To circumvent these perils – the ones facing us today and the *even more ominous ones* looming in the near future – we must understand that their causes are *far deeper* than those rooted simply in ignorance and prejudice. We can pin our hopes only on a change in the course of history – *even harder to achieve* than progress in the development of ideas. (1987c: 24; my emphasis.)

The very clear difference in tone between the two texts is, of course, intentional. Lévi-Strauss explained this in his preface to *The View from Afar*:

[I]n order to serve the international institutions, which I felt I had to support more than I do today, I had somewhat overstated my point in the conclusion of 'Race and History.' Because of my age perhaps, and certainly because of the reflections inspired by the present state of the world, I was now [i.e. in 1971] disgusted by this obligingness. (1987b: preface, xiii)

Must one conclude from this that the first text was entirely conventional, and that Lévi-Strauss expressed his true thoughts only in the second, which seems wilfully to retract or destroy, one after the other, any source of reassurance? It is difficult to go as far as this. This author has always given to his beginnings and to his endings a care, an imagination and a musical sense worthy of Proust. The final phrases of his numerous works always contain dark elements, but also flashes of light, following a tonal shading which, even in *The Naked Man* ('his labours, his sorrows, his joys, his hopes and his works will be as if they had never existed' (1981: 695)), never leads to complete gloom. Moreover, one must take into account the problem of history, which Lévi-Strauss has always insisted on portraying as a mere construct, notably in his reply to Sartre (1966b: 256ff.): 'History is therefore never history, but history-for [a group of individuals]' (1966b: 257); historical knowledge is in fact 'discontinuous and classificatory' (1966b: 260); '[history] consists wholly in its method' (1966b: 262); and 'whatever its value (which is indisputable) historical knowledge has no claim to be opposed to other forms of knowledge as a supremely privileged one' (1966b: 262–3). Therefore, there cannot be any 'equivalence between the notion of history and the notion of humanity', despite some philosophers' views that historicity constitutes 'the last refuge of a transcendental humanism' (1966b: 262).

We would be exaggerating the meaning of this set of propositions were we to conclude that all forms of history or historical representation contain an equal dose of arbitrariness, and should be labelled *a priori* as non-truths. The point is only that historical narratives retain some affinities with myth, and obey a series of functions and constraints that are not entirely explained – and, in consequence, that a 'scientific' or exact history is the most improbable of things unless, precisely, it springs from a critical or sceptical awareness of its own status and processes. Applied to the evaluation of the present and the future, this form of historical scepticism implies a qualification upon even the most pessimistic of viewpoints. Indeed, at the end of *Race and Culture*, the ultimate hope for a 'change in the course of history' cannot, in spite of everything, be taken for an empty possibility; the same clause, however, appeared in a discussion about the future of art:

We have no idea what will happen tomorrow in this domain, and I do not believe that we are able to foresee it: either a disintegration, the self-destruction of pictorial art preparing for its own disappearance, or a new departure ushered forth by this sort of Middle Ages in which we currently find ourselves. (1961a: 162)

Two forms of philosophical awareness seem to be intertwined here: the Spinozan awareness (albeit in a negative form) of a powerful necessity weighing down on cultural diversity in a destructive and instantly catastrophic manner; the Bergsonian awareness of a remaining time, 'creator of unforeseeable newness'. From the latter, in *Race and History* (1952a) springs the idea that 'humanity is rich in unforeseen possibilities, each of which will, when it appears, always strike man with astonishment' (1978b: 361); an idea also expressed in the following observation, from *Tristes Tropiques*:

If men have always been concerned with only one task – how to create a society fit to live in – the forces which inspired our distant ancestors are also present in us. Nothing is settled; everything can still be altered. What was done, but turned out wrong, can be done again. (1973c: 393)

Moreover, there is the fact of ethnological thought. Lévi-Strauss never imagined that humanity could find its salvation in the scientific work of a few people. The text of *Race and Culture*, among others, indicates the opposite. But if, according to one of Lévi-Strauss's favourite themes, '[t]he world began without man and will end without him' (1973c: 413; see also 1981: 694–5), we cannot say that, in the world the ethnologist finds in front of him, his own view stands for nothing. *Tristes Tropiques* ended on an ecstasy arising from nature and the contemplation 'of a mineral more beautiful than all our creations', 'the scent that can be smelt at the heart of a lily', or the 'brief glance . . . one can sometimes exchange with a cat' (1973c: 414–15). However, if 'during the brief intervals in which our species can bring itself to interrupt its hive-like activity', it can 'grasp . . . the essence of what it was and continues to be, below the threshold of thought and over and above society', then it is impossible not to have an 'analogous' experience (one needs only to remove the last few words from the formula) in the contemplation of 'the immense riches accumulated by the human race', even outside the 'narrow furrow' that the West persists in digging (1973c: 393). And even if ethnology is the product of remorse – the remorse of the West – a world open to ethnological experience remains richer (even in potentialities) than a world from which this possibility is absent. This is already a key to the last point which we are going to deal with.

5

The interest in 'untamed thinking' is not a primitivism

In a whole series of texts, Lévi-Strauss opposed the wisdom of so-called 'primitive' societies and cultures to the arrogance and irresponsibility of industrial societies. Among these texts, perhaps the most famous is a few lines written for the enquiry 'Witnesses of our Time' (*Le Figaro littéraire*, 25 November 1965). In response to the question, 'what testimonies of the last twenty years would you bury in a time-vault destined to be found by archaeologists in the year 3000?' Lévi-Strauss wrote: 'Documents relative to the last "primitive" societies, on the verge of disappearance; specimens of vegetable and animal species soon to be destroyed by man; samples of air and water not yet polluted' (1978b: 286). And he added: 'Better to leave them [our far-off successors], some evidence of so many things that the misdeeds of our generation and the next will have forever deprived them of knowing: the purity of the elements, the diversity of beings, the grace of nature, and the decency of men' (1978b: 287). Written during the most optimistic years of the second part of the twentieth century, well before the emergence of ecological preoccupations, these lines seem to convey an uncompromising condemnation. And, in fact, Lévi-Strauss does not provide any ready-made answer to the question of whether, in the Western world, any benefit could counterbalance the destruction of natural and cultural equilibriums. The West has certainly made considerable progress, but only in the direction it has 'chosen' (all societies or civilisations having apparently 'chosen' to invest their inventiveness in a determined direction; see 1978b: 339–40) – essentially, in the invention and the mastery of machines (1978b: 342). But what is gained on one count is lost on others; and one is left wondering whether, from a comparative viewpoint, there are any obvious advantages for Westerners? For the ethnologist:

They [societies] all offer their members certain advantages, with the proviso that there is invariably a residue of evil, the amount of which seems to remain more or less constant and perhaps corresponds to a specific inertia in social life resistant to all attempts at organization. (1978b: 387)

But if Western societies can only provide these advantages for their members at the cost of destroying external equilibriums, is this not a determining motive for favouring models of societies which have remained outside 'the cursed cycle' of exploitation and segregation, over those exemplified by Western civilisation?

The terms of this question are too absolute.

Certainly, the structural reconstitution of the ways and rules of 'untamed thinking' is not without a very high level of participation in this mode of thought. For the ethnologist, far from being a simple object, untamed thinking is that to which he tries to give body in the heart of his own language and, conversely, it inhabits him. In the same way, experiencing the concrete world of so-called primitive societies – not only their rites and myths, but also the material and natural environment of which they bear the stamp – necessarily implies a high degree of subjective investment on the ethnologist's part: in a certain way he inhabits this world even when he is not on the spot. One must simply underline that this investment, this way of taking on 'primitive' modes of thought, is not an identification *of anything or anyone in particular*: it is rather an identification – there again remarkably Spinozan – *with an impersonal totality*. And, to this extent, one must not fear that the ethnologist will ever forget *who he is*. That he has a supposedly difficult relationship with his society of origin does not mean he will choose, from the societies he studies, another one in which to settle. A difficult page in *Tristes Tropiques*, written with reference to Rousseau, indicates this fairly explicitly:

> The study of these savages leads to something other than the revelation of a Utopian state of nature or the discovery of the perfect society in the depths of the forest; it helps us to build a theoretical model of human society, which does not correspond to any observable reality, but with the aid of which we may succeed in . . . pass[ing] a valid judgement on our present state. (1973c: 392)

Therefore, if the ethnologist is searching for a 'model', this model does not belong to any society in particular; and, in theory, the construction of this model will bring her to a critical examination of her own society.

Also, on an intellectual level, the very least that can be asked of us is that we dismiss the great ethnocentric oppositions: that, for example, between a 'pre-logical mentality' and rational thought. Even the distinction, which one might be tempted to uphold, between a symbolic mind (that of 'primitive' or, in general, popular cultures) and a conceptual mind, must not be too rigid, if it is to characterise the difference between untamed thinking and the mode of thinking which the ethnologist represents. Rather, the terms to retain are those exposited in chapter 1 of *The Savage Mind*:

> [T]here are two distinct modes of scientific thought. These are certainly not a function of different stages of development of the human mind but rather of two strategic levels at which nature is accessible to scientific enquiry: one roughly adapted to that of perception and the imagination: the other at a remove from it. (1966b: 15)

But, even when it accepts that it shares with mythological thought a form of *bricolage* (1966b: 16–22), ethnological thought cannot forget its self-reflexive mastery of itself. It cannot, therefore, forget that it coincides with a certain apex of scientific thought, which is historically determinable, whilst at the same time being characterised by the highest degree of freedom in relation to any preconceived frames of reference. The 'Finale' of *The Naked Man* reads to this effect:

To adopt the viewpoint of scientific knowledge is therefore not equivalent to smuggling in the epistemological frameworks peculiar to one society to explain other societies; on the contrary . . . it is to accept the fact that the newest forms of scientific thought may be on a par with the intellectual procedures of savages, however lacking the latter may be in the technical resources that scientific knowledge, during its intermediary phases, has allowed us to acquire. (1981: 637)

And on the previous page, the great complexity of things is explained in a long sentence:

cultural relativism would be puerile if, in conceding the richness of civilizations different from our own, and the impossibility of arriving at any moral or philosophical criterion by which to decide the respective values of the choices which have led each civilization to prefer certain ways of life and thought while rejecting others, it felt itself obliged to adopt a condescending or disdainful attitude towards scientific knowledge which, however harmful it may have been, and further threatens to be, in its applications, is *nevertheless a mode of knowledge whose absolute superiority cannot be denied.* (1981: 636; my emphasis)

However, this is relevant only to the extent that one understands that 'it's not a question of the supremacy of the observer, but of the supremacy of observation' (1991b: 154). The ethnologist could never carry out a regression; rather, he/she is committed to enlargement. And one cannot deny that this enlargement is that of Western culture itself, which should find renewed strength in this fact, rather than appearing weakened by it. Everything detestable in this culture lies precisely in a self-satisfied isolationism, which, added to an incomparable voracity, inevitably contributes to its own unhappiness as well as to that of others. By virtue of a complexity about which one should ask to what degree it has been characteristic, one finds that this tendency to isolation has had as its counterpart a movement of openness which dates back to antiquity, and to which, notably, belong the works of Montaigne and Rousseau. This same openness remains to be cultivated. And Western culture, so described, is not at all antinomic, but at one with the effort to uphold a 'solid' and 'lively' system of 'values'. Only when this has been achieved will Western societies reveal themselves capable 'of sustaining or generating intellectual and moral values powerful enough to attract people from outside, people they wish to have adopt these values' (1991b: 153).

6

All things considered, must one retain the word 'humanism'? If this word designates in 'man' something exclusive to hold on to, then it is to be feared that 'man' will receive from this very privilege a sort of mystical status, and foremost that he will shroud himself in an overtly mystified cloak. The first step in removing the idea of humanism from the realm of verbose hypocrisy is to understand and declare that 'man' does not ask to be taken care of, and nor – and even less so – does any determined form of humanity. A form of thinking that is useful to humanity will necessarily look beyond the human, in the direction of its entire substructure and environment; in short, *the interest found in all forms of diversity* could well constitute humanism's real definition. Such is the final lesson of *The Origin of Table Manners*:

> In the present century, when man is actively destroying countless living forms, after wiping out so many societies whose wealth and diversity had, from time immemorial, constituted the better part of his inheritance, it has probably never been more necessary to proclaim, as do the myths, that sound humanism does not begin with oneself, but puts the world before life, life before man, and respect for others before self-interest. (1978c: 508)

This would be the only consequential form of concern for the self – to borrow a term from the Stoics, that of a complete 'oikeiôsis'. But one must add that if this concern is to be demonstrated by actions, it needs neither a programme nor a proclamation: on the contrary, Lévi-Strauss knows their vanity all too well. His humanism has nothing rhetorical about it; it is entirely practical. As such, there is no need to search for it anywhere else but in the ethnologist's work, in each turn of the analysis, and in each acclimation of sight. The ethnologist's duty is to open and leave open, and to prejudge nothing of the rest. This includes even its own effect:

> What is possible? I do not know. By dint of circumstance, ethnologists find themselves as being the unworthy trustees of an immense sociological and philosophical experience – that of societies which we call primitive or without writing – which is being obliterated and therefore our role was to preserve what we could. And if you ask me: 'what lesson have you learnt from this?' I will offer you this one for all it is worth; and as to whether this lesson can serve today's or tomorrow's man? I do not know! (1961a: 65)

One must also take into account the time factor, which on this occasion is also a number factor. After writing the above study, circumstances allowed me to send a copy of it to Claude Lévi-Strauss. A few days later, I received the following letter (I would like to thank Lévi-Strauss for allowing me to reproduce it here):

12 January 2006

Dear Colleague,

You possess an impressive knowledge of my writings. I admire the art with which you arrange your quotations to offer interpretations that are suggestive and always insightful.

I thank you for this. If, however, I were to have any reservations, it would be as regards your tendency to put them all on the same level – to juxtapose, for example, passages from Tristes Tropiques in which my old socialism lingers, and the uncompromising pessimism of my later work.

However, my thoughts have much evolved in the course of time (for instance, between 1952, when I believed it was possible to play according to the rules set by UNESCO, and 1971, when I decided that the best way to help this organisation was to confront it with its own contradictions).

How can we explain this evolution? Two sets of factors come into play, I believe – some internal, the others external.

1. Faced, as were those of my generation – you explain this very well – with the postulate of humanism, but convinced by the experience of ethnology of its limitations, I initially set out in search of the conditions of possibility of a renewed form of humanism. I have, through trial and error, searched for these conditions in very diverse directions – hence my apparent contradictions – only to realise that they destroyed one another and that this critique (in the Kantian sense) of humanism gradually emptied it of its substance.

2. Above all, every day brought to my attention with renewed urgency the catastrophe of the passage, in my lifetime, of the global population from 1.5 billion at the time of my birth, to 2 billion when I was in Brazil, to 6.5 billion today and 9 tomorrow; and as a consequence our planet will become less and less hospitable and will witness the irreversible destruction of numerous forms of life. Confronted with the sheer scale of this phenomenon, against which nothing else matters, to speak of humanism has become futile to me. Evaluated in these terms, the notion of humanism no longer holds any meaning.

[. . .]

I would like, dear colleague, to express my gratitude for your indulgent attention . . . with kindest regards,

Yours sincerely,
Claude Lévi-Strauss

Translated by Yves Gilonne and Jonathan Cottrell.

REFERENCES

Descola, Philippe 2005. *Par-delà nature et culture*. Paris: Gallimard.
Foucault, Michel 1997. *The Order of Things*. London: Routledge.
　 2001. *Dits et ecrits*, volume II. Paris: Gallimard.
Heidegger, Martin 1946. *Ueber den Humanismus*. Frankfurt: Klosterman.
Lefebvre, Henri 1971. 'Claude Lévi-Strauss et le nouvel éléatisme', in *Au-delà du structuralisme*. Paris: Anthropos, pp. 261–311 (first publ.: *L'Homme et la société*, nos. 1 and 2, Paris: Anthropos, 1966).
Sartre, Jean-Paul 1963. *The Problem of Method*. Translated by Hazel E. Barnes. London: Methuen.

2   Lévi-Strauss and history

Michael E. Harkin

Of all the methodological and theoretical issues raised in the human sciences by structuralism, none is more vexed than its relation to history. Part – but only part – of this conundrum is resolved by analysing the various components of the term 'history'. There remain, nevertheless, certain problems in imagining a truly structuralist history, which we will explore below. However, distinguishing 'history' in at least four senses is helpful at the outset. First, and simplest, is the sense of the word meant by professional historians. To paraphrase Wittgenstein, history is what historians do. In this limited sense, we certainly see grounds for accommodation between history and structuralism, and, indeed, for a structural history of the sort produced by Fernand Braudel. Second is what Lévi-Strauss himself means by the term in at least one key passage: philosophical history, of the universal sort, whether in its Hegelian, Marxist, or evolutionist versions. (That is, historical models that assume a universal model of progression in all times and places (1966c: 257).) This he had little use for (although certainly he employs other aspects of Marx's thought) in the sense that such a schema presupposes the very questions that structuralist anthropology wishes to explore: the way that society is organised functionally and symbolically in relation to its own history and to the material world. Third is the sense of history as philosophical historicism, as opposed to universalism. (That is, the methodological and theoretical focus on the local and historically particular, as opposed to the grand sweep of history.) Although one can easily see structuralism as a universal philosophy in the tradition of the *philosophes*, with its emphasis on the global nature of human thought, it also can be seen as a version of Boasian diffusionism (see Darnell 2004). Fourth is history in the sense of diachrony, the passage of time and the change that it produces. This is an area in which structuralism can often seem to be in the business of denying or suppressing history. Certainly, it is more orientated towards synchronic analysis, on the model of Saussurian–Jakobsonian linguistics. To these four senses we may add a fifth: the degree to which societies acknowledge diachrony. Here, perhaps, is the root of the view that structuralism and history are incompatible. Lévi-Strauss divides societies into 'hot' and 'cold': those that embrace history and those that suppress it. Structuralism itself often is thought to be 'cold' in this sense. However, this understanding rests on a confusion of map and territory, as well as on the conflation of Lévi-Straussian structuralism with other structuralisms.

Social science, human science

A large part of the Lévi-Straussian programme during the 1950s and early 1960s was directed towards establishing the institutional identity of anthropology, which in France lagged far behind its status in the United States and Great Britain. Hence, Lévi-Strauss was faced with the problem of finding a space for anthropology, which could be done – both from a practical and a meaningful perspective – only in relation to neighbouring disciplines. As for sociology, still benefiting from the prestige of Durkheim, Lévi-Strauss was relatively scathing about it, in part owing to poor personal relations with the doyen of French Sociology, Georges Gurvitch (Johnson 2003: 15). For Lévi-Strauss, sociology had failed to fulfil the promise of its Durkheimian–Maussian origins as a method of examining unconscious thought in society, and had become, instead, overly implicated in its own society. This positioning of sociology as a 'domestic' social science both undermined its claims to objectivity, and ceded the field of the 'savage' to anthropology. Moreover, by employing the term 'social science' to refer to sociology, while reserving the term 'human science' for anthropology and history, Lévi-Strauss clearly was signifying that the latter were unique in being universal, and had, moreover, superseded the traditional humanistic disciplines such as philosophy. While the traditional humanities were hopelessly embedded in a Eurocentric perspective, the human sciences were capable of dealing with cultural products such as art and religion globally. The relation to history, then, becomes crucial within the context of this strategy. Rather than make the difficult argument that anthropology was *sui generis*, being able to align it with an established prestigious discipline was helpful. The metaphor of complementarity is used in this situation; anthropology deals with the spatially distant; history, with the temporally distant: 'The anthropologist respects history, but he does not accord it a special value. He conceives it as a study complementary to his own: one of them unfurls the range of human societies in time, the other in space' (1966c: 256). If anthropology and history could be properly articulated in this sense, then the frontiers of knowledge in the post-war, post-colonial world would belong to them. Indeed, there was evidence that this was happening. Unlike the 'great man' historiography of the nineteenth and early twentieth centuries, the Annales School demonstrated certain affinities with structuralism, in particular a concern with system and unconscious phenomena. Lucien Fèbvre pursued questions of the *mentalité* of an epoch along lines suggested by Durkheim and Mauss, and thus parallel to those of Lévi-Strauss. Fernand Braudel, whose work transcended the timeframe of traditional narrative history, explicitly acknowledged Lévi-Strauss, calling his own history of the *longue durée* a 'structuralist' style of history (Braudel 1980: 31).

Some years earlier, Lévi-Strauss had proposed a different sort of complementarity, which was republished in *Structural Anthropology*:

The fundamental difference between the two disciplines is not one of subject, of goal, or of method. They share the same subject, which is social life; the same goal, which is a better understanding of man; and, in fact, the same method, in which only the proportion of research techniques varies. They differ, principally, in their choice of complementary perspectives: history organizes its data in relation to conscious expressions of social life, while anthropology proceeds by examining its unconscious foundations. (1967c: 18)

The trope of complementarity was evidently the means by which Lévi-Strauss imagined the relation between the two fields, even as he poured different contents into the same mould. Indeed, as recently as 2001, he reiterated this position, claiming that his critique of history predated the rise of the Annales School:

The article in question [published as chapter 1 of *Structural Anthropology*] was first published in 1949 and dealt with the state of traditional history before the advent of the Annales school, so it tried to establish a kind of contrast but at the same time a complementarity . . . Now I would say that history and ethnology are the same thing, with the slight difference that we study societies spread out in space whereas history studies societies spread out in time. (Massenzio 2001: 420)

Given the founding of the Annales School in 1929, and the post-war prestige of Marc Bloch as both a scholar and martyr of the Resistance, one has difficulty seeing how Lévi-Strauss could have been writing about contemporary historiography without taking into account the Annales School. Even if this claim were supportable, there does appear to be a consistency throughout his thought on the matter for over fifty years.

The trope of complementarity is so powerful that it seems to obscure other sorts of distinctions. Indeed, seeing the two fields viewed as so thoroughly complementary is strange, on both the spatial–temporal and conscious–unconscious axes. This fact would seem to support the common criticism of structuralist thought as being little more than a dressed-up form of binary logic, fond of placing complex phenomena into little boxes. Moreover, Lévi-Strauss's various statements are in some ways contradictory. How could anthropology apply the 'same method' as history, or indeed be the 'same thing', when clearly the experience of field research – even for Lévi-Strauss, who completed relatively little of it in proportion to his publication – was fundamental to the former? Indeed, although he was never a master field worker, his memoir *Tristes Tropiques* continues to define the experience of anthropological field research for the lay public. While it is true – and this is what I believe he is alluding to in the 2001 interview – that the methods of anthropology have been widely borrowed by historians, and vice versa, this development is far from complete; indeed, the group of scholars who apply both approaches (and who form loose groups under the rubrics of 'ethnohistory' or 'historical anthropology') remains relatively small within either discipline.

The 'debate' with Sartre

The trope of complementarity seems instead to be a sort of Derridian alibi, which 'covers' a variety of positions, most of which in fact marginalise history with respect to anthropology. Indeed, plentiful evidence exists that Lévi-Strauss's view of history as a companion field was in a strong sense asymmetrical. While the spatial distancing of ethnographic fieldwork was viewed as an epistemological asset – *le regard eloigné* – the distancing of history faced certain temporal-epistemological horizons (similar to what Foucault calls *épistémés*). Lévi-Strauss argues this point using schoolboy-familiar French history: the Revolution and the mid-seventeenth-century Fronde:

We are still 'in focus' so far as the French Revolution is concerned, but so we should have been in relation to the Fronde had we lived earlier. The former will rapidly cease to afford a coherent image on which our action can be modeled, just as the latter has already done. What we learn from reading Retz [Cardinal Retz, a contemporary of Mazarin and memoirist of the Fronde] is that thought is powerless to extract a scheme of interpretation from events long past. (1966c: 254–5)

This passage must be read against the background of his 'debate' with Sartre over the *Critique of Dialectical Reason*, and more generally against the notion of world-historical action, which requires, axiomatically, a comprehension of one's historical 'moment'. In other words, to be an actor 'within' history, as opposed to those 'without', one must be aware of the precise stage of unfolding of the class conflict pertaining to one's time and place (see Gow 2001: 16). Thus, the issue in 'reading' the events of the Fronde is, in effect, the problems of translating the past political situation into the recognisable terms of class struggle, which, by definition, bridges the time span between the two sets of events. This assumes that 'history' is something other than what Lévi-Strauss considers it to be; it has its own reality and logic, whereas for Lévi-Strauss it is ontologically and epistemologically indistinct from culture and the human sciences. Additionally, Lévi-Strauss presents here a more radical critique of the possibility of historical understanding, as opposed to the simple preservation of information about the past. Thus, our understanding of the French Revolution is as a 'myth', about which we may ask, 'Under what conditions is the myth of the French Revolution possible' (1966c: 254)? This dynamic applies not only to those who, like Sartre, wish to deploy the myth to contemporary ends, but more generally to the possibility of situating one's own life and society with respect to the past. This is part and parcel of the professional historian's narrative craft: to assemble the details of lives and actions past in a manner intelligible to contemporary readers.

As our ability to maintain 'focus' dissipates with time, we are like the myopic who can no longer see panoramas but only the close details of things in front of him. Similarly, historical understanding dissolves into the particularistic detail of what Sartre calls 'the contingent', ultimately arriving at the point of incomprehensibility. We cannot know the past as other than bits of information, without the synoptic power of myth, which is to say contemporary myth. As George Steiner commented, 'Our sense of history, with its dates and implicit forward motion, is a very special, arbitrary reading of reality. It is not natural but culturally acquired' (1970: 176).

Here, Lévi-Strauss is travelling the well-trodden ground of historians and philosophers of history. Herbert Butterfield's 1931 *The Whig Interpretation of History* makes much the same historiographic point, although in the more limited sense that British history had tended to be viewed through the lens of British cultural and political whiggishness. By the 1970s, Hayden White's synthesis of the problems of historical representation and the linkage of political perspective and literary genre had achieved a degree of generality and sophistication, allowing it to be applicable to all historiography (White 1973). However, in Lévi-Strauss we see a more profound sense of epistemological pessimism. Not only is it objectively impossible (as well as intellectually insupportable) to maintain a myth of world-historical action with regard to all times and places, but it is equally hopeless to construct an intelligible history of any sort, at least without moving beyond the bounds of history itself into, of course, anthropology: 'As we say of certain careers, history may lead to anything, provided you get out of it' (1966c: 262; see Hartog 2005).

Lévi-Strauss's notion of 'myth' as it applies to history is worth examining. On one level, this word can of course be read as a discipline-specific insult, along the lines of calling physicians 'quacks'. Quite likely Lévi-Strauss did intend to be provocative in this way, as he makes clear in this same chapter that history enjoys an unearnt prestige among the human sciences, and has become the last bastion of the old transcendental-humanism rearguard. Clearly, taking the historians down a peg was good institutionally for anthropology, which could then step into the breach. Beyond this, the indictment of history is both more profound and less scurrilous when we consider that, for

Lévi-Strauss, myth was the universal condition of humankind. All significant thought in all cultures was embodied in myth, and Western culture was only a partial exception. The exception entailed scientific discourse, of which anthropology was certainly part, as a means of getting beyond myth. However, that which dealt specifically with a society's own conception of itself is by definition a myth. Myth is a projection of a culture's values and sense of being onto a transcendental plane: precisely what he believes Sartre is doing. What is particularly significant and ironic from the standpoint of the discipline of history is the tendency of myth to obliterate change, whether in the extreme case of 'cold societies', which deny diachrony, or the case of Western 'hot' societies, which believe rather that change is both constant and continuous. The discipline of history is based on the illusion that historical epochs seamlessly succeed one another, leading to the present:

History seems to restore to us, not separate states, but the passage from one state to another in a continuous form. And as we believe that we apprehend the trend of our personal history as a continuous change, historical knowledge appears to confirm the evidence of inner sense. (1966c: 256)

The illusion of continuity of a time span crossing a variety of irreversible thresholds, such as the rise and fall of regimes, the development of new technology, and – a topic of particular concern to Lévi-Strauss – demographic change, can be maintained only on the plane of myth. The origin of this illusion as Lévi-Strauss imagines it in this passage is surprising: the sense of continuous change characteristic of the individual consciousness of time passing. The unspoken implication here is that, just as Sartre and Heidegger had argued that Western consciousness was founded on a denial of death – the ultimate discontinuity – so historical thought was based upon a denial of historical rupture. The historiographic charter myth is, then, a posing of the existential question in a particularly Western way. The non-being of historical cultures cannot be comprehended, any more than the individual life can be seen to end at death. Historical fantasies about the Renaissance as a continuation of fifth-century Athens thus are the counterpart of metempsychosis (Sahlins 1993).

The role of enabling deity in this system is the very idea of change itself:

History seems to do more than describe beings to us from the outside, or at best give us intermittent flashes of insight into internalities, each of which are so on their own account while remaining external to each other: it appears to re-establish our connection, outside ourselves, with the very essence of change. (1966c: 256)

In a relativistic universe, this 'very essence of change' actually is quite similar to the denial of change. Just as one travelling by car or train notices only the changes in the rate of travel, not the velocity itself, so the Western world, accustomed to the idea of steady, 'pure' change, is upset only by the alteration of this process (whether imagined as progress, evolution or revolution) of political inflections on the common consciousness (see Lévi-Strauss 1961b: 237). History, by presenting the artful illusion of internality to times and places obviously external to the present, comforts us with their constructed familiarity. The past may be a foreign country, but it is one equipped with cosy tourist amenities.

An analogous situation is found in historical method, which is rooted in the notion of a distinct data set specific to history: a collection of historical events and facts, which appears as given, but which upon reflection 'resolves itself into a multitude of individual psychic movements' (1966c: 257). That is, at any point a historical event can be maintained as such only with difficulty: the 'Battle of Waterloo' threatens to break down into a multitude of individual life histories, and behind these are the conscious and unconscious mental processes that can be said to be the base level of reality underlying the narrative fiction. As we move along this scale towards the more real, we also lose explanatory power and, ultimately, meaning. This problem of 'infinite regress' afflicts historians in a second way as well. Even allowing for these specious historical 'facts', by what principle does the historian select which set of facts to relate? That is, why tell the story of the Battle of Waterloo from the perspective of the French, not the English, or the officers, not the enlisted men? For that matter, why tell the story of the Battle of Waterloo at all, as opposed to something entirely different? Of course, the answer lies in the politics and sociology of the present: history is 'never history, but history-for' (1966c: 257). This statement, with its Heidegerrian echoes, is not Lévi-Strauss's final word on the matter; if it were, there would be little difference between him and Sartre (1966c: 257–8). Rather, it points the way to a profound historiographic solipsism. Just as the historian must select from among the impossibly broad field of human events a narrow set of constructed facts, the consumer of history must select among an infinite number of histories, each supposing a fictitious community of common values and interest, when in fact each is a singularity (1966c: 258). The perniciousness of this is twofold. On the one hand, this plenitude of histories is self-cancelling. In a remarkable turn of phrase, Lévi-Strauss states that 'a truly total history would cancel itself out – its product would be nought' (1966c: 257). While this nihilism is primarily rhetorical and not supportable – the sum total of Western histories would surely be a cacophony, not a simple cancellation, as of out-of-phase sound waves – it does succeed in undermining the ground of historiography, which is the assumption of both stable historical fields and stable communities.

A second pernicious effect of the fiction of continuity – among both historical eras and communities – is the need to identify a category of otherness. Although relegated to a footnote, this point is worthy of much greater consideration than we can give it here. Directed specifically at Sartre, it is nevertheless an indictment of Western historiography in general: 'The price so paid for the illusion of having overcome the insoluble antinomy (in such a system) between my self and others, consists of the assignation, by historical consciousness, of the metaphysical function of the Other to the Papuans' (1966c: 258). On one level, this may be read as a simple indictment of ethnocentrism in Western thought. The more we affirm the commonality of a European, Western or 'Judaeo-Christian' identity, the more we emphasise our separation from those on the outside. In a more sophisticated reading, Lévi-Strauss seems to be suggesting that by denying the Other within (that is, the absolute separation among individuals even within the same community, and even more so among different communities), we project it onto the category of the Other, always present, always waiting to be filled with content. This operation – a sort of Freudian totemism – is the opposite of sublimation. If we repress the differences that really exist in the social and natural world and which, in the structuralist account constitute the very basis of consciousness, we are forced to be blinded to our common humanity with the Papuans, or the Bushmen, or the Kwakiutl, or whoever fills the current role of primitive Other. In fact, the history of these representations of the Other in the Western imagination – from Herodotus to medieval fabulists such as 'Sir John Mandeville' and clerics such as Savonarola and Las Casas, to the artists published by De Bry, and so on through the pages of 1960s *National Geographic* – is itself a rich field of historical study (see Hartog 1988: 288).

Hot and cold societies

It is useful to mention here that Lévi-Strauss has himself been unfairly accused of the same sort of thing, in often wilful misreadings of his opposition of 'hot' and 'cold' societies and some of the statements made in his UNESCO publications. It is evident, however, that it is here that his claims for anthropology as a 'human science', replacing the older, ethnocentric, transcendent humanism, are realised. Not only does he reject the absolute separation between 'the West and the rest', but he demonstrates that our readiness to assume such a divide is the product of a series of intellectual errors that no self-respecting 'savage' would have made!

The passage in which the opposition of 'hot' and 'cold' societies first appears in English is worth quoting at length:

[T]he clumsy distinction between 'peoples without history' and others could with advantage be replaced by a distinction between what for convenience I called 'cold' and 'hot' societies: the former seeking, by the institutions they give themselves, to annul the possible effects of historical factors on their equilibrium and continuity in a quasi-automatic fashion; the latter resolutely internalizing the historical process and making it the moving power of their development. (1966c: 233–4)

Of course, contrary to several prominent misreadings of this concept, 'cold' societies do not actually live outside of history, in the sense of the passage of time and irreversible change to individuals and even to the system itself (see Gow 2001: 15–16). Moreover, this distinction does not represent an absolute opposition between two mutually exclusive modes of being in time. Although it is a reasonable mistake for the reader to make – given Lévi-Strauss's fondness for logical dualisms, as opposed to stochastic distributions – from the standpoint of a global ethnology, this is not the case. Nonetheless, from the culture-internal standpoint – including that of the West, and its myth-system of written history – the hot/cold opposition does appear to be absolute. More than two decades after the publication of *The Savage Mind*, Lévi-Strauss had this to say:

When we speak of 'primitive' society we put the word in quotes so that people know that the term is improper and has been imposed on us by usage. And yet, in a way, it is suitable; the societies we call 'primitive' are not that way at all, *but they wish to be*. They view themselves as primitive, for their ideal would be to remain in a state in which the gods or the ancestors created them at the origin of time. Of course, this is an illusion, and they can no more escape history than other societies. But this history, which they mistrust and dislike, is something they undergo [*subissent*: 'submit to']. (Lévi-Strauss and Eribon 1991b: 124–5; italics mine)

What is particularly striking in reading this passage in the present is its applicability to religious fundamentalists, whether in Saudi Arabia or Kansas, who wish to erase, literally, the traces of history. This points to a significant and powerful extension of the hot/cold distinction into the present era, when only a few of the original 'primitives' persist. Moreover, it validates what I think lay behind Lévi-Strauss's thinking on this matter in the first place. Given his insistence on a cognitive universalism, what he even at points calls 'human nature', it would be surprising if this desire for changelessness did not exist in all societies, albeit in different expressed forms. We will return to this issue below, in a discussion of the UNESCO publications.

However, to return to the model Lévi-Strauss is developing here, the nature of some societies is to resist change, just as it is ours to 'make a cult to it' (Lévi-Strauss and Eribon 1991b: 125). In each case, the common assumption supports a 'status quo', whether 'static' or 'progressive'. To use slightly different language, we could say that the self-identified 'primitives' employ an ideology of stasis to maintain the illusion of changelessness. Like certain mid-twentieth-century British anthropologists, they could not contemplate the prospect of change in their societies: even the gradual pressures of demographic change could be too much to deal with. The major means of effacing change is to absorb it, either into myth or into kinship. Lévi-Strauss gives numerous examples of both in his oeuvre. Thus, societies may delete, or add, a clan in order to maintain symmetry in the face of demographic change. In one instance, based loosely on ethnographic fact, Lévi-Strauss imagines a society that has three clans – bear, eagle and turtle, representing earth, air and water – losing population to the point that the bear clan becomes extinct. At this point, in order to maintain the tripartite nature of society, the turtle clan must be subdivided. Although the earth/air/water distinction is lost, it may be replicated at a lower level (in the opposition between grey and yellow turtle, in this example). Thus, the structure may be 'shattered', but 'if the structural orientation survives the shock it has, after each upheaval, several means of re-establishing a system' (1966c: 68; see Hénaff 1998: 223). This sense of rebuilding a system, which Lévi-Strauss elsewhere calls *bricolage*, is captured in the quotation from Franz Boas: 'It would seem that mythological worlds have been built up, only to be shattered again, and that new worlds were built up from the fragments' (1966c: 21).

On this model, history is the reality of entropy against which organisms and structures must constantly struggle. The event then comes to be taken in something like its medical sense: always a shock and a threat to the system. Societies, like recovering patients, must overcome them as best they can. While they cannot deny the changes that have been wrought – scars, missing limbs or the like – on the plane of synchrony, they can suppress memory of the trauma, i.e. diachrony, and replace it with a more comforting narrative. To extend the metaphor further, the anthropologist, like a pathologist, can reconstruct the series of events leading up to the present state, but only by carefully reading the signs and rearranging the patient's narrative. In 'cold' societies, diachrony is routinely suppressed, to the point that any hint of time's passage is erased; the ancestors and contemporary people may dwell together in a 'dreamtime'.

Hot, cold and warm

There is a certain degree of sample bias in this perspective of 'cold' societies achieving a phoenix-like resurrection in the wake of destruction, which, in my view, skews the global picture considerably. Surely the cultures recorded by Boas and other Americanist anthropologists, on which Lévi-Strauss bases the majority of his theoretical discussions in *The Savage Mind* (1966c), were in a unique situation, having been brutally assaulted and even annihilated in the European invasion. Some were more successfully persistent, but this is almost certainly the result of geographic good luck, rather than inherent cultural dispositions. My view is that most indigenous American cultures were like the Osage, as recorded by J. O. Dorsey and discussed by Lévi-Strauss. The Osage were in fact aware of their past migrations and the changes effected by them. When they adopted a fierce group of outsiders into their society as the third group, the erstwhile balance between peace and war groups was disturbed. The solution was to reduce the number of clans in the two warlike groups from seven each, to seven between them, thus preserving, structurally if not demographically, the balance between peace and war (1966c: 69). That is, they possessed a historical consciousness not significantly different from that of European societies before the cult of progress. While formally maintaining a pre-existing division of society, not unlike, say, the Three Estates of pre-Revolutionary France, they kept an oral record of the events leading up to the current state of affairs. Moreover, as Lévi-Strauss has noted elsewhere, such origin narratives provide commentary and critique on contemporary society (see 1976a: 173). This is not to deny that certain groups, perhaps including the Australian Aborigines Lévi-Strauss cites for this purpose, were relatively 'cold'. However, I see most non-Western groups sitting in a metaphorical Roman tepidarium, rather than in either a caldarium or a frigidarium.

The above statement probably is not one with which Lévi-Strauss would disagree, at least not strongly. The critical point, however, is one of emphasis. In most of his oeuvre, the primitive is invoked, not pejoratively, certainly, and not without the recognition that to be primitive, at least as much as to be modern, requires a certain amount of work. At the same time, he follows the bias inherent in anthropology, its own structure of the *longue durée*, of selecting for maximum demonstration effect. Franz Boas, with whom Lévi-Strauss in a sense apprenticed as an Americanist anthropologist, disdained the sort of text that would have provided evidence of native historical conscious-ness. In some cases such texts were collected under the rubric of 'tales'; in others they were not collected at all, and were termed 'idiotic' (Stocking 1968: 204). Much like the Osage story discussed above, groups such as the Kwakiutl and Heiltsuk were possessed of a well-developed sense of history (Harkin 1997).

One particular subset of the 'lukewarm' societies is what we could call the 'island' society, as described by Marshall Sahlins, with particular reference to Hawai'i. This is a type of society (and it does indeed appear to be a type, given similar findings by anthropologists working elsewhere in the Pacific) that, although insular, defines the source of value and power as beyond the horizon (see 1985b: 7). In the case of the Hawai'ians, the sea beyond the horizon merged with heaven, so that visitors from afar, whether conquer-ing Polynesian heroes or Captain Cook, were imbued with the sacred. This ideology functioned internally as well; royalty were categorically both from overseas and possessing great mana (Sahlins 1985: 73–103). In an area more familiar to Lévi-Strauss, the Northwest Coast, groups such as the Kwakiutl and Heiltsuk believed the ultimate source of wealth to be a land beneath the sea. This predisposed them to see the European explorers and fur traders, and possibly the Chinese before them, as sources of wealth and power. Thus, the indigenous people of both places were more than willing to establish political, mercantile and cultural relations with outsiders, although they could not, of course, foresee the inevitable threat to their way of life that would follow.

Much of the 'classic' Northwest Coast cultural complex recorded by Boas and analysed by Lévi-Strauss was thus the product of post-contact history. Well-known phenomena such as potlatches and totem poles were, if not exactly post-contact inventions, elaborations of traditional themes in the context of increased wealth and new forms of technology from European sources. For example, the finest degree of craftsmanship exhibited in wooden masks would not have been possible without metal tools. Moreover, the diffusion of certain dances and dance societies, including the famous 'Cannibal Dance', would not have occurred in the pre-contact era, because of the great dangers inherent in long-distance travel. In such cases the post-contact world did not introduce entirely new cultural phenomena, but rather intensified existing cultural patterns, at least up to the point of the loss of sovereignty and the establishment of colonial regimes. This seems to be the diagnostic feature of the 'island' society, and perhaps of 'lukewarm' societies more generally.

The Story of Lynx: an alternative history of the Americas

A relatively recent example of Lévi-Strauss's thinking about historical processes is seen in his analysis of a series of structurally related myths about lynx, coyote and other creatures linked by fraternity (1995b). His theme in this book is less the suppression of the diachronic perspective in favour of the synchronic, as in earlier discussions of mythology, and more the way that structures of thought produce culturally distinctive historicities. As in *Mythologiques*, he assumes a common cultural-mythical system in North and South America. The myths discussed in this book all deal with forms of pairing, particularly twins and siblings. He sees a series of transformations linking a range of opposed terms, e.g. fog and wind, pervading the Americas, and constituting a specifically American dualism. (For readers inclined to think of dualism as an empty form at the heart of structuralism, this is a surprising and stimulating turn.) Specifically, he believes that the American dualism is open-ended and complementary, as befits the trope of a long-lost brother. Siblings, including twins, are always differentiated in some way through the events of the myth. Ultimately, myths about purported twins really are about the impossibility of identity between siblings: a point that is expressed in details such as different sex or the sequence of birth, or indeed as different fates of the twins. This represents, according to Lévi-Strauss,

[th]e progressive organization of the world and of society in the form of a series of dual splits but without the resulting parts at each stage ever being truly equal: in one way or another, one is always superior to the other. The proper functioning of the system depends on this dynamic disequilibrium, for without it this system would at all times be in danger of falling into inertia. (1995b: 63)

This constant offset between paired sets – like that between the firing of cylinders in an internal combustion engine – drives the world forward. Moreover, it provides a creative tension, between the attempt to establish equivalence and the impossibility of doing so. This impossibility is at root existential, because the attainment of equivalence is only ever achieved in the context of a non-human world (i.e. heaven), and its occurrence constitutes a threat to human existence. Ethnographically, twins were nearly universally feared, and often one of the pair was killed. Among the Heiltsuk, twins were associated with both the society of salmon and the world of the dead, and were not expected to live long lives (see Harkin 2007).

This general state of affairs has far-reaching implications for relations between self and Other, including the whiteman:

What these myths implicitly state is that the poles between which natural phenomena and social life are organized – such as sky and earth, fire and water, above and below, Indians and non-Indians, fellow citizens and strangers – could never be twins. The mind attempts to join them without succeeding in establishing parity between them. This is because it is these cascading distinctive features, such as mythical thought conceives them, that set in motion the machine of the universe. (1995b: 63)

Whites thus could be assimilated into this system, but never as precise counterparts to Indians. That is why, in both myth and praxis, whites generally have been seen in terms of some asymmetrical kinship relation, especially younger or elder brother. Even the famous practice in North America of referring to the white government as 'father' implies, particularly in matrilineal cultures, a relationship of alliance rather than identity.

What is particularly striking, from the perspective of historical anthropology, about these myths is that we have examples, at least in Brazil, of both pre-contact and post-contact versions. The pre-contact versions are cosmogonic; ones collected in the nineteenth century also include the whiteman, without altering in any significant way the structure of the myth. In one such myth, this development reaches the point of identifying a culture hero with the emperor of Brazil, Pedro II (1995b: 54). Thus, Lévi-Strauss's argument that this particular version of dualistic thought provided a general orientation to the world, including whites, is convincing. The problem is that it does not seem that he goes far enough with this line of thought. Although successful in positing a connection between mythical thought and historicity in a general way in the context of the Americas, this book still does not give an adequate picture of any particular ethnographic or ethnohistorical setting, a 'grounding of these myths in fuller ethnography' (Yalman 1996). We could, given sufficient data, move well beyond Lévi-Strauss's view that the historical becomes embedded in mythical structures (of whatever sort) to what Marshall Sahlins has called 'mytho-praxis': a perspective that explores the undeniable pragmatic aspect of mythical thought (Sahlins 1981; 1985: 54). That is, the mythical thinking – of Europeans as well as indigenous people – robustly affects their historical actions, and their actions, in turn, affect myth and structure, in a sort of feedback loop. Sahlins's own work, deeply influenced by Lévi-Strauss as well as Saussure, weds structuralism to rich ethnographic and historical scholarship, producing accounts of specific societies, particularly Fiji and Hawai'i, that are more satisfying than the overgeneral description of American Indians that Lévi-Strauss produced. Of course, the sheer scope of *The Story of Lynx* (1991a; 1995b), embracing all of the Americas and elements of European history and philosophy, as well as the relative lack of documentary evidence, would never allow its subject matter to be fleshed out in this way (see Gow 2001: 204). Anthropologists and historians who have deep and specialised experience with specific cultures are responsible for completing the picture. In the final analysis, the indigenous people of the Americas interacted in specific ways with whites, which can be seen in large part as a function of their cognitive habits. Not only their predisposition to see whites as, say, younger brothers, but the subsequent chain of events following contact must be seen as flowing from their worldview, if they are to be granted any sort of meaningful historical agency.

Lévi-Strauss does broach the issue of historical praxis, without giving it sufficient attention, when he contrasts the mental world of the Indians with that of the whites. If Indians conceive of dualism as complementary, for Europeans the concept of dualism is rather one of opposition, and is self-cancelling. Thus, in encounters between the two groups, the American side was generally welcoming to the whiteman, because that was appropriate to their mythical schemas. Although the welcome may have been mixed with fear, mistrust or pity, the appearance of the whiteman did not in any fundamental way upset their world-view. The Europeans, likewise, sought and usually found confirmation of their own folk anthropologies, such as the notion of 'Plinean' races and, above all, the agency of Satan in human affairs (1995b: 218–19). Thus, the existence of indigenous peoples simply fulfilled a sterile dichotomy long predicted. This explains the significant disconnect between the beginnings of empirical description of American Indians, by observers such as Thevet in Brazil in the 1570s and White at Roanoke in the 1580s, and the persistence of the depiction of Plinean races (in the De Bry publications, for example) into the seventeenth century, and Satanism well into the twentieth.

Race, culture and history

The two publications Lévi-Strauss undertook for UNESCO in 1952 and 1971, *Race and History* (1952a) and *Race and Culture* (1971b), are significant to an understanding of his view of the modern world, a view that he rarely addresses elsewhere. Also interesting are the titles of the two works, which, taken together, are an acknowledgement of his Boasian inheritance. (Something similar could be said about *The Elementary Structures of Kinship* (1949a; 1969a) and its allusion to Durkheim.) Clearly, race was never a central aspect of Lévi-Strauss's own research, and his statements on race per se read as if they could have come from Boas's *Race, Language, and Culture*: 'The original sin of anthropology . . . consists in its confusion of the idea of race, in the purely biological sense (assuming that there is any factual basis for the idea, even in this limited field – which is disputed by modern genetics), with sociological and psychological productions of human civiliza-tions' (Lévi-Strauss 1961b: 220). 'Always disconnect' could be the motto for this approach to race, i.e. showing that it has no relation to culture or non-biological phenomena, under any circumstances. In addition to agreeing with the Boasian orthodoxy of the time, which was no doubt why this publication was originally solicited and proved so successful for UNESCO, Lévi-Strauss's own notions of the universal mental capacity of humanity were quite important to other aspects of structuralism. In particular, the existence of a global propensity to construct meaning by relations of contrast and oppo-sition was a necessary first step to his analyses of myth and kinship. If, by contrast, certain groups (whether biological races or not is irrelevant) experi-enced the world in terms of Lévy-Bruhlian 'participation', establishing global principles of structural analysis would be impossible.

A second aspect of the Boasian paradigm was resistance to cultural evolu-tion, which Lévi-Strauss expresses eloquently:

When . . . we turn from biology to culture, things become far more complicated. We may find material objects in the soil, and note that the form or manufacture of a certain type of object varies progressively according to the depth of the geological strata. But an axe does not give birth to an axe in the physical sense that an animal gives birth to an animal. Therefore, to say that an axe has developed out of another axe is to speak metaphorically and with a rough approximation to truth, but without the scientific exactitude which a similar expression has in biological parlance. (Lévi-Strauss 1961b: 227)

He goes on to connect this 'false evolutionism' with premodern philosophical traditions and the philosophical history against which he struggled elsewhere, calling it a 'pseudo-scientific mask for an old philosophical problem' (Lévi-Strauss 1961b: 228). This finally merges with the notion of progress, which he believes to be the defining myth of Western society.

However, Lévi-Strauss's contribution to the debate was not limited simply to espousing Boasian orthodoxy. Indeed, he strikes a contrarian tone early in *Race and History* (1952a) by refusing to contribute to the literature on 'the contributions made by various races of men to world civilization' (Lévi-Strauss 1961b: 219). He believes that such a catalogue would be questionable on at least two grounds: the idea that one can speak of world civilisation in this cumulative sense, and the fact that the notion of 'races' and indeed of hierarchy (for how else to read 'contributions'?) would be preserved. This rejected approach, reminiscent of the more insipid forms of 'multicultural-ism', is one that he came to believe characterised the UNESCO project as a whole (1985b: xiii–xiv; Izard 2001: 12–13). Even though he strongly rejected racism, he had little use for the notion that the world could ever attain a state of global amity; what is more radical, he did not believe that such a thing would even be desirable (1985b: 24). This is the pessimistic side of structur-alist thought, expressed in other documents, most notably *Tristes Tropiques*, but most particularly in the UNESCO publications.

One surprising source for this line of thought is Gobineau, the nineteenth-century French anthropologist often considered the father of scientific racism. Gobineau's fundamental belief was not that races were naturally ranked in a hierarchy, but that each race possessed a special character, and that this character was destroyed through miscegenation (Lévi-Strauss and Eribon 1991b: 149). While Lévi-Strauss obviously is not concerned about racial miscegenation, he is very concerned about the analogous question of increas-ing communication between previously separate cultures. The two problems are precisely analogous because Gobineau believed that the destruction of difference resulted in a state of global entropy, and that organised systems could function only as self-contained and distinct units. This notion proved attractive to Lévi-Strauss, who had viewed first-hand the destruction by absorption of previously tribal cultures in Brazil, and knew very well the grim history of what others would call the world system. A basic principle of structuralist theory is that meaning is created in the space between different elements; to the degree that difference is effaced, meaning is as well. This is a problem not just of linguistic meaning, but also of meaning in the sense that we commonly express in the phrase 'meaning of life'.

Communication among cultures is itself neither inherently good nor bad. Certainly, cultures that remain absolutely alone and insular are unlikely to develop the creative spark that produces great literature or technology (Lévi-Strauss 1961b: 252). This is not simply because of the action of cultural diffusion, at least not in the normal sense of the term. Rather, the existence of an outside group, which is considered inferior by the in-group, often indeed subhuman, provides a necessary foil to the established norms and values, and to the development of a specific cultural ethos (Lévi-Strauss 1961b: 224–5;

1985b: 7). When borrowing occurs, as it does frequently, it is accompanied by a series of mental gyrations that result in the borrowed idea being placed in a new context. In terms of myth and plastic art, this results in the famous transformations and inversions that exist between variants (e.g. 1982; 1990b; 1995b). Obviously, this would be more difficult with items of technology such as fish hooks, but even these take on a cultural imprimatur through decoration, related myth and ritual, and the like (as, for instance, the halibut hooks of the Tlingit, an example familiar to Lévi-Strauss). Thus, one can see that a culture left out of the circulation of such ideas would be at a disadvantage, and not only because it lacked access to the ideas themselves, but because it lacked the opportunity to develop a sense of its own identity in relation to others.

The other pole is no better. A surfeit of communication is equally harmful because it threatens to overwhelm the boundaries of culture:

> It is differences between cultures that make their meetings fruitful. Now, this exchange leads to progressive uniformity: the benefits cultures reap from these contacts are largely the result of their qualitative differences, but during these exchanges these differences diminish to the point of disappearing. Isn't that what we are seeing today? (Lévi-Strauss and Eribon 1991b: 149)

Lévi-Strauss is not referring exclusively to the swamping of previously isolated cultures, although this is part of the picture. Rather, he sees a more serious problem that will leave us all in a global monoculture. In the past, certainly, cultures rose and fell, particularly in the context of the rise of empires and nation-states. Thus, Picts, Celts, Saxons and others combined to form the British nation, and occasionally groups reassert language and identity even when embedded in a nation-state, such as various Celtic groups in Britain and elsewhere (Lévi-Strauss and Eribon 1991b: 153). However, the drivers of this process in the present day seem uniquely powerful and irreversible: demographics and technology.

In his earlier UNESCO publication, Lévi-Strauss holds out the possibility of cultural 'coalitions', which would operate rather like trading blocs on the cultural level. Individual societies would choose to open themselves up to certain others, while at the same time maintaining adequate barriers (Lévi-Strauss 1961b: 256). However, even in that more optimistic publication, he recognises the threat of monoculture, in which 'the differences in their contributions will gradually be evened out, although collaboration was originally necessary and advantageous simply because of those differences' (Lévi-Strauss 1961b: 257). He holds out another possibility – one that he emphasises in *Race and Culture*, and which seems to have been borne out by events: 'the emergence of antagonistic political and social systems' (Lévi-Strauss 1961b: 256). This development may be necessary: '[B]y shifting the grounds of diversity, it may be possible to maintain indefinitely, in varying forms which will take men unawares, that state of disequilibrium which is necessary to the biological and cultural survival of mankind' (Lévi-Strauss 1961b: 256). To that the contemporary reader is tempted to reply, be careful what you wish for.

Race and Culture strikes a somewhat more pessimistic note, although, as Lévi-Strauss points out, the two essays share the same framework and even some of the same text (Massenzio 2001: 424). (A bowdlerised version of excerpts from both recently was published by UNESCO (Lévi-Strauss 2001b).) The main burden here is disentangling the question of racism from what we might call simple cultural prejudice. Scientific racism has lost its object: essentialised, primordial races of the sort imagined by Gobineau cannot be reconciled with the more sophisticated knowledge of traits encoded in the human genome that existed even in 1970. Instead, then we were beginning to ask interesting questions about the interplay of inheritance and environment. (This view, however, leaves out forensic and other approaches in physical anthropology based on skeletal morphology, which still refer to race in essentialising language (1985b: 4–5)). If racism is a dead letter in the scientific community, then the most important tasks are to spread the news to a wider public, and to stop confusing that public by the conflation of racism with the lesser evils, indeed the necessary evils, of preference and prejudice. Lévi-Strauss admits to a healthy dose of these evils himself: he likes Japan and Japanese culture, does not like Arabs, did not 'fit in' with Pakistanis and so forth (Lévi-Strauss and Eribon 1991b: 151–2). This account is refreshingly honest and realistic, but the problem is that the modern nation-state cannot embrace such a perspective, but rather is bound to assert some form of 'multiculturalism'. This is seen particularly clearly in contemporary France, with the rise of the far right, controversies over religious freedom and display, and the novels of Michel Houellebecq, among other things. This is not merely a problem in France, the homeland of the Declaration of the Rights of Man, but in any modern nation-state (the Netherlands, the United Kingdom and the United States providing particularly apt examples), because these states are constituted as part of (and in turn constitute) a liberal world order. Where, then, will be the barriers that Lévi-Strauss imagines can be established to break up the excessive flow of information (and persons) across national and cultural boundaries? Is the Academie Française up to the task? Much more likely is a continuation of the process of breaching the levees of culture, and violent reactions against it: what Benjamin Barber calls 'jihad vs. McWorld' (1995).

The situation at present is one of great peril for anthropology, as it is for humanity itself. At the very moment when the insights of anthropology – structuralist or otherwise – would be most useful, it is increasingly shut out of the places where knowledge of these processes could be studied: not only in countries with poor 'security environments' of the sort written about by Bernard-Henri Lévy (2004), but in communities of all sorts, including in the West, where the barriers thrown up to the outside world are increasingly rigid and at the same time increasingly obviously constructed. Fieldwork in aboriginal communities in the Americas, Australia and elsewhere is becoming ever more problematic, especially for younger anthropologists. At the same time, fundamentalist cults on the rise in the United States, Latin America and the Islamic world increasingly deny our common humanity by inflaming the divisions that exist and by creating new ones. The danger is not that anthropology will disappear, but that it will be torn between mere advocacy and historical study of the archive left behind by previous generations of ethnographers. Lévi-Strauss imagines the latter to be an acceptable future, but such an approach sacrifices the vitality derived from fieldwork, and the disciplinary advantage possessed now by anthropology (Lévi-Strauss and Eribon 1991b: 146). In a final irony, Lévi-Strauss, who began his academic career by marginalising humanistic history, foresees a future in which anthropologists will become 'philologists, historians of ideas, specialists in civilizations now accessible only through documents gathered by earlier observers' (Lévi-Strauss and Eribon 1991b: 146). This appears to be simply an updated version of the dictum, attributed to the Victorian historian F. W. Maitland, that 'anthropology must choose between being history and being nothing' (Evans-Pritchard 1962: 190).

REFERENCES

Barber, Benjamin 1995. *Jihad vs. McWorld*. New York: Times Books.
Braudel, Fernand 1980. *On History*. Translated by Sarah Matthews. Chicago: University of Chicago Press.
Darnell, Regna 2004. 'Text, Symbol, and Tradition in Northwest Coast Ethnology from Franz Boas to Claude Lévi-Strauss', in Marie Mauzé, Michael E. Harkin and Sergei Kan (eds.), *Coming to Shore: Northwest Coast Ethnology, Traditions, and Visions*. Lincoln, NE: University of Nebraska Press, pp. 7–22.
Evans-Pritchard, E. E. 1962. *Social Anthropology and Other Essays*. New York: Free Press.
Gow, Peter 2001. *An Amazonian Myth and Its History*. Oxford Studies in Social and Cultural Anthropology. Oxford: Oxford University Press.
Hartog, François 1988. *The Mirror of Herodotus: The Representation of the Other in the Writing of History*. Translated by Janet Lloyd. Berkeley: University of California Press.
    2005. 'Le Regard éloigné: Lévi-Strauss et l'histoire', in Michel Izard (ed.), *Lévi-Strauss*. Paris: L'Herne, pp. 313–19.
Harkin, Michael E. 1997. *The Heiltsuks: Dialogues of Culture and History on the Northwest Coast*. Lincoln, NE: University of Nebraska Press.

2007. 'Swallowing Wealth: Northwest Coast Religious Beliefs and Ecological Practices', in Michael E. Harkin and David Rich Lewis (eds.), *Native Americans and the Environment: Perspectives on the Ecological Indian*. Lincoln, NE: University of Nebraska Press, pp. 211–32.

Hénaff, Marcel 1998. *Claude Lévi-Strauss and the Making of Structural Anthropology*. Translated by Mary Baker. Minneapolis, MN: University of Minnesota Press.

Izard, Michel 2001. 'Preface', in *Race et histoire, race et culture*. Paris: Albin Michel/ Éditions UNESCO, pp. 7–27.

Johnson, Christopher 2003. *Claude Lévi-Strauss: The Formative Years*. Cambridge: Cambridge University Press.

Lévy, Bernard-Henri 2004. *War, Evil, and the End of History*. Translated by Charlotte Mandell. Hoboken, NJ: Melville House.

Massenzio, Marcello 2001. 'An Interview with Claude Lévi-Strauss', *Current Anthropology* 42: 419–25.

Sahlins, Marshall 1981. *Historical Metaphors and Mythical Realities: Structure in the Early History of the Sandwich Islands Kingdom*. Ann Arbor, MI: University of Michigan Press.

1985. *Islands of History*. Chicago: University of Chicago Press.

1993. 'Goodbye to *Tristes Tropes*: Ethnography in the Context of the Modern World', *Journal of Modern History* 65: 1–25.

Steiner, George 1970. 'Orpheus with his Myths'. In E. Nelson Hayes and Tanya Hayes (eds.), *Claude Lévi-Strauss: The Anthropologist as Hero*. Cambridge, MA: MIT Press.

Stocking, George 1968. *Race, Culture, and Evolution: Essays in the History of Anthropology*. New York: Free Press.

White, Hayden 1973. *Metahistory: The Historical Imagination in Nineteenth-Century Europe*. Baltimore: Johns Hopkins University Press.

Yalman, Nur 1996. 'Lévi-Strauss in Wonderland: Playing Chess with Unusual Cats', *American Ethnologist* 23: 901–3.

3 Structure and exchange

Abraham Rosman and Paula G. Rubel

Why do groups exchange? Why do the Arapesh say 'Your own pigs, your own yams which you have piled up, you may not eat' (Rosman and Rubel 2004)? You must give them to others. Malinowski also raised this question, asking why men give their finest yams to their brothers-in-law rather than keep them (1965: 188–9)? Why does Lévi-Strauss argue that groups must give their sisters and their daughters to others, rather than keeping them for themselves (1969b)? The answer to all of these questions is the same. By giving your own yams, your own pigs, your sisters and your own daughters to others, you create networks of social relationships, since the rule of reciprocity compels them to give you an equal return.

The things distributed at ceremonies are clues to the nature of the social structural relationship of exchangers. Before one discusses social structure and exchange, one must first deal with the concept of structure. Structuralism as a theoretical concept has had a long history in fields like linguistics, philosophy and biology. Piaget contrasted structuralism with 'the atomistic tendency to reduce wholes to their prior elements' (Piaget 1970: 4). Structuralism's most famous exponent in anthropology, by far, was Claude Lévi-Strauss who applied the theoretical framework of linguistics to the analysis of culture. The linguistic concepts which Lévi-Strauss drew upon were those of Ferdinand de Saussure, Troubetskoy and most importantly Roman Jakobson, who was Lévi-Strauss's friend and colleague. Lévi-Strauss was also influenced by the theoretical views of Franz Boas (a debt he acknowledges in *Structural Anthropology* (1963a: 6ff.). In the introduction to the *Handbook of American Indian Languages*, Boas discusses the way in which each language and each culture provides systems of classification of persons, time, space, colours, plants, birds and relatives, etc. Boas also noted that linguistic and cultural structures are unconscious (1911: 67). Unconscious structures became a key idea in Lévi-Strauss's method of analysis. Following Troubetskoy, Lévi-Strauss noted, 'First, structural linguistics shifts from the study of conscious linguistic phenomena to study of their unconscious infrastructure; second it does not treat terms as independent entities, taking instead as its basis of analysis the relations between terms; third, it introduces the concept of system . . .; finally, structural linguistics aims at the discovery of general laws' (1963a: 33). Structuralists adopted several critical distinctions which had been made by Saussure. The first was the distinction between *langue* and *parole*. *Parole* refers to verbal behaviour, and *langue* refers to the unconscious underlying structure including grammar and syntax. Saussure also distinguished between synchrony, the analysis of a language at a particular point in time, and diachrony, the study of a language as it changes through time. These two types of analyses cannot be done simultaneously. Lévi-Strauss applied these principles to the study of culture.

Lévi-Strauss was greatly influenced by the works of Marcel Mauss, particularly *The Gift*. In his *Introduction to the Work of Marcel Mauss*, he points out that the 'notions of "unconscious category" and "category of collective thinking" [are] synonymous' (Lévi-Strauss 1987a: 35). As we have noted above, this idea of unconscious categories or structures is also present in linguistic theory. In *The Gift*, Mauss talks about total social facts in reference to the potlatch. Total social facts involve systems, and all have synchronic, historical and physiological–psychological dimensions (Lévi-Strauss 1987a: 26). According to Lévi-Strauss, 'What happened in that essay [*The Gift*], for the first time in the history of ethnological thinking, was that an effort was made to transcend empirical observation and to reach deeper realities . . . the social . . . becomes a system, among whose parts connections, equivalences and interdependent aspects can be discovered' (Lévi-Strauss 1987a: 38). In his discussion of *The Gift*, Lévi-Strauss recognises Mauss's model-building. The parts of the system are: "transferable", "substitutable", their operations can be reduced to a small number, and such systems can be defined in terms of types . . . the types become definable by these intrinsic characteristics; and they become comparable to one another so those characteristics are no longer located in a qualitative order but in the number and the arrangement of elements which are themselves constant in all the types' (1987a: 38, 39–40). As will be seen later in this chapter, we have used this idea to develop the concept of the potlatch type society.

One of the areas to which Lévi-Strauss applied linguistic distinctions was the realm of kinship. In 1949, he published two landmark works. The first was the article 'Social Structure' (in *Anthropology Today* (1949)), which laid out his conceptions regarding the principles of structuralism. In 'Social Structure', Lévi-Strauss deals with the 'communication' of women, goods and services, and messages. This communication between groups in a society occurs through language, through the exchange of goods and services (usually referred to as economics), and through the exchange of women (which is kinship). These forms of communication operate at different rates. In computing the communication rate of intermarriages, and that of messages occurring in a given society, the differences are of 'the same magnitude as, let us say that between the exchange of heavy molecules of two viscous liquids through a not very permeable film and radio communication' (Lévi-Strauss 1963a: 296). Lévi-Strauss's broader concern with communication, kinship and economics indicates that he views culture as a system of signs and symbols, paralleling language as system of symbols. Lévi-Strauss's approach combines the fields of linguistics, kinship and economics within a single unifying structure.

In Lévi-Strauss's view, a structure is a type of model with four characteristics: the elements in the structure constitute a system, and change in any single element brings about changes in all the others; there is the possibility of a series of transformations for any model, the consequence of which is a family of models; it is therefore possible to predict what will happen to the model if one or more element is modified; the model should make clear all of the observed facts (Lévi-Strauss 1963a: 279–80). Lévi-Strauss uses the example of games to illustrate how structural models operate. Games are systems of elements which function according to rules. The game is no more than the totality of its rules. Chess is a favourite example used by the linguist Saussure. The composition of the chess-pieces, whether they are made of carved ivory, wood or potatoes is irrelevant. It is the relationship between the pieces, and the rules governing their moves, which are important. Saussure also pointed out that knowing that chess originated in India and came to Europe via Persia, i.e. the diachronic analysis of chess, is completely separate from the synchronic analysis of the rules of chess. In the study of language, according to Saussure, diachronic analysis was to be kept separate from synchronic analysis, but today analysts have found that synchrony and diachrony interprenetrate one another.

The second landmark work of Lévi-Strauss was *The Elementary Structures of Kinship* (1949a; 1969b), which was broadly comparative. It dealt with the evolution of structures of exchange in which he demonstrated the identity of structures of exchange of goods with structures of exchange of women which were based on marriage rules (Lévi-Strauss 1949a; 1969b). Lévi-Strauss's approach to kinship was concerned with the relationship between groups rather than their composition, just as structural linguists like Saussure had looked primarily at the relationship between phonemes, not their composition. Prior to 1949, the dominant theoretical approach to kinship of Radcliffe-Brown and his heirs focused on the internal composition of unilineal descent groups as expressed in land tenure, legal systems, politics and religious ceremonies. For George Murdock, another important analyst of kinship, the central issue was the ways in which rules of post-marital residence organised descent groups. Marriage, the relationship between groups, and kinship terminology were secondary considerations for both Radcliffe-Brown and Murdock. When Radcliffe-Brown used the term structure, it was in opposition to function and had nothing to do with the relationship between groups.

Lévi-Strauss moved kinship terminology and marriage rules to the forefront. Since groups defined their marriage rules in kinship terms, the kinship terminology was recognised by Lévi-Strauss as the most immediate mechanism for determining who was marriageable and who was not. For some systems, the terminology shouted sister/not marriageable and cousin/wife. Edmund Leach also recognised the role of kinship terminology in analysing relations between wife-givers and wife-takers among the Kachin (1945). From the structuralist point of view, the structure of the kinship terminology is identical to the structure of marriage rules, and the marriage rules tell one about the exchange of women between groups. In contrast, from the viewpoint of Murdock, the kinship terminology was not a determining factor of anything.

Our own approach to structure follows that of Lévi-Strauss. *Feasting With Mine Enemy* (Rosman and Rubel 1971) demonstrates the way in which potlatch distributions, held on various occasions, in six different Northwest Coast societies, followed the alignments of their social structures. The potlatch ceremony on the Northwest Coast was all inclusive in that it embodied not only kinship, but also economics, politics, religion, theatre, performance and all the arts. These potlatch ceremonies are what Mauss long ago characterised as total social phenomena. In our analyses of Northwest Coast societies, we demonstrated that the structural model which was constructed with kinship data, i.e. rules of marriage or descent, was also the model which made potlatch organisation comprehensible, as well as other cultural phenomena, as will be shown below. In each of the areas we have examined over the years, North America, Oceania and Asia, we have looked at the way in which ceremonial exchanges mirrored the social structure, including those organised by kinship and some that were not.

Exchanges are a form of communication which carry meaning. The objects which are exchanged carry two kinds of meanings. There are those meanings which relate to structural position, such as opposition, alliance and hierarchy, and the other meanings which relate to differences in emotion like competition versus peace. For example, among the patrilineal Arapesh, whom Mead studied long ago, a man distributed pearlshell rings to his affines including brothers-in-law, the mother's brother of a child. That child's *rites de passage* may have included scarification of a girl at adolescence, boys' initiation and finally the funeral of that child. In contrast, Arapesh men gave yams competitively to their unrelated exchange partners, their *buanyin*, the amount of which had to be equalled or bettered in the return. Pearlshell rings signified peace, and affines and yams meant exchange partners and competitive exchange (Rubel and Rosman 1978; Mead 1947). Raw food and cooked food frequently have different meanings. Among the Trobrianders, *urigubu*, which was given to sister's husband after every harvest, always involved raw yams called *taytu*. *Sagali*, the funerary distributions, always involved cooked *taytu* (Malinowski 1965). Cooked food given at a feast may mean commensality but it may also mean 'poison'. Among the Enga, the word *te* refers to the most important exchange ceremony and, in addition, means homicide compensation. In societies with fixed rank, when the subordinate, for example, the vassal, gives a portion of his harvest to the lord, that signifies his subordination, and when the lord gives horses or weapons, in return, that emphasises his dominance.

Ceremonial exchange is object specific up to a point. However, over time, substitutions of exchange objects may be made. Among the Enga, the third stage of their *te* ceremonial distribution had involved only cooked pork but in the 1970s cow and goat meat began to be substituted. On the Northwest Coast, before contact, the Kwakiutl potlatch distribution had involved elk skins, but in the nineteenth century after the beginning of the fur trade with the Hudson Bay Company, Hudson Bay blankets began to be substituted for these skins. In all of these instances of object substitution, the structure of the exchange remained the same, and so did the meaning.

The meanings of the things exchanged, and the relationship between exchangers may be subjected to another type of linguistic analysis. Objects exchanged in different ceremonies within a society are contrastive and are therefore structurally identical to phonemes. An example is the pearlshell/ yam contrast of the Arapesh discussed above. Like the phonemes of a language, the items being exchanged and their meanings are contrastive with one another, and they cannot be substituted for one another. When one phoneme is substituted for a different phoneme, the meaning of the word does change. When one accepts an invitation to dinner, one cannot substitute money for flowers or wine, or the meaning would change as in phoneme substitution. When meaning changes, the structure will change. Giving money would mean payment for the meal, which turns the giving into a commercial transaction like that in a restaurant. Wine means appreciation for being invited. Object substitution in a single ceremony, as in the Enga *te* where cow meat was substituted for pork, is identical to the way in which allophones constitute members of the same larger class. In linguistics, when one allophone is substituted for another, the linguist asks the question, has the meaning of the word changed? The answer is no. In substitutions in exchanges, such as cows for pigs, the meaning of the exchange did not change.

One of the early criticisms of structuralism was that it did not deal with history, that is, changes which occur diachronically through time. This chapter will deal with two important aspects of diachrony. On the one hand, structures may remain the same through time, though substitutions of exchange goods take place, as we have noted above. On the other hand, structures may be transformed through time, but not disappear. In the nineteenth century, the Tlingit had a four-part exchange structure whereas, as we shall see later, today they have a moiety structure, itself weakened by marriages within the same moiety. The societies we will discuss below have undergone enormous changes over the past century as a consequence of contact with the Western world, Christianisation, modernisation and most recently globalisation. For some of these societies, like those of the Northwest Coast, the relationship between ceremonial exchange and social structure was more easily discerned a hundred years ago. However, as a consequence of the effects of the forces enumerated above, the social structure, the concomitant pattern of exchanges, and large-scale ceremonies like potlatches have been greatly transformed. In the modern context, features relating to the political economy are important in the potlatch, while the kinship, religious and symbolic functions have declined in significance.

[* * *]

We will use several classic ethnographies to illuminate the relationship between structure and exchange. We will describe societies with flexible rank, which we have called potlatch type societies. We will use examples in two different ecological settings, the Northwest Coast of North America and Oceania, to demonstrate how in the nineteenth century such societies had the same pattern of structure and ceremonial exchange. More recently, as a consequence of different historical circumstances, they have been transformed and are now organised differently.

By the late nineteenth century, anthropologists had already recognised that societies on the Northwest Coast varied in their social structure. Some were matrilineal like the Tlingit, Tsimshian and Haida, while others like the Kwakiutl and Nuchalat were cognatic. However, anthropologists like Ruth Benedict and Homer Barnett who studied the potlatch did not recognise that the potlatch ceremony differed in relation to the variations in the social structure as we shall demonstrate below. The Tlingit, described by Swanton in 1905, had, by that time, become involved in the Canadian canning industry (1908). At this time, Tlingit society was divided into two exogamous matrilineal moieties, Raven and Wolf, each containing many lineages related to one another by matrilineal descent. The lineages and their leaders were ranked within each moiety. Matrilineages lived avunculocally (men moved to live with their mothers' brothers) in large wooden houses which contained several families. The families and the places in the house that they occupied were also ranked with respect to one another. There was a preference for marriage with Father's Sister's Daughter, or the female referred to as *at*, the Tlingit term for father's sister's daughter as well as father's sister. Each matrilineage had two other matrilineages in the opposite moiety with which

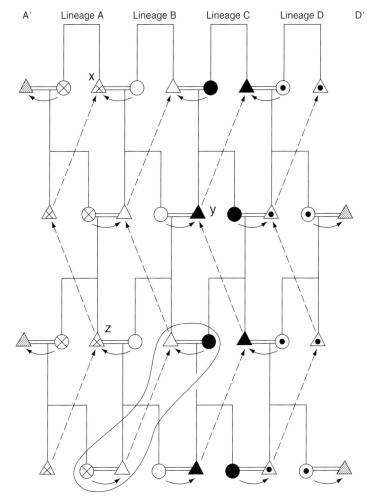

Figure 1 Structure of FaSiDa marriage.

it intermarried, both giving and receiving women in alternate generations from each of these two matrilineages. This resulted in a four-part structure (Rosman and Rubel 1971: chap. 3). (See Figure 1. Structure of FaSiDa Marriage.) The Tlingit had Crow kinship terminology, which is another manifestation of this structural model.

For the Tlingit, there was only one important occasion for a potlatch, the death of a chief, and the assumption to chiefly position of his successor, one of his sister's sons. Who became the next chief depended upon which sister's son was able to amass sufficient support and property to hold this potlatch.

It was also the event at which younger members of the chief's lineage received new names. Seating at a Tlingit potlatch separated the host and his matrilineage from the two groups of guests from the opposite moiety, who were members of the two lineages with which the host group intermarried. The host lineage was seated at the back of the house, opposite the entrance. Affines of the deceased chief were seated on one side, and affines of the new chief, on the opposite side. The affines of the deceased chief from the opposite moiety had provided funerary services for him, and erected a totem pole in his honour. The affines of the new chief built a new house for him. The distributions at the potlatch were in return for these services. There was no competition between host and guests, in contrast to what occurred at Kwakiutl potlatches. The Tlingit host and guests were in opposite moieties which were equal in rank and did not compete. Instead, the two groups of affines in the same moiety competed in song contests at this potlatch. In a Tlingit potlatch witnessed by Swanton, one group of affines of the host says to the other, 'I am holding your daughter's hand.' Swanton explains this phrase in a footnote by saying, 'The daughter of one Wolf [moiety] man being the wife of another, and vice versa' (1908: 440, footnote B). If one looks at Figure 1, the daughter of Man x in Lineage A, Wolf Moiety, is in Lineage B, Raven Moiety. She must marry a man, y in Lineage C, Wolf Moiety. 'Vice versa' means that marriage also goes in the opposite direction, that is, the daughter of y marries a man z in Lineage A. Swanton's statement only makes sense with the structural model based on the preferential marriage rule for Father's Sister's Daughter. At first this ethnographic information seems incomprehensible, but it is clear that the structural model of the type which Lévi-Strauss proposed explains it.

Other societies on the Northwest Coast also potlatched, and shared much the same ecological setting, but had different social structures from the Tlingit. The cognatic social structure of the Kwakiutl included ranked kin groups called *numayms,* and tribes. The presence of cognatic descent and a rule of primogeniture regardless of sex meant that one could be a member of mother's or father's descent group or both, or even mother's father's descent group. This resulted in a system of kin groups with overlapping memberships. The frequency of Kwakiutl potlatches, their functions and the occasions for potlatching were different from that of the Tlingit. While the Tlingit had one major potlatch which honoured the deceased and affirmed succession, among the Kwakiutl there were many occasions for potlatching. *Numayms* competed for individuals to become members by giving them names at potlatches they hosted. Through the lifetime of an individual, particularly one of a chiefly family, he or she received names of increasingly important rank from the competing *numayms* from which he or she was descended, mother's side or father's side, at potlatches held to mark various *rites de passage*. Primogeniture was the important factor in the bestowal of names. People competed by claiming higher and higher rank. Shaming one's rival in a different tribe or *numaym* was one of the ways of competing. There was competition within *numayms*, between *numayms*, and between tribes and between their chiefs. Ranking was manifested at potlatches by where individuals were seated by the host *numaym*, and the order in which they received property. Tlingit competition was completely different. In terms of Lévi-Straussian models, the Kwakiutl structural model is based on the rule of primogeniture, regardless of sex, generating a cognatic descent system, while the Tlingit structural model is based on a rule of marriage.

In contrast to the Northwest Coast, which had a single type of ecology but different social structures and structures of exchange, two societies in different parts of the world with different ecologies and totally different and unrelated languages may have the *same* type of social structure. Such a structural similarity is in no way due to historical connection. Trobriand society in the Massim area of Papua New Guinea is structurally identical to the Tlingit. Both are also potlatch type societies. The Tlingit were hunters, gatherers and fishermen, while the Trobrianders were agriculturalists who concentrated on yam production. Both societies had the capacity to accumulate large surpluses, which enabled them to hold large 'potlatches'. Like the Tlingit, the Trobrianders had matrilineal descent groups, Crow kinship terminology and a preference for Father's Sister's Daughter marriage. Trobriand men were supposed to marry the person whom they called *tabu*. *Tabu* is the Trobriand term for father's sister, and father's sister's daughter. This marriage rule applied primarily to chiefs, but nevertheless it could generate a structure of relationships between the clans or *dala*, or subclan which they headed. Matrilineal descent groups or clans were internally ranked and hierarchically ordered. A chief was succeeded by one of his sister's sons. The first sister's son who was able to amass enough goods to hold a *sagali* or mortuary feast (which was like a potlatch) for his maternal uncle, the chief who had died, would become the new chief. The affines of the deceased chief performed mortuary service for him, and the *sagali* recompensed them for this (refer to Figure 1). The pregnancy of the sister of the chief was also the occasion for a *sagali*. Her pregnancy was important in order to perpetuate the leadership of the matrilineage. The father's lineage of the new chief and his sister performed a series of services during her pregnancy. The pregnancy *sagali* was in exchange for these services (refer to Figure 1) (Rubel and Rosman 1970). The father's lineage of this new chief has given him his principal wife and is currently paying *urigubu*, a yearly payment in yams, to him. The *sagali* payment at the pregnancy ritual for his sister is a reversal of that *urigubu* payment, just as the mortuary *sagali* was a reversal of an earlier *urigubu* payment.

At a Tlingit potlatch, the two sets of affines are recompensed at the same time – one, the affines of the deceased chief for mortuary services which honour him; the other, the affines of the new chief, for honouring the reproductive future of the matrilineage by building the chief's house. Among the Trobrianders, the two clans that intermarry with the host clan are guests at two separate *sagali*, funerary and pregnancy. The structure of the two Trobriand *sagali* is identical to the structure of the major Tlingit potlatch (see Figure 1).

In addition to exchanges with affines, the Trobrianders had several other kinds of exchange systems, in contrast to the Tlingit. There was a competitive harvest exchange between villages – *kayasa* – which in recent times has come to be held in conjunction with a ritualised cricket game, and the competitiveness of this exchange carried over to the cricket game. This represents a change in the elements of the *kayasa* structure rather than a change in the structure itself. The Trobrianders also carry out *kula* exchange, which has the same structure as matrilateral cross-cousin marriage. Chiefs and sometimes wealthy commoners have *kula* partners on other islands, which may be different culturally and linguistically. The goods exchanged were two kinds of shell valuables: red shell necklaces which moved clockwise, and white armshells which moved counterclockwise. Like the Kachin, who had matrilateral cross-cousin marriage, in which each Kachin lineage had its wife-givers and wife-takers, the Trobriand men had separate shell-necklace givers and shell-necklace takers. The structure of the *kula* is quite different from the structure of *sagali*, which reversed direction in the next generation. The Trobrianders conceive of the armshells as female and the necklaces as male, and when they 'meet' (and are exchanged) in the *kula*, they view this as a marriage in a metaphoric sense (Rosman and Rubel 2004: 207).

As noted above, one of the early criticisms of structuralism was that it did not deal with diachrony, or how structures change. Over the more than one hundred years since they were first described, the structures we have identified for the Tlingit and the Trobrianders have changed. The forces for change which we mentioned above have transformed these structures of exchange and their relationship to the social structures to a greater or lesser extent. Here, we will explore the relevance of a continued use of the perspective of structure and exchange for examining these transformed societies. For the Tlingit living in Sitka today, both the social structure and the potlatch system have undergone significant transformation (Kan 1989). Russian Orthodox elders who speak Tlingit tend to be more traditional than those Tlingit who are middle-aged and younger, and do not know the language. The Protestants who missionised among the Tlingit were vehemently against the potlatch, hence Tlingit Protestants tend to be less enthusiastic about potlatching. However, because potlatching has become one of the elements of Tlingit tribal/ethnic identity, its frequency has increased.

The earlier matrilineal system of lineage, clan and moiety has been greatly undermined by the shift from avunculocal to nuclear family residences, and the marriage pattern has been completely transformed. Even moiety exogamy, which was so strong in the past, is often breached, and personal preference determines whom one will marry. The four-part structure generated by Father's Sister's Daughter marriage to which the potlatch structure had corresponded has collapsed into a weakened two-part moiety structure. The inheritance rule in which the traditional heir was sister's son has been violated in that many sons, who fish commercially with their fathers, inherit their fathers' boats. There are conflicts today over collectively owned property like houses and crest objects which belong to matrilineages and matriclans. Such crest objects have become valuable to museums and collectors. According to Kan, 'elders are torn between the desire to help their own nuclear family by selling the artifacts, and traditional rule which demands that these objects be bequeathed to their direct matrilineal descendants with whom they may no longer have strong ties' (1989: 410–11). Potlatch performances now include English summaries of what is said and sung in Tlingit, for the benefit of those who speak only English. However, elders are not in favour of this since translation does not convey the metaphoric meanings which are contained in speeches in the Tlingit language. These speeches also include Tlingit kinship terminology, whose translation into English is very problematic because there are no exact English equivalents for Crow kinship terms.

Among Trobrianders today, the structure of *sagali* appears to be continuing. The changes which have taken place are primarily substitutions of objects in the categories of goods exchanged. As Weiner noted in the 1980s, despite more than a century of Trobriand contact with pearlers, whalers, beche-de-mer traders, gold prospectors, labour recruiters, Christian missionaries, the colonial government and Papua New Guinea national administrators there have not been 'major significant changes in the basic structural features of the exchange system' (Weiner 1980: 276). Jolly points out that gender relations among the Trobrianders have changed. She notes,

Exchanges of women's wealth [banana leaf skirts at *sagalis*] have assumed an inflated and novel significance since Malinowski's time – not only securing the regeneration of Trobriand persons but insuring the perpetuity of Trobriand culture in the face of competing values . . . defending Trobriand traditions and the value of women against both monetary and male values . . . not unselfish persistences but self-conscious resistances to modernity and monetary values. (1992: 38)

Maintenance of tradition is seen as a symbol of resistance and a way of supporting the continuation of Trobriand identity. This is similar to the continuation of the Tlingit potlatch as a way of maintaining Tlingit identity by perpetuating the key ceremonial potlatch exchange in the face of modernisation, and Westernisation. Transformations among the Trobrianders have taken a different form. They altered cricket, utilising cultural material formerly connected to warfare and associating it with modern *kayasa* harvest competition and the competition between political movements (see the film *Trobriand Cricket* by Jerry Leach). A recent description of *kayasa* on the island of Kaileuna, just west of Kiriwina, indicates that it is now a competition between men of a village to see who can grow the most yams (Schiefenhövel and Bell-Krannhals 1996). Though chiefdomship, still present, is a matter of ascribed status, competition in events like *kayasa* is important in local politics today (Schiefenhövel and Bell-Krannhals 1996: 249). Modernisation of the *kula* has meant that power boats have taken the place of outrigger canoes, a substitution of one element for another, but the structure has remained the same.

We have also used the structure and exchange perspective diachronically to examine antecedent forms. Our ethnohistorical research has revealed that the earlier structure from which the Tlingit four-part Father's Sister's Daughter structure developed was a moiety structure of the type found among the interior Athapaskan societies (Rubel and Rosman 1983). The Tlingit potlatch operates today with a two-part matrilineal moiety structure rather than a four-part structure. When the Tlingit structure was transformed with the decline in importance of kinship, and the disappearance of clanship, the competition was no longer based on affinal relations. The competition for power which occurs is among the Tlingit who have now become an ethnic group, or between individuals of different ethnic groups. What were separate societies and tribal groups speaking different languages have become ethnic groups within a larger multiethnic nation. Ethnicity, race and religious differences become the points of cleavage in the larger nation. With regard to the Trobriand four-part structure, Malinowski's field notes hint that earlier in time, the clans in the four-part structure were organised in a moiety structure (Rosman and Rubel 1989). However, there is no evidence that today Trobriand structure has collapsed into a two-part moiety system as the Tlingit system has. On the contrary, the *urigubu*, and *sagali* exchanges continue to take place today maintaining the same structure as earlier.

Lévi-Strauss was concerned with kinship systems where the structure of exchange of goods corresponded to the marriage structure. However, structural analysis can also be used when the structure of ceremonial exchange is separate from the structure of exchange of women and affinal exchange. Among the patrilineal Enga, who live in the Western Highlands of Papua New Guinea, the system of ceremonial exchange, the *te*, is related to the structure of affinal exchange in a different manner from the Tlingit and the Trobrianders. In the *te* exchange system, an Enga man will have two groups of *te* partners, one set in clans to the east of his clan, and the second in clans to the west of his clan. He transmits goods he has received from his eastern partners at their *te* ceremonies to his western partners at the *te* ceremony that

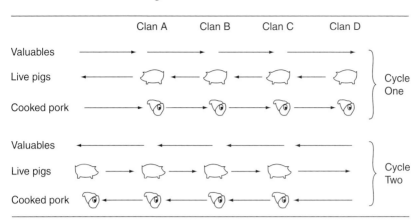

Figure 2 Enga *te* exchange.

he and his clan hosts. The Enga have a system of delayed exchange in which goods move from one group to the next until they reach the end of the chain, when they must reverse and go down the line in the opposite direction (see Figure 2). In the first stage, people give valuables such as stone axes, shells, plumes and small pigs to their partners in one direction. In the second stage, the givers of valuables become receivers of live pigs, which move down the chain as they are passed on at successive *te* distributions held in turn by each clan. At the end of the chain, there is a second reversal when the last receiver of live pigs becomes the first distributor of cooked pork. The distribution of cooked pork completes one cycle of the *te*. Another cycle will begin when initiatory gifts go in the direction opposite to the pork. The structure of the *te* is identical to the structure of exchange of women in Father's Sister's Daughter marriage, though the Enga do not have this preferential marriage rule. Given the pattern of marriage with patrilateral cross-cousin, as among the Trobrianders and the Tlingit, women married in one direction, and in the next generation the direction was reversed (see Figure 1). In phase two of the *te*, live pigs move in one direction, and in the next *te* cycle, the direction in which the live pigs travel is reversed. Structures of exchange of goods, as in the case of the *kula* exchange system, can be identical to structures of exchange of women. As we noted earlier, *kula* exchange has the same structure as matrilateral cross-cousin marriage.

Affinal exchanges among the Enga are different from *te* exchange but are like those found in many other patrilineal New Guinea societies. They go from the husband's patrilineage to the patrilineage of the wife, beginning with betrothal gifts to the bride's family, and ending at the death of the children born of that marriage. *Te* partnerships can develop from affinal relationships.

Enga patrilineal clans, occupying contiguous areas, fought with their neighbours but also exchanged women and goods with them. Since wives often
came from 'enemy' clans, they were considered dangerous. The word *te*
means 'homicide compensation' but *te* is also a sign of peace, since it ends
warfare (Rubel and Rosman 1978: 236). This double meaning recalls the
fact that in German the word 'gift' means poison, in contrast to its English
meaning. Giving and receiving in the *te* exemplifies the ambivalence seen in
exchange in general. The *te* involved competition for wealth, name and status,
and therefore had political significance for groups as well as individuals. Men
lobbied for support by making speeches. Though often the son of a Big Man
also became a Big Man, every man had a chance of becoming a leader. There
was no permanent class structure (Mapusia 1980: 63).

What has happened to the *te* system through time? Besides modernisation
and the end of endemic warfare for a time, Mapusia, an Enga writer, notes that
'Christianity . . . [and] a wave of Western ideologies poured into our society'
(1980: 65). Suppression of warfare was one of the accomplishments of the
colonial administration. As was typical, Westerners assumed that, when
presented with a 'superior' cultural lifestyle, the Enga would automatically
adopt it. Europeans, both government officials and missionaries, Lutheran,
Catholic and Seventh Day Adventist, in their efforts to Westernise the indigenous population had taken a very negative view of the *te* and hoped that with
conversion to Christianity it would disappear. When colonial officials first
encountered the *te* and the potlatch, they saw these exchange systems as
diverting the energies of the people from other more productive pursuits.
People saved, not for investment, but to give away. Missionaries saw the *te* as
a 'satanic' practice. However, it was the most important cultural institution
shaping Enga life. Many Big Men and their followers refused to be converted,
even when threatened with being thrown into hell. When Big Men did convert
and opted out of the *te*, they lost status and friends. Some of those who did
convert to Christianity continued to be involved in the *te*. However, according
to Paki, 'the last great *te* in traditional form took place in 1974' (Paki,
Ambassador Evan, personal communication). During 1974, while doing field
research among the Mae Enga, we observed what seems to have been the last
stage of the last cycle of the *te* to be held, in which halves of pigs, as well as
quarters of cooked cow meat, were distributed by Big Men to their *te* partners
(see Rubel and Rosman 1978: chap. 11).

When 'modern politics' came in, the *te* was used more and more frequently
as an instrument to gain political support, as the potlatch was used among the
Tlingit and the *kayasa* among the Trobrianders. As Mapusia notes, 'During
the previous election campaign, many people have used the system as a means
of winning votes . . . [and as] . . . an important path to gaining support . . . [by]
giving out pigs to as many people as possible hoping these people would be

his supporters when elections are on' (1980: 63). Educated men, who frequently own trucks and trade stores, or work outside of Enga territory, are involved in the modern political system but often continue to take part in the *te* ceremony. The availability of cash has enabled individuals to buy pigs from pig farms if they themselves have not raised a sufficient number. Alternatively, men may attach cash instead of pigs to stakes and boards. Trucks enabled people and pigs to be moved about more efficiently. Traditional leaders were still playing leadership roles in 1980, though strongly challenged periodically by the rising younger generation of men. The education of these younger men and their exposure to a wider world enabled them to explain to other Enga the various changes which were taking place. Traditional leaders were not able to do this. There were a few leaders who were able to have one foot in the traditional arena and the other in the modern, being involved in both modern and *te* politics. In this manner, modern political institutions were grafted onto the local *te* (Mapusia 1980: 70).

As Mapusia concluded in 1980, 'Despite new changes and the imposition of negative attitudes by colonial agents the *te* ceremonial exchange has continued to operate' (1980: 72). When asked about another *te*, older informants said that the *te* was like a great river and now there are too many little rivers. But in Enga Province, businessmen and women, and politicians who wish to win office at any political level from local to national, must successfully manipulate a network of exchange relationships built up with the help of their clans and other clans over many years. The *kula* among the Trobrianders had the same function in that it linked groups different in language and culture.

[∗ ∗ ∗]

Have structures of exchange identified by Lévi-Strauss remained the same, been transformed or disappeared? Large-scale ceremonials like the potlatch, *kula*, *sagali* and the *te*, though reduced in frequency and scope, have not disappeared despite the inroads of modernisation and Westernisation. The structures which these ceremonials encoded, most frequently structures based on kinship, have been transformed. They remain important because they have taken on new functions and meanings. Our examples also represent a continuum of differing degrees of incorporation into larger political entities, and a consequent shift from kinship-based structures to those based on ethnic identity and ethnic groups. Systems of ceremonial exchange like the potlatch, *sagali*, *kula* and *te* had features in common which have enabled them to persist. They represented ways which both individuals and their kin groups used to increase their political importance, prestige and power in the past. Today, they are being utilised as vehicles to gain political support by a new generation of leaders who are operating in transformed political systems in which larger kinship organisations like clans have either declined or disappeared. The *te* among the Enga is now an important vehicle for aspiring political leaders to gain renown, wider reputations and voting support in their campaigns for local and national political office, seeking support from kin as well as non-kin. Trobriand men gain prestige to turn it into political power on a national scale, when their political movements demonstrate superiority in competitive *kayasa* and cricket games. Similarly, the sponsorship of a mortuary potlatch among the Tlingit today demonstrates one's importance and worth, and that of one's kin group. Ceremonial exchange always involves competition and is ultimately about power, which was also its function at an earlier point in time. Today, ceremonial exchange continues because prestige which accrues from the giving is transformed into power on the local and national political scene.

The Tlingit, Trobrianders and the Enga are all now politically part of larger nation-states. More than one hundred years ago, these societies were characterised by what Lévi-Strauss called elementary structures. Today, the remnants of the elementary structures coexist with aspects of what Lévi-Strauss characterised as complex structures. Their social structures, such as the political behaviour and election politics of the Enga and the Trobrianders, in part, can now be analysed utilising statistical models. These societies are therefore less easily analysed in structural terms.

All or parts of the theory of structure and exchange have been critiqued since 1985 by post-structuralists and postmodernists. Recently, the principle of reciprocity, especially, has come under attack. In *The Elementary Structures of Kinship*, reciprocity is central to Lévi-Strauss's idea that the incest taboo marks the beginning of culture (1949a; 1969b). Lévi-Strauss assumes that reciprocity is a cultural universal; it stands at the core of the evolution of culture. James attributes the critique of the concept of reciprocity to the rejection of 'the easy and "naturalistic" generalisations which have sometimes been drawn from readings of *The Gift*' (1998: 17). James supports Alain Testart when he 'questions the facile assumptions of universality behind the apparent general logic of exchange and reciprocity . . . What can it mean to speak, literally, of an "obligation to return"? As a general principle, it does not exist' (1998: 17). Testart cites evidence from potlatch ceremonies, that not everyone who was given property at a potlatch actually made a return. The poor, in fact, may not return goods (Testart 1998: 98). He cites Edward Curtis, an unreliable amateur, as an expert regarding information on the potlatch (Testart 1998: 100, 107–8). Testart does not recognise that Kwakiutl chiefs who distributed in the potlatch represented all of the members of their *numaym* as well as themselves. Thus, even if individual *numaym* guests did not make a return, reciprocity between groups was still operative.

Godelier has noted that Mauss discussed the obligation of gifts to the gods. Godelier contends that in all societies, even modern secular societies, there are sacred objects, retained by humans, which are not subject to exchange, and these provide fixed points relating to the continuity of groups and their identities. Godelier argues that this is the starting point for gift exchange in rank societies (1999: 8, 13, 30). How can the absence of exchange of sacred objects be the starting point for exchange, as Godelier argues? With 'gifts to the gods', sacrifices, there is no reciprocity, since reciprocity is a principle that operates only between humans. They can in no way compel the gods to reciprocate, or make a return; they can only supplicate. This is also why religious acts of charity and philanthropy, often anonymous, do not involve reciprocity and exchange. If there is a return, it may be a blessing or benediction.

The principle of reciprocity has also been questioned by those examining whether or not there is such a thing as a 'pure gift' without any kind of return. In his study of Jain renouncers in India, Laidlaw argues that *dan*, the 'paradigmatic religious good deed', which is food that renouncers receive every day directly from family cooking pots before the family eats, are 'pure gifts' in that no thanks are offered. A general benediction often may be called out by the renouncer when he enters the house (Laidlaw 2002: 47, 48). Is the benediction a return for the food? One might argue that the benediction, 'May you receive the fruit of good conduct' represents a sacred return (Laidlaw 2002: 47). Another interpretation is that the food is being given to the gods through the renouncer, the representative of the sacred, and there is no obligation for the gods to return.

New support for the principle of reciprocity has come from the innovative discipline of evolutionary psychology, which champions reciprocity under the banner of 'social exchange'. Cosmides and Tooby observe that 'humans have evolved a constellation of cognitive adaptations to social life . . . a social map of persons, relationships, motives, interactions, emotions and intentions that made up their social world . . . [The human mind] contains specialized mechanisms designed for reasoning about social exchange . . . it is likely that our ancestors have engaged in social exchange for at least several million years' (Cosmides and Tooby 1992: 163–4). The universality of social exchange, its presence among primate relatives, and palaeoanthropological evidence of reciprocation support this position. In other words 'certain fundamental ways of thinking about social exchange will be the same everywhere, without needing to be socially transmitted . . . [though] social transmission may indeed shape social exchange . . . Consequently, many dimensions along which social exchange varies both within and between cultures, may be instances of evoked culture [that is, culturally transmitted items]' (Cosmides and Tooby 1992: 211; see also Cosmides and Tooby 2004). The human species alone has the cognitive machinery to generate social exchange. Such cognitive machinery must also include the capacity for language, since social exchange presupposes a system of communication, even if only rudimentary. 'The universality of a behavioral phenotype is not a *sufficient* condition for claiming that it was produced by a cognitive adaptation, but it is suggestive. As a behavioral phenotype, social exchange is as ubiquitous as the human heartbeat. The heartbeat is universal because the organ that generates it is everywhere the same. This is a parsimonious explanation for the universality of social exchange as well' (Cosmides and Tooby 2000: 1,260). Long ago, Lévi-Strauss, in *The Elementary Structures of Kinship* (1949a; 1969b) postulated that the incest taboo, which necessitated the exchange of women and social exchange, marked the transformation from nature to culture for the primates who became hominids – human beings. At the very moment when one set of scholars raises doubts about reciprocity, a basic structuralist concept, the research of another group of scholars, the evolutionary psychologists, supports it as a fundamental cognitive adaptation of the human species.

Critiques of structuralism began as early as the 1970s when post-structuralists, some of whom had originally been structuralists themselves, began to question some of its major tenets. Sarup's discussion of Derrida's critique of structuralism sums up the important issues involved. He notes, 'Firstly he [Derrida] doubts the possibility of general laws. Secondly, he questions the opposition of the subject and the object, upon which the possibility of objective description rests. In his view, the description of the object is contaminated by the patterns of the subject's desires. Thirdly, he questions the structure of binary opposi-tions' (Sarup 1989: 43). The empiricist position assumes the possibility of accessing the outside world, and capturing it in an uninterpreted fashion by compensating for the viewer's own language and mind-set and by means of 'back-checking' the translation. The status of science and the objectivity of the language of a description or of analysis are being called into question.

In America, the critique of structuralism has come primarily from post-modernists, who claim that we cannot describe the 'world out there', the idea of knowledge of the outside world, which they call representation. As Geuijen *et al.* note, 'There is no Real World with which different theories can be compared to find out if they are correct' (1995: x; see Marcus 1995). When the postmodernists called into question various aspects of ethnography, anthropologists began to rethink the ethnographic process by which field materials are transformed into ethnographies. Ethnographies have always been the basis for the analysis of structure and exchange. Ethnographies should now reflect the multivocalic nature of culture, human agency, dialogic nature of fieldwork, and anthropological knowledge production. We must pay attention to the role that creative human behaviour plays in effecting change. Saussure long ago pointed out the distinction between *langue*, which represents the structure of a language, and encodes past changes, and *parole*, which represents the idiosyncratic manner in which each individual speaks that language. *Parole* encompasses ambiguity, creativity of expression and the processes of language change, like borrowing, which produces irregularities. *Parole* represents human agency. Transformations in the *te* ceremony and in the potlatch, and the way individuals now use these to advance their own political position represent human agency and creativity. These changes in the nature of ethnographic fieldwork and the way in which ethnographies are produced have not diminished the relevance of structuralism. On the contrary, they have enabled more detailed and productive structural analyses of the type presented in this chapter.

In America, postmodernists have been influenced by the work of Schneider and Geertz, who have questioned what should go into anthropological categories such as kinship, religion and economics, which had formerly been the bases for analysis (Schneider 1984; Geertz 2005: 5). Postmodernists assert that the ethnographic texts which anthropologists had been producing for more than a century were Western representations of the cultures, reconceptualised in Western categories rather than in those of the people themselves. Previous attempts to present what was referred to as the description of a culture 'from the native's point of view', combined with the perspective of the outsider were now seen as inadequate. This replicated what the linguist does in producing a description of a language. Interestingly, what postmodernists are calling into question is whether cultural translation is possible at all. If linguistic translation is a valid enterprise, so is cultural translation (see Rubel and Rosman 2003).

The ethnographic description of a culture is made at a point in time. Postmodernists have criticised anthropologists for writing about cultures, which were seen as timeless, ignoring their contact with Western colonial culture. However, even before postmodernism, anthropologists recognised the need to place their ethnographic research in its relevant historical setting. In this chapter we have placed the societies which we have analysed in their historical frameworks, in order to understand the structural transformations which have taken place, and demonstrate how structures responded to historical forces.

Lévi-Strauss pioneered the development of the structural approach and the focus on structure and exchange. In our analyses, we have taken this approach combining structuralism and exchange into the postmodern, post-structuralist era and shown how structuralism can deal with modernisation, Westernisation and change. The theoretical perspective of structuralism developed by Lévi-Strauss, and more particularly a perspective on structure and exchange, still has explanatory value. Postmodernists support a relativist anthropology, which is much less productive and has less explanatory value than the

78   *Abraham Rosman and Paula G. Rubel*

approach which we have demonstrated here, which is comparative, diachronic and involves model-building. But such a comparative anthropology
must be based on sensitive, detailed and historically situated ethnographies.

Boas, Franz 1911. 'Introduction', in *Handbook of American Indian Languages*, Part 1.
    Washington, DC: Smithsonian Institution Bureau of American Ethnology,
    Bulletin 40, pp. 1–84.
Clifford, James 1986. 'Introduction: Partial Truths', in James Clifford and George
    Marcus (eds.), *Writing Culture: The Poetics and Politics of Ethnography*.
    Berkeley: University of California Press.
Cosmides, Leda and John Tooby 1992. 'Cognitive Adaptations for Social Exchange',
    in Jerome H. Barkow, Leda Cosmides and John Tooby (eds.), *The Adapted Mind:
    Evolutionary Psychology and the Generation of Culture*. New York: Oxford
    University Press, pp. 163–228.
    2000. 'The Cognitive Neuroscience of Social Reasoning', in Michael Gazzaniga (ed.),
    The New Cognitive Neurosciences II. Cambridge, MA: MIT Press, pp. 1,259–70.
    2004. 'Social Exchange: the Evolutionary Design of a Neurocognitive System', in
    Michael S. Gazzaniga (ed.), *The New Cognitive Neurosciences III*. Cambridge,
    MA: MIT Press, pp. 1,295–1,319.
Geertz, Clifford 2005. 'Shifting Aims, Moving Targets: on the Anthropology of
    Religion', *The Journal of the Royal Anthropological Institute* 11: 1–15.
Geuijen, Karin, Diederick Raven and Jan deWolf (eds.) 1995. 'Editorial Introduction',
    in *Post-Modernism and Anthropology: Theory And Practice*. Assen, The Netherlands:
    Van Gorcum, pp. ix–xxvi.
Godelier, Maurice 1999. *The Enigma of the Gift*. Translated by Nora Scott. Chicago:
    University of Chicago Press.
James, Wendy 1998. ' "One of Us": Marcel Mauss and "English" Anthropology', in
    Wendy James and N. J. Allen (eds.), *Marcel Mauss: a Centenary Tribute*. New
    York: Berghahn Books, pp. 3–28.
Jolly, Margaret 1992. 'Banana Leaf Bundles and Skirts: a Pacific Penelope's Web?', in
    History and Tradition in Melanesian Anthropology. Berkeley: University of
    California Press, pp. 38–63.
Kan, Serge 1989. 'Cohorts, Generations, and Their Culture: the Tlingit Potlatch in the
    1980s', *Anthropos* 84: 405–22.
Laidlaw, James 2002. 'A Free Gift Makes No Friends', in Mark Osteen (ed.), *The
    Question of the Gift: Essays across Disciplines*. New York: Routledge, pp. 45–66.
Leach, Edmund 1945. 'Jinghpaw Kinship Terminology', *Journal of the Royal
    Anthropological Institute* 75.
Malinowski, Bronislaw 1965 [1935]. *Coral Gardens and their Magic: Soil-tilling and
    Agricultural Rites in the Trobriand Islands*, volume I. Bloomington: Indiana
    University Press.
Mapusia, Mike 1980. 'The *Tee* Ceremonial Exchange System in the Enga Province',
    Oral History 8 (7): 46–74.
Marcus, George 1995. 'Notes on Ideologies of Reflexivity in Contemporary Efforts to
    Remake the Social Sciences', in Karin Geuijen, Diederick Raven and Jan de Wolf

(eds.), *Post-Modernism and Anthropology: Theory and Practice.* Assen, The Netherlands: Van Gorcum, pp. 1–20.

Mauss, Marcel 1954. *The Gift: Forms and Functions of Exchange in Archaic Societies.* Translated by Ian Cunnison. Glencoe, IL: The Free Press.

Mead, Margaret 1947. 'The Mountain Arapesh III. Socio-Economic Life IV. Diary of Events in Alitoa', *Anthropological Papers of the American Museum of Natural History* 40, part 3: 159–420.

Piaget, Jean 1970 [1968]. *Structuralism.* Translated and edited by Chaninah Maschler. New York: Basic Books.

Rosman, Abraham and Paula G. Rubel 1971. *Feasting With Mine Enemy: Rank and Exchange among Northwest Coast Societies.* New York: Columbia University Press.

   1986. 'The Evolution of Central Northwest Coast Societies', *Journal of Anthropological Research* 42 (4): 567–72.

   1989. 'Dual Organization and its Developmental Potential in two Contrasting Environments', in David Maybury-Lewis and Uri Almagor (eds.), *The Attraction of Opposites: Thought and Society in a Dualistic Mode.* Ann Arbor, MI: The University of Michigan Press.

   2004. *The Tapestry of Culture: An Introduction to Cultural Anthropology* [Eighth Edition]. New York: McGraw-Hill.

Rubel, Paula G. and Abraham Rosman 1970. 'Potlatch and *Sagali*: The Structure of Exchange in Haida and Trobriand Societies', *Transactions of the New York Academy of Sciences.* Series 2, 32 (6).

   1978. *Your Own Pigs You May Not Eat: A Comparative Study of New Guinea Societies.* Chicago: University of Chicago Press.

   1983. 'The Evolution of Exchange Structures and Ranking: Some Northwest Coast and Athapaskan Examples', *Journal of Anthropological Research* 39 (1): 1–35.

   2003. 'Introduction: Translation and Anthropology', *Translating Culture: Perspectives on Translation and Anthropology.* New York: Berg, pp. 1–24.

Sarup, Madan 1989. *An Introductory Guide to Post-Structuralism and Postmodernism.* Athens, GA: University of Georgia Press.

Schiefenhövel, Wulf and Ingrid Bell-Krannhals 1996. 'Of Harvests and Hierarchy: Securing Staple Food and Social Position in the Trobriand Islands', in Polly Wiessner and Wulf Schiefenhövel (eds.), *Food and the Status Quest: An Interdisciplinary Perspective.* Providence, RI: Berghahn Books, pp. 235–52.

Schneider, David 1984. *A Critique of the Study of Kinship.* Ann Arbor: University of Michigan Press.

Swanton, J. R. 1908. *Social Conditions, Beliefs, and Linguistic Relationship of the Tlingit Indian.* 26th Annual Report of the Bureau of American Ethnology for the years 1904–5. Washington, DC: Bureau of American Ethnology.

Testart, Alain 1998. 'Uncertainties of the "Obligation to Reciprocate": a Critique of Mauss', in Wendy James and N. J. Allen (eds.), *Marcel Mauss: A Centenary Tribute.* New York: Berghahan Books, pp. 97–110.

Weiner, Annette 1980. 'Stability in Banana Leaves: Colonization and Women in Kiriwina, Trobriand Islands', in M. Etienne and Eleanor Leacock (eds.), *Women and Colonization.* New York: Praeger Books, pp. 270–93.

4   The future of the structural theory of kinship

Marcela Coelho de Souza

Since the publication of *The Elementary Structures of Kinship* (1949a; 1969a), Lévi-Strauss's work on kinship has acquired a somewhat ambiguous status: foundational, of course – a classic – but a classic whose specific thesis and concepts are frequently thought of as having little relevance to today's anthropology. After forming one of the two grand paradigms that polarised the field of kinship studies in mid-twentieth-century anthropology (the 'alliance theory' that became opposed to the 'descent theory' of British extraction)[1] Lévi-Straussian theses (along with descent theory) fell under the fire of critics from culturalist, practice theory and feminist perspectives, among other tendencies that entered the anthropological scene from the seventies onwards – the decade that saw the demise of kinship itself as an anthropological concept, if not as a legitimate subject of anthropological enquiry.

The news of its passing having been perhaps exaggerated, kinship remains a cherished topic of anthropological research. The field has, nevertheless, re-emerged from the *fin-de-siècle* doubts deeply transformed.[2] Among the multiple aspects involved, the most conspicuous is the status of a conceptual and ideological opposition – that between nature and culture – that is central to Lévi-Straussian kinship theory, to anthropology in general and, more generally still, to modern(ist) thought. A keystone of all of those ideational structures, and of the more material ones we build from them, the dichotomy is today the focus of many of our uncertainties, and the efforts to deconstruct it are perhaps surpassed only by the efforts to reconstitute it – inside and outside anthropology. It is in relation to this that the present relevance of Lévi-Strauss's work on kinship is most salient. We shall see how the anthropological approach to the subject that most explicitly has anchored itself in this opposition is perhaps the one best prepared to work without it – and for good reason...

Alliance and exchange: one or two theories?

The Elementary Structures of Kinship (1969a) opens with an 'Introduction' that includes two chapters, 'Nature and Culture' and 'The Problem of Incest', followed by eight others dedicated to the investigation of 'The Bases of Exchange' – after that, we enter the analysis of the Australian systems and the determination of the different modalities of exchange that constitute the 'elementary structures'. In those ten initial chapters are exposed the essentials of what Louis Dumont (1971) has called the 'general theory' (*théorie générale*) contained in the book, the '*théorie structuraliste de la parenté*', of supposed universal applicability, centred on a structural interpretation of the incest prohibition. Presenting simultaneously the distinctive attributes of nature – universality – and of culture – the coercive or normative character it has *qua* rule, the incest prohibition is not something to be sociologically (or biologically) explained: it is itself an explanatory principle, the partial or negative expression of an imperative that defines the very conditions of possibility of the emergence of society, namely the principle of reciprocity. For a man, prohibited from marrying his own close relatives, to have a wife, he must release his sisters and daughters to others, in order that those others may give him their women. This imperative gives birth to kinship as a field of social relations regulated by a law of exchange which, in some societies, materialises in positive marriage rules – that is, positive injunctions specifying the kinship category, class or group from where to choose a spouse. But even where this does not apply, and the choice of a spouse is not regulated by any such injunctions, the incest prohibition remains, as the minimum form of a rule of exchange and reciprocity that makes possible kinship and society – and culture itself.

Before it, culture is still non-existent; with it, nature's sovereignty over man is ended. The prohibition of incest is where nature transcends itself. It sparks the formation of a new and more complex type of structure and is superimposed upon the simpler structures of physical life through integration, just as these themselves are superimposed upon the simpler structures of animal life. It brings about and is in itself the advent of a new order. (1969a: 25)

According to Dumont, this 'general theory' is to be distinguished from the 'restricted theory' (*théorie restreinte*),[3] 'marriage alliance theory' (*théorie de l'alliance de marriage*). The latter applies only to a specific type of society: those that have 'positive rules' for the selection of a spouse, that is, rules that not only proscribe certain relatives as potential marriage partners, but also prescribe or specify the class or category of relatives from which spouses may be selected. The 'classes' may be clans, lineages or specialised institutions like moieties or Australian marriage sections; but the categories invariably involve the relationship between cross-cousins (that is, the children of a parent's opposite-sex siblings, as opposed to the children of a parent's same-sex siblings). If the bulk of Lévi-Strauss's treatise is devoted to this type of society, its first ten chapters may be described as aiming to determine that

cross-cousin marriage is the simplest expression of the principle of reciprocity, that it is the foundation of kinship itself – that very same principle
expressed by the incest prohibition.

The need to connect these two 'theories' was, and continues to be, put into
question by many critics of and heirs to Lévi-Strauss's theses. Among his
heirs, some of the most pre-eminent – like Louis Dumont and Françoise
Héritier – have preferred to substitute other foundations for the principle of
reciprocity and the notion of exchange: the opposition between mental
categories (affinity/consanguinity), or sexual asymmetry (Dumont 1971;
Héritier 1981).

The suspicions over the notion of exchange are manifold. Some are of an
'empirical' nature, relating to the difficulties in applying it (and the idea of
'reciprocity' in particular) to certain sorts of phenomena.[4] A problem here is
the frequently restrictive or narrow interpretation of the notion of exchange.
We shall come back to this later. Other objections are of a more profound
or basic nature. Among these, many are related to the gender bias in the
presentation of the exchange relations as 'exchange of women'. It was of little
service that Lévi-Strauss insisted that he had been misunderstood; that
from his point of view 'the rules of the game would remain unchanged were
the opposite conventions adopted, with men being exchanged by women's
groups' and that, even if 'a few societies of a highly developed matrilineal
type have, to a limited extent, expressed things that way', treating men as the
objects of matrimonial exchange, the androcentric phrasing simply 'corresponds to what nearly all human societies think and say'; or that another way
to formulate the concept would be to say that 'groups consisting of both men
and women exchange among themselves kinship relations' (Lévi-Strauss
and Eribon 1991b: 105; Lévi-Strauss 1983c: 60; 1987a). These replies do
not seem to have been taken seriously by commentators and critics, who in
general continued to consider the idea of exchange *of women* as a basic
postulate of the theory. This accepted, the theory of course became vulnerable
both to ethnographic objections – demonstrating the inadequacy of such a
description to this or that society, regarding either native representations or
structural description – and to theoretical, political or ideological criticism –
pointing to the 'androcentric, naturalistic or even eurocentric' underpinnings
of the argument (Collard 2000a: 103).

Indeed, it is not impossible to read *The Elementary Structures of Kinship*
as a particular instance of an ideational matrix typical of modernist social
thought that shares with other kinship theories – inside and outside anthropology and social sciences – the same presumption that kinship is the social
construction of natural facts (namely the natural facts of procreation), one that
implies a parallel conception of gender as the social construction of another
natural fact (namely sex or sexual difference). It was on this double terrain

that the most important shifts that have reshaped the reborn field of kinship studies since the nineties have taken place. A number of assumptions were profoundly shaken in anthropological theorising under the impact, in particular, of feminist criticism, and of the new practices of kinship related to the new reproductive technologies. Among them: that kinship is something anchored in relations that, being 'biological', are somehow outside or prior to social relations; that one may correlate that which is female to nature and that which is male to culture (Ortner 1974); and that this correlation may be projected upon the 'domaining' of social life in terms of the opposition domestic/political.[5] On this double account, nevertheless, Lévi-Straussian theory is arguably much less at fault than descent theory. First, the public/domestic dichotomy, which is crucial to the conceptualisation of social structure by British descent theorists in terms of distinct, articulated and hierarchised domains, has limited, if any, value for Lévi-Strauss (Collier and Yanagisako 1987: 5). Second, his treatment of the nature/culture problem, or, more specifically here, of the biological foundations of kinship, as manifest in the place given to 'the family' in the theory, contrasts sharply with the conventional notion of a natural nucleus or base provided either by the parent–child triad or the mother–child pair. He certainly concedes that the 'biological family' is present, and 'prolonged' in human society, since it exists 'prior' to it. But, as he says, 'what confers upon kinship its socio-cultural character is not what it retains from nature, but, rather, the essential way in which it diverges from nature' (Lévi-Strauss 1958a; 1963a: 50). The emphasis here, then, is on discontinuity and on the devaluation of consanguinity as the defining or encompassing dimension of kinship. Kinship as a social fact is *not* a 'recognition' or 'extension' (two key words for the British tradition of descent theory) of natural givens, but a refusal to abide by them.

But there are reasons for doubt. The *way* in question is the object of chapter 3 of *The Elementary Structures of Kinship*: consanguinity (filiation and siblingship) is a natural given; but whereas nature, by the mechanism of heredity, rules over filiation, in the terrain of mating (or marriage) it has no say, and affinity, through the prohibition of incest, comes to occupy this vacant lot and prevent the retention of females by their families, that is, fathers and brothers. The (natural) 'viscosity' of the family is thus contravened by a principle of collective intervention that affirms, against it, the vital requirements of society as such (1969a: 30–1, 41). What we have in this argument is a conventional distribution of the realms of nature and culture in kinship – consanguinity (a connection through common filiation) is opposed to affinity (a connection through marriage) because it is a natural given rather than socially constructed. Despite the value assigned to affinity as the foundation of kinship, this is well inside the traditional anthropological consensus and the cultural conceptualisation of kinship in terms of the duality of nature and law (Schneider 1968) in which it is rooted. It could hardly be otherwise: new ideas cannot but be born from old ones, and often need to be expressed in old languages. But in Lévi-Strauss's work on kinship we do find some significant bendings and torsions of the discourse on the nature/culture distinction that open promising new vistas. Perhaps we should sidestep the direct treatment of the venerable nature/culture opposition and the 'general' theory *as such*. Indeed, Lévi-Strauss himself has confessed that he is less than convinced that his 'preliminaries' in *The Elementary Structures of Kinship* (1969a) (he is referring to the treatment of the nature/culture opposition and the placing of the incest prohibition at the point of 'passage' between them) are required by the overall economy of the book (Lévi-Strauss 1988a; Lévi-Strauss and Eribon 1991b: 100). Taking into consideration, alternatively, some developments inside and outside of the Lévi-Straussian tradition, we may see how both 'theories' (the 'general theory' of kinship as exchange and alliance, and the 'restricted theory' regarding elementary systems) resonate with other, non-Western, conceptualizations of kinship, gender, nature and society – those conceptualisations explored by Lévi-Strauss in his work on Amerindian myths (*mytho-logics*), for instance. In this way, we gain fresh perspectives on old dilemmas. Before exploring these perspectives, let us examine some basic concepts.

Cross-cousins and brothers-in-law: a certain South American relationship...

The Elementary Structures of Kinship is dedicated to L. H. Morgan, from whose *Systems of Consanguinity and Affinity in the Human Family* (1871) it was separated by an interval almost equal to the one that stretches between *The Elementary Structures of Kinship* and us (measured in terms of the extent to which the ethnographic record has grown, this second interval is certainly much longer). This is most apposite. If the greatest discovery of the 'founding father' of kinship studies – the one that established kinship as a distinctive subject in (and of) anthropology – was, in the words of Leslie White quoted by Meyer Fortes (1969: 9), 'the fact that customs of designating relatives have scientific significance', we could certainly say that, among the diverse hypotheses devised to specify that significance, the one put forward in Lévi-Strauss's book deserves pride of place.

The 'new planet' discovered by Morgan (Fortes 1969: 8) – kinship terminologies *qua* systems of 'definite ideas' (Morgan's phrase)[6] – had two very different sides: the classificatory systems that 'confound relationships' in such a way as to assimilate collateral to lineal relatives (applying a single term, typically, to a father and his brothers, and to the mother and their sisters), and the 'descriptive ones' that do not. Classificatory terminologies, or systems, had been the subject of much debate and speculation when Lévi-Strauss entered the discussion. Evolutionary conjectures aside, Victorian anthropologists and ethnographers had been able to connect them to two other conspicuous social institutions in the primitive world: dual organisation (the division of society in two named exogamous groups) and cross-cousin marriage (marriage with the children of one's parent's opposite-sex siblings). The perception of this triple congruence is as old as the vocabulary in question: 'cross-cousin marriage' is a phrase coined by Tylor to describe an arrangement that he interprets as 'the direct result of the simplest form of exogamy', the division of society in two matrimonial moieties (Tylor 1889: 263; Kuper 1988: 99). William H. R. Rivers's work had mapped the various possible connections between specific varieties of such terminologies and diverse features of social organisation, such as special kinds of marriage and group structure, but a general explanation was still wanting.

The Elementary Structures of Kinship was written in New York, between 1943 and 1947, and presented in Paris, in 1948, as Lévi-Strauss's 'main thesis', coupled with a 'complementary thesis', *La Vie familiale et sociale des Indiens Nambikwara* (published that same year by the Société des Americanistes). The 'complementarity' in question is an important one: the Nambikwara play in *The Elementary Structures of Kinship*, a pivotal, if inconspicuous, role.

The decisive moment was Lévi-Strauss's encounter with two Nambikwara bands, speaking different dialects, allied to one another through a convention that made the men in one of them 'brothers-in-law' to the men in the other (and made their 'sisters', wives and vice versa). In the following generation the inter-band marriages would fit the assimilation between affines (spouses- and siblings-in-law) and cross-cousins characteristic of their relationship terminology. If the two groups so united would keep track of their double origin, maintaining, for instance, the separation of their camps, we would have the basis of an exogamous moiety system, a dual organisation as usually conceived. The episode is evoked in *The Elementary Structures of Kinship* (1969a: 67–8), but the first reference to it is an earlier article, 'The Social Use of Kinship Terms among Brazilian Indians' (1943a), where the political dimension of affinity is brought to the fore. Here, the Nambikwara and the historical Tupian groups of the Brazilian Coast are evoked in a discussion of the way certain relationship terms – 'brother-in-law' terms – are used to create a bond between persons previously unrelated, expressing a 'special "brother-in-law" relationship' that worked as an opening device regarding the kinship universe and made possible the establishment of wider social relations (1969a: 67–8; 1943a: 401–3): 'When the technical problem of establishing new social relationships is put up to the Indians, it is not the vague "brotherhood" which is called upon, but the more complex mechanism of the "brother-in-law" relationship' (1943a: 407, note 22). His objective is to show that:

a certain kinship tie, the brother-in-law relationship, once possessed a meaning among many South American tribes far transcending the simple expression of relationship. This significance … is both sexual and political-social; and, owing to its complexity, the brother-in-law relationship may perhaps be regarded as an actual institution. (Lévi-Strauss 1943a: 398)

Despite its anecdotal character, this structuralist primal scene (Viveiros de Castro 2006) is thus central to Lévi-Straussian theory on more than one account. This 'political' dimension of affinity – a topic much developed by Americanist ethnology after Lévi-Strauss – consists not in a dimension that is supplementary to one kinship category or aspect: it informs, in a large measure, the whole 'structuralist general theory of kinship' – the whole understanding of kinship, and ultimately of society, as based on 'exchange', that is, on a connection predicated upon the *difference* between the parties (not on their similarity or identity). We will return to this. As evoked in *The Elementary Structures of Kinship*, the Nambikwara case appears to Lévi-Strauss as one in which, in Lowie's words quoted by him, 'the characteristic features of the sib organization[7] are in some measure *prefigured* among sibless tribes' (Lowie 1919: 28; Lévi-Strauss 1943a: 403; my emphasis). The key is the meaning Lévi-Strauss confers to this *prefiguration* – not a historical prefiguration, but the simplest expression of a principle constitutive of kinship itself. Prior authors had interpreted relationship terminologies like that of the Nambikwara, based on a dichotomy between parallel and cross-relatives, and on the assimilation of cross-relatives to affines (the equation of cross-cousins and spouses, or siblings-in-law if same-sex; of mother's brother and father-in-law; of father's sister and mother-in-law), as an expression of the division of society in two exogamous moieties (for any individual, parallel relatives would be in his/her own moiety; cross-relatives, and in-laws, in the opposite one). When such an institutional division in moieties was not present, as was often the case, the terminology, and the cross-cousin marriage rule associated with it, would be seen as a survival of its previous existence. Not so for Lévi-Strauss, as we read in *The Elementary Structures of Kinship*:

As the dual organization, the kinship system we have just discussed, and the rules of marriage between cross-cousins are in perfect harmony, it might just as easily be said, reversing the previous proposition, that dual organization is the expression, on an institutional plane, of a system of kinship which itself derives from certain rules of alliance. (1969a: 99)

It is not possible to overemphasise the importance of this move, which is not reduced to a mere inversion of the causal priority traditionally conferred to dual organisation over cross-cousin marriage. On the contrary, both, as well as the dichotomous classification of relationships that accompanies them, originate equally 'in the apprehension, by primitive thought, of those completely basic structures on which the very existence of culture rests' (1969a: 101) – namely 'the exigency of the rule as a rule; the notion of reciprocity regarded as the most immediate form of integrating the opposition between the self and others; and, finally, the synthetic nature of the gift, i.e. that the agreed transfer of a valuable from one individual to another makes these individuals into partners, and adds a new quality to the valuable transferred' (1969a: 84). This interpretation of the relationship between dual organisation, cross-cousin marriage and classificatory terminologies is a crucial movement in *The Elementary Structures of Kinship*: it lays the bridge between deduction of the incest prohibition as a universal rule in the origin of culture and the interpretation of concrete systems as elementary structures of matrimonial exchange – that is, the bridge between the 'structuralist general theory of kinship' and the 'restricted theory' of marriage alliance. The 'exceptional importance' (1969a: 121) of cross-cousin marriage, says Lévi-Strauss, rests above all in the arbitrariness, from a biological point of view, of the division of cousins in two distinct classes regarding sexual or marital relations, those of prescribed or prohibited potential spouses (in the above examples, cross- and parallel cousins respectively). Some other explanation must be found. '[V]eritable *experimentum crucis* in the study of marriage prohibitions' (1969a: 143), the institution shows with special clarity 'that reciprocity is present behind all marriages' even in the absence of explicit formulas of matrimonial alliance among groups (1969a: 143); it allows the deduction of the 'general formula' of those phenomena: 'the idea that the *brother–sister* relationship is identical with the *sister–brother* relationship, which are identical with one another' (1969a: 128; my emphasis). 'Before the institutions, and as a condition of their existence, there is in fact the apprehension of a relationship, or more exactly the apprehension of the opposition between two relationships' (1969a: 129). This opposition expresses an underlying structure of reciprocity (1969a: 128–33), in which the distinction parallel/ cross operates as a register of the matrimonial debts and credits between two groups. The sons of two brothers are in the same position vis-à-vis the group of their fathers: they both have a debt to pay, for those women their fathers received the previous generation (their mothers); they are in the same position vis-à-vis the group of their mothers: they have a credit to claim, for the women the group has given in the previous generation (their mothers). Consequently, they cannot exchange sisters. The sons of a brother and a sister, on the other hand, are not in the same position: regarding the same group, one has a debt and the other has a credit. They can exchange sisters. Showing that 'the notion of reciprocity allows the dichotomy of cousins to be immediately deduced' (1969a: 131), Lévi-Strauss not only offers a structural explanation to a widely disseminated phenomenon – classificatory terminologies – but also links it with a general theory of kinship – and of the 'origins' or foundations of society and/or culture:

> In the final analysis, therefore, cross-cousin marriage simply expresses the fact that marriage must always be a giving and a receiving, but that one can receive only from him who is obliged to give, and that the giving must be to him who has a right to receive. (1969a: 131)

Typologies: from elementary to complex, and back . . .

The Elementary Structures of Kinship, apart from the general theory advanced in its initial chapters, presents itself as an exploration of one *type* of system, that which is designated by the title of the book, which corresponds to systems in which 'the nomenclature permits the immediate determination of the circle of kin and that of affines, that is, those systems which prescribe marriage with a certain type of relative, or, alternatively, those, which, while defining all members of the society as relatives, divide them into two categories, viz., possible spouses and prohibited spouses' (1969a: xxiii). Lévi-Strauss's further stipulation that non-unilinear or cognatic systems (*systèmes à filiation indifférencié*) – that is, systems where no descent rule (*règle stable de filiation*) is provided for the constitution of unambiguous groups – 'have nothing to do with elementary structures' (1969a: 105) had the effect of tying the concept of elementary structure to a certain model of 'primitive' society. This model envisaged society in the form of a whole constituted through mechanical solidarity among homogeneous parts – clearly distinct social groups based on kinship, or 'descent', like clans – that, despite being multifunctional, discrete and exclusive, could not constitute each one a society in itself because of their exogamy (they depended on the others to reproduce themselves). This provided an image of society as composed of *segments* whose definition and articulation could be traced back to the encompassing domain of kinship.[8] In contrast, in non-unilinear or cognatic systems, the absence of unambiguous groups that could be defined exclusively in terms of kinship statuses meant that marriage and alliance were dependent not only on kinship criteria, but on something else (typically, on systems of land rights). In elementary systems, then, the skeleton of society was 'internal' to kinship; in non-elementary systems, in contrast, the skeleton was external to kinship, and that meant that individuals could exercise choice, with respect to their marriages, not only regarding personal and aesthetic preferences, but also with respect to social (kinship) categories (provided the incest prohibition was respected) (1969a: 104–5). This measure of choice allowed the societies in question access to a 'historical existence'.

Before we get to history (or in order to get there), we should note that this typology has been much shaken by subsequent developments. But it certainly expresses a strain of argument important in *The Elementary Structures of Kinship*, from which elementary structures emerge as defining a type of society distinct from other types in which alliance, although present negatively, through the incest prohibition, would take very different forms. By the same token, the different formulas of exchange identified by Lévi-Strauss in so-called elementary structures became the basis for differentiating between three types of systems: restricted exchange and two sorts of generalised exchange – matrilateral and patrilateral.[9] Much ink was spent over the fit (or otherwise) between these types and concrete systems, and over the 'reality' of such models or types. Now, those debates have in large part exhausted themselves (not with a bang . . .), and there would be no motive to evoke them here but for the fact that the reason why they ceased to seem interesting helps clarify certain significant ambiguities in Lévi-Strauss's theorising. Lévi-Strauss's preoccupation with social integration – a preoccupation that is manifest throughout *The Elementary Structures of Kinship* – and with social integration of the sort implied in the segmentary image of society alluded to above, is most apparent in two aspects of his theory. One is the already mentioned stipulation that without unilinear groups we have no elementary structures. The other is the contrast he establishes between restricted exchange and the matrilateral version of generalised exchange, on the one hand, and the patrilateral version on the other – in fact, a continuum along which these formulas are graded according to their differing capacities for social integration.[10] Both aspects relate to a distinction to which Lévi-Strauss appeals again and again in *The Elementary Structures of Kinship* (1969a): that between what he calls the 'method of classes' ('which automatically delimit the group of possible spouses') and the 'method of relations', the 'determination of a relationship, or a group of relationships, so that in each instance it can be said whether a prospective spouse is to be desired or excluded' (1969a: 119). The first method (which operates through the prescription or prohibition of marriage with persons in specific groups like clans, lineages, sections) provides, as in the case of dual organisation, 'a global system, engaging the group as a whole'. The second depends on categories or degrees of relationship which differ in extension according to the perspective of each individual Ego, as with cross-cousin marriage. It is then no more than 'a . . . special process . . . a tendency, rather than a system' (1969a: 119), where the unity of the group (if unity there is) would be a derivative by-product of the juxtaposition of a series of non-coordinate local syntheses. In one case, you have society as a totality composed of groups clearly and equally defined from the point of view of every member. In the other, the parts have different shapes and overlapping limits according to each person's perspective: no whole is the same as the other. The distinction is crucial: it may well be the pivot that supports the tension between formalism and functionalism (Héran 1998), or structuralism and Durkheimianism (Viveiros de Castro 1993), that marks *The Elementary Structures of Kinship* and has won the book the judgement of 'pre-' or 'semi-structuralist' (Dumont 1971; Schneider and Boon 1974). For despite Lévi-Strauss's insistence on the fact that both methods are equally capable of generating structures of reciprocity, despite his statement that '[c]lasses or categories, it matters little … the two methods can have equivalent results' (1969a: 315), it is in terms of the distinction between global ('class') and local ('relation') structures that he frames both the concept of elementary structures (making the presence of discrete, sociocentric unilinear groups a criteria for elementarity) and the hierarchy among its modalities.

We are indebted mainly to Louis Dumont for the disentangling of the concepts of elementary structure (his '*alliance de mariage*') and unilineal descent (Dumont 1975a; 1975b) and, more generally, for a heightened aware-ness regarding the import of the distinction between global and local formulas of exchange (Dumont 1971: 98). This double move is at the root of important developments in the study of indigenous South American kinship (Riviére 1969; Overing Kaplan 1973; 1975; Viveiros de Castro 1993; Viveiros de Castro and Fausto 1993). These showed how alliance theory could describe systems *à filiation indifférenciée* like that of the Nambikwara – systems that, for their lack of unilinear groups, had failed to find a proper place in the role played by elementary systems studied in *The Elementary Structures of Kinship*,[11] despite the role that 'a certain South American relationship' had played in the establishment of cross-cousin marriage as the *experimentum crucis* of Lévi-Strauss's theory.

This extension of alliance theory to erstwhile unconquered territory was paralleled by other deployments in the field of non-elementary structures. The work of Françoise Héritier (1981) opened the way for the exploration of so-called semi-complex structures – systems which regulate marriage only through negative injunctions (as do complex structures, based solely on the incest prohibition), and approximate elementary ones because of the socio-logical phrasing of marriage prohibitions (enunciated in terms of groups instead of degrees of relationship as in the case of the incest prohibition and complex structures). Showing how these negative injunctions were articulated to specific, statistically verifiable, positive tendencies (to marry relatives, or to repeat alliances made by relatives, as soon as permitted by the system of prohibitions), she vindicated Lévi-Strauss's hopes that more sophisticated computational tools could overcome the difficulties encountered when modelling systems that incorporate a lot of randomness and are therefore in a state of permanent turbulence (Lévi-Strauss 1966d: 30).[12] On the other hand, Lévi-Strauss's reflections on what he termed 'House societies' (*sociétés à Maison*) addressed another kind of indeterminacy, regarding the apparently but inconclusively matrilinear, patrilinear or cognatic character of certain kinship groupings (Lévi-Strauss 1979a; 1983c; 1984). His starting point is the social organisation of the Kwakiutl Indians of British Columbia. From the parallels he establishes between their basic social units and medieval noble houses, emerges the notion of the House as

a corporate body holding an estate made up of both material and immaterial wealth, which perpetrates itself through the transmission of its name, its goods, and its titles down a real or imaginary line, considered legitimate as long as this continuity can express itself in the language of kinship or of affinity and, most often, of both. (1979a: 174; 1982)

He sees this type of institution as characteristic of a more differentiated social state, 'where political and economic interests, on the verge of invading the social field, have not yet overstepped the "old ties of blood" '.[13] So here we have another path to history – alongside those of cognatic (non-unilinear) systems and semi-complex structures... Certainly, semi-complex structures, cognatic systems and House societies were never coextensive for Lévi-Strauss. Nonetheless, the 'coefficient of freedom' they incorporated, each in its own way, gives rise to a formal and structural complexity that, in all cases, is seen as the counterpart of *historical* complexity, of the irreducibility of the societies in question to the image of 'kinship-based societies' that framed so much of the anthropology of kinship since its inception (Kuper 1988).

If the future of kinship studies rested on 'whether they can progress from the field of elementary structures where they have been quartered so far, to that of complex structures' (Lévi-Strauss 1966a: 18), as it seemed to do for Lévi-Strauss in the mid-sixties, then there is no reason to fear. Modern societies were undoubtedly 'included in our sphere of investigation' (1966a: 18), but whether we did so 'by applying the same conceptual framework which has proved so valuable for the study of simpler societies?' (1966a: 18) is a moot point.[14] For even among anthropologists working within Lévi-Straussian alliance theory (Lévi-Strauss among them), all these developments lead to a general rethinking of the overall typology of exchange formulas and elementary, complex and semi-complex structures that may cast doubts on the soundness of the whole approach.

Exchange, nature, culture and the Indians (again)

Whatever the insights Lévi-Strauss's theories afford us today, the general framework of *The Elementary Structures of Kinship* appears to be seriously compromised. Perhaps we should, then, abandon the idea of (marriage) exchange as a key to the study of kinship and either find something else to put in its place (like sexual asymmetry) or, better still, abstain from the temptation to put forward general theories making a claim to universal validity and restrict ourselves to generalisations of more limited scope circumscribed to certain cultural-geographical areas, or types of societies? Perhaps we should, indeed, keep to the much more useful task of understanding and describing the theories our subjects have of social relations, including those we are accustomed to subsuming under the anthropological rubric of kinship?

This was a plea made by David Schneider four decades ago. He started by describing the theories Americans have on kinship, an endeavour which did much to clarify how deeply embedded in Euro-American cultures anthropological theories were (Schneider 1968). Of central importance to Americans was the distinction between a realm of natural givens and a domain of man-made rules: the combination of 'substance' (symbolised by 'blood') and a 'code of conduct' ('love' as the symbol for an 'enduring, diffuse solidarity') provided the overall definition of kinship in America, and their interplay accounted for most of its variations. Needless to point out how this conceptualisation resonates with analytical strategies anthropologists had employed to think about other people's kinship – including the taken for granted status of nature as the ultimate grounding for connections that could be 'recognised', activated, *or not*. Against this background, natives and anthropologists alike could then focus on the realm of human action, Schneider's 'order of law' – the order of *relationships* ('social kinship', as opposed to 'physical' or 'biological', in anthropological parlance).

Schneider's analysis, and the 'critique of kinship' thus launched (Schneider 1984), was only one of the factors that lead to the demise of 'traditional' or 'classic' anthropological theories of kinship (others were mentioned in the beginning of this chapter). Its perhaps more crucial effect – the foregrounding and consequent destabilisation of the taken for granted status of the nature/culture opposition – is certainly related to parallel developments in Western society and culture that are well beyond our scope here.[15] I have already commented on how Lévi-Strauss's argument in *The Elementary Structures of Kinship* assumes a 'traditional' distribution of consanguinity and affinity along the same dimensions, which present nature as given and culture as constructed, that is now under suspicion. The time has now come to indicate, as promised, how the notion of exchange enters this picture as a means to sidestep the issue of whether there is, or there is not, such a thing as natural versus social/cultural kinship.

We should start with Lévi-Strauss's recent pronouncement (in the 'Postface' to a special issue of *L'Homme* dedicated to the heritage of *The Elementary Structures of Kinship*) that 'criticisms of the notion of exchange rest on shaky ground and result from the adoption of an excessively narrow point of view'

(Lévi-Strauss 2000: 713; my translation). He goes on to restate positions he had rehearsed many times before. Exchange does not always express itself in positive terms. Sharing is not the opposite of exchange (it is rather that 'it is the form that exchange takes when each taker has a claim to the whole', 2000: 713), and neither is stealing (rapt, or bride capture, can be 'a genuine or symbolic way of getting round the rule of exchange' (2000: 714), or a way to restart the circuit of exchange). Exchange does not necessarily require the existence of exchanging units ... He insists that his famous 'kinship atom' (the *quattuor* made up of a husband, a wife, a child and the mother's (wife's) brother (1958a; 1963a)) is not an institution or unit whose presence, universal or otherwise, could be empirically determined (like the elementary family). It is rather the simplest expression of a fundamental relation (alliance, as between brothers-in-law) that might or might not materialise in this form. He takes parallel cousin marriage as an illustration of the relative character of endogamy and exogamy, and suggests it should be studied along with other types of 'close marriage' (*mariage dans un degré rapproché*) connected with differences in status and prestige between donors and receivers (that is, partners in an exchange relationship).

And yet, by accepting this, have we not so extended the notion as to dilute its meaning and compromise its usefulness? Why cling to a notion that is prone to cause so much misunderstanding?

Lévi-Strauss, in his 'Postface', points to two 'inexactitudes' in the critiques addressed to the notion of exchange that he feels compelled to 'rectify'. First, there is the accusation that his theory supposes that biological ties, the family, exchange units or filiation were prior to social/cultural ties, the group, the exchange relation or alliance. Indeed, there are passages in *The Elementary Structures of Kinship* and elsewhere that could be construed as ambiguous regarding this, passages in which exchange, construed as a structure (a 'psychological constraint') that may arise in whichever non-crystallised form of social life (2000: 717), sometimes recedes into the background in a picture dominated by exchange as an institution that connects substantive groups. But you have to be a very obtuse reader to ignore not only the very many explicit statements to the contrary, but also that alliance theory constitutes a sustained effort to conceptualise kinship on the basis of the second series of notions. And this point is related to the second 'inexactitude', one that drives him to the point of exasperation: 'How many times will I have to repeat that it makes no difference to the theory whether it is men who exchange women or the opposite' (2000: 717; my translation)?

Here, as with the problem of the relative priority of the exchange relation over its terms (units like families and groups, or categories like this or that type of cousin), one must be careful to distinguish contingent fact from structural principle in Lévi-Strauss's theory. For the two points are, in fact, one.

Consanguines, as groups or categories defined through substantial idioms of genealogy or filiation, do not exist prior to the incest prohibition; neither do men and women, as transactors and transacted in matrimonial exchange. A sister is a non-wife, rather than a wife being a non-sister; what constitutes a sister as a sister (matrimonially prohibited) is the need for her to be the wife of someone else, and not a primary relation of identity with the subject. It is, in other words, the imperative of exchange – the incest prohibition. Similarly, it is not the opposition between the sexes as terms or substances (natural or cultural, it does not matter) that makes either subjects or objects of exchange, but the fact that, through the relation of exchange, each sex may appear as a term for itself and as a relation to the other. And it is the incest prohibition that 'transforms difference between the sexes into a relation between relations, defining the terms in terms of the relations that connect them, thus making of the natural complementarity of the sexes a sociological opposition between term and relation' (Viveiros de Castro 1990: 31).

The fundamental meaning of the Lévi-Straussian concept of affinity as an exchange relation resides in the priority he attributes to the relation over its terms. The 'obligation to reciprocate' is not a socially sanctioned norm, but the expression of an internal relation to which the terms cannot be seen to be pre-existent.[16] This relation accounts for both the connection and separation between its terms. That should help us to understand the special quality Lévi-Strauss sees in the brother-in-law relation. Contrasting it with the brother relationship as another possible basis for sociality, he says:

[T]he whole difference between the two types of bond can also be seen, a sufficiently clear definition being that one of them expresses a mechanical solidarity ... while the other involves an organic solidarity ... Brothers are closely related to one another, but they are so in terms of their similarity, as are the posts or the reeds of the Pan-pipe. By contrast, brothers-in-law are solidary because they complement each other and have a functional efficacy for one another, whether they play the role of the opposite sex in the erotic games of childhood, or whether their masculine alliance as adults is confirmed by each providing the other with what he does not have – a wife – through their simultaneous renunciation of what they both do have – a sister. The first form of solidarity adds nothing and unites nothing; it is based upon a cultural limit, satisfied by the reproduction of a type of connection the model for which is provided by nature. The other brings about the integration of the group on a new plane. (1969a: 484)

The functional efficacy brothers-in-law have for one another rests not on their similarity, but on their *difference*. The crucial point to retain here is the concept of affinity as a connection between two subjects mediated by their differential relation to a third (the person who is a sister for me is a wife for you). This is what the Lévi-Straussian incest prohibition and the idea of the 'exchange of women' boils down to. The alternative formulation he suggests regarding the exchange of women – that groups, each made up of both men and women, exchange among themselves kinship relations – hints at this: the 'exchange of women' is a play of perspectives (Strathern 1988; Gell 1999: 68–9).

Lévi-Strauss's concept of kinship is then thoroughly structural – non-substantivist, relational. Consanguinity may still appear as nature and affinity as culture, as usual, but the meaning of this distribution is profoundly altered by the way exchange enters into the picture. For in terms of a view of kinship as marriage alliance, or exchange, their relative weight is inverted (with affinity taking the priority normally assigned to consanguinity as the basic kinship relation). The incest prohibition is a rule that poses affinity as a constitutive relation that defines the realm of kinship, as opposed to a norm (regulative rule that could be broken) defining some relatives as unmarriageable. Affinity may be culture, but is not 'constructed' after consanguinity; it is as given as consanguinity; it is in fact prior to it (Viveiros de Castro 2006).

The dualism of affinity and consanguinity, of nature and culture, in Lévi-Strauss's kinship theory, is an unstable one. Now, dualism is certainly an important motive in Lévi-Strauss's work. The tendency to reduce his structuralism to the enchaining of binary oppositions misses an important point regarding this dualism – a point that is most visible in his writings on Amerindian social forms (see the famous 'Do Dual Organizations Exist?', 1958a; 1963a) and, of course, myth. It would require an entirely new essay to develop the point that the instability noted here resonates with Amerindian social philosophy as it emerges from the *Mythologiques* and *Histoire de Lynx* (1991a), in the form of its 'dualism in perpetual disequilibrium' and its *openness towards the other*. This is a reason why *The Elementary Structures of Kinship* should be read side by side with the *Mythologiques* – this time, not to point to the semi-structuralism of the former compared with the latter, but to explore conceptual tools that could help us to go about trying to describe other people's socialities. Exchange and reciprocity among them. Perhaps we would then realise how a work many times criticised for its level of abstraction, by the little attention paid to specific cultural contexts and native concepts, constitutes, on the contrary, one of those happy and rare moments in the history of anthropology when it becomes difficult to say if indigenous thought has taken the form of the anthropologist's thought or the other way round (see the 'Overture' to *The Raw and the Cooked*).

NOTES

1. Descent theory was developed mainly by British anthropologists (Radcliffe-Brown, Evans-Pritchard and Meyer Fortes, among others) working in African societies. It focused on the articulation of kinship and political domains in social life, as

provided by unilinear descent groups present among many peoples in that continent.

2. For some recent assessments, see Peletz 1995; Holy 1996; Godelier, Trautmann and Tjon Sie Fat 1998; Collard 2000b; Carsten 2004.

3. This has nothing to do with Lévi-Strauss's concepts of 'restricted' and 'generalised' exchange (discussed in this chapter).

4. Among those, parallel cousin marriage (or father's brother's daughter marriage, a practice characteristic of Arab kinship systems that apparently negates the opposition between parallel and cross-cousins), and other endogamic practices touching on 'incest' (like sister–brother marriage in ancient Egypt or half-sibling marriage in classical Greece) that seem to contradict the imperative of exchange.

5. The distinction between domestic and public domains is central to descent theory and its interest in the political-jural dimension of kinship systems. In their analysis, women tend to be associated with the former, a projection that was grasped by early feminist anthropology trying to identify the mechanisms responsible for the seemingly universal domination of women by men. The opposition itself later came under heavy criticism.

6. The object of these ideas – whether they refer to genealogical connections, culturally specific theories of conception, definite social relationships or group organisational patterns – has been a much discussed topic in kinship studies, since the basic positions on the issue were formulated in the beginning of the twentieth century.

7. 'Sib' is a word used in early American writings as an alternative to 'clan'.

8. This was an image of primitive society projected by the Durkheimian concept of 'segmentary society' (see Schneider 1965).

9. These formulas are the outcome of specific modalities of cross-cousin marriage among a definable number of exchange units. So, bilateral cross-cousin marriage corresponds to 'restricted exchange' as reciprocal transfer of women between two groups. Matrilateral cross-cousin marriage entails a diagrammatic distinction between the group from which the father obtained his wife (the mother's brother's group) and the group to which he gave his sister. It corresponds then to a formula of 'generalised reciprocity' between a minimum of three groups, such that A gives to B that gives to C that gives to A ... Patrilateral cross-cousin marriage, in its turn, requires the same minimum of three groups, but differs from the matrilateral modality in that the man marries not in the same direction (group) as his father, but in the opposite direction – inverting the orientation of the circulation of women in such a way that the woman given in one generation (the father's sister, for instance) is given back to the same line (to her brother's son) in the person of her daughter (Lévi-Strauss 1969a: chap. 27).

10. For its openness (it can include from three to any number of partners), and the stability of the relations between the units it entails (women always flow in the same direction), matrilateral generalised exchange is the most integrative formula. Restricted exchange comes second, for albeit the units and their relation can be here equally well defined and stable, it consists in a 'closed structure', where each marriage appears as the counterpart of a previous one, a restitution after which, metaphorically at least, 'the transaction is terminated' (Lévi-Strauss 1969a: 444). Patrilateral marriage, being at the same time closed as the bilateral form, and

triadic as the matrilateral one, represents a discontinuous formula that cannot be translated in laws like restricted (A gives to B and B gives to A) or generalised exchange (A gives to B, B gives to C, and C gives to A).

11. In ethnographic regions where descent groups are the exception rather than the rule, or where 'groups' themselves appear as elusive entities, the constrast between a 'solidarity [which] extends to the whole social group, in achieving a structure' (based on 'collective harmony'), on the one hand, and a solidarity that 'results both mechanically and precariously from the sum of particular ties (Lévi-Strauss 1969a: 445), on the other, ceases to make sense. The very idea of society as a totality appears alien and irrelevant to indigenous conceptualisations and social practice.

12. Semi-complex structures are associated with a kind of kinship terminology that became known in anthropology as 'Crow/Omaha' systems. The degree of randomness that Lévi-Strauss finds in these systems leads him to comment that 'Crow-Omaha systems, though formally akin to elementary structures, allow history to play a part in social life. Instead of acting as a regulating device which is constantly tending to set the society back on its old tracks, they leave it a certain measure of freedom which may lead to change. Thus it can be said that with the advent of Crow-Omaha systems, history comes to the foreground in the life of simple societies' (Lévi-Strauss 1966d: 20).

13. '[A]s Marx and Engels used to say. In order to express and propagate themselves, these interests must inevitably borrow the language of kinship, though it is foreign to them, for none other is available. And inevitably too, they borrow it only to subvert it' (Lévi-Strauss 1982 [1979a]: 187).

14. But see Segalen and Zonabend 1987 for comments on some such 'applications'; cf. Segalen 1991 and other articles in Héritier and Copet-Rougier 1990; 1991; 1993.

15. A relevant example of what I am alluding to is the new reproductive technologies that push to the limits the old regime of the nature/culture opposition regarding kinship: for what happens when man-made 'rules' (in the form of technology and of the juridical framework that is supposed to regulate its use) are revealed as that which constitute the 'nature' (the physical bonds) that should be the (given) measure (Strathern 1992a).

16. Created in it, they only subsist while remaining within this relation. As a result, while the partners may or may not reciprocate, for sure, non-retribution does not so much imply the dissolution of the relation as the dissolution of the partners – constituted by these relations, persons do not remain the same 'outside' of them (they will be recomposed on the basis of other relations). This way of putting the question is related to the way in which Melanesianists have thematised the partibility of the person. The discomfort of Melanesian and South American ethnographers with the image of society projected by the segmentary model leads to exploration of alternative vocabularies to those of group definition and articulation; the (gendered) person and the body, their modes of construction and decomposition, provided the matrix for such an alternative conceptualisation of indigenous sociality. But this required a sustained effort to keep the person as a relational construct – avoiding the reification implied in the idea of the person as social role or status, as the sum of rights and duties (that is, of the social relationships) that defined it in British anthropological tradition. What was thus

'reified', native discourse and practice seemed to indicate, could (must) also be decomposed – and the native techniques to do that were those of (gift) exchange (Strathern 1988).

REFERENCES

Carsten, Janet 2004. *After Kinship*. Cambridge: Cambridge University Press.

Collard, Chantal 2000a. 'Femmes échangées, femmes échangistes: à propos de la théorie de l'alliance de Claude Lévi-Strauss', *L'Homme* 154–5: 101–16.

2000b. ' "Kinship studies" au tournant du siècle', *L'Homme* 154–5: 635–58.

Collier, Jane F. and Sylvia J. Yanagisako 1987. 'Introduction', in J. F. Collier and S. J. Yanagisako (eds.), *Gender and Kinship: Essays Towards a Unified Analysis*. Stanford, CA: Stanford University Press, pp. 1–13.

Dumont, Louis. 1971. *Introduction a deux théories d'anthropologie sociale*. Paris: Éditions de l'École des Hautes Études en Sciences Sociales.

1975a [1953]. 'Le Vocabulaire de parenté dravidien comme expression du mariage', in *Dravidien et Kariera: l'alliance de mariage dans l'Inde du Sud et en Australie*. Paris: Mouton, pp. 85–100.

1975b [1957]. 'Hiérarchie et alliance de mariage dans la parenté de l'Inde du Sud', in *Dravidien et Kariera: l'alliance de mariage dans l'Inde du Sud et en Australie*. Paris: Mouton, pp. 7–83.

Fortes, Meyer 1969. *Kinship and the Social Order: The Legacy of Lewis Henry Morgan*. Chicago: Aldine.

Gell, Alfred 1999. 'Strathernograms: or, the Semiotics of Mixed Metaphors', in *The Art of Anthropology: Essays and Diagrams*. London: The Athlone Press, pp. 29–75.

Godelier, Maurice, Thomas R. Trautmann and F. Tjon Sie Fat 1998. 'Introduction', in T. Trautmann, M. Godelier and F. Tjon Sie Fat (eds.), *Transformations of Kinship*. Washington, DC and London: Smithsonian Institution Press, pp. 1–26.

Héran, François 1998. 'De Granet à Lévi-Strauss', *Social Anthropology* 6 (1–2–3): 1–60; 169–201; 309–30.

Héritier, Françoise 1981. *L'Exercice de la parenté*. Paris: Gallimard/Le Seuil.

Héritier-Augé, Françoise and E. Copet-Rougier (eds.) 1990. *Les Complexités de l'alliance, I. Les Systèmes semi-complexes*. Paris: Éditions des Archives Contemporaines, pp. ix–xxii.

1991. *Les Complexités de l'alliance II*. Paris: Éditions des Archives Contemporaines.

1993. *Les Complexités de l'alliance, III. Économie, politique et fondements symboliques (Afrique)*. Paris: Éditions des Archives Contemporaines, pp. i–xviii.

Holy, Ladislav 1996. *Anthropological Perspectives on Kinship*. London: Pluto Press.

Kuper, Adam 1988. *The Invention of Primitive Society: Transformations of an Illusion*. London and New York: Routledge.

Lowie, Robert 1919. 'Family and Sib', *American Anthropologist* 21 (1): 28–40.

Ortner, Sherry B. 1974. 'Is Female to Male as Nature to Culture?', in M. Z. Rosaldo and L. Lamphere (eds.), *Women, Culture and Society*. Stanford, CA: Stanford University Press, pp. 67–88.

Overing Kaplan, Joanna 1973. 'Endogamy and the Marriage Alliance: a Note on Continuity in Kindred Based Groups', *Man* 8 (4): 555–70.

1975. *The Piaroa, a People of the Orinoco Basin: A Study in Kinship and Marriage*. Oxford: Clarendon Press.

Peletz, Michael G. 1995. 'Kinship Studies in Late Twentieth-century Anthropology', *Annual Review of Anthropology* 24: 343–72.

Rivière, Peter 1969. *Marriage among the Trio: A Principle of Social Organization.* Oxford: Clarendon Press.

1993. 'The Amerindianization of Descent and Affinity', *L'Homme* 33 (2–4): 501–17.

Schneider, David M. 1965. 'Some Muddles in the Models, or, How the System Really Works', in M. Banton (ed.), *The Relevance of Models for Social Anthropology.* London: Tavistock, pp. 25–86.

1968. *American Kinship: A Cultural Account.* Englewood Cliffs, NJ: Prentice-Hall.

1984. *A Critique of the Study of Kinship.* Ann Arbor, MI: University of Michigan Press.

Schneider, David M. and James A. Boon 1974. 'Kinship vis-à-vis Myth: Contrasts in Lévi-Strauss' Approaches to Cross-cultural Comparison', *American Anthropologist* 76 (4): 799–817.

Segalen, Martine 1991. 'Mariage et parentèle dans le pays bigouden sud: un exemple de renchaînement d'alliance', in F. Héritier-Augé and E. Copet-Rougier (eds.), *Les Complexités de l'alliance, I. Les systèmes semi-complexes.* Paris: Éditions des Archives Contemporaines, pp. 177–206.

Segalen, Martine and Françoise Zonabend 1987. 'Social Anthropology and the Ethnology of France: the Field of Kinship and the Family', in A. Jackson (ed.), *Anthropology at Home.* London and New York: Tavistock Publications, pp. 109–19.

Strathern, Marilyn 1988. *The Gender of the Gift: Problems with Women and Problems with Society in Melanesia.* Berkeley: University of California Press.

1992a. *Reproducing the Future: Anthropology, Kinship and the New Reproductive Technologies.* New York: Routledge.

1992b. 'Parts and Wholes: Refiguring Relationships in a Post-plural World', in A. Kuper (ed.), *Conceptualizing Society.* London: Routledge, pp. 75–104.

Tylor, Edward B. 1889. 'On a Method of Investigating the Development of Institutions; Applied to Laws of Marriage and Descent', *The Journal of the Anthropological Institute of Great Britain and Ireland* 18: 245–72.

Viveiros de Castro, Eduardo B. 1990. 'Principios e parâmetros: um comentário a l'exercice de la parenté', *Comunicação do PPGAS* 17: 1–106.

1993. 'Alguns aspectos da afinidade no dravidianato amazônico', in M. Carneiro da Cunha and E. B. Viveiros de Castro (eds.), *Amazônia: Etnologia e História Indígena.* São Paulo: Núcleo de História Indígena e do Indigenismo da USP/ FAPESP, pp. 149–210.

2006. 'The Gift and the Given: Three Nano-essays on Kinship and Magic', in Sandra Bamford and James Leach (eds.), *Genealogy Beyond Kinship: Sequence, Transmission, and Essence in Ethnography and Social Theory.* Oxford: Berghahn Books.

Viveiros de Castro, Eduardo and Carlos Fausto 1993. 'La Puissance et l'acte: la parenté dans les basses terres de l'Amérique du Sud', *L'Homme* 33 (2–4): 141–70.

Part II

Myth and mind

5   The two natures of Lévi-Strauss

Philippe Descola

It is common knowledge that the contrastive opposition between nature and culture plays a crucial role in the works of Claude Lévi-Strauss: he has used it in such a variety of contexts and for so many purposes, that for many it has come to embody one of the main characteristics of his way of thinking.[1] It is also well known that Lévi-Strauss attributes to Rousseau the merit of having, in practice, founded the field of ethnology by inaugurating, in *Discourse on the Origin and the Foundation of Inequality*, a strand of thinking on the possible links between nature and culture (Lévi-Strauss 1978b: 35). In other words, the problem of the tension between these two domains lies not only at the heart of structural anthropology, but is also what defines, according to its founder, the domain to which ethnology is dedicated and thanks to which it can claim a certain autonomy within the human sciences. However, the role attributed to this conceptual pair is not easily circumscribed in Lévi-Strauss's thought: it is at once an analytical tool, the philosophical stage upon which the story of our origins is played out and an antinomy that must be overcome. This conceptual pair is given a plurality of sometimes contradictory meanings, which account for its great productivity and the ensuing difficulties of interpretation. The aim of this chapter is to contribute to the clarification of this question by means of what is at once a critique and a tribute, because progress can only be made on the path one has chosen thanks to the advances made by previous generations and, from this point of view, the twentieth century, in anthropology, will undoubtedly remain the century of Lévi-Strauss, since his thought, even if one rejects it, has stamped its mark on our conception of this science, its aim and its methods. My debt to him is greater still, for both personal and intellectual reasons; indeed, it was Lévi-Strauss who first incited me to take up the very question at the core of this chapter, that of the relations of continuity and discontinuity between nature and culture. It is thanks to him that this question became, early on, the main focus of my research and professional activity. However, to build on solid ground, one must test one's foundations, draw up their plan and sometimes adjust their layout. Such is the purpose of what follows.

[* * *]

In the 'Gildersleeve lecture', given in 1972 (Lévi-Strauss 1987d: 101–20) in the United States under the title of 'Structuralism and Ecology', Lévi-Strauss offers the most explicit account of his conception of the role played respectively by mental processes and ecological determinants in the operations carried out by mythical thought when it arranges certain elements of the natural world into signifying systems. This was for him a way of answering, in the very place in which they arose, the accusations of idealism brought against him by an increasing number of North American anthropologists who believed that the constraints exerted on a society by its environment and that society's adaptive responses to them were the origin and the cause of most of its cultural specificities. Taking up an argument that he had already developed in *The Savage Mind*, Lévi-Strauss wanted to show that there is nothing automatic or predictable in the way that a society selects certain aspects of its habitat and endows them with a particular meaning, integrating them into mythical constructions. Indeed, neighbouring populations often select totally different distinctive features in the same animal or plant, or, conversely, attribute an identical symbolic function to species belonging to different genera or even kingdoms. However, the arbitrariness in the choice of distinctive features attributed to such and such a component of local ecosystems is counterbalanced by the fact that these elements are organised into coherent systems which can be seen as the result of transformations obeying a small number of rules. In short, although the myths of neighbouring tribes often use, in the pursuit of the same ends, totally distinct features of the fauna and flora, the structure of these myths is not random; it is organised according to mirror effects of inversion and symmetry.

As one might have expected, the 'Gildersleeve lecture' failed to convince the North American materialists of the soundness of structural analysis and even gave rise to the famous controversy between Lévi-Strauss and Marvin Harris, then professor at the University of Columbia and leading figure of the 'cultural ecology' school (Harris 1976; Lévi-Strauss 1983a). The paradox of this deadlock is that Harris does not appear to have realised that structural anthropology, far from wallowing in a haughty 'mentalism' – as he reproached Lévi-Strauss with doing – was, on the contrary, based on a far more radical naturalism than that upheld by the advocates of geographical determinism. While it is true that Lévi-Strauss has always proclaimed his indifference to what he calls, using Marx's terms, the 'order of infrastructures', he has also never wavered from the idea that nature conditions the intellectual operations by which culture receives an empirical content, nor from his conviction that the day will come when it will be possible to interpret culture in purely organic terms, as the natural result and social mode of apprehension of modifications in the structure and functioning of the brain. From this dual tendency springs an often uneasy cohabitation between a scientific programme formulated in classically dualistic terms – it assigns to ethnography, aided by history and technology, the study of the material base of society and to structural anthropology, that of ideology – and a resolutely monist theory of knowledge, which treats the mind that gives meaning to the world as a part and product of that same world.

The 'Gildersleeve lecture' offers a vivid example of this paradoxical combination. Rejecting the opposition between mind and matter, Lévi-Strauss claims that social life is marked by two simultaneous and complementary determinisms: the first, which is of a techno-economic type, enforces upon the mind constraints resulting from the relation a society has with a particular environment; the other reflects the requirements inherent to the workings of the mind and always manifests itself as identical, regardless of the differences of environment. The first determinism requires that the ethnologist be informed of the objective properties of the natural objects which the mind selects in a given cultural context in order to assemble them into signifying totalities, such as myths or taxonomies. It is therefore necessary to have a good knowledge of the ecological environment of a society if one wishes to analyse its ideological productions, since the latter reveal a compromise between certain traits of the natural habitat and the laws that govern symbolic thought. Lévi-Strauss himself has always devoted a meticulous attention to the flora, fauna and astronomical and climatic cycles particular to the places from which the myths that he studies originate. This methodological precaution is necessary in order to establish rigorously how narratives of neighbouring societies use different characteristics of the local ecology to fulfil similar mythical functions.

However, structural anthropology is above all a form of semiology or even psychology, and Lévi-Strauss has essentially focused his attention on the manifestations of the second type of determinism, that which derives from the mind, not so much in order to isolate cognitive universals, but to account for how the mind operates in varying cultural and geographical contexts, and how it is subjected to the effects of attraction and distortion that result from the specificities of the social and physical environment. This is why Lévi-Strauss, faithful to his project of drawing up an inventory of the mind's 'constraining frameworks' such as it emerges from ethnographic experience, gradually turned away from the domain of social reality which had taken up the first part of his career to devote himself to the study of the various expressions of mythical thought. Indeed, nothing guarantees that the constraints that he had exposed in kinship systems are of mental origin; they might be the mere reflection in human consciousness of certain requirements of social life objectified in institutions. Lacking any immediate practical function, mythology does not present the same ambiguity and reveals to the analyst, in a particularly pure form, the operations of a mind no longer condemned to organise a reality exterior to it, but free to compose with itself.

Even though Lévi-Strauss asserts that mental determinants and those of the natural habitat are symmetrical, he does not grant them the same importance in his work. Indeed, the physical environment is often relegated to a second-ary role, that of providing the mythical mind with the materials on which it draws, which is undoubtedly a useful function, but does not reflect to its full extent the possibilities of interaction between a given society and its geo-graphical environment. Thus, the materialists are right to criticise Lévi-Strauss for his lack of interest in the impact of ecological factors on all those aspects of social life that cannot be assigned to symbolic activity. Indeed, this does not enter into his project, since he chose to focus his attention on 'superstructures', taking up a line of enquiry that, according to him, Marx had only just started to sketch out. At this level of anthropological research, nature is something like a huge reservoir of observable properties in which the mind is free to select objects that it will then convert into signs. In short, this nature-encyclopaedia is first of all 'good to think with' (*'bonne à penser'*, to use Lévi-Strauss's phrase); it offers a springboard for the taxonomic imagi-nation, a pretext for the strange combinations that weave the web of myths; it is the vast and teeming given that is presupposed in the objectification of a world grasped through codified utterances. This nature, planted like a stage set for the theatre of the mind, contrasts not only with the massive and ruthless nature of geographical determinism, but also with the other nature whose effects Lévi-Strauss often evokes: the organic nature of our species, which provides us with the means of perceiving sensible objects and attributing meaning to them, the biological machinery that guarantees the unity of our mental operations and offers the hope of grasping the rules that govern them. While nature, construed as exterior to humankind, remains in an ancillary position, in its bodily manifestation it takes on a key role in a theory of the faculties which refuses to discriminate between subjective states and cosmic properties.

Lévi-Strauss is well aware of the contradiction entailed by this dual con-ception of nature. This is why he tries to offer a solution to it, one in which one may perceive certain echoes of Merleau-Ponty's phenomenology. In the last pages of the 'Gildersleeve lecture', this bodily nature is defined as an organic milieu, akin to the physical milieu, and all the more linked to it for the fact that humans can only apprehend the latter through the mediation of the former.[2] There must therefore be a form of affinity between the information transmitted by the sense organs, their cerebral encoding and the physical world itself. What is this affinity based on? On the fact, Lévi-Strauss tells us, that the immediate data of sensory perception are not raw material, a kind of exact copy of perceived objects, but consist in distinctive properties abstracted from reality through mechanisms of encoding and decoding which are inscribed in the nervous system and function according to binary oppositions: contrast between movement and immobility, presence or absence of colour, differences in the outlines of objects . . . Structures are not, therefore, pure artefacts of the intellect shaping freely a plastic reality. In fact, the mind never ceases to structurally process information that is itself received already structured by the senses. This may be true, but do the sense organs themselves have a structuring or a structural activity? Do they operate an encoding of *stimuli* by contrasting distinctive features, or do they simply lay bare a coding already present in external reality? Lévi-Strauss clearly retains the second option when he claims that the structural properties of nature are not, in essence, different from the codes used by the nervous system to decipher them, or from the categories that the mind uses to account for the properties of reality. In short, 'the mind operates in ways that do not differ in kind from those that have unfolded in the world' (1987d: 118–19). This structural homology of the sign and the object it denotes anchors the signifying process in nature, renders it dependent upon the binary structure of objective reality which explains and guarantees the isomorphism between language and the world.

By embracing a physicalist theory of knowledge, Lévi-Strauss can thus reject philosophical dualism, while continuing to implement a perfectly dualistic methodology. Indeed, in his analysis of myths, he does not approach the physical environment in a naturalistic way, as a set of causal effects, structural properties and molecular assemblages which are coded, decoded and recombined by the perceptive and cognitive machinery. This would require scientific tools which we are still far from possessing. External nature is rather called upon as a kind of lexicon of distinctive features from which the sense organs and the brain are said to draw to produce texts according to syntax of their own. And, if the analysis of myths is possible, ultimately it is precisely because the lexicon of non-human natures used by different cultures varies with their environment, while the natural grammar of the understanding used to organise these elements into utterances is invariant. Hence, the paradox of structural anthropology is that it appeals to a monist conception of the mind and world in order to legitimise a method of analysis in which natural relativism – the diversity of environments – plays a role elsewhere devolved to cultural relativism.

Lévi-Strauss did not, as the 'Gildersleeve lecture' might lead us to believe, convert to monism late and under the influence of neurosciences. It was an early intuition which he has reformulated throughout his life and which the advances made in biology confirmed at the right time, providing his argument with a certain element of empirical legitimacy. As early as *The Elementary Structures of Kinship* (1949a; 1969b), we already encounter the idea that the roots of culture are to be found in nature, in the organic foundations of the working of the mind, which do not differ from the laws of social and physical reality. But this belief is expressed in a philosophical language which is so reliant on dualistic categories that many hasty readers failed to see that the distinction established in principle between nature and culture, in the opening chapters of the book, was no more than a device the aim of which was to enable him to reject any substantive opposition between these two domains.

Let us briefly recall the demonstration. For reasons that can partly be explained by the academic conventions of the time, Lévi-Strauss felt the need to introduce his doctoral dissertation on *The Elementary Structures of Kinship* with some genetic consideration. Relinquishing for the time being the essence of his structural method, he tries to isolate a logical foundation on which to base his analysis of marital institutions, a first trigger responsible for all the ensuing dynamic of social life. This primal base, as is well known, is the prohibition of incest. As the only universal rule, it represents an originary synthesis which expresses the passage from nature to culture. It is natural because it is a given for the whole of the human species and cultural because it takes the form of a norm which is variable in its formulations, but not in its principle. The prohibition of incest, the true moment of birth of social life, is what makes the exchange of women necessary; it expresses 'the transition from the natural fact of consanguinity to the cultural fact of alliance' (Lévi-Strauss 1969b: 30). At some unspecified stage in the process of hominisation, an irreversible transition between a state of nature seems to have occurred in which behaviour is not yet governed by rules and a state of culture character-ised by exogamy and reciprocal exchange, the primary conditions of exis-tence of the marital institutions that Lévi-Strauss would go on to analyse.

If one is to limit oneself to a superficial reading of the methodological chapters that introduce *The Elementary Structures of Kinship*, what undoubt-edly comes to the fore is this outrageous dualism, this sudden conversion of nature into culture which the theoreticians of the social contract, from Grotius to Rousseau, had already hypothesised although they never granted it the slightest historical validity. However, the idea of such a radical rupture is denied by numerous subsequent passages in this work which are interspersed, as if in passing, with technical developments on the nature of kinship systems. Here we learn that culture merely codifies determinants imposed by nature – the sexual instinct or our ability to apprehend biological relations as systems of opposition[3] – and that it does so according to cognitive schemata that pre-exist the norms that translate them. These schemata are sorts of categorical imperatives inscribed in the architecture of the mind – the necessity of rules, the notion of reciprocity and the synthetic nature of the gift (1969b: 84) – and therefore formal structures which constitute 'the indestructible basis of marriage institutions, and the incest prohibition whereby the existence of these institutions is made possible, and of culture itself, the advent of which is constituted by the incest prohibition' (1969b: 440). In other words, the prohibition of incest and the exchange it institutes are efficient causes of social life, but the movement inherent in the prohibition springs from biological and psychological constraints that are more fundamental since they derive from the organic nature of man. And, in order to already escape the dualism of human nature and physical nature that such a conception implies, Lévi-Strauss does not hesitate, in the conclusion to his work, to embrace Engels and his *Dialectics of Nature*, prophesising in his wake that 'the laws of thought . . . are the same as those which are expressed in physical reality and in social reality, which is itself one of its aspects' (1969b: 451). The marked contrast between nature and culture stated at the beginning of *The Elementary Structures* was thus only a philosophical fiction, a kind of thought experience without ontological implications, but which even the shrewdest critics took seriously.[4] Thus, to dispel any misunderstanding, Lévi-Strauss made sure of specifying, in the preface to the second edition, that the opposition between nature and culture is 'neither a primeval fact, nor a concrete aspect of universal order. Rather it should be seen as *an artificial creation of culture*' (1969b: 29; my italics).

An 'artificial creation', undoubtedly, but also a relatively late one and one that is historically determined. This is, at least, what one must add if one is to take seriously what ethnography teaches us about the multiple continuities between humans and non-humans that are established in the cosmologies of many non-modern societies. This, however, is not the path that Lévi-Strauss seems to follow when he tackles the ideological productions of these societies. In this area, despite his own denials, he does indeed sometimes give in to the temptation of treating the opposition between nature and culture as a 'primeval fact' and 'a concrete aspect of universal order'. In the structural analyses of myths, the properties, substances and entities that he isolates in the narrative chain are incorporated to contrastive matrixes which are often organised according to the very axis of the nature/culture opposition; as if, playing on the antithesis between the raw and the cooked, honey and tobacco, dirt and adornment, the bush fires and the cooking fire, the anonymous authors of mythical stories had had the vague intuition that these pairs of distinctive traits are distributed on either side of a more fundamental duality, which is not apprehended as such but already present in the texture of things.

Certainly, no one will question that some contrasts are universally perceived between different states of matter, properties of beings or features of organic modes of action or processes, or that pairs of opposites such as full and empty, supple and rigid, high and low, right and left, life and death, hot and cold, container and contained, offer everywhere an adequate physical framework for organising symbolic systems. However, nothing entitles us to think that the antinomy between nature and culture was, before the modern era, a common means of structuring some of these contrasts between prominent elements of the world, even at an implicit level. One may be willing to admit that no society is indifferent, for example, to the various transformations of foodstuffs. The raw, the cooked, the rotten or the boiled belong to mental categories, if not always lexical ones, which humanity as a whole has learnt to use. But should one analyse these categories by using the nature/ culture polarity as a main axis, as Lévi-Strauss does with dazzling virtuosity in the 'culinary triangle' (Lévi-Strauss 1965a)? One recalls that, according to him, the 'roasted' is universally on the side of nature and the 'boiled' on the side of culture, for the former is closer to the 'raw', since it is never evenly cooked, whereas the latter is supposed to connote a more advanced state of civilisation, since it requires a container and the mediation of water. However, if the conquest of fire represents the accession of humanity to culture, as Lévi-Strauss was keen to show throughout *Mythologiques*, then nothing justifies the claim that the 'roasted' is less cultural than the 'boiled'. The opposition between nature and culture cannot be placed on a graded scale without stripping it of its relevance and operative strength. This problem comes out all the more because the nature/culture axis is far from exhausting all the contrasts between the 'boiled' and the 'roasted' that Lévi-Strauss himself develops in his article, which include: internal cooking versus superficial cooking (inside/outside), family consumption versus celebratory meal (endo-cuisine versus exo-cuisine), feminine cooking versus masculine cooking, preserving of meat and juices versus loss (economy/prodigality), cooking at home versus cooking outside, etc.

By attributing the significance that he does to the opposition between nature and culture in his analyses of modes of cooking, Lévi-Strauss exposes himself, among other things, to great logical difficulties when he tries to articulate the roasted and the boiled to the rotten and the smoked. Indeed, the boiled and the rotten present similarities that many languages have marked. However, in the nature/culture 'key' – to use a Lévi-Straussian metaphor – the boiled is the most cultural form of culinary preparation, whereas the rotten is a natural elaboration of a natural category, namely the raw. Why then should pottery, the archetypal cultural invention, produce a type of food – boiled food – which is mostly assimilated to the rotten, in other words, to a state that uncooked food reaches spontaneously? A similar contradiction affects the category of the smoked. It is the mode of cooking which, according to Lévi-Strauss, is closest to the cooked and is therefore the epitome of culture. Among Amerindian populations, however, the green wood rack used to cure meat must be destroyed after use, unlike what happens with boiling, where the utensils are kept preciously. Smoking therefore – the most cultural way of preparing food – requires the cancellation of the cultural means that made it possible; whereas the mode of cooking that requires one of the most potent symbols of culture (pottery) produces food in a state close to the natural. Far from enabling the distribution of properties, states and processes in a field of symmetrical oppositions and correspondences, the nature/culture dichotomy introduces paradoxical inversions and contiguities.

The solution adopted by Lévi-Strauss to solve these paradoxes is to claim that the opposition between nature and culture disappears when it is mediated by cooking: 'Everything functions as though the lasting possession of a cultural acquisition entailed . . . a concession made in compensation to nature: when the result is long-lasting, the means must be precarious and conversely' (Lévi-Strauss 1965a: 27; my translation). In other words, the preservation of food through smoking is lasting because the medium – the wooden smoking grill – is precarious, whereas the preservation of boiled food is precarious because the medium – the utensils – are durable. Cooking therefore articulates nature and culture by dividing and reversing qualities and states that pertain to these two categories, at the expense of an unavoidable dissymmetry. Even if we can concede Lévi-Strauss's point that dissymmetry is the price to pay for structure to give to myth its dynamism, we may nonetheless ask ourselves whether the elegant demonstration of the 'culinary triangle' could have been made without conjuring up the nature/culture axis. Rather than starting from an opposition which, as the analysis shows, does not delimit two clearly defined fields of predicates, it may have been better if he had restricted himself to a system of contrasts that express phenomenal properties of matter and action. Lévi-Strauss actually puts forward and uses these contrasts: the distinction between elaborated and unelaborated or between spontaneous processes and triggered processes, the range of possible mediations between food and what transforms it (fire, air, water, fat), the types of cooking imple-ments (flat, concave, convex, open, closed) and the degree of immersion in a liquid, etc. These offer a series of combinations which can account for all cooking methods and the meanings which are attached to them, without calling upon an ontological distinction which is not proven to be universally shared.

In several instances, notably in the *Mythologiques*, Lévi-Strauss seems compelled to resort to analytical artifices because he attributes a too literal and substantive value to the opposition between nature and culture, even if it does not fit the data. This is the case, for example, with his analysis of the relations between illnesses and fishing and hunting poisons in South American mythology (Lévi-Strauss 1964a: 279–8). Lévi-Strauss defines poison as a point of isomorphism between nature and culture in as much as it is a natural substance that enables a cultural activity. However, curare and several other Amerindian poisons are the result of a long and complex preparation involving fasts, sexual prohibitions and multiple other precautions. By the time they are used for hunting or fishing, they have already ceased to be 'natural substances' and become products of human activity, i.e. the result of a technical transformation. Furthermore, curare, like weapons, tools, ornaments and salt, is the much sought-after object of intense intertribal exchanges that have a long history. If salt and curare are part of these exchanges, it is because of the transformations they have undergone in their confection: they are conceived as analogous to other craft products and not as raw materials. Finally, the definition of poisons given by Lévi-Strauss could equally well be applied to all the artefacts produced by the Amerindians: a blowpipe, a bow, a pottery piece, ornaments, maybe even a house are, like poisons, the result of the transformation of natural substances which fulfil, once they have been elaborated, a cultural function. Lévi-Strauss never considers artefacts as mediators between culture and nature; on the contrary, he uses them as symbols of culture standing in opposition to natural substances. He says of pottery clay, which one could construe as being the epitome of a natural substance fulfilling a cultural function, that it constitutes 'one of the raw materials of culture' (1964a: 254), and presents it as standing in opposition, in myths, to the clay of termitaries, a symbol of nature. Why should we grant to clay what is denied to poisons, and vice versa?

The above analysis of hunting or fishing poisons is integrated in a masterly analysis, in which Lévi-Strauss brings to light the dialectic of small and large intervals present in Amerindian mythical thought. According to him, poisons are 'chromatic' entities, since they operate an imperceptible transitivity from nature to culture, while having 'diatonic' effects since they decimate the animals which fall victim to them: a maximum continuum thus engenders a maximum discontinuity. The hypothesis is fruitful but there is no need to call upon nature and culture to show that poisons belong on the side of the continuous. Some of their intrinsic properties can testify to this just as well. Fishing poison dissolves gradually in water, creating a layer that drifts along the current. Once mixed with water, it no longer has precise limits and its visibility depends on its degree of dilution. It is indeed 'chromatic'. As for hunting poisons, some of them remain virulent for a very long time; such a length of conservation, which outlasts that of most artefacts produced by the Indians, predisposes these toxic substances, employed each time in minute quantities, to be used to symbolise that which is continuous. Let us add that curare, which exists in the form of a hardened paste when cold, becomes liquid when heated to coat projectiles. It is therefore also 'chromatic' in the sense that it exists in different states that are separated by imperceptible gradations. Unlike 'nature' and 'culture', which are philosophical abstractions that are difficult to transpose outside of their original context, all these physico-chemical properties of poisons are well known among Amerindians, and therefore exploitable in the concrete logic to which their myths give shape, the articulations of which Lévi-Strauss has admirably brought to light.

For, if there is an area where the distinction between nature and culture does not operate, it is that of Amerindian myths, which recount the unusual stories of a time when humans and non-humans were not differentiated, a time when, to take Jivaro examples, it was normal for Nighthawk to do the cooking, for Cricket to play the viol, for Hummingbird to clear gardens or Swift to hunt with a blowpipe. In those days, indeed, animals and plants mastered the arts of civilisation, communicated unhindered between themselves and followed the principal rules of social etiquette. For as much as we can judge, their appearance was human, and only a few clues – their names and strange behaviour – testify to what they would transform themselves into. Indeed, each myth relates the circumstances in which a change of form occurred, tells the story of how a plant or animal that previously existed as a potentiality came to be actualised in a non-human body. In fact, Jivaro mythology explicitly underlines this change of physical state by signalling the completion of the metamorphosis by means of the apparition of a particular anatomical trait or the uttering of a distinctive sound, particular to a species. The Amerindian myths do not therefore evoke the irreversible passage from nature to culture, but rather the emergence of 'natural' discontinuities from an original 'cultural' continuum within which humans and non-humans were not clearly distinguished. This great movement of speciation does not, however, lead to the constitution of a natural order identical to the one we know since, if plants and animals from now on have different physical traits from humans – and thus habits which correspond to the biological apparatus particular to each species – they also have in most cases preserved, up to now, the inner faculties they enjoyed before their speciation: subjectivity, reflexive consciousness, intentionality, aptitude to communicate in a universal language, etc. These are therefore persons, wearing an animal or vegetal body, which they occasionally discard, to lead a collective life akin to that of humans: the Makuna, for example, say that tapirs paint themselves with roucou to dance and that peccary play the horn during their rituals, while the Wari' claim that the peccary makes maize beer and that the jaguar brings its prey home for his spouse to cook.[5]

For a very long time, these types of statements were treated as testimonies of minds alien to logic, incapable of distinguishing reality from dreams and myths, or as simple figures of speech, metaphors or puns. But the Makuna, the Wari' and many other Amerindian tribes who claim such things are no more blind or credulous than we are. They know that the jaguar devours its prey raw and that the peccary wreaks havoc on the maize plantations rather than cultivating them. The jaguar and the peccary, they say, see themselves as accomplishing gestures identical to those of humans, and imagine themselves in good faith as sharing with the latter the same technical system, the same social existence, the same beliefs and aspirations. Thus, in myths as in daily existence, the Amerindians do not consider what we call culture as the privilege of humans since many animals or plants are deemed to believe they possess it, and live according to its rules. It thus becomes difficult to argue that these people are conscious of, or intuit, a distinction between nature and culture akin to the one that we have adopted, when all their ways of thinking seem to contradict this.

Therefore, despite warning us not to take such a distinction too literally, Lévi-Strauss has not always managed to escape the temptation to consider it as a universal fact of human experience. However, this is perhaps stretching criticism further than one needs to as, first of all, the ethnographic information Lévi-Strauss possessed at the time when he was composing his tetralogy was still very patchy and incomplete, limited for the most part to collections of myths. The intensive research that has been led since on the Indians of South America has revealed unexpected perspectives on their cosmologies and their modes of thinking, which the author of *Mythologiques* obviously could not have taken into account at the time. Above all, one feels that Lévi-Strauss uses the nature/culture opposition in his analyses of myths as a form of generic label, or semantic short cut, rather than as a true antinomy expressing an intrinsic dimension in the apprehension of the world. It is in fact an abbreviated designation enabling him to subsume, without too many circum- locutions, contrastive groups of qualities and states which the people, whose myths he is studying, distinguish, although they do not feel the need to differentiate them according to their place on the nature/culture axis. This is the case, as we have seen, of the very fruitful intuition that the Amazonian poisons have a 'chromatic' character and 'diatonic' effects, even though it is difficult to subsume them under contrasting ontological categories without violating local conceptions. This mostly typological use of the opposition between nature and culture may also explain why the ethnologists of indige- nous America are unanimous in acknowledging the heuristic scope of the ethnographical conclusions Lévi-Strauss draws from his analysis of myths, even though they doubt the relevance of such an opposition for the societies with which they are familiar.

[* * *]

If I have lingered on this aspect of Lévi-Strauss's work, it is because he is often considered, notably by Anglo-Saxon anthropology, as the main advo- cate of an unmitigated dualism and the heir to an intellectual movement which, originating with Descartes and assimilated to French rationalism, strove to dissociate nature from culture, body and mind, sense and sensibility, objectifying systematically the thought and the institutions of non-literate civilisations, thanks to binary oppositions that are as abstract as they are unverifiable. One had to do justice to this caricature, which has become the dominant *credo* in the United States, while pointing out the ambiguities of some of Lévi-Strauss's formulations, source of many misunderstandings among his readers. Because if we want to find examples of a literal use of the opposition between nature and culture, it is not so much in his work that one must search, but rather in that of authors who have been influenced by him, applying some of the basic processes of the structural analysis like recipes, without really understanding to what extent this was inseparable from a monist theory of knowledge that counterbalanced the dualism of his method.

It is also true that Lévi-Strauss's position on this matter testifies to the difficulties anthropology encounters because of its more or less explicit adhesion to the belief that the world can be distributed into two isolated fields of phenomena, the interdependence of which must be demonstrated. Apprehended in their most excessive formulations, the terms of the debate make all mediation impossible: either culture is shaped by nature – whether composed of genes, instincts, neural networks or geographical constraints – or nature acquires form and substance only as a reservoir of potential signs and symbols upon which culture draws. Obviously, between the 'abysmal determinism' and the 'airy imagination', to use Augustin Berque's expressions, many authors – anthropologists, geographers, philosophers – have attempted to find a middle road, a dialectical escape from the confrontation of these two dogmatisms (Berque 1986: 135, 141). At equal distance between positivist militants and the advocates of an uncompromising hermeneutics, they have strived to reunite the ideal and the material, the concrete and the abstract, the physical determinations and the production of meaning. But such efforts of mediation are condemned to remain vain for as long as they are based on the premises of a dualist cosmology, and as long as they imply the existence of a universal nature which the various cultures would encode or adapt to. On the axis that leads from a totally natural culture to a totally cultural nature, there is no middle ground, only compromises that bring us closer to one pole or another. Furthermore, the problem is as old as anthropology itself; as Marshall Sahlins puts it very well, anthropology is like a prisoner condemned for more than a century to pace his cell, confined between the wall of the mind's constraints and that of practical determinations (Sahlins 1976: 55).

I would be prepared to concede that this type of prison has its advantages. Dualism is not harmful in itself, and one would be somewhat naïve to stigmatise it for purely moral reasons, as do the eco-centric philosophers, or to make it responsible for all the evils of the modern era, from colonial expansion to the destruction of non-renewable resources, and the reification of sexual identities or class distinctions. We are indebted to dualism for providing, along with the idea that nature obeys its own rules, a formidable springboard for the development of sciences. We also owe to it, alongside the belief that humanity becomes more civilised as it increasingly controls nature and its own instincts, some of the advantages, notably political, that the aspirations to progress have encouraged. Anthropology is daughter to this movement, to the scientific mind, and the faith in evolution, and there is no reason to blush at the circumstances of its birth or to welcome its disappearance in atonement for its youthful sins. But its role does not accommodate this heritage very well; its role being to understand how people who do not share our cosmology could have invented for themselves realities that are distinct from ours, thus testifying to a creativity that cannot be judged according to our own accomplishments. And this is what anthropology cannot understand when it treats our own reality as a universal fact of human experience, when it assumes that our ways of establishing discontinuities in the world and perceiving constant relations, our ways of distributing entities and phenomena, processes and modes of action into categories are predetermined by the texture and structure of things.

Of course, we do not apprehend other cultures as completely analogous to ours – this would not be very plausible. We have a tendency to see them through the prism of part of our cosmology only, like so many unique expressions of Culture in as much as it contrasts with a single and universal Nature. These are very diverse cultures therefore, which nonetheless all belong to the constitutive canon of what we mean by this double abstraction. Because it is deeply rooted in our habits, this ethnocentrism is very difficult to extirpate: to most anthropologists, as Roy Wagner remarks accurately, the peripheral cultures of the modern Western world 'do not contrast with our culture, or offer counter examples to it, as a total system of conceptualisation, but rather invite comparison as "other ways" of dealing with *our own reality*' (Wagner 1981: 42; italicised by the author). To use the modern dualism of nature and culture as the standard of all world systems restricts us to a form of benevolent cannibalism, to the repeated incorporation of premodern peoples' objectifications of themselves into our own objectifications of ourselves. For a long time considered radically 'other', and as a consequence used as foils to civic morality or as models of extinct virtues, 'savages' are now considered as our almost transparent neighbours; they are no longer the 'naked philosophers' praised by Montaigne, but proto-citizens, proto-naturalists, quasi-historians, economists in gestation, in short, the hesitant precursors of a way of apprehending things and people which we, or so we think, have uncovered and codified better than anyone else. This is a way of paying them homage, undoubtedly. However, by making them part of our common lot, it is also the best way of eclipsing their contribution to the intelligibility of the human condition.

Translated by Yves Gilonne and Boris Wiseman.

NOTES

1. This essay was first published in French in Michel Izard (ed.), *Claude Lévi-Strauss*. Paris: Éditions de l'Herne, pp. 296–305.
2. Lévi-Strauss's unstated reference here is the French physiologist Claude Bernard (1813–78).
3. *The Elementary Structures of Kinship* 1969a: 62–3: 'above all because women are not primarily a sign of social value, but a natural stimulant, and the stimulant of the only instinct the satisfaction of which can be deferred, and consequently the only one for which, in the act of exchange, and through the awareness of reciprocity, the transformation from the stimulant to the sign can take place, and, defining by this fundamental process the transformation from nature to culture, assume the character of an institution'; 1969a: 136: 'But if, as we try to show here, it is true that the transition from nature to culture is determined by man's ability to think of biological relationships as systems of oppositions'.
4. Cf. Leach 1970: 112; a mistake Yvan Simonis does not commit in his excellent analysis of Lévi-Strauss's naturalism (Simonis 1968: 33–67).
5. For the Makuna, Århem 1990: 108–15; for the Wari', Vilaça 1992: 55–63.

REFERENCES

Århem, Kaj 1990. 'Ecosofía Makuna', in F. Correa (ed.), *La selva humanizada. Ecología alternativa en el Trópico húmedo colombiano*. Bogota: Instituto Colombiano de Antropología, pp. 105–22.
Berque, Augustin 1986. *Le Sauvage et l'artifice. Les Japonais devant la nature*. Paris: Gallimard.
Harris, Marvin 1976. 'Lévi-Strauss et la palourde. Réponse à la Conférence Gildersleeve de 1972', *L'Homme* 16 (2–3): 5–22.
Leach, Edmund 1970. *Lévi-Strauss*. London: Fontana/Collins.
Sahlins, Marshall 1976. *Culture and Practical Reason*. Chicago and London: University of Chicago Press.
Simonis, Yvan 1968. *Claude Lévi-Strauss ou la 'passion de l'inceste'. Introduction au structuralisme*. Paris: Aubier-Montaigne.
Vilaça, Aparecida 1992. *Comendo como gente: formas do canibalismo Wari'*. Rio de Janeiro: Editora UFRJ.
Wagner, Roy 1981 [1975]. *The Invention of Culture*. Chicago and London: University of Chicago Press.

6   On anthropological knowledge

Claude Imbert

It was in the fifties that Lévi-Strauss explicitly focused on anthropological knowledge, at a decisive moment indeed. A deep, to many readers troubling, difference opposes *The Elementary Structures of Kinship* (1949a; 1969a) to a series of later, connected books beginning with *The Savage Mind* (1962b; 1966b). It testified to a completely new approach to ethnographic understanding. Lévi-Strauss himself confirmed the break. In between, ten years had passed, devoted to an epistemological reflection, echoed in homages paid to Mauss, Durkheim and Rousseau. Lévi-Strauss had definitely turned to a question first raised by Mauss, who left it unanswered, standing as a sealed legacy. When Lévi-Strauss came back from New York, he might have decided either to start new fieldwork in the Pacific or to pursue his theoretical research, turning to some *non-elementary* structures of kinship. These would have supplied a link of sorts to confront contemporary social constructions of family relations in post-war Western societies. Although he never forgot his concern for civil life, he finally chose a third option, precisely to reconsider anthropological knowledge as such.

Three enigmas surfaced out of his preceding experiences. One is closely bound to structuralism, another to his Brazilian fieldwork and the third to Mauss's limited success in *The Gift*. All have to do with the very possibility of anthropology as a science. The uncontested achievement of *The Elementary Structures of Kinship* (1949a; 1969a) had come at an excessively high price. To confirm his argument and give it a decisive perspicuity, Lévi-Strauss resorted to a mathematical representation, a specific application of group theory supplied by the mathematician André Weil. The conclusion to his study of kinship systems left open a two-sided question: *How* do native peoples master a highly sophisticated institution without any mathematical support? *Why* would the demonstration be unsatisfying to scholars if it was not confirmed through a more familiar or respected device, such as mathematics? Either a substantial part of what had been captured as a structure escaped anthropological understanding, or the anthropologist's mind was dependent upon rational procedures too specific and complex to be abstracted from their mathematical symbolism. But nobody would agree that the rules of kinship originated in biology or were the product of a mere casual empiricism. Could those rules be attributed to the unconscious and, if so, what kind of unconscious? Not a Freudian one: Lévi-Strauss insisted that the prohibition of incest had to be rethought as preferential marriage, as a choice submitted to a qualification that embedded the objectivity of an exchange process. He had also paid great attention to kinship denominations, for which he was borrowing from Marcel Granet, who was the first to give a structural representation of family relations, in his case as it applied to ancient China (see Granet 1939).[1] Lévi-Strauss's title, *The Elementary Structures of Kinship* (1949a; 1969a), quite contemporary with Merleau-Ponty's essay *The Structure of Behaviour*, was a declaration, a strategic variation on Durkheim's *The Elementary Forms of the Religious Life*, a claim for rationality, and a way out of the usual concepts of experience, rather than a dogmatic use of the notion of *structure*. Such a fleeting use nevertheless promised to bridge human sciences and exact sciences. It took advantage of a semantic proximity with the notion of *form*, so common during the first decades of the twentieth century that it escaped conceptual transcendentalism without scandal, as Cassirer did in his *Philosophy of Symbolic Forms* (1953). It overlapped with a classical approach, since a new science, as was anthropology, badly needed further elaboration. It should also be recalled that Lévi-Strauss turned to mathematics to elucidate a process of *transformation* and *generativity*, two decisive features which went beyond the limits of a phenomenological, first-order description of facts, forms and things.

The fieldwork in the Matto Grosso region of Brazil had also left an enigma, most evident and humiliating. The undecipherable face paintings of the Caduveo women manifested a knowledge that challenged the ethnographer. These women were able to reproduce the schema of their face paintings on a sheet of paper, producing a two-dimensional graphic which denied the anatomical construction of the face. This schema was an essential element of their identity and of social relations. It displayed an intelligibility which could neither be mapped onto our mimetic/narcissistic relation to the image nor captured through our classical descriptive stance. Its intelligibility, as claimed by natives, was embedded into another and no less sophisticated symbolism which disturbed and challenged any process of translation.

Mauss's *The Gift* (1954) had convinced Lévi-Strauss that the act of exchange was the real matter of human sciences and its leading thread. Nevertheless, and because of his intimate relation to Mauss's writings, he could easily show how far Mauss remained trapped in a Kantian approach. Mauss considers the object of exchange in the terms of an object of experience moving from one donor to the other, instead of focusing on exchange as a framing operation. The three formulas of the gift were conceptualised on the same pattern as the Kantian formulas for morality; they were made dependent upon the same modalities: *you must give, you must accept, you must give back*. Mauss tried to elicit, from some archaic legislations described in his first pages, a confirmation encompassing the whole domain of exchange, including modern market exchange and the common use of money. As a legal and universal principle, exchange encompassed, for Mauss, the contemporary and problematic payment of war compensations, as stipulated in the 1921 Versailles Treatise, and made possible the avoidance of unrealistic requirements, injustice and resentment. Evidently, Mauss did not, and could not, affect the course of history. More generally, an intimate Kantian conviction, which equated social relations and obligations, blocked his ethnographic approach. In the same homage, contained in his *Introduction to the Work of Marcel Mauss* (1950a), Lévi-Strauss underlined Mauss's contrasting achievement in his cross-current interest in magic. He also insisted on Mauss's decisive essays on language, psychology and body techniques, and how far he contributed to reshaping ethnographic fieldwork. Nevertheless, like Moses, Mauss was left out of the Promised Land.

Those three unsolved puzzles – the way native populations treated their own kinship structures, the Amerindian face paintings and the limits of Mauss's thought – called for a unified solution which was to deeply affect the usual epistemological stance, infatuated with a common conception of experience, a Kantian canon tacitly used as a universal phenomenological metalanguage. In response, Lévi-Strauss engaged in structuralism, until it dissolved into what has been another *De Emendatione Intellectus* – to use Spinoza's words – for our present time.

Structuralism revisited

As a preamble to any close reading of Lévi-Strauss's writings, it must be reasserted that he never opted for a kind of formalism that rearranged, at the surface, the ethnographic material. Structural anthropology has been able, negatively, to rub out the usual descriptive syntactical protocol of predicative phenomenology. Positively, it has been an effort to break the code of sensibility, a code able to distribute again and again intelligible relations onto an array of symbolic marks, a process that occurs at a fleeting limit between consciousness and the environment. It is not the place, here, to follow in detail Lévi-Strauss's use of the notion of *structure* in his many writings, but it is essential to scrutinise the specific shape it took through its uses. So, instead of revisiting structuralism, arguing *pro* and *con*, it is better to ask: *what is and what ought to be structuralism*? Thus paying homage to the well-known and decisive essay by Richard Dedekind, published in the last decades of the nineteenth century, *Was sind und sollen die Zahlen*, an essay to which the naïve notion of number did not survive (Dedekind 1963). In the same mood, let us sketch an overview of what was required of the notion of *structure* and what it provided.

In *mathematics* it was introduced as an algebraic structure, depending on sets and the mapping to which they are by definition submitted, a mapping upon which, moreover, an operation may be axiomatically defined. What André Weil provided came from a very specific mathematical domain, a part of set theoretical algebraic group theory through which a *transformation* may be characterised. So, he met Lévi-Strauss's main requirement, that of a minimal inductive transformation, able to map the process of exchange along generations. So far so good; as noted earlier the remaining problem was to understand the implementation of this transformation on non-mathematical supports (kinship relation), and its symbolic tracing in human minds, where admittedly it never exists in its perfect state and norm. It was nevertheless quite clear that no equation, which cancels a debt or concludes a deal, could be a sufficient description of what Mauss conceived as an encompassing social phenomenon. Mauss did not miss the point, but his approach affected the formulas of gift exchange with a deontic modality that blurred the process and submitted its reactivation to a prior, transcendental, moral law. As a consequence, instead of capturing a process as such, he was led to combine juridical concerns with economic considerations, encapsulated in a theory of money for which some surprisingly long notes had been inserted in *The Gift*.

Surprisingly enough, in the same decades, the 1920s–1930s, the notion of structure, identified at the surface level of denomination, or at the quite unconscious level of phonology, offered a key to a universal characteristic of human languages. Better than an invariant property, it brought to the fore an operation rooted in substitutions, oppositions, choices and transformations out of which each language selects its own array of possibilities. Some of these transformational aspects were not ignored in Lévi-Strauss's *The Elementary Structures of Kinship* (1949a; 1969a). They contributed to suggesting an organisation of mind capacities, never thought of before, able to replace the metaphysical, largely homonymic linkage between mind, reason and language. Phenomenology, definitely straining under the weight of the Husserlian notion of apophantic predication as a fundamental syntax devoted to declaration, was put at a loss. Once mathematics had left its Euclidian stance, phenomenology was driven to declare a state of crisis in science, and indulged the apotropaic notion of a primitive mentality.

A third usage came to the fore later on, in Chomsky's structural linguistics, which identified human language specificity as an escape from the behaviour loop and ascribed generativity to syntactical structures. The notion as such had been transferred from the so-called *Frege–Russell type systems* of logic to linguistics, in the late-blooming years of analytical philosophy. If we leave aside that affinity between quantificational logic and linguistics, which turned out to be more limited and specific than had been hoped, and stick to transformation and reiteration, we find another way into the problem raised by Lévi-Strauss, namely would it be possible to delineate a further case of transformation, so akin to mathematics, that would open onto a style of intelligibility not submitted to the predicative and conceptual stance of classical epistemology? In the fifties, this question was still unanswered.

The direction of Lévi-Strauss's thought was shaped by further evidence of a structural mediation, of a more cognitive type, recurring in an epistemological structure whose prototype and paradigmatic virtue Wittgenstein did not miss, although no doubt, at the time, Lévi-Strauss and Wittgenstein did not know about each other's work. One recalls how Wittgenstein, in long-unpublished notes, was led to conceive a way out of truth functional calculus, which clearly was unable to grasp some of the deepest structures of language, by resorting to a logic of *colours* – a simplified map encapsulating primitive oppositions and associations, limited in number, along with a scale of intensities and degrees. Such a model could afford as many interpolations between any pair of opposite poles as is convenient. It revealed a structural level of organisation of qualities which could be substituted in place of any phenomenological theory. We know that in the years that followed the *Tractatus*, Wittgenstein never lost interest in the possibility of a logic of colours framing some language games.

It is in the light of the above that the line of enquiry opened by Lévi-Strauss after the fifties takes on its full significance. After he had excluded that a phenomenological approach and its predicative syntax might provide an absolute norm and pattern for experience and language, he considered how the qualitative structure of sensibility, including voice emission and reception, might encode a symbolic organisation – by which I mean a way of communicating with the environment and other living beings, be they animals or humans. This new approach would contribute to unifying the many forms of communication and exchange that exist before or outside a field in which language had been submitted to a syntax endorsing an overwhelming phenomenological physics. Let us note, by the way, that such slow syntactical processes and conceptual shifts specify a historico-anthropological distribution or genealogy of logics.

It would not be impossible to follow in Lévi-Strauss's writings, from 1960 to the end of the 1970s, his effort to shift from the level of Saussurean linguistics to the phonological level of Russian linguistics, then to a level where qualities function as cognitive mediators. Lévi-Strauss explored an unknown territory, at the limit of brain physiology and consciousness, where human sensibility emerges as articulated systems of differences, with degrees of intensity, and preferences. His findings opened onto a system of knowledge and communication, more directly connected to the neuro-cognitive organisation of knowledge, an organisation that has been later empirically documented by clinical and educational research, which is generally accepted today. To put it in a nutshell, we are nearer to a Wittgensteinian conception than to a Chomskian conception. Sticking to the linguistic notion of structure would be misleading. On the contrary, the phonological array of qualitative values and differences is a part, surely not the least important, of a *logic of qualities*. Viewing structuralism against such a background, which surely was not clear to Lévi-Strauss from the start and was further elaborated in the four volumes of the *Mythologiques*, we are nearer to the problem that lies at the core of his successive approaches to fieldwork, ethnography and anthropology: negatively, to avoid propositional unities – to which the *mythemes* occasionally offered a substitute – positively, to promote a logic of qualities (compare the oppositions raw/cooked, naked/clothed, etc.), to address a man deprived of the European common dressing of language, divested of a propositional *cogito* and its phenomenological stance, no longer a subject facing an object, a human being most able to implant on his/her cognitive abilities different and new symbolisms – which is a common experience today. Lévi-Strauss experienced a brutal and illuminating affinity between a yet unsealed fieldwork and what is required by modern life. More on this later.

In fact, the very notion of a *logic*, in keeping with the Greek featuring of logic, was challenged: such qualified scales, charts, collection of samples, as investigated independently some years earlier by Wittgenstein, do not fit easily into a discursive propositional arrangement. Rather, they suppose a mental map of sorts, as used in classifications, trees or denominative systems, and cannot be fairly appreciated using the categories of a propositional grammar. This was the problem that occupied Wittgenstein just after the *Tractatus*. Both were driven away from preferred syntactical paths to explore a tentative operation of thinking, especially without the accredited framing and operation of a *sensus communis*.[2] Turning to mythology Lévi-Strauss focused more directly on symbolism, and its capacity to recombine and transform, identifying syntax with the immanent transformation of a symbolic system, discovering *why* and *how* such a syntax is adherent to exchange, of which it is an immediate mark and to which it is related through mechanisms of feedback and control and with which it is therefore contemporary. To be clear: *The Raw and the Cooked* is concerned with a division within a symbolic, social process; it does not pertain to a phenomenological description. Its operations are not from the start a qualification of something, they are primarily a mental coding, although they appear as a local adherent coding, loaded with a difference inherent in the opposition between, let us say, the taste of *honey* and that of *tobacco*. As such, the *Mythologiques* contains a lot of information on the way a living being extracts differences and mappings from the chaos of what is not even a world, and about our mental equipment.

We are introduced to a way of communicating not included in the collection of usual *logics*: whether developed in immediate proximity to spoken language, which was the case of the logics that dominated from the Greeks to Kant, or whether they emerged from this narrow channel, as has been the case since Frege. Hence, Lévi-Strauss's innovative title: *Mytho-logiques*.

So, once pushed back to its neuro-psychological level, the notion of structure was endowed with an effective epistemological role. It articulates an objectivity, depriving the opposition of subject and object of its metaphysical authority. Lévi-Strauss was now able to reopen his former enigmas, in particular to develop a system of oppositions and preferences which left aside the digital code of assertion/negation, bringing to the fore a no less powerful operator: a scale of qualitative differences which implies opposition and intensity, and allows the unlimited insertion of further differences and oppositions. When Lévi-Strauss engaged in that new problematic, music was the first model that he proposed for it. Then, some visual artefacts were recognised as being endowed with the same properties, once our way of looking at them had been freed from the Western conventions of representation – however useful and productive these conventions may have been for our Greek legacy. Here, sexual difference and its symbolic markings could be integrated as a syntactical operation underlying the rules of kinship, mythology and masks. Here, we are out of our secular naturalism. Here, any kind of asymmetry or lameness, depending on the proper liability of the support – geometrical, visual or mythological – on which it is inscribed, might be converted into a fair symbolic expression of incest, etc. Lévi-Strauss had dissolved the classical and long-frozen frontier between sense data and language into another syntactical organisation. He assumed as his own challenge an opposition between the *sensible* and the so-called *intelligible* which Kant took from Plato, applied to the case of Newtonian mathematics, formulated in his 1770 dissertation and resolved by means of a transcendental phenomenology of experience.

Here is the ground on which Lévi-Strauss may be fairly appreciated, that of his making of these new epistemological tools, which especially requires one to capture the specificity of human efficiency and foster the contemporary development of the human sciences. *The Savage Mind* (1966b) and the four volumes of the *Mythologiques* opened a way out of the propositional pattern of traditional, phenomenological logic and its obsessive ambition of universal translation. After he had recognised similar structures on heterogeneous supports, Lévi-Strauss was able to rephrase his former enigmas. Hence, the shift that occurs between 'Indian Cosmetics' (published in *VVV* in 1942)[3] and *The Way of the Masks* (1975; 1982a). His encounter with Caduveo facial paintings had elicited a long-lasting effort to capture a meaning, which he interpreted first according to the art of cosmetics inspired by Baudelaire (see the latter's 'Éloge du maquillage' in *The Painter of Modern Day Life*, 2003), then through a family resemblance with playing cards and coats of arms and thirdly, as it was displayed on its most explicit support for symbolic transformations, masks. Here, the iconic elements, now invested with their own logical-syntactical properties, revealed through a finite array of visual components that were being constantly recombined like the phonetic values that make up words, a production of meaning that was neither geometrical nor analogical. They displayed an intelligibility not yet accounted for by any theory. In the end, the three vexing challenges (the Caduveo facial designs, the mathematical representation of kinship structures and the limits of Mauss's theory of exchange), apparently disconnected, had been better than resolved. As soon as they were reshaped according to their proper articulations and symbolic contexts, they were simply and simultaneously blown away. As always, the solution was underlying, but invisible as long as those scattered enigmas had not yet been correctly formulated (as Lévi-Strauss often said himself, giving a precious indication about his own epistemological progress). Over the course of thirty years, the notion of structure had developed, and its immanent, defining property of being transferable, from one support to another, from one field to another, brought to the fore. It had also been fitted with its consequent transformational capacity and syntactical generativity and connected to its cognitive level.

All this has qualified Lévi-Strauss as an Americanist whose contribution is widely recognised in the field of kinship and Amerindian research. Is that all? Lévi-Strauss's guiding thread had been to track the elements of some inductive thinking instead of focusing on local reports and translations resulting in a collection of anomalies. He preferred to explore an operation rather than analyse the disturbing scattered evidence provided by a local culture; he preferred relation and transfer over propositional synthesis. Moreover, such a disturbing reappraisal of what was formerly called *data* was simultaneously deeper, more general, competing for universality and nevertheless able to promote minute and local explanations, directly useful to the ethnographer, precisely because it captured the immanent productivity of a cognitive and vital attitude. The time had come to recognise that nothing is given. Lévi-Strauss had uncovered the contradiction which limited Mauss's achievement. At the same time as he dissolved what appeared to be a gift to reveal a process of exchange, Mauss maintained a position of knowledge articulated to a receptor of sense data and its conceptual, juridical Kantian wording. The conflict could only confirm the importance of ethnology, limited and deficient as it was when confined to mere fleeting data, as long as anthropology was subjected to a phenomenology, in its many guises: naïve, critical or merely propositional. The real question was to be settled in between, in a reworking of both poles: the ethnographical field experience and anthropological intelligence. Conversely, the framing of fieldwork was linked to the equally difficult task of its exposition, which means conducting a demonstration and making it palatable to the scholar's mind – an achievement so specific and nevertheless so essential that it truly constitutes a second fieldwork of sorts, as Marilyn Strathern so convincingly argued.[4] Here, the question is more that of a deep modification of the anthropologist's mind than of a mere epistemological determination. We are at a point when the challenge of modernity was akin to the anthropological predicament and vice versa. The problem loomed in different guises, from the fleeting and weak notion of a primitive mentality, much discussed at the time in philosophical contexts although it had no impact on anthropological research as such, to the arrogant position of colonialism. In both cases a baffled intelligence was unable to identify a production of intelligibility it denied. In a short period of time, the enclosure of the European mind affected like a plague the European metropolis. In so doing it developed an oversimplified and grotesque version of its supposed Aryan past and, like Hugolin, devoured its own children in the tower of its fascinated ambitions. It would take a long time to settle the predicament in its anthropological terms, although it was here necessary to unveil the grim face of colonialism, as well as the unspeakable barbarism and philosophical blindness to which Europe was submitted, which reached their culmination in the first years of the 1940s.

Lévi-Strauss's options

It is now possible to give full depth and meaning to the choice made by Lévi-Strauss when he came back to Paris at the end of the 1940s. His move towards what looked like another speculative approach to anthropology, which it surely was not, may be followed along two paths. The first was a detailed reconsideration of the discipline, as it was framed and reframed in its oblique relation to Kantian criticism; the second was Lévi-Strauss's rethinking of his own experience, on which he has given many testimonies, starting with *Tristes Tropiques* (1955a) and culminating in a telling but nevertheless cryptic montage, in his introduction to *The Way of the Masks* (1975; 1982a).

Lévi-Strauss's genealogy of the discipline, starting with Durkheim and Mauss, testifies to their ongoing effort to obey the pressure of ethnographic observations. The most important fieldwork publications provided the subject matter of an impressive number of reviews that they published in *L'Année sociologique*. Lévi-Strauss underlines the consequent modifications that took place from Durkheim's *The Rules of Sociological Method* to *The Elementary Forms of the Religious Life*. A homage to Rousseau (see *Structural Anthropology II*, 'Jean-Jacques Rousseau, Founder of the Sciences of Man', 1976b) was the most provocative. Lévi-Strauss, leaving aside Rousseau's more famous *The Social Contract*, underlines a note and a project in *The Discourse on the Origin of Inequality*. There, Rousseau suggested sponsorship of an expedition dedicated to the observation of unknown populations, which would have corrected the misguided conquest of America, and would have enabled laying down the foundations of a social anthropology animated by scientific interest and empathy, a kind of human geography as it was later initiated by Alexander von Humboldt. It would have gone beyond the mere ethical and often short-sighted consideration of men in contemporary society, to reveal virtual forms of life. No doubt, Rousseau did not easily overcome his powerful rhetoric of an ethical claim. Nevertheless, Lévi-Strauss identified in Rousseau's *Botanic Letters* a method of classification, opening a new way to knowledge and a virtual positing of the self as a mere living being, watering down the vindicatory declaration of his *Confessions*. Those epistemological modifications were further elaborated in *The Savage Mind*. So, during all those years, the epistemological challenge was Lévi-Strauss's most decisive concern, although it took him a decade to elaborate a way through, one that would enable him to meet this challenge. The last part of *Tristes Tropiques* (1955a) sheds an oblique light on it. Readers may have remarked, here and there in the earlier chapters, some affinity with Rousseau. The last pages ('The Return') definitively explain away and dissolve the literary motif of the *Confessions*, its plea for a justification, and give it its modern philosophical slant. After visiting the overcrowded cities of the Indian peninsula, Lévi-Strauss comes to Taxila, the furthest point reached by Alexander the Great in his conquests. An altar reminds him of the civilisations that, one after the other, occupied the site. Its base was covered with low reliefs whose styles testified to three distinct traditions: Greek, Bengali (influenced by the Muslim Mogul tradition) and Buddhist (influenced by devotional Tupa art). He himself testified to the presence of the European Judaeo-Christian civilisation. Successive powers had, in the long run, demeaned a preposterous assertion of universality. Taxila was the right place to develop, outside of Europe, a somehow bitter yet sober meditation on a frozen conception of culture, one which has prevailed since Alexander's times, including Hegel and the most part of so-called modernist thinking, as if modernity were pre-empted by Hegel's and Alexander's projects – the common substance to Spengler's sombre views and to the opposite project of Malraux. Soon after, Lévi-Strauss visited a humble Buddhist monastery, a *kyong*, where he was deeply taken by the peace and apparent renunciation of Buddha's disciples. Here, the experience might have induced something of a Schopenhaurian mood, urging him to choose between the destructive vanity of political violence pervading present and past high civilisations, and the impending nihilism of a renunciation. He resisted the seduction of the place and moment and concluded with the words 'I exist.' They were pronounced with the clear design of washing the formula of its first and dubious varnish of dereliction and facticity, which led to a philosophical dead end. Lévi-Strauss declared his existence as a protest, opening onto a new agenda, which was also evident to his friends who, like Merleau-Ponty, had stayed in Paris during the war. Far from being an existentialist declaration in the common mood, it was enough of a single word to insert, at the end of the book, a resolution opposed to any travel to the *end of the night*, a decision to assume and explore his own memory. He would reconsider what had been his own experience during his New York years, about which he had so far said nothing in *Tristes Tropiques* (1955a), and develop to its cognitive and philosophical consequences a modification of the mind as a way out of any transcendental selfishness.

It is most surprising that Lévi-Strauss, coming back from America through India, kept silent in the fifties about those years during which he met the most famous Anglo-Saxon anthropologists, engaged in tremendous research activity, writing and teaching, facing his own situation of exile in a city more akin to *Manhattan Transfer* than to a classical European city. The omission of those crucial years gives to the book something of Flaubert's *A Sentimental Education*, a gap in the succession of years akin to that in Flaubert's narrative: '*Il voyagea, il connut la mélancolie des paquebots. . .*'.

The last chapters of *Tristes Tropiques* no doubt said much more than and something different from the sudden monophrastic vertigo of a sentimental education. They opened a philosophical and anthropological programme, which had been badly missing in the French philosophical world since the Enlightenment. Although Lévi-Strauss kept a long silence on his New York years, they were later evoked as something of a feverish and exceptional experience – a place where, saved from the European threats, he dedicated himself to honour the opened credit of survival. It was also, no doubt, what sustained his determination to reassess not theoretical anthropology as such, but the pursuit of the double play of experience and theory as an ongoing, unfinished, confrontation of fieldwork and its assumption through the delineation of its shared intelligibility. Taking account of the Durkheim–Mauss legacy, he enlarged the scope of philosophy, opening an experimental turn in it. It required the uncovering of some untold but effective intellectual processes, including myths and there iconic implementations.

Anthropology of the present world

All I have learned, I have learned in the States.[5]

It is time to recall some facts about Lévi-Strauss's generation. He was an exact contemporary of Merleau-Ponty and Simone de Beauvoir, all born in 1908, which makes him two years younger than Sartre and four years younger than Jean Cavaillès – a very short gap. Too young to be directly involved in the First World War, they were conscious of the disaster. They became adults in the mid-thirties, were faced with the inevitability of the coming Second World War and were conscious that they had not been given the means to oppose the irrationalism and violence which paralysed any attempt at a European politics. Extremist slogans and violence invaded public space, while that new generation became aware of an intellectual gap, close to a philosophical incompetence and equivalent to a dismissal. Although they were very familiar with classical philosophy, or, indeed, because of that, they turned the inevitability of what they faced into a challenge, that required a deep personal commitment. This became evident in the philosophical impetus which received its most famous expression in the journal *Les Temps modernes* (1945) and was taken forward into the 1980s. Lévi-Strauss's generation was also deeply moved by Stravinsky's *The Rite of Spring*. They became convinced that a new approach to sensibility, aesthetics, etc. must eliminate a conception of *sensus communis* so long and carefully maintained throughout the so-called modern times. From affect to aesthetics and behaviour, and from science to philosophy, classical knowledge was challenged by the new and paradoxical evidence that as far as we know, we do not know how we know.

Lévi-Strauss had written a memoir under the supervision of Célestin Bouglé, a sociologist by training whose research largely outstripped the boundaries of his discipline. Bouglé wrote on the Indian caste system, was very close to Granet and Mauss and created a Centre de Documentation in which Cavaillès and Aron were successively librarian and secretary. The Centre had regular interdisciplinary meetings. Bouglé sent Cavaillès to Germany and Lévi-Strauss to Brazil. In the same years, Lévi-Strauss had also been, for a very short period, secretary to a socialist student movement in the journal of which he published a review of Louis-Ferdinand Céline's *Journey to the End of the Night*, paying tribute to the author's talent, to his diagnostic and realistic portrayal of war time, but contesting his autobiographical first-person writing and vituperation. As he put it: 'How true it is that the principal difficulty of autobiographical novels resides in how well the author and the hero fit together' (1933; 2004a; my translation). Let us not forget that Céline's challenging and prized book remained, as well as Conrad's African novels, a looming concern for Lévi-Strauss.

The assertion 'Yet I exist' (1955a; 1973c: 414), which, after Taxila and a meditation on Buddhism enabled Lévi-Strauss to avoid the dissolution of the self, has been a motto as much as an open problematic for the Lévi-Strauss generation. It does not deliver any programme, nothing more than a protest taking possession of the lowest level of philosophical consciousness. This assertion was now deprived of those Cartesian mediations which related, as a fact, existence to an effective *cogito*, and were connected to canonic propositions whose deduction had been the specific task of any Western philosophy during the last three centuries. It elicited, as its immediate conse-quential step, a process described on the same page by Lévi-Strauss as '*se deprendre de soi*', an expression for which there is no satisfying translation, although it clearly indicates something like a detachment from the self.[6] It underlines the fact that the yet unspoken New York experience, whose meaning Lévi-Strauss developed in the sixties, had two main consequences: the overcoming of a philosophically trivial, propositional consciousness, which had lost its Cartesian mathematical warranty, and a conception of knowledge which cannot deny how deeply it is related to affect and survival. That conviction resulted from Lévi-Strauss's converging experiences as a French citizen removed from his job as a teacher and cast away from his country, as an Amerindian anthropologist unsatisfied by his fieldwork, as a refugee in a new kind of city he had never imagined. Here is the knot of the New York years, so vividly evoked in the introduction to *The Way of the Masks* (1975; 1982a). Here are the connections between Lévi-Strauss's first theoretical results on Amerindian social relations and kinship structures, the evidence that the socio-political collapse of continental Europe came hand in hand with a short-sighted, ideological humanism, and his forthcoming Paris-ian writings from the sixties.

The New York years, through a dialogue with Americanist scholars and first-hand documents, gave access to the Amerindians' shaping of their own culture, and enabled the definitive elimination of a near to naïve expected relation to nature, which did not resist Lévi-Strauss's expedition to the Matto Grosso. It was a decisive first step, to be later confirmed through the four volumes of *Mythologiques*. It opened a new approach to the North Amerin-dian potlatch, now completed with its congenial symbolic articulation dis-played at large in North Californian mythology and masks. So Lévi-Strauss's Parisian writings, surprising as this may first seem, pay a due debt to those New York years. *The Way of the Masks* (1975; 1982a) evokes a visit to the Museum of Natural History, where Lévi-Strauss had a first contact with Boas's collections, displayed in their proper ethnographic context (see 1943b).[7]

This experience was first explained through a rather cryptic reference to Baudelaire's sonnet 'Correspondances'. That paradox opens directly onto its resolution. Lévi-Strauss takes advantage of Baudelaire's use of correspon-dences as a critical entry into his *Salons* and literary reviews. It was enough to dismiss the illusion of a universal aesthetic posture, a non-compromising alternative to a philosophical stance, a complementary resource to translate any kind of experience, a resource supposed to be encapsulated in the common attitude of a museum passer-by. With Baudelaire, such a phenomenological ambition was once and for all dismissed, giving way to a more realistic and sober one, to be elaborated later. It was a long way to conceive of a transmission of meaning through channels more diverse and penetrating than a language underpinned by its propositional, categorial determinations. But, starting with Baudelaire, it was also evident that the substitute for it was not mere emotion. The access to Amerindian high-culture documents required a sophisticated framing, to which Baudelaire, translating Poe and de Quincey, facing the troubling modernity of a metropolis, opened the way. The same insight was confirmed when Lévi-Strauss went to discover further Amerindian relics, with the 'lyrism and probity' cultivated by his surrealist friends. Of course, it was then necessary to go further, to elaborate by means of structural analyses, an anthropological understanding appropriate for a cognitive qualitative symbolism, as suggested earlier. The four volumes of the *Mythologiques* elaborated a syntax which does not have its end in itself and immediately called to reopen Mauss's incomplete approach to exchange. *The Way of the Masks* (1975; 1982a) reassembles, in their documented contextuality, the facts and iconic materials relating to potlatch. It discloses an intelligibility inherent to the symbolic garb of any moment of the ritual. The key is not consumption, as Bataille suggested, but again and again, vindicatory and provocative as it may be, the display through material and symbolic goods, of social exchange under hierarchical family relations.

A later, more narrative evocation of New York testified to those moments which were articulated, during the following years, into successive modes of intelligibility (see 1977a; 1983a and 1987b: chap. 20). Lévi-Strauss's New York experience opened onto another understanding of the Tropics. The very notion of *Tropics* took on a dual significance; it designated the other side of the equator and another, unexplored, side of the mind. That double meaning, inherited from the eponymous journal founded by Aimé Cesaire, was an introduction to a mental geography of sorts, although the comparison might be supported by a climatic similarity which opens the evocation of New York. Indeed, landing in New York in May 1941, one felt immersed in a tropical dampness and a more or less symmetric relation to São Paulo in the New World, which recalls the crossing of a limit. *Tropics* do not point to a place on the earth, but to an experience, to the *passage of a line*. The Amerindian lost culture, to which Lévi-Strauss gave back its potentiality, was an immediate appeal to rectify some one-sided modernist conceptions. The social is mental, such was the insight with which Lévi-Strauss complemented Mauss's legacy – but the mental has its necessary material supports, to which symbolisms owe their existence and objectivity, their communicative intelligibility and their syntactical capacity for development and variation. So there is a telling parallel between Lévi-Strauss's visit to the *kyong* and his visit, some years earlier, to the Museum of Natural History in Central Park, where the exiled Lévi-Strauss understood his own present life in the city as a decisive field-work of sorts, his option to engage in a new scientific environment under the patronage of Boas and Jakobson, but also facing the juxtaposition of cultures, peoples, shops, fashions and temporalities, along Downtown avenues, Brook-lyn, Greenwich village and upper Manhattan.[8] The situation implied a deep anthropological experience of another Diaspora. It also nourished Lévi-Strauss's reflection on modern cities, their historical and cultural layers and the new fragmentation of social units, for which kinship, as diverse and contrastive as it became, remained – according to the anthropologist's insight into our present times – the effective basis, a network to permanent social and affective relations.[9]

Anthropological knowledge

Lévi-Strauss's contribution to Americanist studies and scholarship has been long praised and discussed, from inside as well as from outside the French school.[10] Moreover, in recent years, the problem of the nature of anthropo-logical knowledge has become central to the discipline, enforcing a product-ive loop between ethnological data and fieldwork and their anthropological configuration, a new concern which is itself an anthropological fact. The consequence is not relativism, but a new insight into our own process of modernism which cannot be treated as a mere concern with education, or a disenchantment. It affects the unavoidable, decisive and ultimate dimension of selfhood. Modernism is an unfinished process or quest for an intelligibility which does not pre-exist, either in the mind or in the natural/institutional world, but rather breaks its path from the most adherent forms of life to the highest possible symbolic mediations. In short, what matters is no more the relation of subject to object, a fleeting philosophical problem inseparable from a propos-itional stance frozen in transcendentalism, but to acknowledge the never fin-ished mediation between the two poles, which occurs at what Lévi-Strauss describes, in a dual homage to Max Ernst and Merleau-Ponty, as a 'line of junction' ('*commissure*') between two lips which never close once and for all:

Both view painting as successful when it crosses the boundary between the outer and the inner worlds, providing access to an intermediary zone (the *mundus imaginalis* of ancient Iranian philosophy, as described by Henry Corbin),[11] where, writes Max Ernst, 'the artist evolves freely, boldly, and completely spontaneously'. The line of junction ['*commissure*'] thereby turns out to be more real than the physical and the mental parts, which philosophical tradition and ordinary common sense have dedicated it to unite.[12]

Here, Lévi-Strauss was near to denying the grandiose but sombre finale of *The Naked Man* (1981). What were at stake were the intermediary symbolic systems (channels and supports of knowledge, rituals, techniques, institutions, skills, languages) we introduce between the subject and the external world. Such behaviours, as sophisticated as they may be, in arts and sciences, immersed into rituals or ordinary life, local or general, are all at the same time a contribution to a cognitive scanning of a sort, to be understood without reductionism. On the contrary, the implementation of our strategies of consciousness out of emotion – on linguistic, iconic, technical, conceptual or yet unknown expressions – connected with the plasticity of the brain, is inscribed on our philosophical agenda. The production of images and the yet unqualified echoes of a modernity in search of its configuration, including what Lévi-Strauss himself did, are submitted to new requirements which no words or propositional strategy are able to complete. Here, for better or for worse, the function of diverse museums, incidentally so fashionable at the present time, embodies our social experiment in its urban configuration, the modern dismissal of a canonical subjectivity and the never achieved delimitation of selfhood. They also mediate an explicit relation to successive, compacted, layers of expression now explained and displayed as lost memories. A museum in a city suddenly converts a subjectively familiar or repulsive image into a non-arbitrary access to a virtual process of consciousness. As such it contributes to a philosophical experience of sorts, formerly confined to the quietness of a library – although the window of Descartes's office opened directly onto the streets of Amsterdam, and Amsterdam itself was, at the time, if not the museum of modern Europa, its workshop. We know for how long urban connections – a mental geography indeed, as Lévi-Strauss's *cross-country* explorations of New York were later memorised – have been the blind spot of philosophy. To which blindness Wittgenstein, in his *Philosophical Investigations*, opposed his own comprehension of human philosophical-linguistic production, which he compared to the development of a modern city (1958b: 18).[13]

Moreover, what gave *The Way of the Masks* (1975; 1982a) a fascinating perspective and perspicuity was its chapter 1, in which Lévi-Strauss revealed his own intellectual itinerary, following it through its successive moments and tracing it all the way back to his New York experience. The result is a montage, or better still a Cartesian product which filters what was essential in this experience, condensing it in his concluding masterpiece, so little or rarely discussed. Although minute attention would be required here, our present concern is to focus on the fact that we are at the meeting point of Lévi-Strauss's two approaches to ethnographic material – that adopted before the 1960s and that adopted after the 1960s – two approaches that have so often been loosely related through a vague notion of structure, notwithstanding Lévi-Strauss's protestations. Here, the preceding enigmas – the masks, the local inscription of parenthood and the limits of Mauss's approach – were resolved.

This became possible once the ethnographic evidence was unfolded in its proper terms, under a mode of intelligence pervading local symbolism. It was enough to erase the blurring artefacts of a phenomenological translation, along with its most perverse consequence, the postulation of a primitive mentality. All the material of the potlatch, a part of which Mauss had received from Boas, is reconsidered, and Lévi-Strauss acquitted himself of his debt to both of these predecessors. Exchange is related back to its symbolism, which gives a face to its rituals, moments and iconic features: on the masks and the copper plates which export and replicate in a kind of stenography the masks' meaningful symbolism onto something very near to money but not computable as mere commodities. Moreover, the notion of an object as such had been eclipsed by the quite immaterial meaning inscribed on it, as immaterial as a map or a syntax, whose value lies in its transformations and its ability to encapsulate different semantic contents. That dissolution of objecthood enabled Lévi-Strauss to reveal a much more important and precious use of the masks and related material – that of shaping in units of a quasi-language, at the limit of emotional and sexual affects, the geography of social existence as such, albeit with its lot of injustice and hierarchy, which evidently are never lacking. Such has been the key to reconsidering more generally a process of exchange, passing over its former submission to measure and equation, two distinct processes which neither Mauss nor Malinowski, despite their invaluable contributions to the problem, had been able to separate one from the other. The overwhelming evidence attached to some trivial arithmetic operations excluded from the start the mere possibility of an evaluation warranted by a mental qualitative economy. It is also clear that the whole development of the *Mythologiques*, starting with *The Savage Mind* (1962b) had been in charge of its experimental decoding.

So Lévi-Strauss's *The Way of the Masks* (1975; 1982a) concluded the *Mythologiques* with its positive counterpart. It challenged Georges Bataille's *The Accursed Share* and, no less, Malraux's *The Voices of Silence*. Malraux was very clever to forge oxymorons, which was the result of his long addiction to dialectics mitigated with his personal inclination to tragedy – one should concede that Malraux's personal and direct commitment to contemporary history might be an apology for it. The masks, as explained by Lévi-Strauss, are at the same time a geographical and an economic map for exchange, for activities of fishing and collecting, and for the identification of family relations through the connections that link the various owners, heirs or dowry donors of the masks or their equivalent copper plates. They retain on their face value a panoply of symbols offered to shared values and qualifications. Moreover, they opposed a frontier, soon overpassed, to mere monetary trade. Here, the earlier strands of Lévi-Strauss's former research on split representation, kinship structures, myths and facial decorations converge and reveal the unity of his project. The most important shift may be that Lévi-Strauss opened an access to the Amerindian cycles of exchange exemplified in potlatch ritual, without any numbered or legal evaluation. The attribution of value and its warranty were internal to the social/mental process of exchange, not an external evaluation encoded through arithmetical accounting and legal regulations according to our social conventions, although there is little doubt that our monetary transactions are, now as ever, loaded with analogous hopes, desires, threats and fears.

From an epistemological point of view, Lévi-Strauss opposed a logic of exchange, alliances and affinities construed in terms of a qualitative/analogical scale, to a logic based on discrete mappings and equations, whose units are delineated by, and undivided from, the operations they are used to carry out. This latter logic, often understood as underlying the most encompassing notion of exchange, although it is a modern and specific aspect of a more general social process, received its specification under a post-Galilean logic of arithmetical operations, applied to materials and items which are not from the start comparable. Here special attention must be given to those *economic sentiments* which accompanied the awareness of a decisive modification in the first moments of the English liberal school of economy. Those feelings were neither denied nor explicitly mentioned in the universal notion of exchange which Mauss had in mind, although he evokes social rituals of exchange in drinking parties. Here we encounter two different systems whose relative convenience and value is far outside of our concerns today, although the distinction between the two is of primordial value to anthropologists.[14]

Lévi-Strauss was the first to reassess the project of the Enlightenment, as the condition for introducing a new entry in the d'Alembert and Diderot *Encyclopédie*, that for an anthropology based on ethnography as Rousseau conceived of it. The project appeared in *The Discourse on the Origin of Inequality* (1754–5) as if Rousseau had been conscious that a social contract required much more than a politico-juridical stance. After a century, and more, of national or civil wars devastating Europe, the turn to anthropology, so characteristic of contemporary French philosophical thought, might appear as the seizing of an ultimate opportunity including the chance to overcome errors. This opportunity, available at the time of the Renaissance when Europe met but did not recognise the effectiveness of Amerindian cultures, would have provided evidence as important as the observations led in the Galapagos Islands. It would have prepared a valuable complement to Darwin's masterpiece, escaping the Darwinist cultural derivations and their lethal boomerang effect on European countries.

Among the many things Lévi-Strauss learnt from New York, the least is surely not a new understanding of what anyone at the time was inclined to consider as *art*. The memory of the visit paid to the Natural History Museum corroborates the evident grafting of our iconic symbols and languages on a double web of cognitive emotional capacities and social emulations. Moreover, the material support on which a symbolism develops its specific structure was opened to transformations, circulation and exchange. That embedding of art and representation in the symbolic and material production of knowledge was also an exemplary denial of the position of the viewer and his/her phenomenological posture. Aesthetics, mostly supported by neoclassicist convictions and illustrations, came to the fore at the turn of the eighteenth and nineteenth century, in the area of late German scholasticism, as did phenomenology and ontology, and consolidated the latter discourses, which were under threat from modern science and civil life. Because of its strategic position and the difficulty to find an alternative, neoclassicism acquired mentally and concretely on many buildings the apotropaic function of a facade. An anthropological insight came to replace the aesthetic approach when Lévi-Strauss discovered, in the context of the contrasted effervescent world of 1940s New York, the totemic poles of Northwest Coast Amerindian culture near the modernist buildings of Fifth Avenue and the crooked corridors of modest nineteenth-century houses in Greenwich. The mental geography of the city leaked through its facades, and no less in its antique shops, auction houses and store rooms, as well as in its unexpected museums, all of this experienced at the time of the most tragic episode of the Diaspora. Putting an end to the cautious adjustment of sensibility and understanding – to quote Kant – aesthetics left place to a transient and multiple symbolic process. It was called for as much by the fieldwork as by the alternative faces of a contemporary world multiplying its changing facades as an incitation to grasp their potential intelligibility. That fortuitous but magnified and multiplied ethnographic experience in 1941 New York, imposed as it was by the circumstances, had the decisive advantage of orientating Lévi-Strauss's scientific interest away from an obsolete and inadequate demand for concreteness and immediacy, typical of a mental phenomenological attitude, towards the production of intelligibility as an essential part of exchange and social life. The ethnographer turned anthropologist was summoned to detect an ongoing process of rationality, and its concomitant differentiation in contemporary times. He had to renounce the analytical, if not deconstructive, stance which was a last shelter to post-Galilean philosophy. No doubt if Lévi-Strauss learnt from Boas and his colleagues, from Jakobson whom he so often evokes, he also later resorted to electronic databases and exploratory algorithms independently developed by Shannon in the 1940s.[15] For the first time a philosophical mind opened onto its own necessary and fruitful mobility.

No doubt the tables will turn again and again. Which is why it is all the more instructive to pay homage to Lévi-Strauss's writings as they definitively went beyond historicism and relativism.

NOTES

1. In a late conversation with Didier Eribon, Lévi-Strauss (1991b: 99) reveals that this was the point of departure of his own thinking on kinship systems.
2. See Wittgenstein, *Conversations on Logic*, his project of a philosophical grammar (now more usually referred to as *The Big Typescript*, 2005), the *Blue Book* (1958a) and the collection of *Remarks on Colour* (1978).
3. See Lévi-Strauss 1942a. This was the first volume of *VVV*, a journal published by a group of exiled French intellectuals in New York, between 1942 and 1944. Later, a more extended version of this essay was incorporated into *Tristes Tropiques* (1955a). See, in particular, the chapters on Caduveo body painting.
4. See Strathern 1999, in particular chapter 1, 'The Ethnographic Effect', chapter 2 and the Conclusion.
5. Interview with the *New York Times*, 21 December 1987.
6. The French expression comes from the vocabulary of seventeenth-century spirituality and no doubt tacitly alludes to Jansenism and to Pascal, so opposed to the substantialist position of the Cartesian *cogito*.
7. Partly reproduced in *The Way of the Masks* (1982 [1975]), 'Introduction'.
8. In another contribution to the journal *VVV*, Lévi-Strauss wrote a short obituary of Malinowski in which he mentioned his field experience during the First World War, when he was isolated in the Trobriand Islands until 1918. We also know that, during an official dinner, Boas suffered a heart attack and died in the arms of Lévi-Strauss.
9. See his Marc Bloch Conference, which may be the most comprehensive among Lévi-Strauss's essays on the family as a social unit (1983c).
10. See *L'Homme* 1993, no. 126–8, and 2000, no. 154–5.
11. See Corbin 1972.
12. 1983a; 1987b: 245.
13. 'Our language can be seen as an ancient city: a maze of little streets and squares, of old and new houses, and of houses with additions from various periods; and this surrounded by a multitude of new boroughs with straight regular streets and uniform houses.'
14. The choice between these two systems is underlined in de Quincy's *Confessions of an English Opium-Eater*. See in particular the episode set in a London marketplace on a Saturday evening, where he shares the joys and anxieties of workers spending with much tergiversations and appreciations the salary that they have just been paid, and his later interest for Ricardo, to whom he dedicated a never published essay. See also, more recently, Rothschild 2001. Mauss's hesitation on the topic of money is confirmed by the long notes inserted in his essay *The Gift*, and his specific research on the subject which is contemporary with this essay.
15. See 'New York in 1941' (1985a), where Lévi-Strauss recalls that Shannon was once a neighbour of his, although Lévi-Strauss was not aware of the fact at the time.

REFERENCES

Baudelaire, Charles 2003. 'The Painter of Modern Life', in *The Painter of Modern Life and Other Essays: Charles Baudelaire*. Translated and edited by J. Mayne. London: Phaidon, pp. 1–43.

Cassirer, Ernst 1953. *The Philosophy of Symbolic Forms*. New Haven, CT: Yale University Press.

Corbin, Henry 1972. *En Islam iranien*. Paris: Gallimard.

Dedekind, Richard 1963. *Essays on the Theory of Numbers*. Translated by Wooster Woodruff Beman. New York: Dover.

Granet, Marcel 1939. *Catégories matrimoniales et relations de proximité dans la Chine ancienne*. Paris: Presses Universitaires de France.

Imbert, Claude 2005. 'Le Cadastre des savoirs, figures de connaissance et prises de réel formes', in *Penser par cas*. Paris: Éditions de l'EHESS.

2006. 'Qualia', in *Claude Lévi-Strauss*. Paris: L'Herne; translated in *Qui parle?* Minnesota University Press. 2008.

2008. *Lévi-Strauss: le passage du Nord-Ouest*. Paris: L'Herne.

Rothschild, Emma 2001. *Economic Sentiments: Adam Smith, Condorcet, and the Enlightenment*. Cambridge, MA: Harvard University Press.

Strathern, Marilyn 1999. *Property, Substance and Effect: Anthropological Essays on Persons and Things*. London: Athlone Press.

Wittgenstein, Ludwig 1958a. 'The Blue Book', in *Preliminary Studies for the 'Philosophical investigations' Generally Known as the Blue and Brown Books*. Oxford: Blackwell.

1958b. *Philosophical Investigations*. Translated by G. E. M. Anscombe. Oxford: Blackwell.

1978. *Remarks on Colour*. Edited by G. E. M. Anscombe. Oxford: Blackwell.

2005. *The Big Typescript TS 213*. Edited and translated by C. Grant Luckhardt and Maximilian A. E. Aue. Oxford: Blackwell.

7   The limits of classification: Claude Lévi-Strauss and Mary Douglas

Frédéric Keck

Humans have to classify because they face situations of uncertainty. The problem of classifications is important for anthropology, because exotic societies classify objects in other ways than we do. When confronted with another society, the ethnographer feels that his/her systems of classifications are arbitrary, and that the criteria by which he/she links together objects in the world can be contested: a whale can be considered as a fish or as a mammal, depending on whether you focus on its mode of reproduction or its mode of locomotion. Classifications must then be seen not only as a way of describing the world as it is, but as a way of thinking about an environment on which it is necessary to act. This is why classifications are interesting not only for the anthropologist who wants to understand how other societies see the world, but also for the philosopher, who wants to know how human beings think.

Claude Lévi-Strauss's *The Savage Mind*, first published in 1962, is a book about classifications. After his works on kinship and before his works on myths, Lévi-Strauss takes 'a kind of pause . . . a break between two bursts of effort . . . to scan the scene before [him]' (1970: 9). When they trace genealogies of marriage and descent or when they tell stories of origins and conflicts, human beings always classify, they connect different beings of the world in a coherent framework. While the anthropologist is immersed in kinship systems or mythological transformations, the philosopher can take a step back and think reflexively on this human need to classify. How do humans classify, and why are their systems of classifications so diverse? What does classification reveal about the relation between thinking and the world?

These questions have been answered in the anthropological literature by the concept of totemism: whatever form societies give to their classifications, they all have a common structure, which reflects the structure of society. In *Totemism* (1964b), Lévi-Strauss has radically criticised this notion, showing that the totemic institution imagined by anthropologists was an arbitrary construction, assembled out of several cultural traits linking human groups and natural species. On the ruins of totemism, Lévi-Strauss brings to light a form of thinking that relates all elements of the world in an expanding system of classifications: it is a tendency to 'classify out the universe', to use a phrase he borrows from Tylor. The question he therefore raises is, how do societies build limited classifications with this classificatory dynamic? If classifications can integrate all beings in the world, why do they in fact stop at certain beings that they leave outside of the classificatory net? And why have anthropologists themselves limited these classifications to the totemic identification between men and animals?

If we read *The Savage Mind* in the light of this question, it appears surprisingly close to another book which is its contemporary: Mary Douglas's *Purity and Danger*, published in 1966. In the same way as Lévi-Strauss, Douglas tries to rehabilitate the societies that were once called 'primitive' or 'savage', by showing that their thinking is as coherent and logical as that of Western societies. And much like *The Savage Mind* (1966c), *Purity and Danger* is a book of general anthropology, written as a transition between the two major works of Mary Douglas: her ethnographic study of ritual among the Lele of the Kasai, and her sociological reflection on risk led with Aaron Wildavsky (Douglas 1957; Douglas and Wildavsky 1982). But more profoundly, Douglas focuses the anthropological attention on those beings that are situated at the limits of systems of classification, both in 'primitive' and in 'Western' societies. She raises the question, how does human thought react to beings that appear at the limits of its systems of classification and seem to contradict these systems? I will argue that Lévi-Strauss and Douglas give two different answers to this problem, through myth and through ritual, and that this difference reflects the opposition between two paradigms – structuralism and functionalism.

The logic and semiotics of classifications in *The Savage Mind*

The Savage Mind is a book about the logic of totemic classifications. Anthropologists have explained totemism as an originary institution through which humans identify themselves with animals or plants, either through a collective ceremony like sacrifice, or through individual representations of the similarities between them. Lévi-Strauss shows that these different solutions do not account for the various forms of relations between humans and non-humans in so-called 'primitive' societies. He therefore proposes that totemism should not be explored on the level of sociology or psychology, but rather on the level of logic, that is, as a formal study of relations. The term of logic is surprising. At the beginning of the twentieth century, philosophers had tried to cast the classical logic of Aristotle in new terms, by founding it not on the ordinary grammar of language, but on the principles of mathematics. Lévi-Strauss argues that it is possible to find yet another foundation for logic if we start not with ordinary language but rather with forms of life very remote from ours, connecting human beings, animals and plants. It is not an *a priori* logic, formulated through the individual's reflexive observation of his/her own mind, but a logic *a posteriori*, obtained through the ethnographic study of other societies. There is as much logical inventiveness in contemporary mathematics as there is in 'savage' societies, because human beings have always thought using all the logical means that they have at hand. And therefore travelling to the limits of the world is still a way to explore the domain of logic.

A major shift is needed to adopt such a perspective. The image of 'savages' as animal brutes bound by their daily needs must be abandoned. Members of 'primitive' societies are not limited to the necessity of eating or to questions of life and death or to the emotions of big ceremonies: they think because they are very attentive to the many details of their environment. Their thinking is structured because their perception of the environment is structured: they use the discontinuities of their environment to establish comparisons and draw relations. Take the Pawnee classification as it is described by Lévi-Strauss (1966b: 139–40): the Pawnee, of the High Missouri, make distinctions between four types of trees, which are related to four types of colours, which, in turn, enables them to think the four directions (North–East–South–West) and the four seasons, producing a kind of continuity out of discontinuities. A system of classification allows an orientation in space and time by drawing a map of all the different elements that constitute their environment.

This is why Lévi-Strauss can say that the members of 'primitive' societies think in a similar way to modern zoologists: they build a whole science out of the differences between animals and plants, what Lévi-Strauss calls 'a science of the concrete'. Saying that these differences constitute 'thinking' is a pun: the '*pensée sauvage*' on the cover of the book is a flower, the *Viola tricolor,* which is a way of saying that thinking is profoundly immersed in nature, which can be conceived as a proliferation of differences. Rather than as 'savage mind', it is better to translate the above expression as 'wild thinking', because the form of thinking that Lévi-Strauss describes is not limited to the mind of particular individuals called 'savages', but develops dynamically 'in the wild'. In a recent edition of *The Savage Mind*, Lévi-Strauss refers to Shakespeare's phrase: 'For there are pansies, wild for thought'.[1] Wildness here does not mean incoherence or chaos but an occasion for a dynamic process of thought that is entirely coherent.

Now we can understand the notion of classification: there is a logic in nature because the discontinuities between natural beings can be ordered through classification. But it does not mean that nature is ordered in itself, and that human classifications reflect this order: human classifications are fundamentally diverse, because they depend on the interest that societies have for the elements of their environment. For example, the difference between a wolverine and other kinds of bears is not particularly striking for us; but it is important for the Hidatsa hunters, because the wolverine never gets caught in their traps, while other bears do; therefore, the hunter who has to hide in a trap in order to catch eagles invokes the wolverine to think about his problematic situation (1966b: 50). If you take the system of classification of a given society, you will know what is problematic for this society, what elements of its environment force it to think. When Lévi-Strauss talks about a logic of classifications, therefore, he does not mean an inner logic which would reveal the order of nature through human classifications. If classifications depend on the way humans select discontinuities in the environment according to the problems they face when they act on this environment, the logic of classifications can be retraced only through an empirical enquiry into the kinds of natural entities that are pertinent for a given system of classification. Another example is that of the difference between two types of sage, *Chrysothamnus* and *Artemisia*, that becomes intelligible when we realise that it is linked to the difference between male and female in birth ceremonies: *Artemisia* is linked to the feminine, the lunar, the night, whereas *Chrysothamnus* is linked to the male, the sun, the day; but the opposition between male and female can be displaced onto the female pole itself, between different forms of sage, used in different birth situations (1966b: 46–8). A system of classification relates a set of differences that are pertinent in a particular society.

But can we still speak of a 'logic' if systems of classification depend on the selection of elements in the environment by human interests that appear as arbitrary? Is it really possible to study a logic *a posteriori* (1966b: 35)? Here lies the signification of the famous notion of *bricolage* (literally, an intellectual form of DIY). The *bricoleur* is, like the zoologist, confronted with forms that already have a signification in themselves, but he gives them another signification by relating them to other forms. Therefore, his selection of elements is not arbitrary: it depends on possibilities that are already there in the elements he manipulates. Lévi-Strauss opposes the *bricoleur* to the 'engineer' who imposes a preconceived project on nature. The *bricoleur* does not face the world, as the 'engineer' does, but is part of it, and must establish connections from within the world to produce new significations. The form imposed by the engineer is arbitrary, but the form invented by the *bricoleur* is not, because it depends on the inner possibilities of the materials at hand. As an illustration, Lévi-Strauss imagines a society divided into three clans: bear (linked to the ground), eagle (linked to the sky) and turtle (linked to water) (1966b: 67). If, for demographic reasons, the group of the bear disappears and the group of the turtle increases, the difference between ground and water will be transformed into the difference between yellow turtle and grey turtle. It is impossible to explain this transformation with reference to the intention of an individual or a group: it is a *bricolage* that makes use of already existing differences to produce other differences – as in a kaleidoscope, the same elements composed differently create new figures.

Lévi-Strauss speaks of a 'logic of sensible qualities'. Such an expression is paradoxical only if we conceive logic as purely abstract, outside of sensible things; but there is a logic in the way forms and matter are composed in our perception. Logic is not only the way form imposes itself on matter; there is an intermediary level between form and matter, which is the level of signs. Signs are more abstract than matter; they express something else, but yet they remain attached to a context, like a form that would produce its own matter. The logic of the sensible is therefore a logic of signs. Nature launches signs to humans, which are then transformed into logical systems. To understand this point, it is necessary to refer to the linguistic model that Lévi-Strauss borrows from Saussure. Saussure remarked that the relation between the word and the thing is arbitrary, and that it is wrong to search for the origin of language in a correspondence between words and things. The comparison between languages shows that the same thing can be said by means of different words, or even that language imposes its own discontinuities on the flux of perception. For example, the English 'mutton' and 'sheep' refer to what the French call '*mouton*', but the English choose to differentiate between meat and the animal whereas the French do not. The signification of a word is therefore a product of the relations between signs, a sign being defined as the union of a concept and a mental image, or in the terms coined by Saussure, between a signifier and a signified. If the relations between signifier and signified are arbitrary, the relations between signs are motivated, because they depend on the structure of the whole language: e.g. '*bœuf–œuf*' in French is a significant association because it reproduces the relation '*bovis–ovis*' in Latin. Seen in a synchronic cut, language is a structure in which relations are motivated; seen in a diachronic cut, these relations tend to reproduce themselves, but they are more and more arbitrary because they depend on the hazards of history. When we speak our language, we act as *bricoleurs* who follow the inner constraints of the structure of signs, even if this structure does not correspond to anything in the world. These constraints come from outside of the world of things, from the history of the society where the language is spoken. In the imaginary example developed by Lévi-Strauss, the relation between yellow turtle and grey turtle is homologous to the relation between bear and turtle in the first state of the system, and therefore follows the inner constraints of the system of classification; but as it is transformed by a demographic evolution, these constraints, more and more, threaten to disappear.

Saussure speaks of semiotics as the study of the life of signs in society. Semiotics is a kind of logic in which the relations between the terms are profoundly constrained, but these constraints appear only in the variations of social life. Lévi-Strauss refers to a comparison Saussure draws between the life of language and the life of a tree: 'A tree is, as it were, strongly motivated so far as its lower parts are concerned: it must have a trunk and the trunk must be nearly vertical . . . The part played by motivation, however, diminishes, and that of arbitrariness increases progressively as we turn our attention higher' (1966b: 159). This comparison forces one to conceive of language as animated by an inner tendency towards motivation, which constitutes a kind of countertendency to inertia, as if language were submitted to the laws of thermodynamics. There seems to be in every language a kernel in which signs are particularly motivated, i.e. relations between them are dense and regular, and a periphery on which language tends to dissolve itself into chaos and dispersion. We have therefore to think the limits of a classificatory impulse – Lévi-Strauss sometimes speaks about a classificatory intention – within language, rather than simply oppose structure and history.

The application of the Saussurean model to the totemic problem is enlightening. Anthropologists have tried to understand why social groups conceived of themselves as similar to the animals or plants they took as their totems. But the problem is thus as wrongly put as the problem of the origin of language. The relation is not between the social group and the totem, but between, on the one hand, the relations that are constitutive of the group as such and, on the other, the relations between the various totems. 'It is not the resemblances, but the differences, which resemble each other' (1964b: 77). Totemism is a classificatory system in which the relations between social groups are characterised as relations between animals. Although the relation between a group and its totem is arbitrary, the relation between animals is profoundly motivated, because social groups give great attention to the way other groups conceive themselves through animals. When a clan takes a turtle as a totem, it wants to distinguish itself from the clan whose totem is the bear, a distinction that is also that between water and earth; and this distinction is more important than the clans themselves, since it is perpetuated even when the clan of the bear disappears.

Anthropologists have focused their attention on the relation between groups and natural species because it is profoundly motivated; but while doing so, they have left aside the problems that are raised at the limits of classification, where structure is threatened by history. When he dissolves the 'totemic illusion', Lévi-Strauss faces this problem of history, while revealing the inner logic of the system. The question he therefore raises is, why is the polarity of nature and culture so frequently used as a tool to think logical relations? This point is a major key to the shift that occurs in the demonstration made by *The Savage Mind* (1966b), between chapter 3, 'Systems of Transformations' and chapter 4, 'Totem and Caste'. In chapter 3, Lévi-Strauss shows that different systems of totemic classifications in Australia can be analysed as variations on a few logical relations that are transformed from one society to the other; but nature still seems to be the domain from which logical elements are borrowed. In chapter 4, Lévi-Strauss applies the notion of transformation to a radically different system of classification – the system of castes in India – to show that classifying human groups by means of social and technological professions is only a variation of classifying them by means of animal or vegetal traits. For example, in Bengal, castes identify themselves through animal totems as well as through professional activities, and Lévi-Strauss talks about a contamination of natural classifications by cultural classifications; conversely, in North America, the Chickasaw are supposed to act as the animals they have taken as totems, those whose totem is the wild cat having the reputation of sleeping during the day and hunting at night (1966b: 117–20).

This leads Lévi-Strauss to a profound question: why have anthropologists given momentous significance to the difference between totem and caste, since they are mixed together in actual systems of classification? To this question it is possible to answer, as Bouglé did,[2] that there is an evolution leading from totem to caste, culture replacing nature as sources of classifications for society. But Lévi-Strauss gives another answer that relies not on history but on logic: nature and culture present two systems of differences that are real, and therefore they serve as models for all the other types of differences that the human mind uses to think about the world. Consequently, nature and culture are never perceived as such but only through the contradictions that human activity projects on them. The real, here, is not what classifications represent, but rather the limits to which systems of classification point. 'Castes naturalize a true culture falsely, totemic groups culturalize a false nature truly' (1966b: 127). Between 'true nature' and 'true culture' there lie all the symbolic exchanges through which humans inverse the values of true and false in order to act on a reality that they cannot know as such.

Lévi-Strauss owes a great deal, in this perspective, to the works of Marx on ideology. He declares that 'ideology and superstructures' are 'the subject' of *The Savage Mind* (1966b: 117); 'it is to this theory of superstructures, scarcely touched on by Marx, that I hope to make a contribution' (1966b: 130). This reference to Marx cannot be attributed only to the conjuncture of the debate with Marxist intellectuals, since it was when he was very young that Lévi-Strauss discovered 'the fundamental idea that one cannot understand what is going on inside people's heads without connecting it to the conditions of their practical existence' (1991b: 108). The analysis of the ritual of eagle-hunting among the Hidatsa in chapter 2 (1966b: 48–51), in particular the reference to the wolverine, is a good example of the impact of Marx on his thinking. The hunter is in a contradictory position as he must catch an eagle in the sky while digging a trap in the ground; invoking the wolverine helps to solve this contradiction, as the wolverine never gets caught in traps; but it solves it only at the level of the imaginary, not that of the real situation of the hunter, which remains very uncertain. What Lévi-Strauss borrows from Marx is the idea that systems of classification are ideological constructions that try to resolve a contradiction in human practices by displacing it to the domain of the abstract, where its practical expression is inversed and transformed. What is new in Lévi-Strauss's thinking is the idea that these displacements use entities that are intermediaries between nature and culture.

From the relations between nature and culture in totemic societies, Lévi-Strauss has thus moved to the relation between the abstract and the concrete in all human societies. These domains form the two axes on which the classificatory impulse of 'wild thinking' develops. On these two axes Lévi-Strauss develops what he calls the 'totemic operator' (1966b: 151), which is a means of shifting from one level of abstraction to another, through movements of detotalisation and retotalisation. It would be wrong to think only with three levels of classification: categories, species and individuals. In fact, every individual can be conceived as a species if compared to a more individualised individual: my organism is the species that collects all the individual parts out of which I am composed. And a species can be conceived as an individual if compared to a more abstract species: man is an individual that belongs to the species of mammals, although I belong to the species of men. Take the schema of the totemic operator (1966b: 152). It is clear that individuals do not fall into a species, as in modern classifications. Rather, the species is divided into elements, and the individual is divided into parts, and the totemic operator institutes asymmetrical connections between these divisions. There is a relation not between the individual and the totemic species, but between the head of the bear and the head of the individual, which stands, in each case, in a similar relation to the neck and legs. This schema should not be applied merely to the study of a classificatory system; but it gives an image of the dynamic of classificatory thought, which allows one to understand how the perception of natural species is collectively organised.

This layered model is reminiscent of Bergson's conception of the insertion of different levels of intellectual activity in a single perception. Lévi-Strauss pays homage to Bergson for recognising that the natural species is a logical tool immediately produced at the level of perception (1964b: 97). While Durkheim thought that the totem was a collective representation embodied in an animal, and while Lévy-Bruhl tried to describe participation between men and their totem at the level of affectivity, Bergson saw that perception was structured by language – which does not mean that it has the same structure as language, this discovery belonging to structural linguistics. According to Lévi-Strauss, Bergson understood totemism 'from within'

(1964b: 92) because he saw that there is a logic of relations in primitive classificatory systems, and that science derives from this logic. But Bergson still understands life as a practical necessity, as is shown by the opposition between mystical acts and primitive logic. Lévi-Strauss pushes forward Bergson's model of perception layered in a plurality of levels of abstraction, but he gives it an objective foundation: the genetic structure of life as a plurality of codes expressing each other at different levels of functions. If natural species constitute an intermediary level of abstraction, the way they are used as logical operators must not be attributed to an action coming from outside – like the *élan vital* in Bergson's philosophy – but to the fact that they allow the classifier to connect a plurality of levels of reality. Life tends to reproduce itself by conserving its inner information; the tendency towards order in an increasing production of complexity fighting against a tendency to disorder.

An example allows one to understand this point: the rite of shoe-making in Osage societies. Lévi-Strauss shows that this shoe is particularly valorised by the Osage because it symbolises the strength of the warrior, and is associated with the sky, while at the same time attaching him to the ground: it is therefore a contradictory being, and the ritual must stabilise this logical ambivalence. Sky/ground is the semantic opposition out of which the Osage think all the logical levels of the world in which they act: in the direction of the concrete, earth and water, North and South, East and West, in the direction of the abstract, six and seven, peace and war, right and left. The rising sun is particularly valorised because it is represented with thirteen beams, allowing the stabilisation of all the levels at which the logical instability of the Osage shoe is displaced. Here we see that the logic of classifications does not apply the same form to different matters, but displaces a semantic opposition at different levels of abstraction; these different levels are connected in a single situation, even if the structure of classification is always larger than the local use that is made of it. 'A logical structure – initially a simple opposition – thus fans out in two directions: one abstract, in form of a numerology, and the other concrete, first of elements and then of species. On each level semantic short-circuits permit direct connections with the level furthest away' (1966b: 146).

It is possible, now, to understand what Lévi-Strauss means by universal structures of classification. It would be wrong to think that the same structures are applied indifferently in various contexts: the universality here is not static, as that of an eternal form, but dynamic: it is a movement of 'universalisation'. Whatever the situation humans encounter, its logical instability is the occasion of a proliferation of differences that can extend to all the elements of the world. Every ethnographic situation has its 'local logic' that can or cannot be connected to the more general logic of classification.

The logic of the system need not, therefore, coincide at every point with the set of local logics inserted in it. This general logic can be of a different order. It is then definable by the number and nature of the axes employed, by the rules of transformation making it possible to pass from one to the another, and finally by the relative inertia of the system, that is, its greater or less receptiveness to unmotivated factors. (1966b: 161–2)

If the general logic of classifications is not present in every situation, it is because there are unmotivated elements that tend to limit its movement of extension. Here we find an interesting relation between the transparency of classificatory systems and the obscurity of situations: situations are not obscure in themselves in the face of transparent structures, but become obscure because their elements are so numerous that the logical tools available to the classificatory mind cannot integrate all of them in a system of relations, and must therefore stop their activity.

In chapter 6 of *The Savage Mind* (1966b), Lévi-Strauss describes this movement of extension and the limits it encounters in two directions: universalisation and particularisation. Universalisation is the way a society includes in its systems of classification beings that appear at a level of generality so high that they become threatening: sicknesses and strangers. Every being can find a place in the system of classification if it is conceptualised in terms of pre-existing classificatory systems. Lévi-Strauss speaks of a 'humanity without frontiers' (1966b: 166) to describe this movement by which classificatory systems, while remaining stable and coherent, can open themselves to unknown forms of being in order to attribute them normality and citizenship. In the other direction, Lévi-Strauss describes as 'particularisation' the movement by which classificatory systems allow one to give a place to new individuals who first appear as concrete bodies without a proper name, i.e. without a place in the system. Through an analysis of the production of proper names by a process of selection from a communally shared stock of common nouns followed by a ceremony that makes the names sacred, he shows that the individual becomes a person once a proper name has been given to him or her. Proper names are not therefore radically different from common nouns: they are forged at the limit of the system of classification, at the point where 'a society declares its work of classifying to be complete' (1966b: 215). There is a threshold where society renounces classification of individuals and can only point to them; but this threshold is not universal: it depends on the ethnographic conditions of the classificatory activity, which allow a society to extend its classifications or not.

It is now time to summarise the progression of Lévi-Strauss's demonstration in *The Savage Mind*. On the ruins of totemism, construed as an institution identifying men and animals, Lévi-Strauss has discovered a classificatory logic that starts from the intermediary level of the specific operator to extend itself to all elements of the world, in two directions: a horizontal axis linking nature and culture; a vertical axis linking the abstract and the concrete (logically), humanity and persons (sociologically). 'In the same way that, on the logical plane, the specific operator effects the transition to the concrete and individual on the one and the abstract and systems of categories on the other, so, on the sociological plane, totemic classifications make it possible both to define the status of persons within a group and to expand the group beyond its traditional confines' (1966b: 166). The shift from the logical to the sociological analysis is important, for it allows us to raise the problem of the limits of classification at the historical level: that of the event. Classificatory thought must be conceived as an impulse that takes the occasion of any event to affirm its proliferating movement; every event raises a problem, but it is also a chance to widen the scope of classifications. Events can occur on the four poles of wild thinking: newborn babies produce new forms of individuality, new sicknesses produce new categories, new forms of nature or culture produce new specific operators.[3] Wild thinking does not ignore the event, but its inner tendency is to integrate the event into previous classifications, by dividing it into parts that can be related to already known forms of being. The structuralist method is a cartography of the possibilities of the human mind that opens onto a critical enquiry on the kind of problems that different societies raise when they encounter the four limits of their classifications: the particular, the universal, nature or culture.

The event is finally the name of what happens at the limit of classification. It is difficult to conceptualise the event not because it is radically new, but because it has not yet found its place in a classificatory system. Therefore, it appears as irrational, and the only reaction that seems fit is emotion. But if classificatory systems are analysed from the kernel where they are the most motivated, they can be extended to this limit where they still produce order and signification. 'Classificatory systems thus allow the incorporation of history, even and particularly that which might be thought to defy the system' (1966b: 243). Classificatory systems transform what appears emotionally into dynamic structures through inversions of their constitutive parts. Can this be related to the idea that modern thinking transforms dangers into risks by including them in a grid of rationality, such as that of risk? In what sense may one conceive of the new events that appear at the limits of classification as sources of danger?

Ambiguity and contradiction in *Purity and Danger*

Let us now compare *The Savage Mind* to *Purity and Danger*. Mary Douglas operates, like Lévi-Strauss, a dissolution of a presumed institution to open a new field of enquiry in the possibilities of human thought. The problem of impurity – why do humans perceive things as unclean? – has been misunderstood because anthropologists have confused it with the concept of the sacred, that is, with the effect of a prohibition which separates, among all things, those that are pure and those that are impure. This solution to the problem relies on the concept of a religious institution that categorises reality by means of clear collective representations; but it leaves aside all those individual perceptions producing the mere feeling that something in the world does not fit in its place. Mary Douglas links this criticism of the theory of the sacred to a methodological reflection on ethnographic enquiry. Anthropologists have been led to look for the sacred principle that organises society because they look for explicit meanings as dictated by their scholarly training and theoretical views; but ethnography teaches them to become attentive to all those implicit meanings by which individuals perceive the world collectively and practically. Purity is a question that relates to the socially determined modes of perception of beings that the concept of the sacred tended to obscure – in the same way as for Lévi-Strauss the study of wild classifications allows description of the variety of perceptions of natural beings that the concept of totemism tended to reduce.[4]

In this perspective, Mary Douglas rehabilitates the domain of magic and witchcraft that anthropological theories of religion had discarded as irrational and individualised. Magic is a structured perception of the environment that does not rely on the representation of a rule, but rather on the shared feeling of a danger. Dangerous beings are those who do not find a place in classificatory systems at hand, and who oblige human thought to reframe classifications. Magical reasoning is therefore much more ambitious than religious reasoning: it does not apply a transcendental rule to empirical cases; it transforms existing classifications to include beings that do not yet have a place. As Evans-Pritchard has shown,[5] magical reasoning searches for a cause for all events in the world, and is not satisfied until every being has its place in an order of supernatural causes. Science derives therefore as much from magic, with its unreasonable attempt to generalise determinism, as from religion, with its fixed frames of rationality.

On this point, Lévi-Strauss and Douglas agree, and both try to analyse the human mind at the level of the structured perception of unknown beings, rather than of the representation of a rule. But they differ on the psychological model they use. We have seen that Lévi-Strauss refers to structural linguistics to show that unknown beings can be decomposed into signs and connected to a system of signs by a classificatory dynamic. Douglas refers rather to the psychology of *Gestalt* according to which perception selects in the environment what interests the subject for his or her action on the surrounding world. The question of the arbitrariness of classifications, therefore, is raised very differently. For Lévi-Strauss, a classificatory term is considered as arbitrary as long as it has not been connected to other terms of the classificatory system.

For Douglas, it is arbitrary because it depends on the construction of the subject, who can reduce its arbitrariness by modifying his/her classificatory system. 'In perceiving we are building, taking some cues and rejecting others. The most acceptable cues are those which fit most easily into the pattern that is being built up. Ambiguous ones tend to be treated as if they harmonised with the rest of the pattern. Discordant ones tend to be rejected. If they are accepted, the structure of assumptions has to be modified' (Douglas 1966: 36).

Notice the 'we' in Douglas's psychological analysis. It assumes that we, as human beings, can reproduce for ourselves the kind of reasoning that leads to magical behaviour. This analysis follows the classical empiricist description of perception as something assembled on the basis of formal resemblances, while adding to it a capacity for selection inherent in form. Beings are perceived on the basis of the similarities between them, which tend to produce by repetition a schema that allows the mind to integrate other beings. This schema then becomes a form, which means that its contours, first vague because linked to the necessities of action, become sharp and clear. Beings that were first perceived as similar then appear as different; therefore, certain beings are perceived as ambiguous, that is, belonging to two different sets of classifications. The perception of these beings produces a situation of discrepancy and uneasiness: it must either modify its classification to integrate these beings, or select in the characteristics of the unknown beings those that are pertinent for an established classification. Symbolic entities are those that do not fit in available taxonomies, and are therefore the object of a supplementary treatment.[6]

By settling for one or other interpretation, ambiguity is often reduced. For example, when a monstrous birth occurs, the defining lines between humans and animals may be threatened. If a monstrous birth can be labelled an event of a peculiar kind the categories can be restored. So the Nuer treat monstrous births as baby hippopotamuses, accidentally born to humans and, with this labelling, the appropriate action is clear. They gently lay them in the river where they belong. (Douglas 1966: 59)

It is interesting to compare this famous analysis of the monster in *Purity and Danger* to the analysis of the newborn in *The Savage Mind* (1966c). For Lévi-Strauss, newborn babies also raise a problem because they do not have a place in the system of classification, and society must undergo a complex process to create a proper name that suits him or her. But the newly born does not appear at the limits of two classifications in the eyes of a subject: rather, as being at the limit of the classificatory impulse, that is, at the point where classification stops its movement and recognises the sacred character of the person. Here we see that Lévi-Strauss does not rely on a psychology of similarities, but on a semiotics of the life of signs. Every sign presents itself as double, and the life of the mind consists in establishing relations between these double entities; but once this life extinguishes itself, signs appear as they are, double entities that appeal desperately for relations. A newborn is both an individual and a person, and appears both inside and outside of the system of classification. Semantic oppositions come first for Lévi-Strauss; they do not result from the classificatory activity but they are its initial condition. It is therefore possible to oppose the model of 'exhaustion' that is developed in Lévi-Strauss's works, according to which the process of division inherent in classification, in the end, leaves outside of itself a residue,[7] and the model of ambiguity in Douglas's work, according to which a process of perception leaves beings at the limits of two classifications.

This difference appears clearly in the use both authors make of the logical notion of contradiction. For Lévi-Strauss, the classificatory impulse of 'wild thinking' comes from the existence of contradictions in the way societies perceive the world on which they act; these practical contradictions are then inversed and displaced at the more abstract levels of classificatory thought, through the use of specific operators such as mythical symbols. Contradiction is a condition of action in an environment that presents itself as uncertain and dangerous. For Mary Douglas, contradictions are produced by those who contest widely accepted classifications, and become dangerous for society itself. Indeed, witches use the ambiguities in perception to assert a counter-power against ritually imposed classifications: they thus become the representatives of those beings that are excluded by the process of classification. Douglas moves here interestingly from the psychology of perception to the sociology of power. Power tends to reproduce the classifications that appear spontaneously in perception, and particularly through the repetition of these classifications in rituals. But power opposes itself to counterpowers that come from the threats of witches. 'Witches are the social equivalent of beetles and spiders who live in the cracks of the walls and wainscoting. They attract the fears and dislikes which other ambiguities and contradictions attract in other thought structures, and the kind of power attributed to them symbolises their ambiguous, inarticulate status' (Douglas 1966: 102). Contradiction is not only a logical operation, which could be seen as a theoretical projection on social practices: it is a confrontation between two forces that contradict each other. Douglas observes that the social system is 'at war with itself' when pollution defies the categories of cleanness, since beings that appear as clean can, observed from another point of view, be seen as unclean. It is interesting to notice that while for Lévi-Strauss magic extends the scope of classifications by its tendency to 'classify out the universe' by the means of signs – a view Douglas considers as aesthetic (Douglas 1967) – for Douglas magic is a contestation of religiously accepted classifications, which opens a much more political perspective.

Douglas's reasoning on the limits of classifications can thus be described as dialectical. She shows that a contradiction is appropriated by power when ambiguous animals, instead of being rejected outside of the limits of classifications, are put at the centre of the social system, as in the ritual of the pangolin she has studied among the Lele of the Kasai (Douglas 1957). The pangolin 'contradicts the most obvious animal categories. It is scaly like a fish, but it climbs trees. It is more like an egg-laying lizard than a mammal, yet it suckles its young. And most significant of all, unlike other small mammals its young are born singly' (Douglas 1966: 168). It is then worshipped as its human counterpart, twins (who have a human appearance but are born double like animals), because it is a sign of fertility. The rite of the pangolin is very powerful because the contradiction, instead of being encountered from the outside, at the limits of the system of classification, is integrated at the centre of the system, and tends to be reproduced although it relies on a contingent basis. The contingency of natural classifications is transformed into a social necessity once it is inscribed in the ritual act by which society creates its order.

Here Douglas refers to the philosophy of Sartre. Like Lévi-Strauss, she shows that the dialectical reason, reserved by Sartre to modern and historicised societies, also operates in 'primitive' societies.

If they could choose among our philosophies the most congenial to the moments of that rite, the pangolin initiates would be primitive existentialists. By the mystery of that rite they recognize something of the fortuitous and conventional nature of the categories in whose mould they have their experience. If they consistently shunned ambiguity they would commit themselves to division between ideal and reality. But they confront ambiguity in an extreme and concentrated form. They dare to grasp the pangolin and put it to ritual use, proclaiming that this has more power than any other rites. So the pangolin cult is capable of inspiring a profound meditation on the nature of purity and impurity and on the limitation [of human contemplation on existence]. (Douglas 1966: 170)

But notice the difference in the reference to Sartre between the two authors. For Lévi-Strauss, the classificatory dynamic of wild thinking is dialectical because it is the effort to extend itself to all beings in the world, starting from a contradiction which reveals that all beings can be related to other beings because they appear as double in problematic situations. For Douglas, it is dialectical because it can absorb the contradiction at its margin and bring it to the centre. Both are fascinated by the philosophy of Sartre, but for different reasons. If for Lévi-Strauss Sartre produces a new myth by integrating the event that is the French Revolution into the different levels of classificatory thought, for Douglas he discovers in the experience of impurity ('nausea') the possibility of founding a new ritual that gives meaning to the world by the recognition of its contingency and contradiction.

This allows one to compare more generally myth and ritual as two ways of dealing with the limits of classification. Myth starts with the feeling of a contradiction inherent in practices, and it elaborates classifications to find logical mediators between the terms of the contradiction. For myth, unknown beings are a real contradiction, because they stand at the limit between being and non-being, and therefore this contradiction cannot be solved but only displaced. Ritual starts with an ambiguity, that is, with beings at the limits between two systems of classification, and transforms it into a contradiction, when counterpowers gather around this ambiguity, and then solve the contradiction by putting it at the centre of society. For myth, on the contrary, there is no ambiguity: the difference between terms is sharp and clear, and it is a starting point for a proliferation of differences. The point when differences cease to proliferate is not the resolution of the initial tension but a point of exhaustion: at this point, classificatory systems cannot produce any more differences, only a confusion between beings. Ritual unifies all beings in the world in a single action; myth tries to unify them in a narrative that preserves their difference.

If myth and ritual appear, following the reflections of Lévi-Strauss and Douglas, as two ways of dealing with the limits of classification, then structuralism and functionalism can be seen as two alternative paradigms in the anthropology of danger and risk. Mary Douglas has famously applied to the emergence of the rationality of risks in the American culture her thesis on the social perception of unknown beings; she shows that institutions, not individuals, build up intellectual grids to master the risks that occur in their environment. But this implies that institutions are like organisms which react to the dangers they face by rationalising them in the form of risks. Douglas even speaks of a choice between forms of institutions, which presupposes that institutions have a kind of intentionality (Douglas and Wildavsky 1982: 195). Lévi-Strauss's *Mythologiques* applies the discovery of the totemic operator to the Amerindian continent, where forms of diffusion, transformation and exchange are traced without any relation to a human intention. The problem of unknown beings then becomes that of the possibility of integrating new events in a classifying dynamic that has covered a whole continent, and the encounter with the West appears as a catastrophe that has exhausted and devastated the Amerindian mythical impulse. Structuralism, in this perspective, describes the encounter with unknown beings as the source of a tension between the universal possibilities of the human mind and an event which threatens to render thought impossible. The event that occurs at the limits of classifications can thus be conceived in two alternative ways: as a danger, transformed into a risk by a ritual that integrates contradictions, or as a catastrophe, divided and discarded by a mythical proliferation of differences.

NOTES

1. William Shakespeare, *Hamlet*, act IV, scene 5, quoted in the Pléiade edition of Lévi-Strauss's *Œuvres* 2008.
2. Bouglé 1993. Bouglé was a close friend and supporter of Durkheim. His essays on caste first appeared in 1900.
3. For a development of this point, see Keck 2004.
4. Mary Douglas pays homage to Lévi-Strauss for his dissolution of totemism and discovery of an analogical style of thought in Douglas 1967 and Douglas 1999: 23–4.
5. See the quotation of Evans-Pritchard in Lévi-Strauss 1962b: 23–4, and Douglas 1966: 1.
6. For a discussion of this point, see Sperber 1975.
7. For an illustration of the model of exhaustion, see 'How Myths Die' in Lévi-Strauss 1978b: 256–68. Myths can die when their structure becomes blurred if they pass certain thresholds without reconfiguring another structure: they are then transformed into legends.

REFERENCES

Bouglé, C. 1993. *Essais sur le régime des castes*. Paris: Presses Universitaires de Paris.
Douglas, M. 1957. 'Animals in Lele Religious Thought', *Africa* 27 (I): 46–58.
  1966. *Purity and Danger: An Analysis of Concepts of Pollution and Taboo*. London: Routledge & Kegan Paul.
  1967. 'The Meaning of Myth, with Special Reference to "La geste d'Asdiwal" ', in E. Leach (ed.), *The Structural Study of Myth and Totemism*. London: Tavistock.
  1999. *Leviticus as Literature*. New York: Oxford University Press.
Douglas, M. and A. Wildavsky 1982. *Risk and Culture: An Essay on the Selection of Technological and Environmental Dangers*. Berkeley: University of California Press.
Keck, F. 2004. *Lévi-Strauss et la pensée sauvage*. Paris: Presses Universitaires de Paris.
Sperber, D. 1975. 'Pourquoi les animaux parfaits, les hybrides et les monstres sont-ils bons à penser symboliquement?', *L'Homme* 15 (2): 5–24. (Reprinted in *Method and Theory in the Study of Religion* 8 (2), 1996: 143–69.)

8   The local and the universal

Eric Schwimmer

Lévi-Strauss is a many-sided genius, so that it is still partly an open question what part of his work will survive after he crosses the Acheron. His heritage may overstep the limits of ethnology. Any description of his work focused on existing academic disciplines could miss whatever may prove to be the essence of his work. I have chosen the theme of local versus universal knowledge, because from one perspective a group's bodily and external universe is the sum of all it can know, but each group's universe differs from all others. Yet, humanity also has a common universe: some similarities are more potent than differences. This is one great question structuralism was set up to consider. It involves analysis of exacting factual data, as well as much methodological discovery, philosophical awareness and literary descriptive power.

The peoples I studied, such as Mâori and Orokaiva, still perceived themselves, in 1960, as wholly enveloped in their own local system of thought. Today, their civilisations are not lost but their myths have been ordered by a new calculus, aimed at relating the core of their historical universe to another one, global in its range, contemporary in its forms, inspired by abundant objective knowledge and a metaphysical source of moral rules. As such transformations were not a field of anthropological study fifty years ago, it was only with the help of structural methods that I could hope to model the transformed relations of these plural universes, to discover by what hidden logic they took shape and how new frames were created to cope with new experiences.

The reading list of structuralism begins in the sixteenth and seventeenth centuries in Europe, as early as Hobbes, Montaigne, Rabelais, Cervantes, Spinoza, who were all immersed in their transition from the Middle Ages to modernity. Deeply attached to the universe that was passing away, they were also deeply critical, disturbing, mental wanderers, creating a new discourse for an intelligible world. Lévi-Strauss's final monograph, *Regarder, écouter, lire* (1993a; 1997) offers a panorama of a humanist, largely aesthetic heritage of the seventeenth to the nineteenth centuries that followed on from these founders and formed the seedbed of today's anthropological structuralism. It reveals a list of significant ancestors, artists like Poussin, Ingres, Rameau, and brilliant theoreticians, notably an all but unknown musicologist,

Michel-Paul-Guy de Chabanon (1785). While these forerunners presented putatively universal theories, they referred only to European civilisation, until comparisons with Persian, Chinese and Japanese world-views began in the late eighteenth or early nineteenth centuries.

The role of structuralism, however, has always been to construct bridging or mediating models to connect local and universal perspectives. Its basic obstacle lay in the mainstream's Cartesian postulation that clear, distinct *knowledge* is derivable only from universal propositions. The rules of that epistemology treat symbolic systems, founded on local traditions, values, doctrines, rituals or art forms, as lying beyond the scope of scientific *knowledge*. Although Western philosophy, since Kant, has greatly clarified and attenuated the contradictions between science and religious beliefs, it led to a rigid separation, between on the one hand, scientific knowledge, or 'truth', and 'laws', stated in universal propositions, in an abstract '*if – then*' form, with clear and distinct specifications; and, on the other, *a priori* judgements religious or secular, often stating constant connections or sequences, but denied scientific status, even though some such studies did bring together autonomous indigenous symbol systems, synthetically linking possible experiences in the consciousness of a social group. Structuralism set the universal proposition alongside the existing sciences, by reviving and updating much of Kant's rigorous methodology, but replacing the 'transcendental subject' by the researchers' empirical observation of collective understandings. Here researchers' identification with the group studied is reduced to a minimum by the selection of cultures differing as much as possible from their own, by maximising translation difficulties, and by thus separating them by a grid of basic communal constraints, permeable only due to their common humanity (1964a: 19; 1969d: 11).

In this ethnographic context, the researchers' verities and those of the community studied become 'mutually convertible, hence acceptable to many other outsiders at the same time'. It is in this sense that a degree of universality may be conferred on local knowledge. The present chapter aims to follow Lévi-Strauss's steps towards this basic objective: first, in the field of elementary structures of kinship, then with local cognitive universes and finally with mythology. Before turning to this, however, it is desirable to set out Lévi-Strauss's concept of an ethnographic kind of humanism, a humanist kind of anthropology and a theory of an optimal cultural diversity – a universal concept inspired by information theory, signifying a state equidistant between entropy and disorder, offering a safe maximum of creative tension.

The three humanisms

In his first period, Lévi-Strauss wrote a brief popular essay on the local/universal antinomy entitled: 'The Three Humanisms' (1956a; 1973a: 319–22;

1976d: 271–4). Stating what he took to be essentials of his own role and the role of anthropology in world history, the essay also professed a belief in the future of humanism, in a new 'ethnological' form (see Kambouchner's essay in this volume).

The genesis of ethnological humanism lay in great voyages, planned or accidental, in migrations and colonisations, whose exotic stories were passed on orally or written, in maps and in imaginative inventories. Its practical genesis as an academic discipline, transforming these stories presenting cultural differences rather than resemblances (1983a: 50; 1985b: 26), came later, in the wake of necessities of state administration of human groups, ruled by external or internal colonialism. Anthropology was therefore deeply affected by the end of the colonial world order, and the transformation of administrative necessities.

Lévi-Strauss's brief note was thus doubly polemical, contesting prophecies about the death of anthropology but also about the death of humanism. He argued that anthropology was the most ancient form of humanism, predating colonialism, but providing Western civilisation with a self-knowledge derived from familiarity with other civilisations. From ancient literature, the Renaissance had recaptured forgotten notions and methods and, moreover, acquired new perspectives by confronting those culled from other times and places. When the youth of the Western elite was taught the Classics since the sixteenth century, it was thus initiated not only in languages and texts, but also in an intellectual quasi-ethnographic method, tantamount to a technique of imagining life in a different civilisation. Roman and Greek antiquity taught the West that no fraction of humanity can aspire to self-understanding, except by dialogue with other civilisations. That lesson is apt to survive colonialism.

In the eighteenth and nineteenth centuries, this kind of 'humanism' expanded to match the progress of geographical exploration. China and India were included in the range of academic studies, under the name of 'non-classical philology'. Humanism thus entered a second phase, invading new territory. Methods of study retained the same philological focus as for classical antiquity.

Towards the end of the nineteenth century, ethnology began to introduce the West to a third stage of humanism: the so-called 'primitive' societies, which were still disdained and not counted as civilisations at all, became objects of humanistic study. Research thus reached its ultimate limit of geographical extension, leaving humanity with nothing further to discover about itself. ('The only remaining inquiry can now be in depth, where the end is not yet in sight.') Study of these last civilisations, mostly non-literate, lacking in figurative monuments, could no longer be philological or historical, so that it now became necessary to equip humanism with new tools of investigation, either by increasing distance (as in physical anthropology, prehistory, technology) or by increasing depth, and, hence, by attaching great importance to the minutiae of the mental lives of the inhabitants.

Though this vision of humanistic anthropology is occasionally put forward in Lévi-Strauss's writings, its practical implications never become wholly explicit. It can be best introduced by considering the professional subdivisions into which he broke down the field of anthropology and identified the context of the term 'humanism'.

The three components of anthropology

Lévi-Strauss's subdivisions of anthropology primarily mark dimensions of fields of study. The term 'anthropology', discussed above, 'aims at a global knowledge of man' (1963a: 353) but the two other terms (ethnography, ethnology) are area specific. Ethnography aims at recording as accurately as possible the ways of life of particular groups. Ethnology, on the other hand, utilises data provided by the ethnographer for comparative purposes (1963a: 2), and thus 'represents a first step toward synthesis – geographical, historical or systemic. It includes ethnography as its first step and is an extension of it' (1963a: 352). Though Anglo-Saxon schools are described as teaching social or cultural 'anthropology', their programmes focused primarily on local and area studies. If Lévi-Strauss soon occupied an eminent and influential international position in anthropology, this was due to two factors: a widely felt need for new universal propositions in anthropology, but also his success in local fields of enquiry which he never relegated to an ancillary position.

Accordingly, the first ten chapters of Lévi-Strauss's *The Elementary Structures of Kinship* (1949a; 1967a; 1969b) were treated at first as interesting meta-theories, concerning the incest prohibition, the principles of reciprocity, the basic unit of kinship, the mother's brother and the marriage system ... They aroused discussion in the academy, where anthropologists lost no time in finding objections, often misunderstandings, sometimes real contradictions between deductions from structural theory and what seemed to be established fact. The ensuing debates were the more heated due to the profession's wariness of *a priori* theoretical predictions.

His *Race and History* (1952a; 1952b), published by UNESCO, widely distributed as a booklet, proposes a blueprint of humanism. It explains that, unlike coalitions, 'isolated cultures cannot hope, by themselves, to create the conditions of a truly cumulative history' (1983a: 39; 1985b: 17). It offers eloquent theoretical support to the birth of the globalisation movement.

When, on the other hand, Lévi-Strauss updated that text under the title of *Race and Culture* (1971b; 1985b), his second essay met with much demur by UNESCO and officials concerned with international cultural cooperation. While it kept to the 1952 blueprint of indigenous thought, and its 'wisely conceived humanism'

(1983a: 35; 1985b: 14), it argued also that the globalisation process is rapidly reducing the number of the world's autonomous cultures, and thus the diversity of potentially available sources of cultural knowledge (1983a: 40; 1985b: 18). Its plea for 'a certain optimum of cultural diversity' (1983a: 15; 1985b: xiv) was not based on pragmatism alone, but maintained that the necessary proximate cause of the diversity of cultures is the effort of each to be distinct from the surrounding ones, i.e. the effort to be *itself*.

Not only was this 'optimal cultural diversity' model repugnant to UNESCO, but also to almost the whole scholarly world, which opposed it on two mutually contradictory grounds: either a commitment to pure persistence of all local cultures, or else a belief that local culture is an expendable anachronism and should be rapidly dissolved. This concerted opposition tends to marginalise any models favouring *optimal* diversity.

The objections to 'optimal diversity'

During the post-war period, several universalising trends competed for attention, notably psychoanalysis, phenomenology and Marxism. All these trends, more or less consciously but inevitably, bore marks of the world-views of Western local cultures in which they originated. Anthropological structuralism classified these trends as blind to cultural diversity and treated all their interpretations of non-Western cultures as ethnocentric Western projections.

Thus, the Freudian theory of child development, with its stages of oral and anal development, is assumed to be universal. A brilliant psychoanalyst, E. H. Erikson, tested this theory among the Yurok of Central California (Erikson 1943), on the basis of highly credible observations of childrearing, but sought also to extend his conclusions to an interpretation of the Yurok world-view as a whole, invoking as evidence mythic data drawn from various societies residing much further to the South. Lévi-Strauss argued (1985e: 215–16; 1988b: 162) that nothing authorised Erikson to draw on Yurok practices to interpret the ethos of other societies. He argued that the relations between mother and child, the discipline of physiological functions, distinctive attitudes to feeding and excretion, the acquisition of wealth, etc., described in Erikson's field data, were peculiar to Yurok and not extensible elsewhere. 'Rather, we are presented with a logical and philosophical problem that has been raised in diverse societies.'

The question raised here should not be confused with the more complex question of 'cultural relativism'. Lévi-Strauss is posing the problem of 'the apparent antinomy between the unicity of the human condition and the seemingly inexhaustible plurality of the forms in which we apprehend it' (1983a: 51–62; 1985b: 26–8). The theory of cultural relativism can explain the plurality of forms, but takes no account of the historical circumstances by which these societies were cut off from universal scientific discoveries (1971a: 569–570, 1981: 636–7). Erikson's approach, on the other hand, elucidates universals of the human condition but attaches no meaning to the plurality of forms. It is only in ethnological humanism that the antinomy between these two perspectives is made into a basic object of enquiry.

This debate involves major general issues of epistemology, arising in the context of global decolonisation in the second half of the twentieth century. The anthropology of the dominant colonial nation-states, founded on Darwinism and functionalism, gave little weight to logical and philosophical aspects of the cultural systems of the rest of the world. This was not just due to the colonialist sentiments of enquirers but Western cultures lacked conceptual tools for the adequate interpretation of deeper levels of non-Western systems of thought. *The Savage Mind* (1962b; 1966b) was a major contribution to the filling of this gap.

Yet, this book did not end opposition to the concept of optimal diversity, which was as inconvenient to schools of phenomenology as to the Freudian school, though on different grounds. Paul Ricoeur, in a famous debate with Lévi-Strauss, asked how a structural type of enquiry would give access to the meaning of mythic texts without leaving an 'irreducible residue' (Groupe philosophique d'ESPRIT 1963c; 2004c: 174–5). 'If I do not understand myself better by understanding these texts', asked Ricoeur, 'can I still speak of "meaning"? If meaning is not a component of self-understanding, I do not know what it is.'

Lévi-Strauss answered:

Meaning is always reducible. In other words, behind all meaning, there is non-meaning, and the contrary is not true. The myths of a society are the discourse of that society, a discourse that has no personal emitter. It is collected in the way of a linguist who goes out to study a poorly known language whose grammar he is trying to establish ... If I had to deal with that problem, which God forbid, I would see it as a variant of biblical mythology and I would sort the one alongside the other.

The debate was inconclusive, as we may well put more personal thinking into our mythological enquiries than we consciously know of or would admit. Lévi-Strauss's strongest argument against Ricoeur was that we might not understand things from the inside and from the outside *at the same time* (2004c: 177–8, 181, 184). That difficulty led Lévi-Strauss to split anthropology into two distinct subdisciplines: ethnography that tries to understand from the inside; and ethnology that enquires, from the outside, into the unicity of the human condition (1963a: 351–3).

The third major universalising movement opposed to structuralism was Marxism. Though Lévi-Strauss was a staunch anti-colonialist, Marxist doctrine argued that anti-colonialism is a form of, and should be placed in the service of, the class struggle. This would, however, challenge the foundation of established systems of local thought and established practices of class alliance in contemporary tribal societies, as well as the principles of humanistic ethnology. Althusser, one of the rare Marxists who understood structuralism, published a useful analysis (1974), listing numerous structuralist positions he identified as Spinozan. He nominated Spinoza as Lévi-Strauss's spiritual ancestor. Even if affinities are admitted, however, most Spinozan positions listed by Althusser differ from structuralism. It may well be nonetheless that structuralism, Marxism and structuro-Marxism all have some deep mythic family likeness to Spinoza.

Lévi-Strauss's primary philosophic debt has been to Kant. In a published conversation, he recalls that he was enchanted, as a student, by Kant's idea that the real is unknowable and that we grasp none of it except through the distorting prisms of sensibility and understanding (Hénaff and Lévi-Strauss 2004: 105). This is an idea he might also have found in Spinoza. What distinguishes Lévi-Strauss from his predecessors is his radical materialism.

This appears in the dominant role of internal bodily functions and of ecological/economic determination in his analysis of transformation of mythic systems. His documentation abounds in sardonic contradictions, e.g. in the relation between women and tapirs, highly erotic in the majority of myths, but anchored realistically in the virtues of tapir meat in the kitchen; or in the art of embroidery with porcupine quills, practised in highest forms by tribes where porcupines are almost non-existent. A key Arapaho myth (1978d: 203–4) describes the heroine as having learnt this art in winter from porcupine friends who had hardly any quills to give her; it would have been better if she had come in summer time.

From local to universal models

As early as *The Elementary Structures of Kinship* (1949a; 1969b), Lévi-Strauss's universal models are constructed to resolve paradoxical data. His prolonged argument with Leach bore largely upon the matrilateral cross-cousin marriage system of the Kachin. E. R. Leach was the first major British figure to support Lévi-Strauss's critiques of functionalism and of functionalist comparative methods, to treat culture as a symbolic system, to encourage the use of mathematical models and recognise, at least in theory, the importance of studying unconscious aspects of social systems (Leach 1961). A highly competent field worker, he discovered that Kachin has two marriage systems, *gumsa* and *gumlao*, each with its own distinct rules (Leach 1954: chap. 6). When Lévi-Strauss studied the dated but fairly credible literature about Kachin, Leach's data were unavailable. *The Elementary Structures of Kinship* (1949a; 1967a; 1969b) therefore inferred *inter alia* a paradox between Kachin ideology of equality, and the hidden but really over-heavy economic cost of their bride price prestations. In the absence of a mediating mechanism, this cost would be incompatible with an egalitarian marriage system. This objection unsettled relations between Lévi-Strauss and Leach seeing that the theoretical conclusions of the former diametrically opposed the field data of the latter. Leach's own discovery of the two marriage systems led both scholars to the inescapable conclusion that the system contained heavily indebted wife-takers, who fell into debt-slavery, and these circumstances caused the egalitarian *gumlao* villages to adopt *gumsa* rules in time, while continuing pressure on the wife-takers led eventually to mass migration and the establishment of new *gumlao* villages.

This anecdote brings out the skills of Claude Lévi-Strauss in deducing the inner logic of enigmatic local kinship systems, not only of Kachin but also others in Brazil, and concerning Murngin in Australia, Mundugomor in Papua New Guinea, Lele in Africa, always in places where functionalist fieldwork of high quality had taken place, but some structural principle had been neglected. Such detective work certainly built up the reputation of Lévi-Strauss among Anglo-Saxon ethnographers, who often kept to their former theoretical positions, unsure whether they had been beaten by science or by magic.

Yet, the question remains whether such deductions were really yielding universal fundamental mental structures. We saw above why psychoanalytical, hermeneutical or Marxist blueprints did not produce better results, but early structural methodology often could not detect unconscious mental activity, e.g. explain why, at the time of study, Kachin had an egalitarian self-image. What is the objective basis of their ideological commitment to equality? What are their deeper feelings about the iron constraints of their matrilateral cross-cousin marriage system? Why do they invariably address their love songs to forbidden categories of partners? Even though studies of the Kachin marriage systems cover ecological, economic potential, feasting rituals and political issues, they are mute about mental operations that the mythic codes can often reveal.

As the road from local to universal structural concepts and tools was gradual and complex, it may be useful to trace its stages. During the first phase (from 1940 up to about 1960), the tools came from two main sources, the phonology of Trubetzkoy/Jakobson and the sociology of Marcel Mauss. Trubetzkoy (1933: 227–46) proposed four basic operations for structural linguistics: (1) shifting from the study of *conscious* linguistic phenomena to their *unconscious* infrastructure; (2) not treating *terms* as independent entities but taking *relations* between terms as the basis of analysis; (3) *showing* and elucidating how phonemes are always part of a concrete phonemic *system*; (4) discovering *general* laws, either by induction or 'logical deduction, which would give them an absolute character' (Lévi-Strauss 1963a: 31).

While Mauss's influence on structuralism is pervasive, its core lies in the concept of 'total social phenomenon', defined by Lévi-Strauss by three attributes: (1) a form that is common to the various manifestations of social life (1963a: 363); (2) incarnated in an individual historical experience; (3) offering a system of interpretation accounting for all physical, physiological, psychic and sociological aspects of behaviour. This model accounts for unconscious phenomena, the primacy of relations and local-level systems but Lévi-Strauss did not regard Mauss's *Essay on the Gift* as a truly universal theory of exchange, on the grounds that the famous 'three obligations: giving, receiving and giving in return' do not suffice to form a structure; they leave an epistemological gap to be plugged by local metaphysical notions such as Mâori *hau* (or *utu* or *mana*). Their basic weakness is being revealed by current ethnography such as Metge (2002), but is foreshadowed by Lévi-Strauss (1950a: xxxviiiff.; 1987a: 46).

Lévi-Strauss presupposed, like Spinoza but unlike Descartes, that our world is in principle intelligible, though the true significance of many signifiers is still obscure. By implication, perceived phenomena fall into two categories: those of which we have adequate objective knowledge, and those that become intelligible only if we add a notion that exists in an imagined world transcending sense perception, a 'floating signifier' (1950a: xlix; 1987a: 63). This theory may be classified as universal, in that it enables us to set up a universal catalogue of symbolic categories. *Totemism Today* (1962a; 1963d) explored a specific, concrete case of such paradoxical kinds of knowledge: humanity has adequate knowledge of social units such as clans which are, objectively speaking, made up of members of the same species and form a continuous series with the same physical, physiological, psychic and sociological characteristics. On the other hand, the distinctiveness of specific bounded communal units, while an important social fact, is more difficult to establish objectively. Totemism resolves that problem by postulating that each social unit is attached to a natural species as floating signifier (totem), so that, in an imagined world of possibility, each social unit is linked to a natural species, and the set of such species evidently forms a discontinuous series. These perspectives are founded on paradoxical kinds of knowledge.

This is indeed a universal theory, more informative than Mauss's, because many relations exist even between humans whose totems are different. As totemic systems also postulate the existence of relations between different *totems* and of homologies between intra-human and intra-totem relations, choices of totems made by human groups are not altogether arbitrary but take account of factual ecosystem relations between non-human beings. Such relations had been recognised by Lévi-Strauss's predecessors, notably Radcliffe-Brown (1951). Totemism therefore provides not only a catalogue of categories, but also a universal system of relations between categories, human or non-human.

Yet, the most specific 'isomorphism' between Spinoza and Lévi-Strauss lies in seeking and finding *something* 'adequate' that is omnipresent in the confused ideas of the first kind of knowledge, and that can mediate between the first (purely local) and the second (universal) kinds. According to Spinoza, there is in all our bodily modifications *something* that can be conceived naturally: all bodies have common properties; all are modes of extension; all participate alike in movement and rest, in variable degrees, some being quicker or slower than others. These modes are present in the whole and the parts of all things, in any of the body's affections. If conceived as such, they constitute adequate knowledge, but in fact they remain halfway between percept and concept (*Ethics* Part II: propositions 37–8; Matheron 1988: 71). Lévi-Strauss, especially in *L'Origine des manières de table* (1968), likewise draws on notions of periodicity to show how, in Amerindian myths, it mediates between animistic views of the universe and rational, quantitative notions about seasons, age groups, day and night, life and death.

Pre-constrained elements

The next phase of Lévi-Strauss's study of universals, in *The Savage Mind,* went on to explore in greater depth the nature of 'floating signifiers', whose theoretical status had been left rather vague. Did that concept offer a general, wholly materialist theory of symbolic thought or did it just serve to interpret specific cultural systems? The opening chapter of *The Savage Mind* (1962b; 1966b) begins by postulating that, while the Cartesian tradition of Western philosophy distinguishes *percepts* from 'knowledge' (where the latter term refers to clear and distinct universal *concepts*), humanistic anthropology recognises two distinct modes of scientific thought. The first is roughly adapted to the level of perception and imagination; the other at a remove from it, as though there are two different routes of arriving at the necessary connections that are the object of all science. During the Neolithic, the first route led to man's mastery of great arts of civilisation: domestication of animals, weaving, pottery, agriculture. There may be no necessary connection between perceptible qualities and objective properties, but there is often at least an empirical relation between them (1962b: 24; 1966b: 15).

Descartes did not recognise such mastery as evidence that it was based on a kind of knowledge, but Spinoza did so. For Spinoza, this 'first kind of knowledge' is a depository of tradition, imagination, religion and magic, exempt from philosophical enquiry, while the second kind is made up of clear and distinct universal concepts. There is also a 'third kind of knowledge: intuitive science', to which we attain if we perceive the exact relation between a thing and the divine substance on which it depends. Structuralism claims the 'floating signifier' to be 'a pledge of all art, all poetry, all mythic and aesthetic invention' (Lévi-Strauss 1950a: xlix; 1987a: 63). It is a strictly materialist theory of the intuitive production of symbolic systems, elements of which – *signs*, symbols or 'mythemes' (see *infra*) – are irreversibly locked together in social memory, in *languages* (verbal or non-verbal) and in *vocabulary*.

Lévi-Strauss immortalised this theory by the image of a *bricoleur* (handyman), keeping a collection of used carpentry items in his tool shed, recombining for every new production, some such items that proved useful in the past and reusing them (after subjecting them to certain operations). As these stocked *signs* already have *meanings*, circumscribing their later use, they are 'pre-constrained' (1962b: 29; 1966b: 19).[1] Elements may be added but 'every choice that is made will involve a complete reorganisation of the structure, which can never be the one vaguely imagined nor another one which might have been preferred' (1962b: 29; 1966b: 19). Unlike Western literature or folklore, the *bricoleur's* operations are bound by the cast-iron rigidity of typical traditional mythic and ritual symbol systems. The term 'pre-constrained' implies that structural 'transformations' are viewed as radical new departures by their creators.

The Savage Mind was less concerned with transformations than with the initial task of setting up an alternative system of logic, intermediate between percepts and concepts, from whose minimal units (mythemes) local human groups created ageless *imagines mundi*. Vestiges of such cosmic images survive in modern life, ancillary and peripheral, but deeply – unconsciously – anchored in the human mind.

Myths: the ethnological level

The first sentence of *The Raw and the Cooked* (1964a; 1969d) suggests that 'empirical categories, such as those of raw and cooked, fresh and rotten, soaked and burnt, etc., definable with precision through mere ethnographic observation of a particular culture, can serve nonetheless as conceptual tools to detect abstract notions and link these together in propositions.'

A simple illustration of the construction of such propositions is the ironic ending of *The Jealous Potter* (1985e; 1988b) where Lévi-Strauss gives a 'structural' explanation of the Oedipus complex. He proposes a triangular model, whose apex is Tiresias (the inspired prophet who knew who Oedipus was but nobody believed him). The other angles are a messenger revealing that Oedipus did not know his true parents, and a servant who had him adopted in babyhood, though instructed to kill him. These three characters are the only ones to have had 'knowledge' (in the Kantian sense) of Oedipus, the last two from actual experience, and Tiresias from *a priori* knowledge based on the possibility of experience. From the viewpoint of Freud, Ricoeur or Marx, this structural triangle is meaningless, but 'let us remember that American Indians attach special sacredness to stories that seem vulgar or even obscene or scatological to ourselves' (Lévi-Strauss 1985e: 266; 1988b: 204). Thus, ethnological humanism seems committed to universal propositions in the Kantian sense.

The first volume of *Mythologiques* (1964a) already introduces all these perspectives. Its *methodology* rules out the postulation of any 'myth of origin', as the primal source of any local system of thought is hidden in the mists of history. Enquiry thus begins with a 'myth of reference', supposedly arbitrarily chosen, made up from a pre-existing stock of immutable mythemes. Ethnographically, *The Raw and the Cooked* (1964a; 1969d) hardly goes further than the speakers of Gé, Tupi and Chaco languages of Eastern Brazil, again because the *method* requires a very gradual expansion from the Bororo and Gé initial groups of myths to others of similar culture that can be used for purposes of ethnological comparison. Even so, most comparisons are 'formal', i.e. based on the texts alone, but that is not due to the method, but to the state of the ethnological record. The later volumes cover far more tribes, languages and regions, from South to North America, and far more ethnological information is supplied.

The epistemological question whether such ethnological records can yield valid universal propositions hangs on Kant's criterion for valid propositions: the necessary link between what the myth says and the possible experience of those who offer it. Now, the universe of myth is made up of earth, sky, waters; cosmic forces, periodicities; animals, plants, heavenly bodies and above all humanity. The stories speak of bodies, of sufferings and satisfactions, love and hatred, encounters and exchanges, events and journeys, unintended consequences, gifts of knowledge but also strategies, deceptions, trickeries. They are keys to moral, intellectual and aesthetic questions arising in real life. Told as evening entertainment, these myths are templates for interpretations of hidden connections in a meaningful universe.

In *The Structural Study of Myth* (1958a; 1963a), Lévi-Strauss describes a method for breaking down myths into minimal units called *mythemes* that cannot be identified by purely linguistic criteria: 'they should be looked for at the sentence level. At the first stage of research, we should proceed tentatively, by trial and error, guided by the basic principles of all forms of structural analysis' (1958a: 233; 1963a: 207). The *mytheme* concept is cumbersome, but there is no advantage in simplifying the minimal unit (e.g. to the single word), as words have multiple meanings that cannot be fully traced without reference to all sentences that introduce them.

Even though specific mythemes may be rigid in content, there are many ways of linking them to new myths. They may be negated, inverted, recoded or may serve a new message. Such logical operations are sensed, rather than stated, by informants. Outside observers need to deduce the transformation rules by structural analysis and align the actual transformations, links of isomorphism and other relations. Lévi-Strauss thus establishes systems of logical classification distinguishing, say, between three kinds of sound, then shows that the same classification is made between kinds of taste, smell, touch, and that – in these myths – what is said about one of the senses is symbolically applied to the others also (1964a: 161; 1969d: 153). His term 'isomorphism', though never formally defined, is indicated by figures illustrating 'zoological transformations' (1971a: 606; 1981: 677), but generated by an algebraic function. Isomorphic mythemes are aligned in series called *axes*, either within the myth of reference or within the same *group* of myths.

Gradually, a nebula of axes is traced, denser at the centre than at the periphery, which at no stage becomes crystallised into a stable, determinate system. Myth-logic is as devoid of finality as of origin. However far enquiry is extended, the beginning or end of an axis cannot be adequately known. Myth-logic seeks no synthesis of axes, no hidden unity in its texts, no resolution of its confusion of contraries. A multiplicity of axes, sequences and themes is essential to it. The structural analytical method attaches crucial importance, however, to the spirals formed when an enquiry, moving from axis to axis, finds its way back to previously established models. The range of these models is widened by data added at each revolution of the spiral.

The universal propositions of the ethnology of *Mythologiques* emerge from the way images or tonalities of humanity are brought together in a consciousness. Striking features of this consciousness are (1) knowledge of the connections between different parts of the cosmos; (2) moral rules generated within a cosmic system of relations ruled by no transcendent authority; (3) events intelligible in terms of forces within that relational system; (4) constant search for information about material facts of that system, especially its relations in time (periodicity) and in space (the right distance between things); (5) forces internal to the human body, as an integral part of the cosmic schema. Although literary power was necessary to give credence to Lévi-Strauss's construction of this kind of mythic cosmos, its foundation needs to rest on a maximum of methodology. This methodology is no cover-up of literary imagination, but integral to his objective, as demystification has to be based on an infrastructural anchor of objectivity.

Myths: epistemological novelties

The epistemological question that arises is that the concept of 'myth' in itself cannot be clearly demarcated. It has too many links with religion, ritual, politics and psychology to be treated as an aesthetic genre. Above all, it should not be identified as a system of symbols or tropes, but rather echo Lévi-Strauss's and Bakhtin's (1968) affinity with Rabelais's interest in intimate *realia*. The only clear epistemological clue we are given is that myth, to Lévi-Strauss, is an autonomous domain of the mind. A myth can never be transformed into anything but another myth. On the other hand, as a depository of a strongly synthetic kind of possible experience, relevant to all aspects of the lived-in universe, myth is a vehicle of ontic and moral knowledge in all provinces of life. Its universality does not lie in the very diverse interpretations of systems of content, but in the unconscious logic used in creating new myths from existing stocks of mythemes.

It is in this tracing of the unconscious dynamics of myth-logic that structuralist methodology updates Kant by drawing on Jakobson's linguistics and on mathematical logic. In particular, classification and interpretation are no longer viewed as separate operations, but each mytheme, without having meaning in itself, can produce meaning in a system where it is opposed to another and because of that opposition (1985b: 145). For instance, the myths are presented by excellent summaries that – by the author's own admission (see Bellour 1979: 165) – have a double function: as 'not just a resumé, but rather the extraction of a secret architecture … an approximation to the model one is trying to construct'. One might conclude that the 'universe' set up by that model has a clearly identifiable centre (France). The quotations given at the head of many chapters in *Mythologiques* and some parallels drawn from regions far from America give the same impression. The text of *Mythologiques* is, indeed, full of examples of such 'double articulation', where one level of meaning interprets local materials while the other envisages what Bakhtin (1986: 126) might have called a universal super-addressee.

Such devices do not, however, suffice to set up credible universal propositions. Different universes (in the sense of Lotman's *semiospheres*, 1990) could well be set up in other centres, say in Japan or China or India or Brazil or Egypt. On the other hand, as the geographical range of comparison widens, and as the style and construction of the tales becomes more complex and 'literary' where the enquiry moves in a northerly direction, the basic unity of *Mythologiques* is not lost. Instead, in addition to universal mental structures like periodicity or Amerindian/Oceanic techniques like the earth oven, it relies increasingly on a deeper level of analysis, requiring the use of complex models whose universality rests on analogues of advanced mathematical logic.

Thus, *Mythologiques* is on firmer ground when it jokingly resolves the Oedipus event into the action of three personages – Tiresias, the messenger and the servant, and when it qualifies this trio as 'the same canonical triangle' (1985a: 265; 1988b: 203) that appears in the canonical formula for myth in *The Jealous Potter*. It is on this, and on other related mathematical objects, that we should principally rely to identify the methodological core of Lévi-Stauss's project of ethnological humanism.

Ethnology and mathematical logic

Lévi-Strauss devoted his first major work to the worldwide classification of kinship systems on the basis of modalities of marriage exchange, attempting, by a few basic principles, to account for many elementary kinship structures distributed over a wide geographical area. In many social systems, systematic study, with the help of talented informants, can account satisfactorily for their elementary units and principles of operation, but in others, informants' data are confused and classifications invented by social scientists offer no solution. Such was the case of the Murngin of Arnhem Land (Australia), the society where Lévi-Strauss first used mathematical tools for the objective formal analysis of marriage classes. The study, done by André Weil, a mathematician, showed proofs, by relational logic, that, at the time of the study (prior to the Second World War), Murngin currently had two (logically incompatible) marriage systems.

When reporting these findings (1967a; 1969b: chap. 14), Lévi-Strauss points out that no culture could preserve its individuality under Weil's conditions and that, if Murngin had been split concretely into two subsocieties, this would have been noticed by two excellent ethnographers who had worked there. Hence, Murngin must have been able to live with two incompatible systems of marriage, using subtle arrangements that varied from place to place. Lévi-Strauss also showed (1962b: 205–11; 1966b: 157–8; Kelly 1935) that Aborigines had effective mathematical techniques of their own for dealing with structural transformations taking place everywhere in their communities. He mentions 900 Aboriginal survivors from thirty tribes, haphazardly regrouped in a government camp, under conditions that made the upholding of traditional beliefs and customs highly improbable. Yet, their first response to the regrouping was to adopt common terminology and correspondence rules so as to harmonise tribal structures that, in the whole region, were based on moieties and sections. If asked about his section, an individual might reply: 'I am so-and-so in my own lingo – that is Wungo here.'

Lévi-Strauss could quote some indices enabling groups to make choices between names available in the new locality. These refer to distinctive life ways and perceptible qualities local moieties ascribed to themselves, and turn out to be homomorphous to the life ways and qualities of totem animals of those moieties. The Aborigines' thought processes are unwittingly mathematical, in that they reduce qualities of groups to schematic, mathematical terms and functions in order to solve an implicit equation of the general form (a: b:: x: c), where x is the section name they find most appropriate for their new locality.

If the characteristics of (a, b, c) can be fully stated, it is easy enough to solve such an equation, but Aboriginal informants speak only of (a), the universe of their own moiety, where numerous relations (contiguous residence, aquatic or igneous nature, common activity, possession) may be motives for claiming a common moiety name, whereas a symbolic father–son relation between two totems (in matrilineal societies) would be a sign that these totems are in opposite moieties. If choice of the name (x) were inspired also by historical events or aesthetic imagination, regrouping might become an occasion for a radical cultural transformation.

The canonical formula of myth, enounced in 1958 (1963a: chap. 11) is not only the most complex, but also the most fundamental of the mathematical objects used by Lévi-Strauss. Though he never said that *myth* is a category for which applicability of the formula is a necessary and sufficient condition, the formula is an index of the mythic mode, distinguishing it from other literary *modes* (see Schwimmer 2001), like folktale or novel. Each mode predominates in the literatures of one epoch of culture.

The canonical formula for myth is $[F \, x \, (a): F \, y \, (b) \; \neg \; F \, x \, (b): F \, a^{-1} \, (y)]$. I refer to it here briefly, from the viewpoint of the relation of the local to the universal. The first time we find it quoted in the *Mythologiques* is in *From Honey to Ashes* (1966a: 212; 1973d: 249), but that reference is still somewhat intuitive, and not yet clearly founded on theoretical data analysis. In *The Origin of Table Manners* (1968: 269–98; 1978d: 327–61), we find an account of a quadripartite structure based on a mathematical object called the Klein group. The group of myths presents a universe ruled by Sun and Moon, Summer and Winter, nomadism and sedentariness, hunting and agriculture, war and peace (1968: 260; 1978d: 316–17). The general theme analysed by Lévi-Strauss is the structure and mathematics of seasonal variations. Its background is the mythic war waged by an omnipotent Sun and its denizens, masters of the universe, to subdue the Moon and most earthlings. In line with Amerindian philosophy, the struggle ended in a 'Red Baton' peace ritual, where the Sun agreed to a Compact alternating his power with that of the Moon on a seasonal basis. Other myths convey a similar balancing message by the image of Sun and Moon sitting at the extremities of a canoe, with someone tending the cooking fire at the centre.

The main heroes of the cosmic wars are, on one side, ten bachelor brothers, who double as thunderbirds and are looking for wives, and a similar group, doubling as poisonous snakes, on the other. The narrative universe of myths analysed comprises at least four distinct structures: links of kinship; of biological behaviour (e.g. rules of menstruation); of cultural behaviour (e.g. pearls and ornaments); and links that unite humanity with the universe (e.g. seasonal periodicity). Lévi-Strauss analyses these in detail, using Klein group mathematics but his text and figure portray a deep non-commutative change not expressible in Klein group mathematics. I reanalyse them here, using Morava's method, so as to illustrate the power of the canonical formula.

The canonical formula

The Klein group is simpler than the canonical formula, but it has limitations as a universal model for myth. It covers current mythic operations like opposition and inversion, either singly or doubly and in any direction. On the other hand, it is locked into four standard positions, structurally inadaptable to external and internal realities of environmental or historical change. Structuralism has often been accused of lack of flexibility in this regard, but the real issue may be subtler. In the Kantian terms on which Lévi-Strauss often relies, structure and history are perceived as an antinomy but its poles are not always in perfect equilibrium. In terms of research strategy, a scholar is often in a position of redressing a balance that has been disturbed by his predecessors. Over the last fifty years of perceived contradiction between structure and process, Lévi-Strauss took up the neglected field of structure, without ever denying the importance of process.

Scubla (1998) rightly wonders why, after setting up a fully adequate canonical formula for myth in 1955, Lévi-Strauss never developed it systematically until thirty years later (1985e: 70–80; 1988b: 50–8). He rightly remarks that this model continued to guide Lévi-Strauss's thinking during the years of its seeming dormancy, but the fact remains that he preferred to rely on the more static Klein group rather than the more dynamic canonical formula. In this context, it is significant that he learnt the use of the Klein group model only after Marc Barbut (1966) explicated it. On the other hand, no credible interpretation of the more complex canonical formula was published until Petitot (1988). An alternative reading of the formula has since been proposed so as to relate it to local diversities as well as universal forms. An American mathematician, Jack Morava (2003), discovered that it is a 'consistent mathematical system', professionally known as 'a non-trivial anti-automorphism of the quaternian group of order eight'. He was amazed to find that Lévi-Strauss had managed, by pure intuition, to put together a mathematical 'critter' of such complexity. Scubla (2004: 218, note 8) confirms (see also Schwimmer 2003) that Morava's interpretation is not a formalist monstrosity, but a convenient *vademecum* for working anthropologists.

Unlike Petitot's morphodynamics, it can be used for modelling structural-historical change in specific cultural systems. Morava points out that the relation between the left- and right-hand sides of the formula is readable either as a general equivalence relation, or as marking a non-commutative transformation in the state of the world. When deep structural changes occur in the world, these are expressed in a new character (y), appearing in the last element of the formula, i.e. in $[\mathrm{F}\, a^{-1}\, (y)]$.

Does this formula (to quote Scubla 1998: 30) 'resolve some great contradictions that forever trouble the human mind'? That may not quite have been its purpose, but as Scubla also writes (Scubla 1998: 19), the formula's schemata and processes are basic in anthropological theory. Its place in ethnological humanism is that of 'an image, a picture, a graphic design that could facilitate the intuitive grasp of a chain of relations' (Lévi-Strauss 1984: 13; 1987c: 4). Let us apply this to the myths of peacemaking between heavenly bodies. For this purpose we transform each of the four symbols of the left-hand side of the canonical formula to obtain the right-hand side. We can write this as: $(x \neg x, a \neg b, y \neg a^{-1}, b \neg y)$, where function (x) stands for universal omnipotence. The opposite function (y) stands for consensual authority. Symbols (a, b) stand for any of several pairs of tale characters, as Lévi-Strauss's model covers four distinct structures. For example: in the structure of Biological Behaviour, two heroines (a, b) are both classed as non-wives in their groups. Heroine (a) obeys the menstruation rules but (b) catastrophically breaks them.

Looking at the transformation of the four symbols and at Lévi-Strauss's figure, we note first that (x) is merely transformed into itself. Seeing that Sun and Moon each predominate for half of the year, celestial omnipotence continues all the year round. One unchanging element always occurs in canonical myth equations, as *all* myths have at least one component as an armature preserving the continuity of the culture. The transformation from [F x (a)] to [F x (b)] signifies, for example, that, after gruesome experiences, heroines learn not to break menstruation rules. Above all, it signifies that the erotica of the Red Baton ritual led to a Compact reducing by half the omnipotence of the enfeebled wintry Sun and its denizens (1968: 270–1; 1978d: 328–30).

The two transformations occurring in the last term of the formula, $[F\ a^{-1}(y)]$, are more complex. The symbol (a), no longer a character, transforms into a function, and is inverted into (a^{-1}). That is what Lévi-Strauss calls a twist. Then, character (b) is sent to (y), which is thus turned into a character. Canonical formulas have a double twist. First, servants of the Sun, such as Thunderbirds, cease their assaults for the season – a peace constrained by the ritual Compact. These creatures turn from characters into a function and come to symbolise the consensual authority of the Compact. Then, the new character (y) is no longer the Moon but specifies the ritual and mathematical actors. The two convoluted lines of the figure (1968: 297; 1978d: 360) show each side predominating for half of the year, but becoming subordinate thereafter. The power of this canonical formula lies in its ability to show *mathematically* the cultural genesis of a universal notion of seasonal periodicity, resulting from rational criticism of confused ideas.

While the canonical formula can be useful in casting light on double twists, it is only one of a number of mathematical analogies Lévi-Strauss exploits from time to time. When exploring universal symbols mediating between life and death, he uses dyads or canonical triangles, or chooses the Klein group when a quadripartite system seems appropriate. His main purpose being the elucidation of complex cognitive systems, he selects, among a fairly wide range, the mathematical object that best suits particular data. The broader purpose of *L'Origine des manières de table* (1968) is to show that periodicity is halfway between percepts (experience of the body, observation of nature), and an adequate understanding of objective process. For this reason, a long description is given of disputes about calendar mathematics, reminding of devices in pre-classical ancient Rome, to reconcile the ten lunar months to the solar year, which was known to be longer. The myth presents the leap from the end of ten lunar months to a beginning of the new solar year – a leap that is visible in Lévi-Strauss's drawing (1966a: 297).

In the end, as we know, *Mythologiques* is – consciously – as circular as Joyce or Proust. The foundation of its epistemology is the canonical formula, which interprets a complex system of unconscious universal rules for transforming myths, hence also for a logical construction of symbol systems. This rule system remains a nebula unless it is stated in mathematical language, enabling humanity to become conscious of at least some formal constraints on symbolisation. In this respect, *L'Homme nu* (1971a) is a first step that badly needs supplementing by further research. Its ethnology and epistemology (halfway to global and conceptual) are unified by a literary power of synthesis such as characterises the great myths of the Neolithic age. It is not a document to change the world, but just to hear, touch, see and smell it. It may be as indestructible as the life experience that underlies it. Its final message is that myth-logic necessarily happens. Humanity creates cultures on a foundation of counterfoil of existing mythic notions, and the way this happens can become intelligible, even if it may always be imperfectly known. Some have thought that Lévi-Strauss is a man of the eighteenth or nineteenth century, but an approach as elemental as his could put him earlier still, as though Montaigne, Rabelais, Cervantes or even Spinoza were calling his cue.

NOTE

1. Minimal units of myth (*mythemes*, see below) already have meaning on the level of language and vocabulary: 'empruntant un néologisme à la technique du batiment, on dirait que les mythèmes sont "précontraints"', i.e. they are like ferroconcrete subject to continuous stress while setting (1973a: 173; 1976d: 143).

REFERENCES

Althusser, L. 1974. *Éléments d'autocritique*. Paris: Hachette Littérature.
Bakhtin, M. M. 1968. *Rabelais and his World*. Cambridge, MA: MIT Press.
    1986: *Speech Genres and Other Late Essays*. Austin: University of Texas Press.

Barbut, Marc 1966. 'Le Sens du mot structure en mathématiques', *Les Temps modernes* 246: 791–814.

Bellour, Raymond 1979. 'Entretien avec Claude Lévi-Strauss', in Raymond Bellour and Cathérine Clément (eds.), *Claude Lévi-Strauss, textes de et pour Lévi-Strauss*. Paris: Gallimard, pp. 157–209.

Chabanon, Michel-Paul-Guy de 1785. *De la musique considérée en elle-meme et dans ses rapports avec la parole, les langues, la poésie et le théâtre*. Paris: Pissot.

Erikson, E. H. 1943. 'Observations on the Yurok: Childhood and World Image', *University of California Publications in American Archaeology and Ethnology* 35 (10): 257–302.

Groupe philosophique d'ESPRIT 2004 [1963] 'Autour de *La Pensée sauvage*. Réponses à quelques questions', *Esprit* 301: 169–92.

Hénaff, Marcel with Claude Lévi-Strauss 2004. '1963–2003: l'anthropologue face à la philosophie. Entretien', *Esprit* 301: 88–109.

Jakobson, R. 1973. *Questions de poétique*. Paris: Seuil.

Kant, Immanuel 1949 [1783]. 'Prolegomena to Every Future Metaphysics that May Be Presented as a Science', In *The Philosophy of Kant*. New York: Modern Library.

Kelly, C. Tennant 1935. 'Tribes on Cherburg Settlement (Queensland)', *Oceania* 5 (4).

Leach, Edmund R. 1954. *Political Systems of Highland Burma: A Study of Kachin Social Structure*. London: The London School of Economics and Political Science. 1970. *Lévi-Strauss*. London: Fontana/Collins.

Leach, Edmund R. (ed.) 1961. *Rethinking Anthropology*. London: Athlone Press.

Lotman, Yuri M.1990. *Universe of the Mind: A Semiotic Theory of Culture*. Bloomington: Indiana University Press.

Maranda, Pierre (ed.) 2001. *The Double Twist: From Ethnography to Morphodynamics*. Toronto, Buffalo and London: Toronto University Press.

Mason, Richard 1997. *The God of Spinoza: A Philosophical Study*. Cambridge: Cambridge University Press.

Matheron, Alexandre 1988. *Individu et communauté chez Spinoza*. Paris: Minuit.

Metge, Joan 2002. 'Returning the Gift – *Utu* in Inter-group Relations', *Journal of the Polynesian Society* 111: 311–38.

Morava, Jack 2003. 'On the Canonical Formula of C. Lévi-Strauss', online: http://arxiv.org/abs/math.CT/0306174 (accessed 1 December 2003).

Petitot, Jean 1988. 'Approche morphodynamique de la formule canonique du mythe', *L'Homme* 106–7: 24–50.

Radcliffe-Brown, A. R. 1951. 'The Comparative Method in Social Anthropology', *Journal of the Royal Anthropological Institute* 81, parts I and II.

Schwimmer, Eric 2001. 'Is the Canonical Formula Useful in Cultural Description?', in Maranda (2001): 56–96.
    2003. 'Ethnographic Fieldwork and the Canonical Formula', Communication presented at HOMO Congress, Budapest, November. MS published on CEDEROM, *Information Society Heritage and Folklore Text Analysis*, online: http://itm.bme.hu.homo2003 (accessed 1 December 2003).

Scruton, Roger 1998. *Spinoza*. London: Phoenix.

Scubla, Lucien 1998. *Lire Lévi-Strauss. Le Déploiement d'une intuition*. Paris: Odile Jacob.

2004. 'Structure, transformation et morphogenèse ou le structuralisme illustré par Pascal et Poussin', in Michel Izard (ed.), *Claude Lévi-Strauss*. Paris: Éditions de l'Herne, pp. 207–20.

Spinoza, Benedictus de 1992 [1677]. *Ethics*. Translated by S. Shirley. Indianapolis: Hackett.

Tanner, Adrian 2003. 'The Cosmology of Nature, Cultural Divergence and the Metaphysics of Community Healing', in John Clammer, Sylvie Poirier and Eric Schwimmer (eds.), *Figured Worlds: Ontological Obstacles in Intercultural Relations*. Toronto, Buffalo and London: University of Toronto Press, pp. 189–222.

Trubetzkoy, E. N. 1933. *Psychologie du langage*. Paris: F. Alcan.

Marcel Hénaff

Innovative thinking always operates on the uncertain border between light and darkness. On the side of light, it formulates new, explicit, clearly defined concepts, putting them forward for debate, hoping to convince while taking the risk of being contradicted or even rejected. On the side of darkness, it draws from a reserve of notions which lies within of the realm of the commonly shared views of an epoch or an established discipline and its traditions. Lévi-Strauss's thinking about the concept of symbolism illustrates this in exemplary fashion. This concept derives from a long philosophical and hermeneutic history. At the turn of the twentieth century, the most prominent figures of British religious anthropology – Frazer, Robertson-Smith – and those of the French school of sociology – Durkheim, Mauss – made it one of the major concepts of their theoretical work. From his earliest works, Lévi-Strauss has proposed to use it in a specific way and has elaborated, in this connection, original positions. He writes in 1945: 'No social phenomenon may be explained, and the existence of culture itself is unintelligible, if symbolism is not set up as an *a priori* requirement of sociological thought' (1945a: 517–18). He also adds: 'Sociology cannot explain the genesis of symbolic thought, but has just to take it for granted in man' (1945a: 518). A few years later in the *Introduction to the Work of Marcel Mauss*, he specifies: 'Any culture can be considered as a combination of symbolic systems headed by language, the matrimonial rules, the economic relations, art, science and religion' (1950a; 1987a: 16). Further to his 1945 claims, he adds: 'Mauss still thinks it possible to develop a sociological theory of symbolism, whereas it is obvious that what is needed is a symbolic origin of society' (1987a: 21). We can already acknowledge here two important claims: symbolism is a primary fact which enables us to understand the very institution of society, and every element of a culture is an expression of this symbolism.

These are powerful and precise claims. They are formulated in texts that just precede the publication of *The Elementary Structures of Kinship* (1949a) or that immediately follow it, such as the *Introduction to the Work of Marcel Mauss* (1950a), often considered to be the manifesto of structuralism. These positions have been judged intellectualist or even formalist. It was thought that they could be summed up as follows: Lévi-Strauss founds reality on the symbolic. This is a first example of misunderstanding or even misinterpretation. Lévi-Strauss never speaks of 'the symbolic'. This form of nominalised adjective was first coined by Lacan (Roudinesco and Plon 1997) in the fifties, in the wake of his reading of Lévi-Strauss. Some will object to this reminder by saying that even if Lévi-Strauss does not mention 'the symbolic', no one illustrates better what this term means. In short, if he did not use the expression himself, maybe he should have done. As a result, many do so for him and take this as the basis for their criticisms. Today, it is no longer necessary to take part in this kind of controversy. It is infinitely more interesting to try to understand precisely the concept of symbolism that Lévi-Strauss has developed throughout his works, to evaluate its scope and relevance and – if necessary – its limits or obscurities. One interesting approach would consist in tracing the emergence of the concept and its transformations as his texts evolve from one period to another, establishing a conceptual genealogy. This is what I have undertaken in a previous work (1998, see in particular chapter 5). This study will be of another kind; it will endeavour to be systematic, i.e. it will aim to grasp Lévi-Strauss's thinking about symbolism as a coherent doctrine. It will also present aspects of it which are insufficiently formulated and explore affirmations that need to be questioned or criticised. From this perspective, we can already point out that the question of symbolism presents itself in his works in two main aspects, which must be considered together.

According to a first aspect, symbolism, perceived as the very condition of the formation of any human society and therefore of all culture, appears first of all as a constructed order, as a group of terms and relationships articulated according to rules – for example, a kinship system. In this way, symbolism constitutes an implicit pact and a system of mutual recognition; it is coextensive to the very idea of institution. It is also a system of differences, the best model and most complete expression of which is probably the system of language. More generally, it is that by which the order of culture asserts itself as distinct from nature.

But this first aspect cannot be separated from a second aspect which concerns the mode of expression of symbolism. What is its specificity, compared to other forms of expression such as signs or images? Lévi-Strauss has seldom discussed these points directly. However, one discovers throughout his work that the specificity of a symbolic system is not to signify or illustrate but to *operate*, i.e. to belong to the realm of performance as in the case of a ritual or a mathematical demonstration, or a musical variation. This is the concept of symbolism that Lévi-Strauss presupposes – without explicitly mentioning it – in his reading of myths.

What, then, should we make of the concept of symbolic order as institution and as culture, with which we began? How should we articulate these two apparently very distant aspects of symbolism? Or – to put it more succinctly – may one think of a kinship system or a language as being 'symbolic' in the same sense as an initiation ritual or a geometrical design on a piece of pottery? What these manifestations of symbolism have in common is not obvious at first glance. Is this because of an excessively broad use of the concept of symbolism of which one should be suspicious, or, on the contrary, is it because we have not yet grasped this concept at a sufficiently deep level?

The emergence and formation of the symbolic order: society, culture, kinship

What does it mean that we need to explain the symbolic origin of society rather than formulate a sociological explanation of symbolism? In what way is symbolism a primary fact? It is striking that when palaeontologists wish to identify the markers of specifically human activity, they spontaneously resort to the notion of symbolism.[1] This is apparent, for example, in the archaeological material concerning Neanderthals. What is often considered to be the surest indication that they belong to the human species is the rare presence of decorated or incised objects and the attested existence of burials. And yet, more generally, these incisions, engravings, drawings or site arrangements are themselves nothing but a testimony to a symbolic activity that implies a more essential condition of possibility. How may we define it? May one find the definition of such a condition in Lévi-Strauss's texts? If we do, in his case it is not by way of a conclusion to an archaeological enquiry (for that is not his profession) but as a logical requirement implied in the existence of societies observable today, in particular those whose way of life has remained the closest to what it was in the most distant past.

Exogamy and the incest taboo

In *The Elementary Structures of Kinship*, Lévi-Strauss does not discuss symbolism directly. However, it is probably in the course of this work that he offered the most important and coherent hypothesis concerning a *symbolic origin of society*. For this reason we must return to the initial argument put forward in this book, even if it seems well known or too well known, for the lesson that it contains for the present discussion may not yet have been drawn from it.

The preliminary question, considered insoluble, that Lévi-Strauss confronts in this enquiry on kinship systems is that of the universality of the incest taboo. His treatment of this question has sometimes been viewed as something like a superfluous preamble preceding the main demonstration – this was the case, in particular, of Anglo-American anthropology (see Needham 1971). It is, on the contrary, of capital importance not only for the rest of this work but also for the conception of society that Lévi-Strauss proposes. In many respects, it provides the key to the entire edifice of Lévi-Strauss's theory of symbolism or the symbolic order. In short, one may turn to his answer to this question to understand what he means by 'symbolic origin of society'.

Let us briefly remind the reader – who may be unfamiliar with this debate – what it implied. Anthropology, since its birth in various disciplinary guises (social, cultural, religious) in the last decades of the nineteenth century, was deeply interested in the question of the prohibition of incest, less in fact in an attempt to solve it, than as a form of scholarly exercise enabling daring minds to formulate exciting hypotheses on the origins of human society. Indeed, theories multiplied. They were either of a biological nature (assuming an unconscious knowledge of the risk of degeneration linked to the non-respect of the prohibition); of a psychological nature (lack of sexual interest for partners who are too close); or of a socio-historical nature (an ancient abduction of women had evolved into a peaceful exchange; or an old taboo relating to menstrual blood had become an interdiction relating to sexual relations with women belonging to one's own group). In the 1920s/1930s, most anthropologists, confronted with the contradictory nature of these diverse explanations, preferred to consider the question unsolvable and left it aside, in much the same way that linguistics had renounced trying to account for the origin of language.

It is in this context of suspicion about this issue that Lévi-Strauss, in the opening chapters of *The Elementary Structures of Kinship* (1969a), reopened the debate, approaching it in a manner that was to cause surprise. Following sound methodology, he assumes that a sociological problem should be explained in sociological terms. What observation establishes beyond doubt are the consequences of the prohibition of incest: to make possible or rather impose exogamic exchange. This entails that fathers and brothers cannot take their daughters or sisters as wives; they must relinquish them to another group (a clan or moiety or any other accepted exogamic group) who, in compensation, will do the same to ensure a balance of exchanges. It is therefore as if a fundamental need for reciprocity founded the incest taboo which, as a result, appears less as a negative rule prohibiting relations with close partners than a positive rule ensuring matrimonial exchanges between groups.[2]

This simple explanation, in keeping with the most commonly made ethnographic observations, shed a sudden light on the old enigma, but left in the dark an essential question: what could be the reason for this need for reciprocity which not only initiated matrimonial exchange but made it compulsory? It is in his answer to this question that Lévi-Strauss paves the way to an understanding of the symbolic order and the notion of a symbolic origin of society. For, in the light of the present argument about the emergence of a symbolic order, the existence of exogamy carries with it another major implication which remains to be explained.

Society as institution and the passage from nature to culture

What defines the symbolic order, according to Lévi-Strauss, is that it consists in a set of rules that is entirely separate from the natural order (even though these rules relate to natural facts). It is precisely this separation that the prohibition of incest implies or creates. Indeed, we know that in all living species biological reproduction implies the union of two partners of opposite sex. Nature does not prescribe anything else. The choice of partners remains undetermined. The social rule emerges between this necessity and this indeterminacy; it stipulates which partner is acceptable or allowed or, on the contrary, prohibited. The rule therefore applies to a natural fact – the necessity of a sexual union – and endows it with cultural value: the union becomes prohibited or permitted. What was a natural necessity becomes a choice; union becomes an *alliance*. In this sense the incest taboo is indeed the articulation between two worlds or rather its formulation brings about the passage from one order to the other. By this we mean that the cultural universality of the rule grafts itself directly onto the natural universality of union. However, revealing this articulation still does not help to explain why the human species, unlike other animal species, deems it necessary to specify the choice of partner, nor does it explain the modalities according to which this choice is made. The existence of the incest taboo shows precisely this: that the initiative of making unions is taken away from the 'natural' group of blood relations (consanguines) to be entrusted to the social group; the latter comes to prevail through the imposition of rules; and this is what brings about culture. What is surprising is that this social rule exists in *all* societies and, in this respect, attains the same universality that characterises natural laws. In other words, it is society as an institution which asserts itself here:

The prime role of culture is to ensure the group's existence as a group, and consequently, in this domain as in all others, to replace chance by organisation. The prohibition of incest is a certain form, and even highly varied forms, of intervention. But it is intervention over and above anything else; even more exactly, it is *the* intervention. (Lévi-Strauss 1969a: 32)

This precedence of the social group over consanguines (which we may translate as the precedence of society over the family) reveals the positive nature of the incest prohibition: it is in no way a moral prescription nor does it translate some obscure preventative biological reaction. It simply and essentially means that for every woman relinquished by her consanguines, another one will be made available by another group of consanguines. This *mutual recognition* is precisely what operates the shift from the natural necessity of union to the instituted rule of alliance, and thus explains why we have a human society and not just a biological group. In other words, this means that a wife cannot be claimed from those who stand in relation to her as fathers or brothers. Prohibition, in this way, constantly puts a young woman in an external position with regard to the group of consanguines; she is freed from her dependence on them; she is necessarily destined to be passed on to another group and is, therefore, in principle 'available', generally, to all those in search of a wife in the other group: 'the first logical end of the incest prohibition is "to freeze" women within the family, so that their distribution, or the competition for them, is within the group and under group and not private control' (Lévi-Strauss 1969a: 45).

Thus, human society, without ceasing to be a group of animals, without escaping the constraints imposed on other living creatures, nonetheless asserts itself as belonging to another realm, one that is defined as *culture*. The prohibition of incest therefore has a finality and only one finality: to ensure that the consanguinal group is exogamous, to remove it from the realm of nature so as to enable the social group to exist as such, to affirm its authority over the consanguinal group. It is only through the obligation of exchange born from *mutual recognition*, through the interdependency created by the movement of receiving and returning, that a truly social bond of *alliance* recovers and transfigures a natural bond of sexual co-operation. It is this movement and obligation that prevents the social group from splitting into 'a multitude of families, which would form closed systems, monads without doors or windows, and which no pre-established harmony could prevent from proliferation and antagonisms' (Lévi-Strauss 1969a: 479).

Gift, reciprocity, alliance

To explain these acts of reciprocity, Lévi-Strauss turned to Marcel Mauss's *The Gift*,[3] where he found the most comprehensive and appropriate theoretical formulations for the analysis of his data. Drawing on his reading of various ethnographic accounts (such as those of Boas, Malinowski, Best, Thurnwald and many others), Mauss collected in this essay a large number of testimonies relating to the ritual exchange of gifts in the traditional societies of North America, Melanesia and India, and compared them to similar rituals in the societies of ancient Europe (Roman, Germanic, Celtic, Scandinavian). The geographical and spatial diversity of Mauss's examples is such that it allows him to view the phenomenon of gift exchange as general. On the basis of these numerous testimonies, Mauss is able to reveal a number of findings and conclusions. (1) These exchanges of gifts are not mere displays of civilities, they consist in practices that involve society in all its dimensions (political, economic, legal, religious); ritual gift exchange is a 'total social fact';[4] it is therefore the very essence of the group that is expressed and put into play through exchange. (2) This exchange is composed of three gestures or moments which are inseparable: to give, to receive and to return; each of these gestures entails the other two; exchange takes the form of a ternary structure of reciprocity. (3) What characterises ritual gift exchange is at once its festive and its compulsory nature; there are circumstances under which it is obligatory to give, just as the beneficiary is obliged to accept (or he risks provoking a conflict) and later offer a gift in return. (4) In the act of giving, what is given is the donor himself; a part of him goes to his exchange partner (hence the use of magic to protect this substitute for the self). (5) Through this mutual exchange, the partners come to an agreement with one another and gain respect, prestige and status.

In this movement of mutual gift exchange, Mauss barely mentions matrimonial alliances. Lévi-Strauss, by contrast, understood remarkably that such alliances constituted its most important expression. This is why, in *The Elementary Structures of Kinship*, having shown that the prohibition of incest is above all a positive rule that requires exogamic exchange, he goes on to give a more general explanation of it in chapter 5: 'The Principle of Reciprocity'. It is a *principle* since we notice its application in all gift-giving practices: this reciprocity is precisely the way a human group asserts itself as such, since it is this very reciprocity that underpins the necessity of exogamy and thus the universality of the prohibition of incest, and *therefore* the passage from nature to culture.[5]

'Exchange, as a total phenomenon, is from the first a total exchange, comprising food, manufactured objects, and that most precious category of goods, women' (Lévi-Strauss 1969a: 61). This is an important remark since it enables us to view the institution of marriage within a broader perspective and thereby understand the incest taboo in relation to the total system of culture, of which it is perhaps the cornerstone (since it is the condition of its existence) but of which it also an element among others. 'The system of prestations *includes* marriage, but also *keeps it going [le prolonge]*' (Lévi-Strauss 1969a: 66–7). Indeed, prohibition enables and requires exogamy; it forces each group to relinquish women to other groups (in each case, it does so according to special rules and conditions). But what is then important to remark is that this gesture of gift-giving is inseparable from a set of other prestations which make of it a syncretic expression of reciprocity. One can thus understand why any breach of the obligation of reciprocity (for example, the solitary consumption of celebratory food) takes on an *incestuous*[6] dimension and, symmetrically and conversely, why matrimonial alliance involves all forms of reciprocity. 'It would then be false to say that one exchanges or gives gifts at the same time that one exchanges or gives women. For the woman herself is nothing other than one of those gifts, the supreme gift among those that can only be obtained in the form of reciprocal gifts' (Lévi-Strauss 1969a: 65).

Reciprocity therefore defines a specific area: that of *goods or people* that cannot be privately appropriated. Even though they can be the objects of a private use or relation, they remain, by essence, that which enables the institution of the community. From this point of view, reciprocity is indeed a principle: it cannot be derived from the existence of society; it opens up the possibility for society to exist as an institution. It is no more than what makes the various modalities of exchange possible. The initial and founding relation is the *mutual* exchange of *gifts*: it has an agonistic nature, it is an act of *recognition* of the group as such, an emancipation from the natural circle of consanguines, an expression of the symbolic order of alliance. One may reinforce this idea by comparing the different ways in which great apes (gorillas, chimpanzees, bonobos and orang-utans) and humans recognise their own kind. For the former, this takes place through a series of complex postures comprising gestures, vocal messages and displays of authority or allegiance, of trust or rejection.[7] Humans, however, are the only beings for whom mutual recognition occurs and is displayed through giving the other *goods* as a *token* of and substitute for the self. What confers upon these goods their exceptional value and determines their status is nothing other than the fact that the donor is present in them as such, that this gift is a part of him- or herself, better still: it condenses him/her into the given object.

Such is the fundamental function of the ceremonial gift (which is not a mere variation of the exchange of goods that would not involve money).[8] This token and substitute represents the commitment of the donor to his or her partner. It is the offer and guarantee of an alliance, the most important form of which is marriage. It is in this respect that a human society, beyond its regulatory processes, is already rooted in convention and supposes, at every level, the need for mutual recognition. And this alliance, this exchange of tokens, is also, according to the most ancient tradition, what defines the gesture of symbolism.

Symbol, pact and reciprocity

We must indeed consider the etymology of the term *symbol*. It reveals that the Greek verb '*sumballein*' means to put (*ballein*) together (*sum*), to join or assemble. This refers to a well-known practice in the Greek or Roman tradition, whereby a piece of pottery is broken in half, each partner then keeps one part which, later on, he or she fits to the other along its random fracture line, thus testifying to their pact. The fact that the '*symbolon*' has

always been assimilated to a form of alliance or agreement is a crucial point
which we will later need to elucidate. As Edmond Ortigues, author of one of
the best studies on the subject, puts it:

> The *sum-bolon* consists of the correlation between elements devoid of intrinsic value
> which, when put together (*sum-balló*) or mutually adjusted, enable nonetheless two
> allies to recognise each other as such, as allied to each other (*sum-ballontes*). Or again,
> symbols have distinctive and contrastive values, offering possibilities of meaningful
> combinations which assert a rule of mutual exchange or obligation: your law will be
> my law. Two ideas seem essential: (1) the principle of symbolism is a mutual bond
> between distinctive elements, the combination of which is meaningful, and (2) the
> symbolic effect is a mutual bond between subjects who recognise each other as tied by
> a pact, an alliance (divine or human), a convention, or a law of fidelity. (Ortigues
> 1962: 61; my translation)

This helps us to understand how every community is constituted through
the process in which a *mutual recognition* is established through a symbolic
pact. The process of symbolisation marks, first of all, the entry into a realm of
public recognition, a community of sharing: a *koinonia*. This is the very
process of human development, as palaeontologists know very well (see
above, note 7). An implicit pact becomes the invisible base of all convention
and communication. This is why – following Benvéniste or Jakobson –
Ortigues presents this symbolic structure, which is immanent to language
itself, as the condition of the process of signification. There is indeed, in
language, an implicit, non-conscious level which is truly symbolic and composed of all the contrastive and differential elements (at the forefront of which
are the phonemes) which enable the very emergence of the sign. The horizontal relationship of interdependence between the differential elements
enables the vertical relationship of reference to a signified:

> Symbols are the founding elements of a language, considered in their interaction to one
> another as constitutive of a system of communication or alliance, a law of reciprocity
> between subjects. Whereas the sign is the union of a signifier and a signified, the
> symbol initiates a relation between a signifier and other signifiers. Whereas the sign
> points towards a signified belonging to a different order than the signifier, the symbol
> belongs to an order of signifying values which presupposes itself in its radical alterity
> to any given reality. (Ortigues 1962: 61; my translation)

> Language can only *speak about* (something) in as much as it has the internal structure
> of *speaking to* (someone). The sign *expresses*, but symbols constantly *testify* to the
> structure of language as such … The sign offers a meaning and presupposes a
> language. The symbol belongs to the genesis of this presupposition itself. (Ortigues
> 1962: 65; my translation)

It is from this point of view that one may understand symbolism as an
implicit pact and this in its essential relation to the structure of ceremonial gift
exchange construed as the founding act of mutual recognition, in other words

as *alliance*, the consented union of the same and the other. It is also on this point that we should take on board Lévi-Strauss's lesson. He saw that human society can only come into being through the global break that is the emergence of the symbolic order construed as a system of differential terms, which is the condition of any mutual recognition, of any articulated discourse, of any possibility to grasp an order in the world; one might say, of any possibility of having a world and not just an environment.

A first recapitulation is needed at this point. For Lévi-Strauss, the prohibition of incest institutes society simultaneously as the order of culture, as a system of differences (a set of terms and relations governed by rules) and as the realm of alliance. It is all of this, he believes, that makes up the *symbolic order*, and constitutes the advent of a truly human society. *This is also why he can speak of a symbolic origin of society.* This formulation is acceptable precisely in as much as it refers to the literal conception of the symbol as marking an implicit pact, a process of alliance, an acceptance of rules which transcend natural regulatory processes. The logic of the incest taboo teaches us that *human society emerges in the form of relationships of alliance.*

However, a major difficulty arises at this point. How can we articulate this concept of symbolism as alliance, this *sym-bolon* construed as pledge or pact (in the manner that the 'symbol of the Apostles' designates the Christian *Credo*), with what is commonly understood when one refers to the symbolic dimension of a gesture (for example, to salute), of an object (a cave painting or mask), of a place of worship (a temple) or a practice (such as a sacrifice)? This second use of the word has become prevalent and one wonders, therefore, how one may apply it to kinship systems, language, techniques and knowledge. In other words, it is as if from the moment that Lévi-Strauss interprets society as the order of culture, he also sees all of its activities and productions as symbolic. Does this not risk giving to the otherwise rigorously founded concept of symbolic order an excessively broad scope? It is all the more difficult to answer this question as the two uses of the concept of symbolism seem to have increasingly diverged over time.

The function of symbols and their effectiveness

One may find in Lévi-Strauss's works themselves the elements of a solution to the above difficulties; for he too uses the concept of symbolism in this second sense. This is exemplified in an essay, published in 1949 (1972b), entitled 'The Effectiveness of Symbols' (it is worth noting that it is contemporary with *The Elementary Structures of Kinship* (1949a; 1969a)). It is perhaps here that we will find the bridge we are looking for to link the two conceptions of symbolism outlined above. We will then have to ask ourselves whether this dimension of symbolism – its effectiveness – is maintained in the rest of Lévi-Strauss's works. We will find, surprisingly, that it is, but without Lévi-Strauss explicitly laying claim to it. Or at least, this is what perspectives from studies by other authors will show.

Symbolic effectiveness

In the text that bears this title (1972b), Lévi-Strauss does not give an explicit definition of symbolism. It is a concept whose meaning can be derived, as it were, from the examples he analyses. These relate to a ritual carried out by the Cuna Indians of Panama in which a shaman treats a woman undergoing a painful childbirth. The ritual is accompanied by an incantation which provides a dramatic representation of the patient's body and its organs, which are assimilated to various sites (paths, gorges, mountains). The ritual conjures up a whole emotional geography; the pain and the illness themselves are represented through intense images. A whole story unfolds in which the patient is made to participate mentally. Her body is turned into the site of a dramatic struggle between evil spirits and protecting spirits. The uterine world is represented as a stage inhabited by threatening animals that the ritual will expel; the body comes to host a whole cosmos. Each figure and each action is precisely described. In short, the patient is enticed into a mythical world and made to conceive of her body and what she feels as a network of places and figures. She is made to imagine a dramatic sequence which starts with the conception, is followed by the pregnancy and ends with the birth in progress, in which she participates along with her internal guests. It is the whole of this system of representation that may be called symbolic, i.e. the animals and characters whose expressions and actions are assimilated to the organs, feelings, states and actions of the patient.

How may one explain the *symbolic effectiveness* of the cure? It is situated simultaneously on two levels – that of the specific realm and functioning of its symbolism (which is different from the realm of the sign or that of ordinary language) and that of its social dimension (which it shares with language and sign systems in general).

With respect to the first level, Lévi-Strauss, in order to explain how organs and psychological states may be translated into animals and characters, invokes an '*inductive property*', by which formally homologous structures, built out of different materials at different levels of life – organic processes, unconscious mind, rational thought – are related to one another' (Lévi-Strauss 1972b: 201). This is indeed something very particular, specific to symbolism, which relies on the coalescence of a figure and a meaning, or rather on the fact that *the intelligible operations of symbolism are carried out directly on sensible elements*. These operations are carried out at a different level from articulated language and conscious discourse[9] and are precisely what

Lévi-Strauss calls *pensée sauvage* ('untamed' thinking, in the botanical sense of the term 'untamed').

But another aspect of the shamanic cure is just as important and probably explains its success, since the patient manages to overcome her pain and the birth takes place:

That the mythology of the Shaman does not correspond to an objective reality does not matter. The sick woman believes in the myth and belongs to a society which believes in it. The tutelary spirits and malevolent spirits, the supernatural monsters and magical animals, are all part of a coherent system on which the native conception of the universe is founded. The sick woman accepts these mythical beings or, more accurately, she has never questioned their existence. What she does not accept are the incoherent and arbitrary pains, which are an alien element in her system but which the shaman, calling upon myth, will re-integrate within a whole where everything is meaningful. (1963a: 97)

Here, Lévi-Strauss clearly indicates what he deems essential in this process: the individual cure consisted in conjuring up collective representations. The fact that the patient is made to take part in an internal dramatisation of the various figures evoked, according to known forms of narrative and representations, means that it is through an entire familiar social and cosmic world that she faces her ordeal; she projects her body into this world which, at the same time, is internalised by her. Symbolism only exists through this relation. In the end, if the shamanic cure has a symbolic effectiveness, it is through this integration of the individual psyche with representations which are provided by the group and therefore by a tradition. It is as though the illness consisted of a break with the immediate social world and that the first aim of the cure was to reintegrate the patient into her community. This occurs through the mediation of symbolic representations, not only because they have a social origin and form a 'coherent system', but also because the various stages of the cure and the evocations that accompany them consist in a very precise *ordering* of all the elements and figures evoked. 'Both antecedent and subsequent events are carefully related. [Indeed, the aim is to construct a systematic whole]' (1963a: 197).[10] Healing is deemed effective only if the result is apprehended as the recovery of a former state of equilibrium. It must therefore present the patient with 'a resolution, that is, a situation wherein all the protagonists have resumed their place and returned to an order which is no longer threatened' (1963a: 197).

To sum up, in this case symbolism seems to be an operation of figuration based on precise homologies between representations of the body and those of the world. The movement of this operation is construed as an inductive process, the result of which is the integration of the individual into an order of representations both cosmic and social. In other words, what emerges here is the anticipated articulation of symbolic *order* and symbolic *function*. It is because the group exists (is instituted) in and through symbolism that the narratives, images and generally the representations of individuals are always already part of it. The ritual is effective because it unifies the two levels. However, in order to fully grasp this, we must understand the fundamental difference between symbol and sign and spell out the full significance of the notion of effectiveness, which in this chapter has only been hinted at so far.

Symbol and sign

To talk, as Lévi-Strauss does, of a symbolic *effectiveness*, presupposes another better-known and more widely accepted form of effectiveness: technical effectiveness. To join the term *effective* to the adjective *symbolic* is to risk creating something like an oxymoron, since usually the realm of the symbol is opposed to that of reality (as, for example, when one qualifies an action or presence as being 'purely symbolic'). This weak conception seems to contradict what we have just established about the notion of *symbolic order*. We are therefore required to pursue the definition further. This may be done by starting with the notion of symbol such as it is defined in opposition to that of the sign. Here is how Ducrot and Todorov distinguish these two notions:

The practical test that allows us to distinguish between a sign and a symbol is the examination of the two related elements. In the sign, these elements are necessarily different in nature; in the symbol, as we have just seen, they must be homogeneous. This opposition sheds light on the problem of the arbitrary aspect of the sign, a problem brought back into focus in linguistics by Saussure. The relation between a signifier and a signified is necessarily unmotivated; the two are different in nature, and it is unthinkable that a graphic or phonic sequence should resemble a meaning. At the same time, this relation is *necessary* in that the signified cannot exist without the signifier, and vice versa. On the other hand, in the symbol, the relation between symbolizer and symbolized is unnecessary (or arbitrary), since the symbolizer and the symbolized (the signified *flame* and *love*) sometimes exist independently of each other; for this reason, the relation cannot be other than motivated, since if it were not motivated, nothing would compel its establishment. These motivations are customarily classified in two major groups drawn from the psychological classification of associations: resemblance and contiguity. (Ducrot and Todorov 1994: 102)

Unlike the sign, the symbol implies a connivance and even coalescence between the physical medium of expression and the thing evoked. However, like the sign, it belongs to the realm of representation: neither symbols nor signs are 'natural', both require the emergence of another plane, different from the world as it is (even though the elements of which they are made are taken from this world) and therefore separate from it, although separate in different ways. It is this difference between symbols and signs that we need to evaluate. But, for now, this reminder helps us to understand the very concept of symbolic effectiveness. For, the relationship of contiguity that connects form and content in the symbol allows us to understand the *inductive process* which associates mental representations with physical states, as seen in the Cuna cure.

However, the symbol in the singular form is, in fact, nothing more than an abstraction required for the purposes of analysis. No symbol exists in isolation. Symbols always belong to symbolic systems and this on two different levels. The first, which may be qualified as empirical (or encyclopaedic), is that of various cultural systems; the symbolic elements are circumscribed and attributed value through specific interplays of relationships, because they are extracted from a particular environment (a climate, fauna, landscape, flora, techniques, links with other cultures). The second, which is a theoretical or formal level, pertains to the very status of symbolism or of the *symbolic function*, which is to say its institutionalised (in the sense of non-natural) and conventional (in the sense of social reality) character. It is clearly this second level that was privileged by Lévi-Strauss (and, in his wake, Lacan and many others). How may we understand this systematicity without losing sight of the other dimension of symbolism – the effectiveness of the inductive process? In what sense are these two aspects inevitably linked?

Operating schemas

To answer these questions we have to try and understand more precisely the notion of *symbolic effectiveness*. After this initial analysis, the question needs to be reformulated as follows: how can a symbolic system, construed as an implicit pact and a system of reciprocity, also be *effective*? Or rather, how and why must it be effective in order to be symbolic? How must we understand the proposition that the *sign expresses* while the *symbol operates*? No one has answered this question better than Dan Sperber in *Rethinking Symbolism* (1975). His arguments will prove invaluable since they will allow us to understand why and how the use of the musical model in the analysis of myths constitutes Lévi-Strauss's last and most complete elaboration of the question of symbolism even though, paradoxically, this was not made explicit.

Sperber's main argument is summed up in the following claim: 'Symbols are not signs. They are not paired with their interpretations in a code structure. Their interpretations are not meanings' (Sperber 1975: 85). According to him, the mistake of semiologists was to consider symbolic phenomena as if they constituted signs coupled with their meanings. They therefore sought out the message signs held. This meant deciphering symbols while ignoring the specificity of symbolism and leaving the following obvious question unanswered: why does symbolism exist if it must be reduced to something else? Lévi-Strauss seems to have clearly anticipated this problem and his entire theoretical approach seeks to avoid this simplification. Because, in the same way that there is an intelligibility immanent in kinship systems and a classificatory logic operating within the differences of the sensible universe, there is also a thinking process displayed in the very elements and processes of rituals. One must bring to light its elaborations and operations and not reduce them to a signified (meaning) introduced by an external discourse.

Sperber asks the following: if a symbolic device is not a system of signs and does not attempt to formulate a meaning, what is it? He answers, 'Symbolism conceived in this way is not a means of encoding information, but a means of organizing it' (1975: 70). Elements appear as part of systems of homology, symmetry, oppositions, inversions and other logical relations. These operations do not need to be subjected to a search for meaning; thus 'a symbolic opposition must not be replaced by an interpretation, but placed in an organization of which it constitutes a crucial element' (1975: 70). Thus, symbolism is foremost a system whose purpose is to carry out certain operations, it is a tool for creating order. One does not ask what an instrument means but what it is used for, what it enables us to produce. Symbolism produces an order in a set of sensible elements, an order which is intelligible thanks to the homologies, oppositions, inversions, symmetries which it brings to light, interconnects or sometimes institutes. This is to a certain extent what Lévi-Strauss calls 'untamed thinking' (*pensée sauvage*). Such is the use of natural species in the establishment of a system of differentiations in human society, what has been named 'totemism' (1969e); this is also the case of rituals which do not attempt to say something, but to produce, maintain or modify the course of things; finally this is – we shall come to this below – the case of the sequences and levels of a group of mythical tales which do not attempt to express the world but to organise it.[11] Confronted with symbolic phenomena, the traditional questions put forward by semiology (and by hermeneutics) amounted to asking: what does it mean? In short: what is the message of this code? However, the problem is not to establish what symbols mean, but rather to understand how they function, what order they construct, what transformation they accomplish, what world they create.

Mythical narratives

Therefore, there is indeed in Lévi-Strauss another way of thinking the question of symbolism; but it is not explicitly formulated as for him it seems quite obvious; it is the very air his work breathes. One may find an indirect presentation of it in the 'Overture' to the first volume of the *Mythologiques* (*The Raw and the Cooked*, 1964a; 1969d) and in the 'Finale' of the last (*The*

Naked Man, 1971a; 1981). Indeed, according to the conception upheld by Lévi-Strauss since 1950, myths or rather sets of mythical narratives, like all social productions, are symbolic systems. Right from his early writings, Lévi-Strauss subjects these narratives to a structural analysis inspired by linguistics (more specifically, phonology), as he had succeeded in doing with kinship systems. This is the case of the inaugural text published in 1955, 'The Structural Study of Myth' (1955e), or of that of 1960, 'The Story of Asdiwal'. It is still this model that Lévi-Strauss uses in 1962 in *Totemism Today* (1962a) and in *The Savage Mind*. *The Raw and the Cooked*, however, reveals not only an implicit doubt about the limits of the uses of the linguistic model but also a striking attempt to get beyond it, or at least to include it in a new approach. This attempt will be confirmed in the last volume of the *Mythologiques*. Indeed, Lévi-Strauss calls upon *music* (in other words, an *art form* and not a scientific discipline) to provide him at once with a model of exposition and a model of interpretation. On the one hand – at the level of exposition – this involves a vertical reading of myths, focused on their different 'codes', as if they were the superposed staves of a musical score. These 'codes' consist of the various semantic layers of the narrative, as revealed by the astronomical, culinary, matrimonial, technical, zoological and other references. But on the other hand – at the level of interpretation – we are told that myths, like music, cannot be transposed into something else; a myth is elucidated through its narrative variations, just as a musical theme is *interpreted* through its development: 'The myths are only translatable into each other in the same way as a melody is only translatable into another which retains a relationship of homology with it' (1981: 646). Myths and music cannot be reduced to a meaning, they must be received at their own level of functioning, that of the operations induced by their form. This is why the mythographer must limit him- or herself to an exposition which reveals and activates the operations allowed by a mythical schema, like a conductor reads a score and then directs its performance. The aim is therefore not to decipher the meaning of narratives but to understand how they order a world which thereby becomes meaningful. Lévi-Strauss says this explicitly with regard to two central figures of the Amerindian narratives he studies: 'Of the sun and the moon, the same thing can be said as of the countless natural beings mythically manipulated: Mythical thought does not seek to give them a meaning – [it acquires a meaning through them]' (1978b: 221; amended translation). In other words, what mythical thought designates is itself; and in so doing it constructs an order of the world, through its symbols, the tools it uses to carry out its operations.

This is why the reader is also invited to let him- or herself be 'carried toward that music which is to be found in myth' (1969a: 32). This is not a mere metaphor but a formula which Lévi-Strauss uses as the most appropriate means of indicating what his linguistic and semiological conceptions of myths did not allow him to explicitly formulate but which he had, however, so well perceived in his texts on shamanism: the interplay of mythological narratives operates as a form of symbolism; like all symbolism it is above all an inductive process; the relations between the symbolic elements – or rather the symbolic sets – are relations of *transformation*. If the relations between myths are relations of transformation, this means that they are linked like the variants of a single schema, just as a symbolic phenomenon can only be affected by another of the same order. Narratives are not objects to be interpreted but processes to be grasped and developed in the same way that a musical variation 'translates' a theme or a sequence into sound patterns according to certain rules. These variations do not aim to express something else but to complete or extend an operation. Narratives that seem absurd when discussed in terms of their meaning become coherent when discussed in terms of the operations that they perform. Therefore, mythical thought appears to be the most accomplished manifestation of an 'untamed' mode of thought itself construed as the expression of an intelligibility formulated in and through the very elements of the sensible world (figures, sensations, beings, objects).

Conclusion

This elucidation of symbolism, construed as the means of carrying out an operation, is crucial because it allows us to understand the following: a community – a given culture – comes into being through a system of mutual recognition, an implicit symbolic pact by which a social order and an order of the world are instituted. What secures the strength of this pact, and the stability of the social ties it creates, is that this symbolic order is 'effective', in the sense defined in what precedes. It draws us into its networks and its processes; this is its *function* and without it there would be no community and no society in general. This is why it operates neither at the level of conscious will, nor even that of unconscious affects, but at the level of those instruments of figuration – symbols – which, at the same time as they are articulated to one another, bind us together. They ensure that affects constitute effective devices. This is also why symbolisms (and some symbols more than others) have a long memory; our cultures remember them beyond changes of time and place. A good example of this is given by Georges Dumézil, who has convincingly demonstrated that the same three symbolic functions have existed for centuries in all Indo-European cultures although they have taken on subtly different forms: a martial or ruling function, a sacerdotal or spiritual function and a procreative function associated with fertility. Georges Duby traces this model throughout the European Middle Ages – *bellatores*, *oratores*, *laboratories*. It still defined the three orders of society on the eve of the

French Revolution. Beyond or beneath these great institutional structures many other symbolisms shape everyday practices, ways of living together which are passed on from generation to generation. Our languages bear witness to them and remember them. As do, beyond language, our bodies.

Translated by Yves Gilonne; revised by Jean Louis Morhange.

NOTES

1. See André Leroi-Gourhan 1993: chaps. 5, 10, 13; Emmanuel Anati 1995: chaps. 12, 13; Jacques Cauvin 2000: chaps. 3, 7, 11; Ian Tattersall 2004: chap. 5.
2. 'In this way, every negative stipulation of the prohibition has its positive counterpart ... Like exogamy, which is its widened social application, the prohibition of incest is a rule of reciprocity. The woman whom one does not take, and whom one may not take, is, for that very reason, offered up. To whom is she offered? Sometimes to a group defined by institutions, and sometimes to an indeterminate and ever-open collectivity limited only by the exclusion of near relatives, such as in our society' (Lévi-Strauss 1969a: 51).
3. Marcel Mauss 2002.
4. On this key concept see Bruno Karsenti 1997.
5. 'It is a question of a universal mode of culture, although not everywhere equally developed' (Lévi-Strauss 1969a: 53).
6. See Françoise Héritier 1982: 152–79.
7. Cf. Jane Goodall 1986; F. B. M. De Waal 1994; K. A. Bard and S. T. Parker (eds.) 1996; Hans Kummer 1993; De Waal (ed.) 2001.
8. I develop this argumentation in a more detailed version in Hénaff 2002: chap. 4; cf. Marcel Hénaff, 'Gift, Exchange, Play, and Deception', in C. Gerschlager. 2005.
9. Psychoanalysis understands this power of symbolism very well since what the patient says, by virtue of his/her free associations and above all the transference, partakes in this inductive process which is very different from conscious knowledge (which acts more like a screen).
10. The second of these two sentences (in square brackets) has been left out from the English translation.
11. This is above all true of 'myths' in oral traditions. The question is totally different with regard to mythologies which have been reworked by the written tradition.

REFERENCES

Anati, Emmanuel 1995. *La Religion des origines*. Paris: Bayard.
Bard, K. A. and S. T. Parker (eds.) 1996. *Reaching into Thought: The Minds of the Great Apes*. Cambridge: Cambridge University Press.
Cauvin, Jacques 2000. *The Birth of Gods and the Origin of Agriculture*. Translated by Trevor Watkins. Cambridge: Cambridge University Press..
Duby, Georges 1982. *The Three Orders: Feudal Society Imagined*. Translated by Arthur Goldhammer. Chicago: University of Chicago Press.

Levi-Strauss and the question of symbolism

Ducrot, Oswald and Tzvetan Todorov 1994. *Encyclopedic Dictionary of the Sciences of Language*. Translated by Catherine Porter. Baltimore: Johns Hopkins University Press.

Dumézil, Georges 1941. *Jupiter, Mars, Quirinius. Essai sur la conception indo-européenne de la société*. Paris: Gallimard.

1958. *L'Idéologie tripartite des Indos-Européens*. Bruxelles: Latomus.

Goodall, Jane 1986. *The Chimpanzees of Gombe: Patterns of Behavior*. Cambridge, MA: Harvard University Press.

Hénaff, Marcel 1998. *Claude Lévi-Strauss and the Making of Structural Anthropology*. Translated by Mary Baker. Minneapolis, MN: University of Minnesota Press.

2002. *Le Prix de la vérité. Le don, l'argent, la philosophie*. Paris: Seuil.

2005. 'Gift, Exchange, Play, and Deception', in C. Gerschlager (ed.), *Deception in Markets*. London: Palgrave Macmillan.

Héritier, Françoise 1982. 'The Symbolics of Incest and its Prohibition', in Michel Izard and Pierre Smith (eds.).

Izard, Michel and Pierre Smith (eds.) 1982. *Between Belief and Transgression: Structuralist Essays in Religion, History and Myth*. Translated by John Leavitt. Chicago: University of Chicago Press.

Karsenti, Bruno 1997. *L'Homme total, sociologie, anthropologie et philosophie chez Marcel Mauss*. Paris: Presses Universitaires de France.

Kummer, Hans 1993. *Vie de singes: moeurs et structures sociales des babouins hamadryas*. Paris: Odile Jacob.

Leroi-Gourhan, André 1993. *Gesture and Speech*. Translated by Anna Bostock Berger. Cambridge, MA: MIT Press.

Mauss, Marcel 2002. *The Gift: The Form and Reason for Exchange in Archaic Societies*. Translated by W. D. Halls. London: Routledge.

Needham, R. (ed.) 1971. *Rethinking Kinship and Marriage*. London: Tavistock.

Ortigues, Edmond 1962. *Le Discours et le symbole*. Paris: Aubier.

Roudinesco, E. and Michel Plon 1997. *Dictionnaire de la psychanalyse*. Paris: Fayard.

Sperber, Dan 1975. *Rethinking Symbolism*. Translated by A. L. Morton. Cambridge: Cambridge University Press.

Tattersall, Ian 2004. *Becoming Human*. Oxford: Oxford University Press.

De Waal, F. B. M. 1994. *La Politique du chimpanzé*. Paris: Odile Jacob.

De Waal, F. B. M. (ed.) 2001. *Tree of Origin: What Primate Behaviour Can Tell Us about Human Social Evolution*. London and Cambridge, MA: Harvard University Press.

Wendy Doniger

The apparent method

Reductionism and science

Claude Lévi-Strauss first expounded the basic tenets of structural anthropology in *Structural Anthropology* (1958a; 1963a). Many scholars of myth accuse Lévi-Strauss of being coldly scientific, probably because he has insisted that the logical patterns of myths can be expressed in a series of mathematical formulas, particularly what he calls the 'canonical formula' (which has the form a: b :: c : a^{-1}), geometrical abstractions that enable him ultimately to distil a myth into an algebraic formula, expressing a homology between two sets of relations.[1] It is this sort of thing that has driven Clifford Geertz, for instance, to write of the 'extraordinary air of abstracted self-containment' in Lévi-Strauss's work. He goes on to say:

'Aloof, closed, cold, airless, cerebral' – all the epithets that collect around any sort of literary absolutism collect around it. Neither picturing lives nor evoking them, neither interpreting them nor explaining them, but rather arranging and rearranging the materials the lives have somehow left behind into formal systems of correspondences – his books seem to exist behind glass, self-sealing discourses into which jaguars, semen, and rotting meat are admitted to become oppositions, inversions, isomorphism. (Geertz 1995: 48)

This is unfair. Lévi-Strauss has always been interested in the messiest, juiciest aspects of human culture – eating and killing and marrying. Is it just that mythology *is* full of those things, and Lévi-Strauss knows it (i.e. that mythology has a dirty mind)? Or is that he has selected myths that have dirty minds? Or that he imposes his own dirty mind upon the myths that he selects – myths about, as Geertz admits, 'jaguars, semen, and rotting meat'? Hard to say; but the end result is a cold method that analyses the hot content of myths. Yet, he himself insists that he is only revealing structures. What is he repressing, that he keeps insisting he is just interested in the structures (just the facts, ma'am)?

The idea that the study of mythology is a scientific enterprise has haunted and perverted this discipline from F. Max Müller (*Lectures on the Science of*

Language) to C. G. Jung (*Essays on a Science of Mythology*). And the idea that Lévi-Strauss is a wannabe scientist seems to be confirmed by the subtitle of his great multivolume work, *Introduction to a Science of Mythology* (1969d; 1970; 1973b; 1973d; 1978c; 1978d; 1981). Lévi-Strauss later claimed, not without anger, that his American publisher gave his work this title – perhaps to echo Müller and Jung – without his knowledge;[2] his own title, *Mythologiques*, has connotations of art, not of science. Yet, he does insist that he is doing science, in this remarkable passage:

I am convinced that the number of these systems is not unlimited and that human beings (at play, in their dreams, or in moments of delusion) never create *absolutely*; all they can do is to choose certain combinations from a repertory of ideas which it should be possible to reconstitute. For this one must make an inventory of all the customs which have been observed by oneself or others, the customs pictured in mythology, the customs invoked by both children and grown-ups in their games. The dreams of individuals, whether healthy or sick, should also be taken into account. With all this one could eventually establish a sort of periodical chart of chemical elements analogous to that devised by Mendelier. In this, all customs, whether real or merely possible, would be grouped by families and all that would remain for us to do would be to recognize those which societies had, in point of fact, adopted. (Lévi-Strauss 1967d: 178)

In this approach, the component parts of the myth are derived from thick description and then arranged 'scientifically'. The sum total of human thought can be analysed as precisely as the compounds formed from the elements. But here, more than anywhere, Lévi-Strauss is passionate, irrational, megalomaniac. The precision and scope of this periodic table is insanely ambitious (the elements of myth cannot be pinned down like elements and compounds), but it is also even theoretically inane. Listing all the theoretically possible customs and then selecting the ones that actually occur is, I think, a method analogous (!) to the method of catching lions in the old joke: 'Catch two lions and let one go.'

Minimal and other pairs, or, binary oppositions

Myth, Lévi-Strauss argues, is a form of language, and language itself predisposes us to attempt to understand ourselves and our world by superimposing dialectics or dichotomies upon data that may not be binary at all. And underneath language lies the binary nature of the brain itself, which cooks the raw material of human experience on dualistic griddles. Right and left, good and evil, life and death – these are inevitable dichotomies produced by the brain that has two lobes and controls two eyes, two hands. We are split creatures literally by nature, and we process experience like a simple digital machine. Our common sense is binary; the simplest and most efficient way to process experience seems to be by dividing it in half, and then to divide the halves in half, reformulating every question so that there are only two possible answers to it – yes or no. In *Structural Anthropology* (1967c), as well as in subsequent works, Lévi-Strauss asserted that all mythology is dialectic in its attempt to make cognitive sense out of the chaotic data provided by nature, and that this attempt inevitably traps the human imagination in a web of dualisms: each dualism (such as male/female) produces a tension that seems to be resolved by the use of a mediating term (such as androgyny), but then that new term turns out to be one half of a new dualism (such as androgyny/ sexlessness) *ad infinitum*. The dyad of 'integrated' and 'split' is itself a basic contrasting unit in mythology; that is, any split image may be used to form one half of a pair, the other half being the integrated image of which the half is the dissection. The question of whether or not to split something in half may be answered by yes or no. (Most cultures, but not all, have usually answered yes to this question.) On this level, the structure *is* the meaning; the medium is the message.

Yuri Lotman has applied a structural theory (more precisely, a semiotic theory of transformational grammar) to literary texts. He points out that 'a mythological text, because of its exceptional capacity for topological transformation, can boldly make assumptions about the identity and similarity of things which we would be hard pushed to do.' He argues that the need to compress a cyclic view of time and the universe into the linear form of a narrative is the reason why mythological texts abound with 'certain characters identical with each other' (Lotman 1990: 152). Lévi-Strauss's method of analysis, his canonical formula (a: b :: c : a^{-1}), relates what is the same (the two sets of parallel terms: a and c, and b and a^{-1}) to what is different, more specifically, to what is opposed or inverted (the two sets of compared terms: a and b, and c and a^{-1}). To consider multiple variants simultaneously (which is the genius of the structural method), one must choose variants on the basis of their similarity; but to determine the significant oppositions in the myth, one must isolate factors of difference. These factors are defined by means of what linguists call minimal pairs, two terms that change the meaning when they replace one another in the same situation, like *c* and *h* in 'cat' and 'hat'. Minimal pairs are defined by distinctive features. Lévi-Strauss named these atomic elements of myth 'mythemes', in response to the 'phonemes' of his colleague, the linguist Roman Jakobson – the atomic building blocks of meaningful sounds that make up words that are as pure, and as *given*, as the elements of the periodic table. These dyadic structures contribute to a general dichotomisation of thought, and these dichotomies often attract to themselves polarised moral judgements.

One aspect of this polarisation is the prevalence of inversion, a process that Freud long ago taught us, and Lévi-Strauss, to recognise as an intrinsic quality of myth. If a man kills his son, in one variant, the theme might be inverted so that the son kills his father (Ramanujan 1984), in another, through inversion. Geertz, as we have seen, mocked Lévi-Strauss for his inversions, but Lévi-Strauss defended them in, as usual, scientific terms:

Similar inversions occur in optics. An image can be seen in full detail when observed through any adequately large aperture. But as the aperture is narrowed the image becomes blurred and difficult to see. When, however, the aperture is further reduced to a pinpoint, that is to say, when *communication* is about to vanish, the image is inverted and becomes clear again. This experiment is used in schools to demonstrate the propagation of light in straight lines, or in other words to prove that rays of light are not transmitted at random, but within the limits of a structural field ... The field of mythical thought, too, is structured. (Lévi-Strauss 1967e: 42)

One such inversion is precisely the ability of 'the field of mythical thought' to translate a microscopic image into a telescopic image, to move us from the infinitely small to the infinitely large. The myths suggest that, if your microscope is powerful enough, it turns into a telescope, that things really deep down and really far away become one another. Everything has an opposite, and many things become their opposites.

Shoring up the method: jumping off the structuralist bus

Thomas Laqueur remarks, 'If structuralism has taught us anything it is that humans impose their sense of opposition onto a world of continuous shades of difference and similarity' (1990: 19). Yet, the stories retain those continuous shades. Rather than a neat grid, therefore, we would do better to attempt to construct another continuum such as Edmund Leach proposed in his modification of Lévi-Strauss's starkly polarised oppositions: 'We need to consider not merely that things in the world can be classified as sacred and not sacred, but also as more sacred and less sacred. So also in social classifications it is not sufficient to have a discrimination me/it, we/they; we also need a graduated scale close/far, more like me/less like me' (Leach 1979: 166).[3] Or we might construct a Venn diagram of interlocking motifs, in which each variant has some of the themes, but not all, and each arranges them differently, and, more important, interprets them differently.

  Structuralism is a great way to sort out the pieces, the distinctive features, of a myth. Structuralism isolates the themes in a myth; it says, this *is*. But the myth is not a structure; it is a narrative; the myth adds to the structures speculations about the sequence of events, about causation; it says, this happens *because*. Structuralism does not arrange the pieces chronologically or sequentially or causally. The narrative does, and when it changes the arrangement, it changes the point of the story. The myth does not settle for elementary structures; it modifies them and qualifies them in many different ways, and often even rejects them. Mythemes do not behave like phonemes; the rules of language cannot simply be superimposed upon myths, because myth involves subjective structures (aesthetic, political, social) that do not complicate analyses of language.

If a reader of Lévi-Strauss is foolish enough to seek the punch line, to cut to the chase, to turn to the end of the mystery to find out who did it, then that reader is likely to be disappointed. The formula that Lévi-Strauss often provides at the end, holding it up proudly for us to see, like a cat that brings its master a half-masticated mouse, is anti-climactic; often it bleeds the myth of all of its meanings. But before he gets to that end, Lévi-Strauss reveals to us more complex levels of meaning. He tells the stories, and tells about the stories, and suggests many rich patterns of interpretation before he boils it all down to a set of logical symbols. The trick is to jettison Lévi-Strauss right before the moment when he finally deconstructs himself. It is a point that is hard to gauge, and calls to mind the story of the woman on the bus who, when asked by a stranger about a particular stop, advised him, 'Just watch me and get off one stop before I do.' We must jump off Lévi-Strauss's bus one stop before he does. In order to remain truly engaged with our texts, we must wallow in the mess for a while before the structuralists clean it up for us. We must not hasten too quickly to the ultimate reduction; we must linger in the texts.

For, once we have jumped off the structuralist bus, we are likely to find that we are not there yet. We have to get on another bus (political, theological, psychological), or several buses. We need a lot of transfers on the mythic journey. At the beginning stage of the analysis, it is enough to identify certain unifying structures. Later, when we begin to search for the meanings of the structures, and to locate those meanings in particular historical situations, we must venture into the symbolic territory of Mircea Eliade and beyond it into the land of Freud, and Mary Douglas, and many others. But, if one knows what pocket to look in for those transfers, Lévi-Strauss provides them, too. Structuralism is, like myth itself, a neutral construct that could, theoretically, be used to ask any of a number of questions, to address any of a number of problems. Ivan Strenski insists that, in a structural study, 'Myths reveal no religious truths and deploy no supernatural power' (Strenski 1987: 165). I would debate this. The neutral structures are not dependent on religious thought as they are in, say, an Eliadean analysis, but they are open to it at any point. Lévi-Strauss includes the cosmological level in many of his analyses, and we can use other sorts of ideas to flesh it out (as he does not), once we have used the structural method to isolate the structures. Since Lévi-Strauss neither privileges nor excludes religious or political questions in myths, in incorporating such questions into a structural analysis, we would be staying on the structuralist bus after Lévi-Strauss gets off.

If we need a form of post-post-colonialism, surely we also need a form of post-post-structuralism. David Tracy has noted the ways in which the flaws of structuralism can be obviated by other kinds of awareness:

It may well be true that Lévi-Strauss' structuralist methods are sometimes entangled with the bleak beauty of a despairing structuralist ideology, that Foucault's geneal-ogical method is often entwined with a bitter polemic against any form of humanism, that Barthes' semiotic method sometimes seems inseparable from a deliberate, if vitalizing, critical perverseness, that Derrida's deconstructionist methods seem to need the aid of *some* determinate meanings as they spill us and all our classic texts into his vitalizing abyss of indeterminacy. Yet all these ideologies possess, after all, their own truth: a suspicion of the illusions, the alienation, often the death and slackness of all self-congratulatory humanisms. Moreover, the ideologies are not intrinsic to the methods of structuralist, semiotic or deconstructionist explanations. The methods – as methods of explanation – stand on their own either to develop and expand our original understanding or to confront and challenge it at the root. (Tracy 1981: 118)

The trick is to apply the methods without the ideologies, indeed to apply the methods in conjunction with other methods (instead of ideologies).

The actual method

Splitting hares

What answers do we get if we ask structuralist questions of myths? How does the method work out in actual practice? Here is an example. Lévi-Strauss retells a group of stories told among several North and South American tribes: the Tupinambas, the ancient coastal Indians of Brazil (recorded by the French monk André Thevet in the sixteenth century), the Kootenay and the Salish (1995d: 29).

A woman was going to meet the god who would be her husband, and while on her way the Trickster intervenes and makes her believe that *he* is the god; so, she conceives from the Trickster. When she later finds the legitimate husband-to-be, she conceives from him also and later gives birth to twins. And since these false twins had different fathers, they have antithetical features: one is brave, the other a coward; one is the protector of the Indians, the other of the white people . . .

Among the Kootenay, who live in the Rocky Mountains, there is only one fecundation which has as a consequence the birth of twins, who later on become, one the sun, and the other the moon. And, among some other Indians of British Columbia of the Salish linguistic stock – the Thompson Indians and the Okanagan – there are two sisters who are tricked by apparently two distinct individuals, and they give birth, each one to a son . . .

There are two sisters who are travelling in order to find, each one, a husband. They were told by a grandmother that they would recognise their husbands by such and such characteristics, and they are then each deluded by the Tricksters they meet on their way into believing that they are the husband whom each is supposed to marry. They spend the night with him, and each of the women will later give birth to a son.

Now, after this unfortunate night spent in the hut of the Trickster, the elder sister leaves her younger sister and goes visiting her grandmother, who is a mountain goat and also a kind of magician; for she knows in advance that her granddaughter is coming, and she sends the hare to welcome her on the road. The hare hides under a log which has fallen in the middle of the road, and when the girl lifts her leg to cross the log, the hare can have a look at her genital parts and make a very inappropriate joke. The girl is furious, and strikes him with her cane and splits his nose.

A series of sexual deceptions results in the birth of twins to two different fathers. But the last episode takes a different turn, ending in a series of splittings – the separation of the two sisters, of the legs of the older sister, and of the nose of the hare. The violent splittings in the final episode are a displaced reaction to the sexual deceptions which are, themselves, made possible by visual splittings, doubles of identity.

Lévi-Strauss's gloss of this story suggests some of the structural aspects of splitting: 'The elder sister starts to split the body of the animal; if this split were carried out to the end – if it did not stop at the nose but continued through the body and to the tail – she would turn an individual into twins, that is, two individuals which are exactly similar or identical because they are both a part of a whole' (1995d: 29–30). 'Exactly similar or identical' twins are the appropriate product of a sexual act brought about by one individual pretending to be 'exactly similar or identical' to another; and the hare (a trickster figure) is split to compensate for the doubling of the sexual trickster.

Bricolage and mythemes

What does structuralism tell us about myths and how to analyse them? These are closely related questions, for the method mirrors the making. Structuralism gives us a pretty good idea of how myths are made. If you take an early story (more precisely, a story that was recorded early, since no one knows when it was first told) and compare it with later tellings, it is as if the first story was dropped and broken into pieces, and then put together differently – not wrongly, just differently. The broken pieces are the atomic units of a myth, what Lévi-Strauss called 'mythemes'.

In the ecology of narratives, recycling is a very old process indeed. Myths, like all things in constant use, get broken and fixed again, lost and found, and the one who finds them and fixes them is what Lévi-Strauss calls a *bricoleur* – a term he borrowed from the French term for the handyman whom the British used to call a 'rag-and-bones man' (Jacob 1977), who makes new things out of broken pieces of the old. The rags and bones of the stories, the recycled pieces, are the mythemes (Doniger 1998), made in what William Butler Yeats (in 'The Circus Animals') called 'the foul rag and bones shop of the heart'. Scholars of myth now call the process of recycling these inherited mythic themes *bricolage* (a term that Lévi-Strauss made famous, even in English-speaking circles); the myth-maker's toolbox consists of fragments of old stories that can be recycled in new stories (Doniger 1998: 75–9; 138–45). Storytellers can build a potentially infinite number of stories by rearranging a limited number of known mythic themes. Each culture chooses the scraps that it wants to keep; some have proved more recyclable than others.

Each telling of a myth draws upon a network of these rags and bones, a kind of Erector-set of prefabricated pieces, an identikit with which to construct all the faces of a myth. (A colleague of mine once told his under-graduate class that the *Odyssey* was like the Parts Department of Western literature.[4]) Many motifs flow together to make a new story, like the flotilla that goes to Dunkirk in the film of *Mrs. Miniver*: little streams of little boats float silently together, their ranks swelling as they join finally in the broad Thames and the even broader Channel, what Hindus call the Ocean of the Rivers of Story.[5] Each piece has its own previous life history and brings its own barnacles into the story. And there are several good reasons to call the ragbag of themes 'the same' even when it undergoes major transformations in different cultures, or in different periods or sectors of the same culture.

What use is such a grid of themes? It summarises the structure of many variants, from different times and places, and allows us to argue that they are, in some sense, 'the same'. It shows us how a few variables, in permutation, can account for the rough outlines of the thousands of variants in our vast corpus. It enables us to identify stories within our corpus and to see their structural patterns. It alerts us to things to look for in each story; it helps us to see the connections, to determine degrees of affinity between the structures of variants. It makes it possible to trace the recurrent themes through the corpus of myths without discussing each theme every time it occurs. And it helps us to see what is missing from some variants. A comprehensive list shows us all the symmetrical slots of possibility for the themes, but the actual examples of the stories show that some combinations do not seem to occur. Once we have seen this structure, we may use other methods to enquire after the reasons for these lacunae.

The structural method allows us to make an inventory of the network of dialectical themes that make up a corpus of myths, and to map them simul-taneously in two dimensions, vertically within a text and horizontally through several different texts (Doniger 1998: 88–94). People do not often literally talk at the same time in myths, but their various ideas, their symbols, their agendas are running at the same time, as Lévi-Strauss has pointed out: one cannot understand myth as a continuous sequence, but only like a musical score, reading all the lines simultaneously (1995d: 44–54). It should not be surprising to learn that Lévi-Strauss uses Wagner as his primary example of the confluence of opera and myth, since Wagner, the most mythical of all opera composers, invented leitmotifs, themes that function precisely like Lévi-Strauss's 'mythemes', each with its own significance; when they are combined, their various symbolic values are expressed simultaneously.

Lévi-Strauss has characterised the structuralist approach as nothing but 'the quest for the invariant, or for the invariant elements among superficial differences' (1995d: 8). Yet, if we take a closer look at his system, the mythemes do allow for difference as well as sameness. We can structure competing voices as opposed mythemes (Lévi-Strauss does not, but one could), and if we attempt to structure more than two competing voices, we find ourselves once again on a continuum rather than a dialectical grid, which is just where we need to be. The structural mythemes are there, all right, but they must be formulated in such a way that they can be emplotted, not graphed.

But the network of interlacing dichotomies cannot be neatly laid out as a structuralist might wish them to be and paired up neatly like children in the buddy system: nature/culture, man/woman, permitted/forbidden, good/evil, light/dark, integrated/split, known/unknown, etc. The binary categories in these stories tend to generate potentially infinite intermediary subcategories, and different cultures find different ways of blurring the lines between such Western categories as mind and body. Moreover, through the very nature of the dialectic, the splitting that seems to solve the original problem of conflict or ambivalence is in itself a source of new anxiety. The solution to the problem of doubling is a new integration, with new tensions. Thus, the mytheme of male *or* female may yield a new, paradoxical mytheme of male *and* female, and we are off and running on a new and differently conflicted path of androgyny and bisexuality.

The mythemes, moreover, can be arranged in any order, thereby excluding both cause and effect and value judgements. But could there not be other mythemes to include some of what the story mythemes by definition exclude? Why could domination and subversion not be mythemes? And why could causation not be a mytheme, and chronology, time, history? As we will soon see, Lévi-Strauss does, in effect, create a causal, historical mytheme in *The Story of Lynx*. Would this not be one way to take structuralism further than most card-carrying structuralists want to go, into political, theological, ethical territories? Is God a mytheme? For a structuralist, the great existential question would be, Is there a Mytheme?

Repetition and paradox

Films, too, particularly, lowbrow popular movies, B-movies (or even B-minus movies), are constructed, and reconstructed, through *bricolage*. Films provide a rich compost for myths to grow in; they are the *reductio ad absurdum* of many myths, for Hollywood is as much a myth factory as it is a dream factory. To make money, film-makers take what works and copy it, from gross plots and titles (such as the various remakes of *The Prisoner of Zenda*) right down to names of characters and stunning camera angles; motifs circulate and recirculate in Hollywood much as they do in the medieval cycles or in a Wagnerian opera. What we call mythemes when they occur in myths we call clichés when they occur in B-movies; we might better call them cinememes, with its overtone of miming. Whole films recirculate in this way,[6] in what often amount to 'covers', as popular musicians call their explicit revisions of other musicians' songs.[7] This is Hollywood's (and Bollywood's) version of the repetition compulsion. (In *Move Over, Darling*, the 1963 cover of *My Favorite Wife* (1940), Doris Day explicitly refers to the earlier film as one she saw years ago.) This habit has become so notorious that when Alan Bennett's British play *The Madness of George III* was produced as a film for distribution in America, it was retitled *The Madness of King George*, for fear that Americans would mistake the British title for the third in a series of which they had missed the first two instalments. 'A survey had apparently shown that there were many filmgoers who came away from Kenneth Branagh's film of *Henry V* wishing they had seen its four predecessors' (Bennett 1995: 6–7). Such repetitions catch up not just whole plots but the constituent parts of the plots (the man, transformed into a woman, who gazes in solipsistic lust at his own new breasts) and conventional images (the swirling of the sky during a kiss). Turner Classic Movies, on to this, often groups a day's films around a repeated theme; on Mother's Day of 2005 they ran, in sequence, a series of films about mothers who sacrifice themselves for their children: *None But the Lonely Heart* (1944), *I Remember Mama* (1948), *Stella Dallas* (1937), *Mildred Pierce* (1945), *Imitation of Life* (1959) and *Madame X* (1966). Some people call film plots junk food mythology, but really they are comfort food, mythology like mother used to make.

The need to hear the same story over and over again is in part explained by Freud's (1990) insight into the repetition compulsion, the mind's tendency to repeat traumatic events (in dreams or storytelling) in order to deal with them. Structuralism helps us to see what questions are being asked over and over; structuralists are haunted by *déjà vu*. As Terence Cave points out, the sense of cliché that drives the myth 'is also the sense of repetition, a compulsive returning to the "same" place, a place already known, as if one were discovering it for the first time' (1988: 489). But the compulsive repetition of the same mythemes over and over again is also explained by Lévi-Strauss's useful insight that complex human implications that arise out of the dualistic structures seem to emerge as paradoxes. Lévi-Strauss is talking not merely about *mental* constructs and patterns, but about *emotional* needs and conflicts. Where his critics accuse him of reducing myths to logical oppositions, I see him as illuminating human ambivalences. Paradox is not merely an obsession of myth-makers; it is Lévi-Strauss's obsession, too: paradoxes are to him what whales were to Captain Ahab.

Certain enduring and insoluble human dilemmas and paradoxes generate a potentially infinite variety of invariably failed answers and solutions that different storytellers have proposed for them (Lévi-Strauss 1967e). Every myth is driven by the obsessive need to solve a paradox *that cannot be solved*, a mess that cannot be cleaned up (Lévi-Strauss 1963a; 1967e). This is, I think, the greatest methodological contribution that structuralism makes to our understanding of myths. Myths transform the paradox into a narrative that expresses a contradiction; they simultaneously express two opposed paradigms, two major human contradictions, two human truths that are simultaneously true and mutually opposed. The tension between these two paradigms holds us in suspense to the very end of the story, where we often discover that both of them are true.

I am using paradox here as glossed by part of the *Oxford English Dictionary* definition:

A statement or proposition which on the face of it seems self-contradictory, absurd, or at variance with common sense, though, on investigation or when explained, it may prove to be well-founded (or, according to some, though it is essentially true). Often applied to a proposition or statement that is actually self-contradictory, or contradictory to reason or ascertained truth, and so, essentially absurd and false. In logic, a statement or proposition which, from an acceptable premise and despite sound reasoning, leads to a conclusion that is against sense, logically unacceptable, or self-contradictory.

This type of paradox expresses something closer to ambivalence than to logical self-contradiction, something closer to the word's lexical Greek sense: 'against opinion', or, as we would say, 'counterintuitive'. (Calvin Klein's perfume called Contradiction, advertised with the slogan, 'She is always and never the same', would have been called Paradox if it had been made in France.)

The either/ordering of the world is deeply embedded in European thought. What got Greek philosophy off the ground was the notion that, for any state of affairs, there were only two possibilities, A and not-A, and only one could be true. This is what makes possible Platonic dialectic, Aristotelian logic and the Cartesian approach to the mind/body problem. The Greek paradigm casts its shadow over many myths about binary choices, myths that cling to the A/not-A logic. The problem here is that in mythology (and much of human life), A and not-A are often *simultaneously* true, a position that those Greeks and their descendants regard as irrational. From the mythological point of view, consistency is the hobgoblin of people who cannot, philosophically speaking, walk and chew gum at the same time. Other mythologies, notably but not only Hindu, flourish within the realm of the both/and (Doniger 1998: 157–8). For instance, the god Siva is simultaneously both erotic and an (anti-erotic) ascetic; the goddess Sitala ('the Cool One') both brings the fever of smallpox and dispels it.[8]

Unwilling universalism

Because repetition is endemic to myth, Lévi-Strauss points out (1969d: 13), the best gloss on a myth within a culture is another myth within that culture. Myths are self-explanatory, transformations of one another; one myth translates another, or, perhaps, one myth psychoanalyses another. He admitted that the themes that the mytholologist selects as the basis of the analysis 'owe much to the analyst's subjectivity' and 'have an impressionistic character' (1995b: 186). But to say that they are subjective is not to say that they are entirely arbitrary. Their arbitrariness is limited by our responsibility to the data. In comparing two myths, from two different cultures or within a single culture, we may use another myth (from that culture, or from another) to supplement our understanding of a given text. Such a supplement is needed in part, as Lévi-Strauss (1969d: 13) has demonstrated, because of the fragmentary nature of myths themselves (which must be supplemented by the fragments in other, related myths). But the supplement is also needed because of the fragmentary nature of our understanding of myths.

As Lévi-Strauss has not explicitly argued but as his own writings seem to imply (Doniger 1989), these supplementary fragments of myths may be taken from other cultures. Often the best way to understand a myth is by understanding how it differs not only from other myths in the same culture but also from variants in other cultures. Lévi-Strauss himself said it best and most boldly: 'In proposing the study of mankind, anthropology frees me from doubt, since it examines those *differences and changes* in mankind which have a meaning for all men, and excludes those peculiar to a single civilization, which dissolve into nothingness under the gaze of the outside observer' (1967d: 58; my italics). Thus, difference itself becomes a basis for comparison – a comparison made possible only by the assumption that difference has 'a meaning for all men' (and, presumably, for all women). In other words, one of the ways in which we are all alike is in our shared interest in our differences.

As Lévi-Strauss put it with uncharacteristic naïveté (1963a: 208), 'How are we going to explain the fact that myths throughout the world are so similar?' And, more subtly:

Mythic stories are, or seem, arbitrary, meaningless, absurd, yet nevertheless they seem to re-appear all over the world. A 'fanciful' creation of the mind in one place would be unique – you would not find the same creation in a completely different place ... If this represents a basic need for order in the human mind and since, after all, the human mind is only part of the universe, the need probably exists because there is some order in the universe and the universe is not a chaos. (1995d: 11)

If one did not know that the author of this remarkable credo was the great French structuralist, one might have mistaken him, in the dark, for Jung.

Lévi-Strauss met the problem of cross-cultural parallels head on in his attempts to account for certain striking similarities in what he called 'split representation' in the art of Asia and America (a subject that, like the two related cultures that explore it, involves two halves of a single substance):

Do we rest, then, on the horns of a dilemma which condemns us either to deny history or to remain blind to similarities so often confirmed? ... These studies have been jeopardized even more by intellectual pharisees who prefer to deny obvious relationships because science does not yet provide an adequate method for their interpretation ... How shall we explain the recurrence of a far from natural method of representation among cultures so widely separated in time and space? The simplest hypothesis is that of historical contact or independent development from a common civilization. But even if this hypothesis is refuted by facts, or if, as seems more likely, it should lack adequate evidence, attempts at interpretation are not necessarily doomed to failure. I shall go further: Even if the most ambitious reconstructions of the diffusionist school were to be confirmed, we should still be faced with an essential problem which has nothing to do with history. Why should a cultural trait that has been borrowed or diffused through a long historical period remain intact? Stability is no less mysterious than change ... External connections can explain transmission, but only internal connections can account for persistence. (1963e: 247, 258)

The fact of historical diffusion does not get us off the hook of the problems inherent in the hypothesis of independent origination (reinventing the mythic wheel each time from 'the same' experience or some always-already-there Jungian archetype). On the contrary, we need that hypothesis to explain why, in historical diffusion, some elements are retained while others are not. Lévi-Strauss further advanced this point in *The Story of Lynx*, arguing not only that borrowing is never haphazard but also that what is borrowed is not just fitted into a pre-existing structure: the borrowing takes place because of the similarity in structure between myths in the culture that 'lends' them and myths in the culture that 'borrows' them. And what explains this similarity of structure? He is unwilling to say, but his other writings imply the 'internal connections' of a shared mental structure, that is, a 'common origin' not of the myths themselves (as Jung has argued) but of the mental structures that create the myths.

Lévi-Strauss, pinch hitting for Jung (as he does surprisingly often), bails the historian Carlo Ginzburg out of a similar quandary. For although, in opting for historical diffusion, in his magisterial study of witchcraft in Europe, Ginzburg implicitly rejected Lévi-Strauss's hypothesis of (universal) 'structural characteristics of the human mind' to explain why the same phenomena *recur*, he does use Lévi-Strauss's *Structural Anthropology* to explain why they are *retained*, citing the passage about 'split representations' and concluding:

> To understand the reasons for this twofold characteristic – persistence in time, dispersion in space – it seems necessary to follow a different route: ['derivation from structural characteristics of the human mind']. But there is no reason to suppose that these perspectives are mutually exclusive. We shall therefore seek to integrate in the analysis the external historical data and the internal structural characteristics of the transmitted phenomena. (Ginzburg 1991: 217)

Thus, he argues that historical diffusion and Lévi-Strauss's hypothesis of universal 'structural characteristics of the human mind' can be integrated. In this way, Ginzburg, like Lévi-Strauss himself, is able to explain both what happened (history) and why it kept happening (structure), to run with the universalist fox and to hunt with the contextualised hounds (or, as the case may be, hedgehogs).

Unknown historicism

Lévi-Strauss's structural models have, like archetypes, been faulted for being disconnected from history, change, the flow of time: they are said to exist in a Platonic void that would make them equally relevant at all moments in the life of a culture, any culture. But the structural method does not just provide a kind of stasis; the idea of the mediating category in the Hegelian dialectic makes the theory dynamic, as it made Hegel's theory historical: structuralism sees myths as processes of synthesis and change. The lineage of binary oppositions and dialectic comes to Lévi-Strauss not just from Hegel but also from Marx (Lévi-Strauss was a Marxist for many years, and has never really ceased to be one) and from Russian formalism. Alan Dundes divides structuralism into two branches: Vladimir Propp for narrative sequence; Lévi-Strauss for binary oppositions.[9] I would argue that Lévi-Strauss himself incorporated (among the possible mythemes, what Propp called 'moves') – the set, traditional pieces of the plots of the Russian folktales called *skazki*. He also established a more general kind of movement through the process of the dialectic. Moreover, in *Myth and Meaning* (1978a), Lévi-Strauss makes explicit the connection with history that he has, in fact, always intended his structures to have, when he argues for the diachronic aspects of myths (changing through time) as well as their synchronic aspects (transcending the barriers of time). In this short, clear text, Lévi-Strauss squarely faces the issue of chronology, putting historical flesh on the structural bones by tracing the specific cultural development of a corpus of myths (1995d: 25).[10] (In folklore, too, the diachronic philological approach has largely been replaced by structural approaches that are more respectful to subaltern or popular diversity.)

He also raised political aspects of the problem of the same and the different both inside and outside the text in his comparative study of myths of twinship in North America and Europe, *The Story of Lynx* (1991a; 1995b) (another subject that, like the 'split representations', involves two halves of a single substance – a structuralist's dream). Noting the similarity between the myths about the twins in Amerindian thought (as he calls it), on the one hand, and Castor and Pollux (the Gemini, or Dioscuroi) in Western mythology, on the other, he argues that there is a perceived (and real) similarity in the structure of the AmerIndian and European myths, a similarity that extends even to the kind of plants and planets associated in the two continents with the two pairs of twins. Yet, there are striking dissimilarities between the ideologies of twins in the two cultures. The European myth (epitomised, for Lévi-Strauss, by Montaigne) expresses what he calls the ideology of identity, which excludes the Other; it emphasises the similarity of the twins and thus the reduction of the Other to an image of the self, the annihilation of its difference. The AmerIndian myth (epitomised in the famous case of Montezuma welcoming Cortes as a god) expresses what Lévi-Strauss calls the ideology of opposition, really a kind of synthesis or coexistence, which assumes that one must interact with the other; it emphasises the dissimilarity of the twins, and thus the unstable coexistence of self and other. In this Amerindian world-view, nothing and nobody can exist without an opposite with which it coexists in unresolved tension. The mythologies of the twins are therefore not themselves identical twins; there is a profound difference between ideologies that exclude or interact with the Other, that annihilate or coexist with difference.

Here Lévi-Strauss tackles the political implications of mythology more directly than in any of his previous work. The clash between the two cultures and their mythologies had tragic consequences for the Amerindians. Since they defined themselves in terms of their opposites, there already was a place of coexistence for the Europeans (or any other Others) in Amerindian thought, even before these Others arrived in America. But the conquering Europeans never occupied this place; since they thought in terms of identity, and thus of exclusion, they destroyed the peoples whom they confronted in the New World.

There is, of course, a problem in lumping together all the Amerindians – the 'high' Aztec and the Inca, the 'low' Thompson and Tupinamba – as Lévi-Strauss does. This is particularly problematic since, as he himself argues, the Amerindians (all of them, presumably) were so highly sensitive to the Other and hence, presumably, to the differences among their own groups. But one might overcome this problem by applying the paradigm to one group at a time, and, indeed, they may have been largely alike in the particular ways that concern Lévi-Strauss. In any case, this study adds new mythemes to the *bricoleur*'s bag: Europeans/Amerindians = identity/opposition = exclusion of the Other/interaction with the Other = similar/dissimilar twins = annihilation of difference/coexistence of self and other = colonising/colonised.

Unconscious Freudianism

Lévi-Strauss is indebted to Freud for many things: for the concept of ambivalence that underlies his theories of contradiction and paradox, for the structural use of inversion and so forth. His debt is patently evident, particularly in one of his last books, *The Jealous Potter* (1989c), in his use of such Freudian terms as 'secondary elaboration', for glosses of the symbolism of myth, and 'upward displacement' for the substitution of parts of the head for the lower parts of the body. The surrealistic streak in Lévi-Strauss is also ultimately derived from Freud, as Strenski points out: 'It is true that Lévi-Strauss's quest for a logic beyond the surface of myths can and has been linked with Freud . . . This quest for the hidden logic in things [is] common to both Freud and the surrealists' (Strenski 1987: 179). In his analysis of the myth of Asdiwal, Lévi-Strauss refers to latent content and unconscious categories (1967e: 165, 173). More basic still is his emphasis on the importance of irrational forces as a basis of myth. Yet, ambivalence appears in the author, as well as his text, for he came to differ from Freud in denying both his debt to Freud and his universalism. He questions the universality of child psychology and argues that it is inapplicable to the myths of South American tribal peoples because those myths 'were not produced by mankind in general' (1989c: 173). He argues more convincingly that one cannot, as Freud did, apply the single 'psycho-organic code' to a myth, for a myth will always use several codes (1989c: 186–7).

He goes out of his way to reject the obvious psychoanalytical explanations for many stories that he selected in the first place precisely in order to meet Freud on his own turf, to demonstrate that one does not need Freud even in what most of us would regard as the most blatantly Freudian situations. Surely Lévi-Strauss chose the Oedipus myth for his model (in his most famous essay, in *Structural Anthropology*, 1967c: 220–8) precisely in order to set himself up against (and thumb his nose at) Freud; he remarks archly that the Freudian variant is one more variant to which his structural analysis applies.

His exposition of the Oedipus myth is quite clear, works well and yields valuable insights into the cross-cultural theme of the wounded foot (Doniger 1999: 175–85), but it has not been so well received as his analysis of the Asdiwal myth. Why? Because we know the Oedipus myth better and have stronger, preconceived ideas about what it is about? Because it is a work of literature, and structuralism works best on myths, not on literature? Because Lévi-Strauss summarises it brutally, and we miss the parts he leaves out (we would miss them in the Asdiwal too, if we knew them)? All of the above.

The oppositions that his analysis yields have become part of the vocabulary of structuralism. What we inherit from Lévi-Strauss is not merely the fact that there are structures (and some idea of how these structures *work*: inversion, opposition, transformation, mediation), but a sense of what those structures might be (nature/culture, up/down, left/right, male/female, raw/cooked). Yet, we need more than he is telling us to come up with such mythemes ourselves. How does he find them? By intuition, or by reading Freud?

Apparently not. In *The Jealous Potter*, Lévi-Strauss argues that since some of Freud's ideas – 'oral and anal character and so on' (1989c: 131) – were already inherent in the myths of the Jivaro people of Ecuador, Freud was unoriginal, indeed superfluous. He argued, perversely, *against* Freud, that the blatancy of sexual symbols in Jivaro myths was evidence that the Jivaro invented our psychiatric myths better than we did, as well as earlier. He pointed out that there is a 'convergence between psychoanalytic and mythic thought', and, more particularly, that Freud's theory of the primeval Oedipal conflict (expressed in *Totem and Taboo*, in 1913) was like a myth of the Jivaro (1989c: 172). 'As we can see', he remarks, 'the Indians even had psychoanalysts!' And he goes on to emphasise the complete convergence of Jivaro myths and Freudian theories by remarking, tongue firmly in cheek, 'How wise are the Americans in calling psychoanalysts "head-shrinkers," thus spontaneously associating them with the Jivaro!' (1989c: 186).

The convergence, Lévi-Strauss argues, is evident in the founding myth of incest:

It is *Totem and Taboo* in its entirety that, well ahead of Freud, the Jivaro Indians anticipated in the myth that for them plays the part of a Genesis: societies arose when the primitive horde split into hostile clans after the murder of the father whose wife had committed incest with their son. From a psychological point of view the Jivaro myth offers an even richer and more subtle plot than *Totem and Taboo*. (1989c: 185)

So, too, as Geertz remarks, 'Not only does Lévi-Strauss hope to find Rousseau's Social Contract alive and well in deepest Amazon – and so counter such theories of the origins of sociality as Freud's primal parricide or Hume's conventionality – but he thinks that, among the Nambikwara [of Brazil], he has actually and literally done so' (Geertz 1995: 38).

Thus, the myths themselves have beaten the psychoanalysts to the punch in excavating their own secret or latent meaning; Freud is a plagiarist, who stole all his best ideas from the Jivaro head-shrinkers whose heads he claimed to have shrunk. 'Myths don't need any help when it comes to reasoning like a psychoanalyst', he insists (1989c: 186). A Freudian, however, might see this convergence between the Jivaro myths and the psychoanalyst as positive evidence that Freud was right in his analyses of myths; and, in fact, Lévi-Strauss does grant that Freud's greatness lies partly in his talent for thinking 'the way myths do' (1989c: 191). But what he means is that Freud thinks like a structuralist. This is hardly surprising, since Lévi-Strauss got some of his central ideas from Freud, even as he claims that Freud got *his* best material from the myth-makers.

But Lévi-Strauss assumes that the Jivaro invented not only Freud's stories and Freud's theories but also Freud's 'perfectly explicit notions and categories – such as oral character and anal character' (1989c: 185). This, I would argue, is simply not true; it is Lévi-Strauss, not the Jivaro, who thinks like Freud and abstracts from (or imposes on) the Jivaro myths Freudian categories that the Jivaro never attest. Lévi-Strauss implies that he himself can think like the Jivaro (or else how could he represent their thinking to us as he does?); this is also implicit in his assertion that Freud thinks like the Jivaro at those moments when Freud, occasionally, gets it right (for how could Lévi-Strauss know this if he did not know how the Jivaro think?). The argument runs like this: (1) Myth-makers are structuralists; (2) Lévi-Strauss is a structuralist; hence (3) Lévi-Strauss can understand myth-makers; (4) Freud is (sometimes) a structuralist; hence (5) Freud is sometimes right about myths.

Lévi-Strauss simply replaces Freud's universal category of physical desire with his own universal logical category of what might be called logical lust – 'a need to impose a grammatical order on a mass of random elements' (1989b: 196) – which he regards as 'upstream from desire' (1989b: 196). Thus, his analysis of physiological emotions and processes removes the 'physio' from the 'logical' by stating that the head, not the body, produces the myth. Lévi-Strauss beheads both Freud and the Jivaro; he keeps the head of the myth-maker, and leaves Freud the body. His beheading myths are autobiographical; he is killing his intellectual father, Freud, climbing up the ladder of Freud's methodology and then kicking it away. The basic human universal is not sexuality but the structure of myth.

NOTES

1. This is a simplification of the original formula, which will be discussed in more detail in other chapters in this volume. See, in particular, Eric Schwimmer's contribution.

2. Claude Lévi-Strauss, personal communication, Paris, October 1980.
3. Speaking of Lévi-Strauss's *The Savage Mind*, Leach remarks, 'Though fascinated by that work I have also felt that some dimension to the argument is missing' (1979: 166).
4. Personal communication from Steve Gabel, November 1994.
5. *Mrs. Miniver* (1942), written by James Hilton *et al.*, from the novel by Jan Struther; directed by William Wyler; starring Greer Garson and Walter Pidgeon.
6. Sometimes they have entirely new titles but sometimes the same titles, so that versions are distinguished only by their dates (as essential to the identity of films as the vintage is to wines) or, like English kings, by 'I' or 'II'.
7. These recycled elements make it extremely difficult to copyright the plot of a film (see Friend 1998).
8. For Siva, see Doniger O'Flaherty 1973; for Sitala, see Dimock 1989: 130–49.
9. Alan Dundes, introduction to *Sacred Narrative* 1984.
10. This is the historical analysis of 'Harelips and Twins: the Splitting of a Myth', which we considered above only in its purely structural aspect.

REFERENCES

Bennett, Alan 1995. 'Madness: the Movie', *London Review of Books* 17 (3) (9 February): 6–7.

Cave, T. 1988. *Recognitions: A Study in Poetics*. London and New York: Oxford University Press.

Dimock, E. C. 1989. 'A Theology of the Repulsive: the Myth of the Goddess Sitala', in *The Sound of Silent Guns, and Other Essays*. Delhi: Oxford University Press, pp. 130–49.

Doniger O'Flaherty, W. 1973. *Asceticism and Eroticism in the Mythology of Siva*. Oxford: Oxford University Press. (Retitled *Siva: The Erotic Ascetic*, 1981.)

   1989. 'Structuralist Universals versus Psychoanalytic Universals' (review of *The Jealous Potter*, by Claude Lévi-Strauss), *History of Religions* 28 (3): 269–81.

   1998. *The Implied Spider: Politics and Theology in Myth* (The 1996–7 ACLS/AAR Lectures). New York: Columbia University Press.

   1999. *Splitting the Difference: Gender and Myth in Ancient Greece and India* (The 1996 Jordan Lectures). Chicago: University of Chicago Press.

Dundes, Alan 1984. *Sacred Narrative: Readings in the Theory of Myth*. Berkeley, CA: University of California Press.

Freud, S. 1990. *Beyond the Pleasure Principle*. Translated by James Strachey. New York: W. W. Norton.

Friend, T. 1998. 'Copy Cats', *New Yorker*, 14 September: 51–7.

Geertz, C. 1995. *After the Fact: Two Countries, Four Decades, One Anthropologist* (The Jerusalem-Harvard Lectures). Cambridge, MA: Harvard University Press.

Ginzburg, C. 1991. *Ecstasies: Deciphering the Witches' Sabbath*. Translated by Raymond Rosenthal. New York: Pantheon Books.

Jacob, F. 1977. 'Evolution and Tinkering', *Science* 196 (4,295): 1,161–6.

Laqueur, T. 1990. *Making Sex: Body and Gender from the Greeks to Freud*. Cambridge, MA: Harvard University Press.

Leach, E. 1979. 'Anthropological Aspects of Language: Animal Categories and Verbal Abuse', in William A. Lessa and Evon Z. Vogt (eds.), *Reader in Comparative Religion.* New York: Harper and Row, pp. 153–66.

Lotman, Y. 1990. 'The Semiosphere', in *Universe of the Mind: A Semiotic Theory of Culture.* Translated by Ann Shukman. Bloomington: Indiana University Press.

Ramanujan, A. K. 1984. 'The Indian Oedipus', in Alan Dundes and Lowell Edmund (eds.), *Oedipus: A Folklore Casebook.* New York and London: Garland Publishing.

Strenski, I. 1987. *Four Theories of Myth in Twentieth-Century History: Cassirer, Eliade, Lévi-Strauss and Malinowski.* Iowa City: University of Iowa Press.

Tracy, D. 1981. *The Analogical Imagination: Christian Theology and the Culture of Pluralism.* New York: Crossroad.

Part III

Language and alterity

11   Of *The Story of Lynx*: Lévi-Strauss and alterity

Peter Gow

Pedro Manuyama Fumachi, a 31-year-old resident of a poor neighbourhood of the town of Requena on the Ucayali River in Peruvian Amazonia, told the following myth to a researcher from a project on popular religion in the region:

> After the flood a man who had several daughters was bathing, when Jesus Christ passed by, dirty, covered in the mud of the flood. As he passed by he saw the man and his daughters and asked the older one to get rid of the mud that he had, but she was swimming and refused and said, 'Why would I wash this filthy man.' Then the younger one offered to wash God and in return he chose her as the Virgin and raised her to heaven. To punish the older one who had refused, she left the water with scabies. From that day, black scabies exists. (Regan 1993: 151)

Pedro Manuyama's name indicates he is descended from the Cocama people, who dominated the lower Ucayali River at the arrival of the Spanish. His ancestors fiercely resisted conquest until their military defeat in the middle of the seventeenth century, when they finally accepted Jesuit mission life in Santiago de la Laguna on the Huallaga River to the west. They remained there until they began to disperse away from the abandoned Jesuit mission in the early nineteenth century back towards the Ucayali and beyond. The descendants of the Cocama form a major component of the poor riverine peasantry and urban dwellers of the region (see Stocks 1981 and Agüero 1994).

In my first reading of Manuyama's myth, I made little of it. At most, I thought it was yet another example of the tragedy of European colonialism for indigenous American people. Manuyama had been robbed of his birthright, and reduced to living as a second-class citizen in a slum in a place that was once the proud and exclusive territory of his feared ancestors. Defeated as much by epidemic illnesses as by military superiority, the Cocama were then subjected to over a century of Jesuit tutelage in an alien religion, their own cosmology ridiculed, and their own stories scorned. Worse still, that painful tutelage seems to have signally failed, for Manuyama's story reveals a shocking ignorance of the grandeurs of that alien religion, which, had it been understood, might have rendered this brutal historical experience if not justifiable, then at least intelligible and perhaps a little more bearable.

But no, all the Jesuits managed to do is leave Manuyama with this incoherent little story, where God rewards a young woman kind to him by making her the Virgin, and punishes her haughty sister by giving her scabies.

Later, reading Claude Lévi-Strauss's *The Story of Lynx* (1995b), I discovered that Manuyama's little story is a perfectly coherent version of a very widely diffused and ancient indigenous American myth. To find it growing in the mind of a young man in an urban slum in late twentieth-century Peruvian Amazonia suggests that the world is more complex than we are usually willing to admit. The French missionary Thevet recorded a version of this myth in 1555 from the Tupinambá in (what was to become) Rio de Janeiro (Métraux 1928).[1] The many versions of this myth form the subject matter of *The Story of Lynx* (1995b), the last of the three companion volumes to the monumental *Mythologiques*. This book addresses the opposite values given to twins in thoughts of the peoples of the Old and New Worlds, and indeed the nature of the differences between the peoples of Europe and the Americas, issues that reappear in Manuyama's story. It is to these complex issues that the present chapter is dedicated.

A puzzle

As Lévi-Strauss notes, the issues addressed in *The Story of Lynx* (1995b) go back to some much earlier concerns in his work. He writes there:

This book . . . stems from two questions that I had asked myself across a gap of several years without noticing their connection. In 1944 I wondered about the nature of dual organization in South America . . . At the time I was writing *The Elementary Structures of Kinship* and the comparative data I was using (Ch. 6) suggested that dual organization in other parts of the world raises similar problems. Articles published in 1956 and 1960 and my lectures of the years 1957–59 at the Ecole des Hautes Etudes mark the stages of this reflection. Later, as I was working on *The Naked Man*, I encountered a problem that I first thought specific to the mythology of the Salish-speaking peoples in the Northwest of North America. This problem seemed so special to me that I first resigned myself to set it aside. I have, however, alluded to it in various places (see the Index of *The Naked Man* under the entries for 'Wind' and 'Fog'), all the while promising to come back to it someday. In 1968–69 I interrupted my teaching program so as to draft the main lines of this problem in the form of an *intermede* (I called it an interlude) in one of my courses at the Collège de France. On this occasion, I became aware that the two problems – that of South American dualism and that raised by the mythology of the wind and fog in a specific area of North America – were really only one and that the second formed a test illustrating and confirming through a particular case the solution that I had proposed for the first. (1995b: xvi–xvii)

These passages are important, because Lévi-Strauss here notes the slowness with which he came to this resolution, and its importance. In the article from

1944, 'Reciprocity and Hierarchy', Lévi-Strauss addresses a small detail of Bororo ethnography. He returns to this article in *The Story of Lynx*, when in debate with David Maybury-Lewis, he quotes his early position:

A probably unilateral analysis of dual organization has all too often propounded the principle of reciprocity as its main cause and result . . . However, we should not forget that a moiety system can express not only mechanisms of reciprocity but also relations of subordination. However, the principle of reciprocity is at play even in these relations of subordination: this because subordination is itself reciprocal: the moiety at the top spot in one plane concedes it to the opposing moiety in another. (1995b: 236–7)

And he concluded:

It is possible that systems typical of dual organization in South America in which multiple pairs of moieties criss-cross each other . . . can be understood as an attempt to overcome these contradictions. (1995b: 237)

Lévi-Strauss here reiterates conclusions drawn many years before, some in debate with Maybury-Lewis, but now sets them in a much wider frame.

What has changed over the intervening years is precisely his sense of how much wider that frame is, for the analysis of *The Story of Lynx* (1995b) has shown that the myths of the Salish-speaking peoples on the fog and the wind involve impossible twins. This impossibility is true whether in the form of attempts to co-ordinate these two mutually exclusive meteorological conditions, or in the form of the proliferation of twins or pseudo-twins who progressively cease to be twins, such as Lynx and Coyote. And further, it is true even of these people's incorporation of French-Canadian folktales, by treating them, so to speak, as 'twins' to their own myths. All are varieties of a single problem. Lévi-Strauss goes on to propose that the local mythology in which these borrowings abound 'shows itself to be solidly organized, as if in its initial state it had had omissions, empty spaces, while it was awaiting, so to speak, external contributions that would fill them and only thanks to which its structure could be completed' (1995b: 220).

Lévi-Strauss had long noted and pondered on the manner in which apparently equal moiety pairs in South America would be called the 'Strong' and the 'Weak', the 'Older' and the 'Younger', the 'Good' and the 'Bad'. Here, dualism is always asymmetric, and as a consequence dynamic, for indigenous American thought always contains a hollow place ready for the Other. This is in marked contrast to European reaction to the discovery of the New World. He writes: 'the discovery of the New World does not seem to have had much of an impact on European consciousness in the following decades' (1995b: 208). Even Montaigne, famous for his essay on the Tupinambá, does not really react as strongly as might have been thought, for he concludes his reflections on the customs of the Americans with gratitude that he is a Catholic.

The indigenous American people responded in an opposite manner. As in the famous cases of Mexico and Peru, they reacted to contact with the Europeans as the fulfilment of prophecy of a new race of men from the east or of returning gods. Most impressive of all, the Tupinambá myth recorded by Thevet in 1555 tells of the mythic origins of the Europeans as the 'true children' of the demiurge Maire-Monan (1995b: 44). We can assume that the narrator, who, like most indigenous American people, would have experienced this myth as a venerable tradition coming from the ancient past. But it is entirely possible that he had lived through the very first ever encounter between Europeans and the Tupinambá, which had happened only fifty-five years before. As Lévi-Strauss notes, the identification of the conquerors of Mexico and Peru as prophesied voyagers post-dates the events by some time, so may actually have been lived out differently, but the Mexicans, Peruvians and Brazilians had certainly included the Europeans within their cosmologies long before the Europeans began to take the novelty of the New World seriously.

Lévi-Strauss argues that this is because European and American mythologies treat twins very differently. In the former, twins, even if of heterogeneous origin, rapidly converge towards identity, while in the latter, twins, even if initially identical, just as rapidly diverge. For Europeans, the New World was just that, a new version of the Old World, and, if initially novel in its novelty, was destined to be identical to the world they already knew. For the Americans, however, the new people were just that, new people, and their coming implied radical change. Despite what we often continue to hope, that this latter reaction was caused by some powerfully salient and objective marker of the European superiority, horses, guns, beards or whatever, the uncomfortable truth lies in Columbus's dying conviction that he had, in life, been tantalisingly close to China, rather than in an unguessed world.

Anthropology and colonialism

Columbus matters in the *The Story of Lynx* for the French original, *L'Histoire du Lynx* (1991a), was published in a significant year, 1991. As Lévi-Strauss writes:

I believe that it is now possible to trace Amerindian dualism to its philosophical and ethical sources. It draws its inspiration, it seems to me, from an opening to the Other, an opening that manifested itself in a demonstrative manner during the first contacts with the Whites, even though these latter were driven by very opposite motives. To recognize this as we are about to commemorate an event that – rather than the discovery – I would call the invasion of the New World, the destruction of its peoples and its values, is to engage in an act of contrition and devotion. (1995b: xvi)

Public celebration of such an event could only be unpleasant to a man who had spent so many years studying indigenous American peoples, for 1492 marks the beginning of the tragic colonial history of the New World, a violent invasion that was to prove so destructive for local peoples and whose consequences continue to reverberate to this day. Lévi-Strauss was clearly not going to celebrate Columbus, but the fact of the invasion is central to *The Story of Lynx* (1995b), even although, very characteristically, Lévi-Strauss approaches it from a distinctively indigenous American angle – the stories of Lynx themselves.

One of the most impressive features of Lévi-Strauss's work is his willingness to address alterity on the scale at which the other seeks to address it. For him, this approach is central to anthropology as a science, for it puts the other first, and thus becomes the variant, in European thought, of the far more general indigenous American opening to the Other. Lévi-Strauss never hides the parallel careers of colonialism and anthropology. He wrote, in 'The Scope of Anthropology':

What we call the Renaissance truly marked the birth of colonialism and anthropology. Between the two, confronting each other from the time of their common origin, an equivocal dialogue has been pursued for four centuries. If colonialism had not existed, the rise of anthropology might have been less delayed. But anthropology might not have been moved to implicate all mankind (and it has now become its role to do so) in each of its particular case studies. Our science reached its maturity the day that Western man began to understand that he would never understand himself as long as there would be on the surface of the earth a single race or a single people whom he would treat as an object. Only then was anthropology able to affirm itself as an enterprise renewing the Renaissance and atoning for it, in order to extend humanism to the measure of humanity. (1977c: 31–2)

In *Tristes Tropiques*, Lévi-Strauss makes a key allusion to the problem of the relationship between anthropology and colonialism when he writes:

At what point would the study of the wild people of Brazil have afforded the purest satisfaction, and revealed them in their least adulterated state? Would it have been better to arrive in Rio in the eighteenth century with Bougainville, or in the sixteenth with Léry and Thevet? For every five years I move back in time, I am able to save a custom, gain a ceremony or share in another belief. But I know the texts too well not to realize that, by going back a century, I am at the same time foregoing data and lines of inquiry which would offer intellectual enrichment. And so I am caught within a circle from which there is no escape: the less human societies were able to communicate with each other and therefore to corrupt each other through contact, the less their respective emissaries were able to perceive the wealth and significance of their diversity. In short, I have only two possibilities: either I can be like some traveller of the olden days, who was faced with a stupendous spectacle, all, or almost all, of which eluded him, or worse still, filled him with scorn or disgust; or I can be a modern traveller, chasing after a vanished reality. (1973c: 50–1)[2]

By the time European thought can come to imagine the many wonderful things that must have been on display for the first Europeans to visit the Americas, it is far too late. It is like the story of the Spanish priest, the only literate European to see Cuzco before it was stripped to provide Atahuallpa's ransom, but who did not bother to write a description of it.

Powerful as Lévi-Strauss's thought is, I think that at this point it succumbs to its origins. He devotes his last words in 'The Scope of Anthropology' to the wild people, writing of them:

Men and women who, as I speak, thousands of miles from here, on some savannah ravaged by brush fire or in some forest dripping with rain, are returning to camp to share a meagre pittance and evoke their gods together. These Indians of the tropics, and others like them throughout the world who have taught me their humble knowl-edge, in which is nevertheless contained the essence of the knowledge which you have entrusted me to transmit to others, soon, alas, destined to extinction through the impact of the illnesses and – to them more horrible still – the modes of life we have brought them. (1977c: 32)

Timely and important as these words were when and where they were spoken (see also the writings of Darcy Ribeiro collected in *Os indios e a civilização* (1970), who clearly influenced Lévi-Strauss in this respect), they also contain the assumption that the Indians are destined either to die out or to become a poor and deformed version of ourselves. Different in the beginning, the Old and New Worlds are twins, and their destiny is to become identical twins, in the Old World sense.

While not wishing to play down the immense consequences of demo-graphic decline, it is a fact that most of the indigenous peoples studied by Lévi-Strauss in Brazil in the 1930s continue to exist today, many with expanding populations, and continue to be the objects of revealing ethno-graphic accounts. What Lévi-Strauss saw was a very specific moment in the history of indigenous people in Southern and Central Brazil, as the Brazilian government began to increase its powers over these interior areas, and in which indigenous people were treated as obstacles which would either disap-pear or become integrated as Brazilians (see Ribeiro 1970). Thankfully, this situation has changed, and there is increasing acceptance of, and support for, indigenous people and their ways of life in Brazil.

If Lévi-Strauss saw the indigenous people of Southern and Central Brazil at what was the worst moment of their population loss, now we see, throughout Lowland South America, growing indigenous populations. In some cases, this population growth began quite early. Tessmann writes of the Cocama in the early 1920s: 'the Cocama are a vital tribe . . . The number of their children is great, and even although many die, the Cocama still grow considerably' (Tessmann 1999 [1930]: 44–5). This population growth continues to this day. Relatively little attention has been given to this phenomenon, which is surprising given that in many areas, indigenous population densities are beginning to approach pre-Columbian levels.

Part of the reason for anthropologists' failure to address this problem undoubtedly has to do with a pessimism shared with Lévi-Strauss: if they do not die out, they adopt our way of life. The point is made with force by Peter Roe, discussing Yarinacocha near the city of Pucallpa on the Ucayali River: 'the now-Europeanized ex-Cocama, as rural mixed-blood people, are aggrandizing their land holdings in the name of expanding civilization against the still visibly Indian Shipibo-Conibo' (Roe 1982: 81). Certainly, rural and urban people who are descended from the ancient Cocama do not live in ways identical to their ancestors, but is it really fair to call them 'Europeanised'? Superficially, Pedro Manuyama's story might sound Europeanised, insofar as it deals with religious ideas imported from Europe, but as *The Story of Lynx* has shown, it is clearly also very distinctively American.

As *The Story of Lynx* has also shown, Pedro Manuyama's story should not be thought of as syncretic or creolised in any common understanding of these terms, for it belongs to a set of myths that are intrinsically open to the Other. Following Lévi-Strauss, we should really be more surprised if Manuyama's story had not incorporated the thought of the Other. It would seem to me that this story, and by extension the people who tell it, are Europeanised in a distinctively indigenous American way. If the Jesuits wanted to convert the Cocama people to Christianity, and hence to make them twins in the European sense, then the Cocama took on that religion in order to become twins with the Europeans in the American sense.

This point raises an ethnographic and a historical problem. If we assume that people like the modern descendants of the Cocama are Europeanised in our sense, then there is little new knowledge to be gained in studying them. Certainly, the paucity of studies of these people is in marked contrast to the wealth of studies of the 'still visibly Indian Shipibo-Conibo'. This means that we simply know very little about the Cocama, and hence do not even know what we do not know. Secondly, by focusing exclusively on those indigenous American peoples who currently strike us as different, we assume that all that these societies can do is either endure or disappear. We have no idea of how they can, as is obviously the case, expand and transform in history, and how they can use their own ceaseless internal dynamic to use what has been offered to them by the European invasion that they find meaningful and appealing to themselves. We have no developed sociology of recovery.

The sociology of recovery

A potential starting place for such a sociology of recovery appears in several works by Lévi-Strauss that date to the period immediately before 'Reciprocity and Hierarchy': his thesis on the Nambikwara, published long after it was written (1948), the article on war and trade (1942b; 1976e) and the article on the social use of kinship terms (1943a). All three deal with a specific reaction by two Nambikwara bands to the problem of declining population in the formation of a kind of dual organisation. Curiously, Lévi-Strauss does not himself refer to these ideas in *The Story of Lynx* (1991a; 1995b), despite their obvious connection to the issue of dualism in the Americas. In the article on use of kin terms by indigenous people in Brazil, he tells the story as follows:

> During the past twenty years, several epidemics nearly destroyed the central, northern and western divisions of the Nambikwara. Several groups were decimated to such an extent that they could no longer successfully maintain a socially autonomous existence. In the hope of reconstituting functioning units, some of these, therefore, attempted to join forces. In the course of our fieldwork we met and worked with such a merged group made up of seventeen individuals using the northern dialect (Sabáne group) and thirty-four using the central dialect (Tarúnde dialect). Each of the originally distinct groups, however, lived under the guidance of its own chief, although both leaders cooperated. (1943a: 401)

Lévi-Strauss notes that most people in each group, including the chiefs, could not understand the language of the other. He continues that the

> fundamental problem raised by the union of these two groups, namely the nature of the relations to be established between their respective members, was solved by the common statement that all the male members of the Sabáne group were to be acknowledged as the 'brothers-in-law' . . . of the male adults of the Tarúnde group, and conversely, that the latter were to be acknowledged as 'brothers-in-law' . . . by the former. (1943a: 402)

Lévi-Strauss argues that this fusion was facilitated by the specific meaning of the brother-in-law relation in indigenous South American societies where, far from being a simple kin term, it is a much broader socio-political relation.

Lévi-Strauss goes on to show how this same relationship, that between brothers-in-law, ordered the relations between the ancient Tupi of coastal Brazil, the same people among whom Thevet collected the earliest of the myths in *The Story of Lynx* (1991a; 1995b) and the French and other European visitors. The latter, however, failed to fully understand it, and likened it to familiar forms of Christian ritual co-parenthood. Lévi-Strauss comments:

> Since the sixteenth-century travellers and sociologists have failed to devote sufficient attention to the phenomenon, probably because it could readily be interpreted as a development of the imported *compadre* relationship. In our opinion, on the contrary, the brother-in-law relationship, together with its remarkable implications, constitutes an indigenous aboriginal institution based on the pattern of native culture. Nevertheless, it presents a striking example of convergence in which the native and Latin-Mediterranean institutions show numerous apparent similarities overlying important structural differences. (1943a: 398)

Again, Lévi-Strauss points to European obtuseness with regard to indigenous American thought and society.

Although unmentioned in *The Story of Lynx* (1991a; 1995b), this argument has a surprising relevance to it. As well as yet another example of the failure of Europeans to admit the genuine alterity of the indigenous people, it is, in itself, a remarkable piece of New World dynamic dualism in sociological action. The Tupi and the Europeans were able to engage in ongoing dynamic social relations without any genuine understanding, on the part of the latter, of what these relations actually were. Only an indigenous American people could, one suspects, have thrown themselves into close and binding relations with these strangers who hold to diametrically opposed models of what those relations might be. If it was the Europeans who ultimately initiated these new relations by coming to the Tupi rather than vice versa, it was the Tupi who seized the opportunity and imposed on the novel relation their own dynamic form. If the two bands of the Nambikwara could fuse in this manner, why could not the Tupinambá and the French? Can we not see in this relationship, given two contradictory perspectives by its two partners, a sociological version of the Old and New World attitudes to twins, but one that now operates as social relation?

Reviewing the same historical materials as Lévi-Strauss with a rather different question in mind, Viveiros de Castro has discussed the problem of the apparent ease with which the Tupinambá converted to Christianity and the extreme instability of that conversion (1993). He notes that the modern anthropological concept of culture is the scion of the missionaries' concept of faith, for both centre on what people believe. As such, anthropologists have severe problems in addressing why the Tupinambá were so zealous to become Christians, problems they share with their missionaries. What sense does it make, Viveiros de Castro asks, to want to become the Other, but for one's own ends?

The colonial history of the Portuguese and Tupinambá was certainly marked by enslavements and massacres, but also by intermarriages. This, at least, is what a fuzzy Brazilian nationalist myth of origin likes to repeat, although to my knowledge it has not been subject to serious historical analysis from a sociological perspective. It would be fascinating to pursue Lévi-Strauss's insight through the colonial history of that country.

Absent from the article on kinship terms, the theme of asymmetric dualism reappears in 'War and Trade among the Indians of South America', in the same terms as in 'Reciprocity and Hierarchy' and then again in *The Story of Lynx* (1991a; 1995b). Lévi-Strauss writes of indigenous South American societies:

In almost all of the societies there is a division into two moieties, the role of which is to perform ceremonies by turns, and often too, to regulate marriages. However, in South

America, this institution, so wide-spread in other regions of the world, takes on a supplementary character: dissymmetry. At least in the names they bear, these moieties, in a large number of tribes, are not equal. There is thus the couple, 'those of the Strong' and 'those of the Weak', that of 'those of the Good' and 'those of the Bad', that of 'those from Upstream' and 'those from Downstream', etc. This terminology is very close to that which different tribes used to designate each other . . . (1976e [1942b]: 338)

Lévi-Strauss goes on to suggest that some of these dual systems may represent fusions of separate peoples, and again evokes the Nambikwara example described before.

Aside from epidemics, war and trade are what Europeans brought to indigenous American peoples. They also brought an effortless sense of their own superiority, especially with regard to their religion. As Lévi-Strauss has shown in *The Story of Lynx* (1991a; 1995b), indigenous American people were able to rapidly insert Europeans into their cosmology, and asymmetry in their relations with Europeans would have been exactly what they would have expected. Could such an approach shed light on the colonial history of the Americas? Certainly, Lévi-Strauss evokes it in *The Story of Lynx* for the conquests of Mexico and Peru, and it may well be more general. I have argued that precisely this asymmetrical dualism helps to explain certain enigmatic features of the relationships between the Piro people of Peruvian Amazonia and colonial agents, and how these features have been masked by the assumption by those agents that apparent Piro acquiescence was a simple recognition of their superiority (Gow 2001). At least, Piro people have long sought out the goods and knowledge of those they call *kajine*, 'white people', while consistently refusing to become *kajine* or even admitting to their co-humanity.

Failure to explore fully the manner in which asymmetric dualism may have been operative in the colonial history of the Americas is undoubtedly due to its possible tastelessness. After all, indigenous people lost a very great deal more than they ever gained by the invasion, and to attribute those losses in any way to indigenous people themselves is tantamount to blaming the victim. This is certainly true, but a failure to properly explore the potential operation of indigenous ideas and social institutions characterised by dynamic dualism is to compound the full tragedy of the invasion with a refusal to recognise that, even in the midst of disaster, indigenous American people continued to be true to the interior logic of their own thoughts.

A good example of this comes from Elizabeth Ewart's study of the Panará people of Central Brazil (2000; 2003). Already decimated by centuries of violence, these last independent survivors of the historic Southern Cayapó people were subject to very aggressive efforts to end their voluntary isolation in the 1970s and, when that was achieved, to remove them from the lands they occupied and loved. This was accompanied by devastating population collapse that the Panará themselves call 'the time when everybody died': perhaps as many as nine out of every ten Panará people died in the mid-1970s. Slowly, the survivors regrouped, and eventually managed to return to a fragment of their original territory, where they began to recover in numbers and consequently in confidence. But even as they did so, they did not reconstitute their moiety system of 'those of the Base' and 'those of the Leaves'. Where many analysts might simply bemoan a further loss of cultural difference, Ewart, following *The Story of Lynx*, provides a more interesting and perhaps more Panará answer. During the intense internal debates before the Panará made peace, they became polarised between 'the old men', who counselled no, and 'the young men', who counselled yes. One asymmetric dualism gave birth to another. Peace was made, with the unforeseen consequences already noted. But even as they recovered, Ewart argues, the Panará never sought to return to their earlier mode of asymmetric dualism. Instead, they explored the dynamic potentials of a new one, the new peaceful relations between themselves, *panará* and the *hipe*, 'enemies, Northern Kayapó, Brazilians', in a proliferating series of asymmetries and derived symmetries. This late twentieth-century example of dynamic dualism in action, recognised by an ethnographer who was familiar with *The Story of Lynx*, invites us to rethink what we know about indigenous people in the Americas since 1492.

The Lynx in Peruvian Amazonia

It may prove difficult to explore the consequences of Lévi-Strauss's ideas on asymmetric dualism for the colonial history of the Americas, but it is possible to see their effects in the modern social landscape of Peruvian Amazonia, that part of the continent I am most familiar with. Concluding the article on war and trade, he wrote:

> The sociologist must, however, always bear in mind that primitive institutions are not only capable of conserving what exists, or of retaining briefly a crumbling past, but also of elaborating audacious innovations, even though traditional structures are thus profoundly transformed. (1976e: 339)

As I have argued elsewhere, this article of Lévi-Strauss's, with this conclusion, helps us immeasurably to address many features of contemporary indigenous Amazonian peoples like the Piro of the Bajo Urubamba (1991a), and later I explored its further consequences in the light of the analysis in *The Story of Lynx* (Gow 2001). Here, following the clue revealed by Pedro Manuyama's story, I want to explore some further possibilities elsewhere in the region. *The Story of Lynx* sets thought to work, and so finds certain facts that now take on a new light, and reveal features of the world, apparently of little interest, that now take on new meanings.

I have already quoted Roe's account of the 'ex-Cocama' people, which bring us back to Pedro Manuyama and his story with which I began. This term was coined by the archaeologist Donald Lathrap (1970) to denote these people because they often deny being Cocama or even indigenous. He wrote of the 'ex-Cocama' people of the town of Juancito:

> In matters of dress and custom the people are not noticeably different from the inhabitants of the two large cities of eastern Peru, Iquitos and Pucallpa. They consider themselves to be typical representatives of Peruvian culture and would be offended if called Indians. (Lathrap 1970: 17)

This is hardly a potent call to explore the lived world of such people in any greater depth. Even those ethnographers who have taken up the challenge, such as Agüero, the author of an excellent ethnography of Cocama millenarianism, report similar phenomena:

> The Tupí-Cocama, from fear or shame, no longer consider themselves to be indigenous, but rather as 'Peruvians'. There exists, without doubt, a particular kind of covering-up of their own identity due to their historical experience of contact with the white/mixed blood which was considered adverse and negative. Because of this, they have tried to accommodate themselves to the way of life of those they call 'the Peruvians'. (Agüero 1994: 70)

Agüero's claim here, despite its pragmatic obviousness to people like me, is not properly an ethnographic statement, for no evidence is presented that these people cover up their own true identities from fear or shame. All that Agüero shows is that these people no longer consider themselves to be indigenous and now call themselves Peruvians.

This 'ex-Cocama' claim is alien to European thought insofar as indigeneity, while associated with cultural features, is simultaneously a natural identity, indeed a racial one, and hence not supposedly amenable to personal choice. For Cocama people to deny being indigenous, or to claim to no longer be indigenous, can only be a lie from the perspective of European thought. Or, if accusing poor people from Peruvian Amazonia of lying about who they are seems too strong, then we might instead attribute to them negative emotional states, such as fear or shame that might explain why they dissemble about their true identities. But what if we accepted that what these people say about themselves is simply true, and then asked what such claims might mean to them, and consequently to ourselves?

Close scrutiny of the available ethnography shows that Cocama or 'ex-Cocama' people's claims about who they are make sense as long as we do them the simple justice of considering what these claims mean to themselves.[3] These people are not indigenous because, for them, 'indigenous' means something very different from what it might mean to us. For them, 'indigenous people' are *tribu* (Spanish)/*tapɨya* (Cocama), 'wild forest people', as opposed to *gente* (Spanish)/*awa* (Cocama), 'people'.[4] They also claim that their ancestors were *tribu-tapɨya*, but that they were civilised by outsiders, *extranjeros* (Spanish)/*mai* (Cocama), and became *gente/awa*. They continue to carry the traces of their ancestral *tribu-tapɨya* origins as their surnames, such as Manuyama, but they are not *tribu-tapɨya*, they are *gente/awa*. It thus makes perfect sense for them to 'no longer consider themselves to be indigenous'. It also makes perfect sense for them to call themselves Peruvians, given that they call local people without *tribu-tapɨya* surnames precisely *extranjeros/mai*, 'foreigners', that is, non-Peruvians.

From this perspective, what local people in places like Requena say about themselves begins to make more sense. An informant in Regan's study stated, 'Those who have foreign names humiliate those of us who have Peruvian names' (Regan 1993: 111). Another informant, Rosa Sivano Tamani from Nauta, described local social life as follows:

In the city you see two groups: the people of the centre and the peasants or riverbank dwellers and between these groups there is no relation. Each group lives with those of its own group, treating the riverbank dwellers as Indians. There is classism. You see this between the people of the centre and the riverbank dwellers, above all with regard to surnames. (Regan 1993: 111)

Augusto Ahuanari Icomena, also from Nauta, stated: 'In Nauta there are two social classes. Those who think themselves to be of a better race or as white people, humiliate the Indians and speak badly to them' (Regan 1993: 111). Rosa Arcelia Da Silva from Requena, where Pedro Manuyama told his story, said of their shared hometown: 'There are *mestizo* people and Cocama people. No others. They get along well. They are marked off, however, by their surnames. It is not the same to be called Da Silva as to be called Manuyama' (Regan 1993: 112). In Peruvian Amazonia, Da Silva is a surname of obviously foreign (Portuguese/Brazilian) origin, while Manuyama, Sivano, Tamani, Ahuanari and Icomena are surnames of obviously local (Cocama) origin.

Regan's study was inspired by liberation theology, and he quotes these statements as evidence of the nature of class inequality and racial prejudice in the region, and European thought can easily hear in them a better future where such prejudices cease, and it could indeed be 'the same to be called Da Silva as to be called Manuyama'. But Lévi-Strauss's analysis in *The Story of Lynx* suggests a quite different reading of these informants' statements, one closer to indigenous American thought. These people are asserting that local society is organised asymmetric dualism, and that the two groups that compose it could never be equal precisely because there are *two* of them. The divisions by urban location, occupation, race and surnames, which unquestionably arose in the colonial history of Peruvian Amazonia, are treated by people with Cocama surnames as an asymmetric dualism of some considerable complexity. And more, for they have imposed this same asymmetric dualism on their oppressors – as Da Silva, proud of her foreign surname, said: 'there are *mestizo* people and Cocama people. No others.'

That modern towns and smaller rural settlements in Peruvian Amazonia are characterised by complex dualistic structures has been noted by several authors, most impressively by Chevalier for Puerto Inca (1982), but their obvious origin in the ongoing vitality of indigenous American thought has been either ignored or found wanting. After his rich account of the complex asymmetric dualisms of the small town of Puerto Inca, Chevalier argues that these ethnographic data do 'not warrant a historicist explanation that would reduce such arrangements to a mere reflection or prolongation of a pre-Hispanic past into the social present of a "primitive-like" community' (Chevalier 1982: 222). Here, European sociological thought refuses the possibility that modern Amazonian social phenomena could show profound and impressive continuities with the region's past precisely because such phenomena *are* modern, and hence evidence of the progressive assimilation of the pre-Hispanic past into the modern Hispanic present. Yet, surely, if Pedro Manuyama can tell his version of the Story of Lynx in a Christian guise in a shantytown in the late twentieth century, we might expect to find many more such continuities from an indigenous past in unexpected places and unexpected forms.

One world only

These observations on contemporary Peruvian Amazonia suggest that Lévi-Strauss was correct, and that we are confronting unexpected 'audacious innovations'. In the article on war and trade, Lévi-Strauss wrote:

Further, it is beyond doubt that since the discovery of the Antilles, inhabited in the sixteenth century by Caribs, whose wives bore witness still, by their special language, to their Arawak origin, that processes of social assimilation and dissimilation are not incompatible with the functioning of Central and South American societies. More recently, as we have seen, von den Steinen was witness to the same phenomenon in the Arauití village of the Alto Xingú. But, as in the case of the relations between war and trade, the concrete mechanisms of these articulations remained unnoticed for a long time. (1942b; 1976a: 338)

All the necessary facts, therefore, were well known to Europeans, and from the earliest period. What was absent was the requisite sociological imagination.

The grandeur of anthropological thought lies in its remarkable openness to the Other, and its insistence that what we unreflectingly care about most are simply our own local concerns. Whether in the domains of religion, kinship, politics or economics, anthropology consistently points out that there are other ways forward that are viable, other ways of being human. And in doing so, the discipline has developed increasingly precise analytical tools for exploring the variety of ways of being human. However, when anthropological thought has turned to indigenous American people and their ongoing survival, from 1492 into the contemporary world, it has been far less open-minded. Far from having developed a rich analytical vocabulary for exactly how these people have survived and then sometimes thrived, anthropology has only come up with vitiated concepts like acculturation, deculturation, assimilation, ethnicity and even cultural resistance. Despite the volumes that have been written about these terms, none of them has any particular analytical precision, and they are as regularly dropped without regret as they are invented without intellectual passion or commitment.

If Lévi-Strauss's work has not addressed such issues, and if he has seldom shown intellectual interest in what happens to indigenous American peoples when they apparently adopt 'the modes of life we have brought them', then in his rigorous work on mythology, he has provided an explanation of why the conceptual vocabulary with which we habitually discuss the reality of the survival and recovery of the Other, in its indigenous American instantiation, is so very dull and life-less. For this is how European mythic thought conceives of twins: even if they are markedly different at the outset, they progressively become identical. Even as we begin to recognise, through anthropology, their genuine differences from us and the intellectual meaning of those differences, indigenous American people are destined to become identical to us. If this is so, little needs to be explained, and no genuine challenge is presented to anthropological thought. European thought was right all along.

In his reflections on the mythological meaning of twins in *The Story of Lynx*, Lévi-Strauss shows that the New World really is a new world, full of 'great things', to borrow from an early account of Brazil, but now understood in its intellectual rather than its merely utilitarian sense. But it also shows us that the Old World is a new world too, for it forces us to rethink aspects of how Europeans think that we might either take for granted or assume to be natural. Until *The Story of Lynx* (1991a; 1995b), the progressive movement of twins towards identity in European mythology was an isolated fact, if it was ever really recognised at all. With *The Story of Lynx*, this isolated fact can be brought into contrast with the very different situation in the mythologies of the New World, and in that relation it acquires meaning. What that meaning might be has been explored here, following Lévi-Strauss, only in relation to the obtuseness with which Europeans greeted the novelty of the New World, but it doubtless extends much further into European cosmology and sociology.

That exploration remains to be done, but its very possibility resolves the anomalous position of European thought as an anthropological problem. Habitually, European thought sees itself as either self-evident, as a transparent tool for interrogating reality, or simply the correct way to think. This is probably general to all human modes of thought, but with this key difference: European thought has, for the past five centuries, proved uniquely invasive. Even when it allows for dialogue with the thought of the Other, European thought always insists on the last word. *The Story of Lynx* points towards a genuine dialogue, a prolonged conversation between different modes of thought, a conversation that might actually get somewhere. This destination will certainly not be agreement, but might allow that European thought is just one variety of human thought, not its measure.

The idea that European thought is, or should be, the measure of all human thought is a consequence of colonialism, and of events like Columbus's 'discovery'. What we call the Discovery of the New World is really our extreme mythologisation of the acts of one man, Christopher Columbus, as an exemplar of how we all should be, and how some of the sons of Europe stand out from general humanity as special. That Columbus died unaware that he had discovered anything other than a shorter route to Cathay should give us pause about the vaunting powers of European individuals. More importantly, that Columbus found lands already richly inhabited by people should give us pause when we talk about 'discoveries'. The point is especially important in the face of long-known evidence that Columbus discovered a New World that was already known to Europeans, although less exemplary ones, as the American geographer Carl Sauer documented in his remarkable piece of regressive history, *Northern Mists* (1968).

Prevailing winds carried Columbus to the New World and back, while a fog descends on earlier relations. Wind and fog are the impossible twins of the mythologies of the Salish-speaking peoples that Lévi-Strauss addresses in *The Story of Lynx* (1991a; 1995b). There, another history is constantly invoked against the 'Discovery of the New World'. This is the fact that the two worlds were never really out of contact in the first place. If Columbus was always much further from China than he thought, some parts of the New World, and their peoples, were not. If we abandon the view of the peopled Earth centred on the Atlantic, and focus instead on the Pacific, Europe loses it centrality and becomes a strange peripheral district to a world where Asia and the Americas lie much closer together. In *The Story of Lynx* (1991a; 1995b), Lévi-Strauss makes frequent reference to the possibilities that the connections or disconnections he is pursuing may reflect contacts much preceding the age of the invasion, contacts mediated through the Pacific, or at least the Bering Straits. The fanfare of 1992 is set there against a date we can never commemorate because we will never really know when it happened: that day when some of our ancient ancestors chose to really discover the Americas, that new world.

ACKNOWLEDGEMENTS

Earlier versions of some of the ideas expressed here were first aired during a brief third stint as a Visiting Professor at the Museu Nacional in Rio de Janeiro. I thank Eduardo Viveiros de Castro, Tania Lima, Marcio Goldman, Aparecida Vilaça and Elizabeth Ewart for their conversations on *The Story of Lynx* over the years, and Julio Shahuano and Roxane Rivas for conversations about why Cocama perspectives matter.

NOTES

1. That Manuyama, or at least his recent ancestors, spoke a dialect of Tupinambá raises a series of fascinating further historical problems I cannot address here, but see Urban 1996 and Gow 2003.
2. I have translated Lévi-Strauss's *sauvages* as 'wild people'. My concern is not for 'political correctness' but for retaining the rhythm of the original text. The English 'savage' sounds much harder and has a very different evocational field than the French *sauvage*. The soundscape of the French *sauvage* is better evoked by the English *wild*, *wilderness* and so on.
3. See Gow 2003 for full explication and sources for the following argument.
4. I take the Cocama forms from Espinosa 1989.

REFERENCES

Agüero, Oscar Alfredo 1994. *El milenio en la amazonía: Mito-utopía tupí-cocama o la subversión del orden simbólico*. Lima and Quito: CAAAP and Abya Yala.

Chevalier, Jacques M. 1982. *Civilization and the Stolen Gift: Capital, Kin and Cult in Eastern Peru*. Toronto: University of Toronto Press.

Espinosa, Lucas 1989. *Breve diccionario analítico Castellano Tupí: sección Cocama*. Iquitos: CETA.

Ewart, Elizabeth 2000. 'Living with Each Other: Selves and Alters amongst the Panará of Central Brazil', Unpublished PhD thesis, University of London.

——2003. 'Lines and Circles: Images of Time in a Panará Village', *Journal of the Royal Anthropological Institute* (N.S.) 9: 261–79.

Gow, Peter 1991. *Of Mixed Blood: Kinship and History in Peruvian Amazonia*. Oxford: Oxford Studies in Social and Cultural Anthropology. Oxford: Oxford University Press.

——2001. *An Amazonian Myth and Its History*. Oxford: Oxford University Press.

——2003. 'Ex-Cocama: identidades em transformação na Amazônia Peruana', *MANA* 9 (1): 57–79.

Lathrap, Donald W. 1970. *The Upper Amazon*. London: Thames & Hudson.

Métraux, Alfred 1928. *La Religion des Tupinamba et ses rapports avec celle des autres tribus tupi-guarani*. Paris: Libraire Ernst Leroux.

Regan, Jaime 1993. *Hacia la tierra sin mal: la religión en la Amazonía* (second edition). Iquitos: CETA.

Ribeiro, Darcy 1970. *Os Indios e a civilização: a integração das populações indígenas no Brasil moderno*. São Paulo: Editora Civilização Brasileira S.A.

Roe, Peter G. 1982. *The Cosmic Zygote: Cosmology in the Amazon Basin*. New Brunswick, NJ: Rutgers University Press.

San-Roman, Jesús 1975. *Perfiles históricos de la Amazonía Peruana*. Lima: Ediciones Paulinas/CETA.

Sauer, Carl O. 1968. *Northern Mists*. San Francisco: Turtle Island Foundation.

Stocks, Anthony 1981. *Los nativos invisibles: notas sobre la historia y realidad actual de los Cocamilla del Rio Huallaga, Perú*. Lima: CAAAP.

Tessmann, Günter 1999 [1930]. *Los indígenas del Peru Nororiental: Investigaciones fundamentales para un estudio sistemático de la cultura*. Quito: Ediciones Abya-Yala.

Urban, Greg 1996. 'On the Geographical Origins and Dispersions of Tupian Languages', *Revista de Antropologia* 39 (2): 61–104.

Viveiros de Castro, Eduardo 1993. 'Le Marbre et le Myrte: de l'inconstance de le âme sauvage', in A. Becquelin and A. Molinié (eds.), *Mémoire de la tradition*. Nanterre: Société d'Ethnologie, pp. 365–431.

12   Before Babel: Lévi-Strauss and language

Christopher Johnson

> In the first place, we have spoken about the relation between *a* language and
> *a* culture. That is, how far is it necessary, when we try to study a culture, to
> know the language? Or how far is it necessary to understand what is meant by
> the population, to have some knowledge of the culture besides the language.
>
> Lévi-Strauss, *Structural Anthropology*

In a memorable passage at the beginning of *Tristes Tropiques*, following his
famous denunciation of travel and explorers ('I hate travelling and
explorers'), Lévi-Strauss criticises the amateurs of exoticism who travel vast
distances in order to bring back to their European public sensationalised
accounts of cultures which have already been well documented in ethnographic studies (1955a: 9–10; 1992: 17–18). Later in the text, he distinguishes
between this superficial and aestheticised exoticism, which engages
the senses but not the mind, and a more authentic and scientific exoticism,
that of ethnography. Even if the ethnographer and the explorer might share
the same passion for alterity, even if both might endure the same kind
of deprivations in order to obtain their knowledge, the relative status of
this knowledge is not in question (1955a: 37–8; 1992: 38–9). Although the
ethnographer's point of departure is defined by his or her attraction to the
'exotic' and, symmetrically, a certain aversion to his or her native culture,
the destination of ethnology as a discipline, as a *science*, is not exoticism for
exoticism's sake, but a deeper understanding of human nature. Following the
programme outlined by Rousseau in a long note of the *Second Discourse*, the
goal of anthropology should be to acquire a better knowledge of human
diversity in order to obtain a better understanding of the essence of humanity
(1973a: 46; 1978b: 34–5). In this sense, Lévi-Strauss is not so much interested
in the exotic in itself as in what the so-called exotic reveals about cultural
difference, so that the real object of anthropology as a discipline of the exotic
is cultural diversity.

   The concept of diversity is central to the seminal essay published in 1952,
Race and History. At the start of this essay, Lévi-Strauss very quickly
dispenses with UNESCO's question concerning science and racism, in order
to propose the more general question of cultural diversity, asking whether

the observable differences between cultures might not also imply their inequality, and whether there might exist a critical threshold of cultural diversity below which humanity could not move without endangering its existence (1973a: 381; 1978b: 327). *Race and History* can therefore be read as an essay on the origins of cultural inequality, a kind of twentieth-century variant of Rousseau's famous essay, but also as an essay on the properly vital question of the survival of the human race. The big problem, as it emerges in the pages of *Race and History*, is first how to account for the palpable fact, in the immediate post-war period, of the technological, economic and military hegemony of the Western world, and, second, how to deal with what the author judges to be its inevitable corollary, the homogenisation of world civilisation, the threat of a global 'monoculture', as he will express it a few years later in *Tristes Tropiques* (1955a: 36–7; 1992: 37–8). It is not my intention here to engage with the detail of Lévi-Strauss's argument in *Race and History*, but for the purposes of this discussion, it is important to note that, typically, he tackles the problem of cultural diversity by a process of abstraction, constructing models of cultural differentiation based on the ideas of *combination* and (inspired by contemporary developments in information theory) *information*. In other words, he presents different human societies as being made up of sets of cultural traits, the differences between societies being a function of the relative combination of these traits, and the relations between societies being characterised by the communication and exchange of individual traits (1973a: 405sq.; 1978b: 347sq.).

Lévi-Strauss's conceptualisation of cultural difference and culture contact in *Race and History* is an interesting one, if only for the kind of models it mobilises, but it is not unproblematic.[1] However, what I would like to focus on here is the strange omission, in an essay on human diversity, of what for the ethnologist should be one of the fundamental components of both cultural specificity and cultural contact, that is, language, or *languages*. This omission is all the more striking because at the time that Lévi-Strauss was writing *Race and History* there was another, very influential paradigm or theory of cultural difference operating at the intersection of linguistics and anthropology, the so-called Sapir–Whorf hypothesis. The Sapir–Whorf hypothesis considered cultural difference as a function of linguistic difference, and was basically a combination of two principles. First, the idea of linguistic determinism, that is, the idea that our modes of thought, our ways of interpreting the world, perhaps our perceptions, are influenced, or even determined, by the categories of our languages. Second, the concept of linguistic relativism: given the great diversity of languages – a diversity especially visible in the case of the Native American languages studied by Sapir and Whorf, which frequently showed considerable divergences from Indo-European language groups – the world experiences of individuals speaking distinct languages are in a certain sense incommensurable.[2]

It is not my intention to comment on the ultimate value or viability of the Sapir–Whorf hypothesis, which in its so-called 'strong' version, delineated above, has been vigorously contested. What interests me here is rather the absence of any reference to the idea of linguistic relativism in the pages of *Race and History*, and the lack of any substantial reference to the subject in the rest of Lévi-Strauss's work. Significantly, the one instance in which Lévi-Strauss does directly reference Whorf's work – in a text published a year after *Race and History* – he is critical of the type of linguistic analysis Whorf represents. It would be worthwhile taking a closer look at this text, in order to get a clearer picture of Lévi-Strauss's thinking on the relationship between language and culture.

'Linguistics and Anthropology' was originally a paper given at the Conference of Anthropologists and Linguists at Bloomington, Indiana, in 1952 (later published in *Structural Anthropology*). In view of the fact that the paper was delivered in the concluding session of the conference, it is an instructive reminder of Lévi-Strauss's qualities as a speaker, and as an individual capable of providing a critical overview of his discipline and the different theoretical challenges it faces. It is also a revealing indication of the direction his research was taking following his shift in specialisation, after 1950, from kinship studies to the anthropology of religions. As in the programmatic *Introduction to the Work of Marcel Mauss* (1950), one can observe here Lévi-Strauss's strategic delimitation of the terrain that will increasingly be that of the structural study of myth and classification systems, a kind of clearing of the ground before he embarks on the more detailed theorisation the latter will entail. Symptomatic of this gesture of delimitation is his repeated reference to what has *not* hitherto been attempted in the field of anthropology and linguistics. So while much attention has been given to the relationship between specific languages and specific cultures, he argues, the more general question of the relationship between language and culture has been neglected. Recognising the complexity of this relationship, which has until now been viewed as one of causality or inclusion (for example, culture *produces* language; language, along with other social constructions, is a *part* of culture), he points out that it is also one of conditionality (language is the principal medium through which culture is transmitted) (1958a: 77–8; 1977d: 67–8). However, there is a second kind of conditionality which Lévi-Strauss evidently finds more interesting, and which concerns the homologous 'architecture', as he terms it, of language and culture:

But also, from a much more theoretical point of view, language can be said to be a condition of culture because the material out of which language is built is of the same type as the material out of which the whole culture is built: logical relations, oppositions, correlations, and the like. Language, from this point of view, may appear as laying a kind of foundation for the more complex structures which correspond to the different aspects of culture. (1958a: 78–9; 1977d: 68–9)[3]

As can be seen, Lévi-Strauss's strategy here is to raise the question of the relationship between language and culture to a higher level of abstraction, beyond the intuitive or commonplace interpretations which have character-ised more orthodox discussions of that relationship. What such abstraction permits and requires, he suggests, is a closer collaboration between linguists and anthropologists, more rigorous than the kind of 'soft' interdisciplinarity they have traditionally practised, and enabling anthropology finally to acquire the kind of scientific credentials linguistics has obtained in the past few decades – making it, like linguistics, an authentic human science (1958a: 79–80; 1977d: 69–70).

At the same time as Lévi-Strauss recognises the complexity of the language–culture relationship, he also proceeds to simplify that relationship by reducing it to another level of determination, that of the *human mind*. From this point of view, language and culture are 'parallel modalities' of 'a more fundamental activity' (1958a: 81; 1977d: 71).[4] The fact that, over a period of thousands of years, language and culture have co-evolved within the space of the human mind means that it would be unusual if there were not some kind of structural correlation between the two (1958a: 81–2; 1977d: 71–2). This reduction of the problem of language and culture to the 'architecture' of the human mind is what today would be described as a *cognitivist* approach. In other words, the kind of anthropology Lévi-Strauss is proposing is concerned above all with the fundamental structures of the human mind, and the way in which the human mind, to use the vocabulary of information and computer science, *processes* social and cultural experience. This cognitivism, as it might be called, and the accompanying endorsement of a communicational model of language, helps to explain Lévi-Strauss's rejection of Whorf's ideas in the following part of his presentation, ideas which appear to have been a leitmotif of discussions up to this point of the conference:

Whorf and his ideas have frequently been put forward during our discussions. Indeed, Whorf tried to reveal correlations between language and culture, though in my opinion the correlations he established were not always convincing. The reason for this seems to be that he is much less systematic in his analysis of culture than he is for language. He approaches the latter as a linguist (it is not for me to judge how good a linguist), in other words the object he focuses on is not the product of an empirical and intuitive apprehension of reality, but the result of a linguistic analysis involving a considerable degree of abstraction. However, the cultural object with which he compares this is sketchy, and is not developed beyond the level of crude observation. Whorf tries to reveal correlations between objects that belong to two very disparate levels, in terms of the quality of observation and sophistication of analysis that are, respectively, applied to these levels. Let us therefore situate ourselves firmly at the level of systems of communication. (1958a: 83–4; 1977d: 73; my translation)

One can understand Lévi-Strauss's impatience, as an anthropologist, with what he considers to be an under-determination of cultural description in Whorf's work. His brief consideration of Whorf's linguistics presents him as literally getting lost in the complexities of language, and as failing to take account of the detail of the other side of the equation, cultural reality. It seems as if for Lévi-Strauss, this asymmetry invalidates the whole of Whorf's analysis, and he does not consider, for example, whether it might not be possible to rectify this imbalance by complexifying Whorf's treatment of cultural facts. In addition, there is, curiously, no direct mention or consideration of the hypothesis of linguistic determinism itself. Instead, Lévi-Strauss immediately uses what he has presented as the deficiency or failure of Whorfian linguistics in order to propose a *communicational* model for the analysis of linguistic and cultural phenomena. What follows is a series of illustrations of possible structural correlations between language and culture, which focuses for the most part on the domain of kinship structures. In the conclusion to his paper, in a move that mirrors his earlier marginalisation of Whorf, Lévi-Strauss reiterates his gesture of hospitality to the 'uninvited guest' of the conference, that is, the human mind, which it is the task of the new anthropology to elucidate (1958a: 91; 1977d: 79–80).

From the beginning of the 1950s therefore, Lévi-Strauss is proposing that anthropology should be a kind of psychology, and, more precisely, an 'intellectualist' psychology, which deals with the cognitive rather than the affective dimensions of mental phenomena.[5] As is well known, the model he uses to represent the operations of the human mind is taken primarily from linguistics: it is a structural model which originates in the work of the Swiss linguist Ferdinand de Saussure, published at the start of the twentieth century. At the heart of Saussure's theory of language is the concept of *la langue* ('the language'), as expressed, for example, in his key formulation 'In the language itself [*la langue*] there are only differences' (1983: 118; 1986: 166). It would be useful to pause an instant here, in order to underline the strangeness of this formulation for the uninformed speaker of French, the kind of distortion it imposes on the everyday usage of the French term *la langue*. Whereas in its common, everyday usage, the word refers, in the singular, to the specificity of a national language (French, English, German, etc.) or, in the plural, to the diversity of natural languages, in Saussure's theory the definite article of the term *la langue* refers to a subset of *le langage* (simply, 'language'), in other words, it refers to the underlying code which determines linguistic production in all its forms (*la parole*). This inflection of the everyday use of the word, which since Saussure's work has been incorporated into a number of the major French dictionaries, is symptomatic of the counterintuitive nature of the concept of *la langue*: a supplement of discipline, and, in the dictionaries, a supplement of definition, is required to conceptualise an abstract system which would predetermine the structure of not one, but *all* languages.

Lévi-Strauss's introduction of the linguistic model into anthropology is not entirely faithful to Saussure's original conception,[6] and in order to get a fuller picture of his first formulations of structural analysis, one would of course also need to factor in the influence of the linguistics of Jakobson and Trubetzkoy. However, if one looks at Lévi-Strauss's first attempts at the structural analysis of myth, Saussure's influence is nonetheless fundamental. In the now classic article first published in 1955, 'The Structural Study of Myth' (1955e), he uses the Saussurean distinction between *langue* and *parole* – which he takes to represent respectively the 'structural' and 'statistical' aspects of language – in order to propose a third level of symbolisation at which highly structured collective representations such as myth might operate. These kinds of collective representations are indeed, he claims, a kind of language (*langage*), and as such can be submitted to the same methods of conceptualisation and analysis as human language (1958a: 230–3; 1977d: 209–11). Just as the dream was for Freud the royal road to the individual unconscious, so the collective representations of myth are for Lévi-Strauss the royal road to the structures of the human mind. From the foundational 1955 article to the *Mythologiques* and beyond, he is first and foremost interested in the deep structure of myths, the laws of transformation which regulate the relations between myths, that is, their language (*langue*) in its most universal (Saussurean) sense, rather than the particular languages in which they are articulated. Already in 'The Structural Study of Myth', in a 'brief parenthesis', Lévi-Strauss emphasises this priority of *the* language of myth over the *languages* of myth:

A remark can be introduced at this point which will help to show the originality of myth in relation to other linguistic phenomena. Myth is the part of language [*mode du discours*] where the formula *traduttore, traditore* reaches its lowest truth value. From that point of view it should be placed in the gamut of linguistic expressions at the end opposite to that of poetry, in spite of all the claims which have been made to prove the contrary. Poetry is a kind of speech [*langage*] which cannot be translated except at the cost of serious distortions; whereas the mythical value of the myth is preserved even through the worst translation. Whatever our ignorance of the language and the culture of the people where it originated, a myth is still felt as a myth by any reader anywhere in the world. Its substance does not lie in its style, its original music [*mode de narration*], or its syntax, but in the *story* which it tells. Myth is language, functioning on an especially high level where meaning succeeds practically at 'taking off' from the linguistic ground on which it keeps rolling [*sur lequel il a commencé par rouler*: literally, on which it started off rolling]. (1958a: 232; 1977d: 210)

The reader who reads between languages – in this case English and French – will note the interesting divergences here between 'original' and 'translation', the most interesting of which is probably the final sentence, where the French text states that myth literally leaves the ground of its linguistic support, while the English version paradoxically suggests that it keeps rolling on that ground. If one takes the French text as the primary source, then it can be concluded that the English version is simply a mistranslation, though the situation may in fact be more complicated than this.[7] For the moment, however, I would like to retain the ambiguity of this divergence, this hesitation between the two versions, in order to ask whether a total 'take-off', to use Lévi-Strauss's aeronautical metaphor, is ever possible, when it is a question of the radically different and diverse languages in which myth is incarnated. What Lévi-Strauss is proposing here is a kind of *stereospecificity* of myth as a cultural object, which would ensure the universality of our perception of it as a myth, an aesthetics of recognition which in turn would ensure – in spite of the diversity of language and culture – the stability of the 'absolute object' (1958a: 231; 1977d: 210) that is myth. The question I will be asking in the remainder of this discussion will be, quite simply, what happens to linguistic diversity and linguistic alterity when the plurality of human languages are subsumed into *the* language of the human mind?

In 1956 Lévi-Strauss published a short article, 'The Three Humanisms', which was subsequently included in *Structural Anthropology II* (1973a: 319–22; 1978b: 271–4). The first humanism, he argues, was the rediscovery of Graeco-Roman civilisation at the end of the Middle Ages and during the Renaissance. This, he claims, was the first incarnation of ethnology, to the extent that this discovery revealed another world, from the early European perspective an exotic world, an experience which taught us that we can only really understand ourselves by comparing ourselves with what is different to us. The teaching and learning of the languages of antiquity, Greek and Latin, were an integral part of this 'technique of estrangement' (*technique du dépaysement*), as Lévi-Strauss terms it. In order to gain access to this lost world, a linguistic apprenticeship was therefore essential. Even if the languages of antiquity are now what we call 'dead' languages, nevertheless by practising them one acquires an intellectual training, an intellectual discipline which is comparable to the kind of training necessary to the practice of ethnology (1973a: 319–20; 1978b: 271–2). The second humanism, says Lévi-Strauss, was simply the extension of the methods of Graeco-Latin humanism to the other great world civilisations, China and India, for example. In France, this branch of studies is normally designated as 'non-classical philology'. Once again, the study and mastery of languages, in this case less proximate and more diverse languages, was indispensable to the understanding of lost civilisations (1973a: 320; 1978b: 272–3).[8] The third and final stage of humanism, according to Lévi-Strauss, is ethnology itself, which extends the study of humanity to the societies neglected by the more traditional humanisms. Unlike the so-called classical and non-classical civilisations, the societies studied by ethnologists have no 'high culture', so to speak: in most cases, they produce neither durable monuments nor written literatures. The task of ethnology is to provide an external and objective perspective on these societies, but also, through the practice of fieldwork, the participation of the ethnographer in the everyday existence of a particular group, an internal perspective on their everyday experience, their mental and affective life. In this respect, in its desire to embrace the whole of humanity, the 'primitive' as well as the 'civilised', ethnology is a more *democratic* form of humanism than its predecessors (1973a: 321–2; 1978b: 273–4).

It is difficult not to agree with Lévi-Strauss that if we wish to widen our consciousness of the world and therefore of ourselves, it is necessary to open ourselves up to other mentalities, to other modes of thought and existence, in short, to the *exotic*. The practice of fieldwork, the immediate experience of another cultural reality, both objective and subjective, would be the ultimate expression of such openness or exposure. The only problem, and the only reservation one might express here, is that in passing from what he terms classical and non-classical humanism to the modern science, the *human* science of ethnology, it is not only the text which disappears as the privileged mode of access to the other – the societies studied by ethnographers have no texts, they are in Lévi-Strauss's own description 'non-literate societies' (*des sociétés sans écriture*) – but also, it seems, language, or *languages*. While the study of the great civilisations of the past demands a linguistic discipline, a close frequentation and skilled manipulation of their now extinct languages, in the case of non-literate cultures the question of the *practice* of their languages is left in suspense. One can only suppose, and hope, that linguistic competence – advanced linguistic competence – would also be part of the training of the participant-observer of 'exotic' cultures, the privileged mediator of cultural *and* linguistic alterity. It is precisely this question of competence that I will focus on in the next part of this discussion.

It is in the four volumes of *Mythologiques* (1964a–1971a), where some 800 North and South American myths serve as a kind of laboratory case for the study of myth, that one finds the most sustained and sophisticated application of structuralist method. In view of Lévi-Strauss's considerable intellectual investment in this project, it is not surprising to find, in the final volume of the cycle, *The Naked Man* (1971a), an extended defence of structuralism. In the 'Finale' of the *The Naked Man* – the musical metaphor is Lévi-Strauss's – he reviews and responds to the different criticisms, what he calls the 'methodological objections' (*objections de méthode*), which have been directed at structuralism. I will not enumerate these criticisms here, since they are not all of equal interest or relevance to the present discussion. What does stand out, however, and what Lévi-Strauss himself singles out and confesses to being the most serious criticism, is the one concerning language, or rather, *languages*. Lévi-Strauss's explanation, his defence or self-defence, is so interesting, but also so curious and so difficult, that it is worth quoting in its entirety:

None of the objections that I have just briefly reviewed goes to the heart of the problems that these volumes try to elucidate. A much more serious one . . . has been made by certain linguists who reproach me with having, only in exceptional cases, taken into account the diversity of the languages in which all these myths were first conceived and formulated, although not invariably recorded . . . I cannot claim to be linguistically competent, and even among the specialists there is probably no one capable of undertaking the comparative philological study of texts originating in languages which, although all American, differ as much among themselves as those of the Indo-European, Semitic, Finno-Ugrian and Sino-Tibetan families.

Philological analysis has to be resorted to in the case of the dead languages, where the meaning of each term can only be determined by looking at it [*le permutant*] in several contexts . . . In most cases, unfortunately, there is no original text, and the myth is known only in translation, or even through several successive translations made by interpreters capable of understanding a foreign language and who made versions in their mother tongue, which was not always that of the person recording the story.

Hic Rhodus, hic salta: if, in spite of the decisive part played by philology in Professor Dumézil's outstanding works . . . I had made it a preliminary condition that I would study the myths only in the original languages, my project would have been unrealizable, not only by me, since I am not a philologist with expert knowledge of the Amerindian languages, but by anyone else. I had therefore to commit myself to a double wager [*un double pari*], first in making do with such instruments as I could improvise [*en fabriquant d'abord des instruments de fortune*], not of course as a substitute for philological study . . . but to offset to some extent the impossibility of having recourse to philology; then in deciding to await the result before coming to a conclusion about the fundamental problem. The result is now available; I myself at least am convinced that this enquiry, which was undertaken in the face of limitations serious enough to make it theoretically unfeasible [*qui eussent dû théoriquement la vouer à l'échec*], has on the contrary proved most fruitful. This is an accomplished fact we must now argue from, even if at first sight it seems to constitute a mystery, which calls for explanation.

The key to the enigma is, I think, to be found in the myth creation process revealed by my study, and which it alone could demonstrate clearly by being carried through to its conclusion. If, as is shown by the comparative analysis of different versions of the same myth produced by one or several communities, *conter* (to tell a story) is always *conte redire* (to retell a story), which can also be written *contredire* (to contradict), it is immediately understandable why it was not absolutely essential, for the purposes of the rough sorting out I had in mind, to study the myths in the originals, instead of in a translation or a series of translations. Properly speaking, there is never any original: every myth is by its very nature a translation, and derives from another myth belonging to a neighbouring, but foreign, community, or from a previous myth belonging to the same community or from a contemporaneous one belonging to a different social sub-division . . . that some listener tries to plagiarize [*démarquer*] by translating it in his fashion into his personal or tribal language, sometimes to appropriate it and sometimes to refute it, and therefore invariably distorting it. (1971a: 575–6; 1981: 643–4)

As can be seen, there is much, indeed too much that could be said about this passage, and about what one might term the *monolingualism* of Lévi-Strauss's *Mythologiques*. I will restrict myself to the following points:

(1) The state of Babel which, from the outset, problematises any attempt at a general ethnography of the Americas. As Lévi-Strauss points out, the diverse indigenous languages of this continent are frequently more different from one another than are the great language families of the Old World.

(2) The problem of linguistic competence, which Lévi-Strauss himself does not possess. And even if there do exist specialists of one or more of these indigenous languages, it would be impossible for an individual person to cover them all. Nobody has such a competence, it is not *humanly* possible to have such a competence. An integrally philological approach is therefore in principle impossible.

(3) The retreat of the origin, which, interestingly, becomes a 'post-structuralist' motif following Derrida's reading of the *Mythologiques* (1967: 419–21; 1978b: 286–7). Often there is not even any original 'text' of a myth. The 'myth' that one is left with is the product of an extended chain of communication, a series of translations.

(4) Lévi-Strauss's response to this methodological aporia, which is to jump (*Hic Rhodus, hic salta*).[9] This jump is a jump into the unknown, a risk, a wager (*pari*), whose success (or not) can only be judged after the event. As it turns out – and this is, in Lévi-Strauss's own words, the 'mystery' – the adventure has proved fruitful, and the structuralist method has overcome the state of Babel which should from the very start have condemned it to failure.

Lévi-Strauss himself appears to be convinced of the success of the endeavour, but nevertheless seems to feel obliged to elucidate what he calls the 'mystery' of this success. The explanation for this, he suggests, is that myth is essentially a translation or series of translations. It will be noticed here that Lévi-Strauss is referring to 'translation' not only in the restricted, everyday sense of the term – that of the communication and conversation between natural languages – but also, and above all, in the sense of a transformation (opposition, transposition, deformation) operating at the level of the language (*langue*) of myth. Because structural analysis, as it is practised in the *Mythologiques*, is primarily interested in the transformational relationships between myths, the location of a myth is never *in* a language or *in* a culture, but in the space which separates them. This is what allows Lévi-Strauss to assert, following this passage in the 'Finale' and reviving the argument of 'The Structural Study of Myth', that the linguistic embodiment of a myth – its style, narrative mode, syntax and aesthetics – can be detached from what he calls its 'story', 'semantic content' or (using the terminology of information theory) 'message'. What he proposes, therefore, is a 'relative detachment' (*décollement relatif* – the original aeronautical metaphor appears to have disappeared here) of myth, a relative autonomy of a myth's meaning in relation to its 'linguistic base' (*support linguistique*) (1971a: 577, 579; 1981: 645, 648).

One can admire the elegance, and appreciate the theoretical interest, of Lévi-Strauss's defence of the structuralist method vis-à-vis the seemingly intractable problem of linguistic variation. This defence is extended and complicated in the subsequent pages of the 'Finale' in a long digression on myth and music (1971a: 577–96; 1981: 645–67). There is neither time nor space here to enter into the detail of this digression: that would be the task of a separate study involving, among other things, the analysis of Lévi-Strauss's aesthetics. What I would like to question, returning to the aeronautical metaphor of 'The Structural Study of Myth', is whether the 'taking off' of the meaning or message of myth from the ground of its linguistic support can ever be a total one, or whether, as the English version of this passage implied, the aircraft still continues to roll along the ground, its nose raised in the air, perhaps, but the wheels of its rear undercarriage never losing contact with the earth. This is not to say that translation is impossible, nor that 'meaning' is never transmissible between different linguistic universes: it is not necessary here to invoke the so-called 'strong' version of the linguistic relativism of Sapir–Whorf. It is rather that, if one were to take Sapir–Whorf seriously, a proper analysis of the kind of culture contact Lévi-Strauss is referring to when he describes, for example, the passage of a myth from one linguistic group to another would indeed require the grounding of a kind of *super*-philology, an advanced competence in the two or more languages involved in this type of intercultural communication. For the practical reasons mentioned by Lévi-Strauss above, such an approach would in many cases prove to be impossible, and as one multiplied the stages of transmission of a given myth, the problem of appropriate competence would increase accordingly. His solution to this apparent impasse is a thoroughly *technical* one, that is, he circumvents the problem of the plurality of natural language by positing a higher (or perhaps, more accurately, lower) level language which is the universal language (*langue*) of myth, contained in the laws governing the transformations between myths. As he concedes, this solution is not an ideal one, it is not, so to speak, an engineering solution, but rather *bricolage*, the ad hoc construction of instruments of analysis ('in making do with such instruments as I could improvise'), in the hope (the wager) that their application might at some point pay off. His own, retrospective evaluation of this endeavour is, it must be confessed, solipsistic and self-validating: the method is right because it has, in his estimation, worked; the gamble has, in his opinion, paid off, therefore the method is correct. The reader, and more expert commentators of North and South American mythology might not share this methodological optimism, if only because the explanation Lévi-Strauss gives of how myths are created – which, ironically, is based on a wordplay (*conter–conte, redire–contredire*) that has his translator working overtime – appears to be so reductive. Is the reader substantially advanced in his or her understanding of how the 'language' of myth might work in learning that it is based on the binary alternative of the replication and/or refutation of one myth by another, and therefore a necessary process of distortion? Is this a realistic model of how collective representations are actually communicated between cultures? Is such essentially *overdetermined* communication formalisable in any meaningful way? Is such formalisation ultimately necessary?

If Lévi-Strauss's solution to the Babel of myth is a technical one, it is also the reflection of a given state of technological culture at a given point in time. That is, his dream of short-circuiting the complexities of linguistic embodiment could be seen as being symptomatic of a more general trend in twentieth-century science. As I have argued elsewhere, in spite of its importance, the linguistic model is only one of a number of models Lévi-Strauss uses to conceptualise myth in his earlier texts. Among these, models drawn from information theory and cybernetics, along with their instantiation in what in the 1940s and 1950s was the emerging field of computing technology, play a key role (Johnson 2003: 88–103). In fact, what is interesting about this scientific-technological context is precisely the lack of separation between 'pure' and 'applied' science, between science and technology. The founding figure of cybernetics, Norbert Wiener, described this kind of science as 'operational' science: our study of logic, for example, cannot be separated from the experimental investigation of its instantiation in working models such as the computer or the human nervous system (Wiener 1961: 125). Wiener's influence on Lévi-Strauss's early conceptualisation of myth is manifest, not only in the set of terms and concepts Lévi-Strauss borrows from cybernetics (programme, message, coding, redundancy, feedback), but also in his 'operational' view of his own practice of structural analysis. Myth in this sense is a kind of information technology, a 'logical model' or 'logical tool' as Lévi-Strauss puts it (1958a: 229, 254; 1977d: 216, 239), the investigation of which gives insight into the structure of the (human) mind which produces it.

It would be interesting to pursue further here the history of the interdisciplinary matrix from which structuralism emerged in the earlier, formative part of Lévi-Strauss's career, but again this would be the task of another, separate study. For the moment, it is sufficient to remember that the kind of technology

Lévi-Strauss is alluding to when he refers to myth as a logical 'tool' or 'model' is indeed computing technology, in other words, the machine manipulation of symbolic systems. It is commonly understood that the computing technology of the mid-twentieth century was first developed to deal with mathematical and arithmetical problems of a scale exceeding the normal capacities of a specialised human agent: computers were machines which, increasingly, were capable of processing artificial languages more rapidly and more efficiently than was the finite human mind. What is less well known is that from the start, one of the other important applications for which the computer was considered a potential candidate was the processing of natural languages, that is, machine translation. The hope, or ambition, was that if one could go deep enough into the basic structures of human language, then one would be able to reach a level of symbolic abstraction at which the diversity of natural languages – *any* and *every* language – would be mutually convertible.[10] The interdisciplinary implications of machine translation were immediately apparent, as inevitably it mobilised not only information science, but also linguistics and psychology. While Lévi-Strauss himself makes no substantive reference to what Warren Weaver called 'mechanical translation', it is clear that he shares the same kind of optimism and ambition of what, in retrospect, might generically be referred to as the cognitive sciences, that is, sciences which look at the processes of the human mind – including its symbolic behaviour in the production of natural language – in the light of the ambient science of computing technology.[11] In fact, it has been argued that it was the rise of cognitive science that was most responsible for the eventual discrediting and marginalisation of the linguistic relativism paradigm of Sapir–Whorf (Gumperz and Levinson 1996: 3–4; 41–2). One of the fundamental principles of cognitive psychology is the universality of our basic categories of perception and of our *processing* of sense data, activities that are deeply embedded in the long-term evolution of our species. For the cognitive sciences, as they have developed since the 1950s, the relationship between 'thought' and 'language' is a unilateral one: it is thought, or cognitive processes, which inform language, and not the reverse. At a fundamental level, the diversity of natural languages derives from the same mental infrastructure, and they are therefore formally the same.[12] It is this kind of universalism which seems to inform Lévi-Strauss's thinking on myth and, inseparably, his attitude towards language and languages. In his extended defence of structuralism in the 'Finale' of *The Naked Man*, he cites specific areas of contemporary science which appear to confirm structuralism's semiotic-reductionist programme, presenting a 'bottom-up' conception of human thought, consisting of a homology of structures at each level: binarism of the genetic code; binarism of visual perception and smell; binarism of human language; binarism of symbolic and mythical thought (1971a: 605, 612, 617–18; 1981: 678, 684–5, 691–2).

That Lévi-Strauss has put his finger on an important feature of contemporary science, that is, the prevalence of the informational and computing paradigm, is not in question. What is less certain is whether the homology of structures he describes provides a satisfactory map or model of how the human mind might ultimately function, especially when it is engaged in higher-level functions such as language and the kind of symbolic thinking one finds in mythical discourse. In particular, there remains the unanswered question of linguistic determinism and linguistic relativism, the extent to which an individual language might ultimately shape thought and the degree of work – perhaps infinite – that would be necessary to establish an effective correlation between divergent systems of thought/language. Here again, one might ask, does the aircraft ever leave the ground?

In order to move towards some form of conclusion, in the final part of this discussion I will turn from theory to autobiography, not in order to make some kind of *ad hominem* judgement of Lévi-Strauss's thinking about language and languages, but because, as is often the case with Lévi-Strauss, autobiography can illuminate theory – or perhaps more accurately in this case, the choice of theory – in interesting ways. Here, I will take two examples from the autobiographical texts.

The first can be found in Lévi-Strauss's 1988 interviews with Didier Eribon (1988a), where he confesses that he lacks a natural gift for languages:

C.L.-S.   I don't have a gift for languages. I write articles in faulty English, and I can give a talk in English with a hateful accent. [. . .]

D.E.   You never had, like Dumézil, the relentless drive [*volonté*] to learn languages? A consuming passion for foreign languages?

C.L.-S.   For Dumézil, it was not only a passion or a drive, it was a gift! (1988a: 125–6; 1991b: 87)

One could discuss at length the question of the gift, the question of passion and the will, of what is given freely (the spontaneous gift of tongues of the Pentecost) and what is acquired, the product of a long and patient discipline, of an apprenticeship, of experience. Here, I will simply note the reappearance of Dumézil, the *other* structuralist, who in the 'Finale' of *The Naked Man* represented an alternative, philological approach to the study of myth, an approach Lévi-Strauss could doubtless admire but not emulate.

The second example occurs in *Tristes Tropiques* and constitutes what might be called a limit-case, a situation which throws a kind of retrospective light on the other instances of cultural contact related in the 'ethnographic' chapters of the book – Bororo, Caduveo, Nambikwara, Tupí-Kawahib. This is the meeting with the group named Mundé, which apparently has never been cited in the ethnographic literature on the region. Having reached the final stages of his ethnographic expedition, the younger Lévi-Strauss has finally found some authentic 'savages', apparently untouched by civilisation. Unfortunately he has neither the time, nor above all the means, to study them properly; he does not know their language, and does not have an interpreter:

Even though I was ignorant of the language and had no interpreter, I could try to grasp [*pénétrer*] certain aspects of the Mundé way of thinking and social organization, such as how the group was made up, the kinship system and vocabulary, the names of the parts of the body, and the colour vocabulary, according to a chart I always carried with me. Kinship terms and those used for the parts of the body, colours and shapes (e.g., the shapes engraved on the calabashes) often have common characteristics which put them halfway between vocabulary and grammar: each group forms a system, and the way in which different languages choose to arrange or confuse [*choisissent de séparer ou de confondre*] the relationships expressed by means of it allows us to make a certain number of hypotheses, even though they may relate only to the distinctive features of this particular society.

However, although I had set off on the adventure with enthusiasm, it left me with a feeling of emptiness.

I had wanted to reach the extreme limits of the savage; it might be thought that my wish had been granted, now that I found myself among these charming Indians whom no other white man had ever seen before and who might never be seen again. After an enchanting trip up-river, I had certainly found my savages. Alas! they were only too savage. Since their existence has only been revealed to me at the last moment, I was unable to devote to them the time that would have been essential to get to know them. The limited resources at my disposal, the state of physical exhaustion in which my companions and I now found ourselves – and which was to be made still worse by the fevers of the rainy season – allowed me no more than a short busman's holiday [*une brève école buissonnière*: literally, *faire l'école buissonnière* means to play truant] instead of months of study. They were there, all ready to teach me their customs and beliefs, and I did not know their language. They were as close to me as a reflection in a mirror; I could touch them, but I could not understand them. I had been given, at one and the same time, my reward and my punishment. (1955a: 396–7; 1992: 332–3)

This sequence is characterised by two movements, two gestures, which seem to be pointing in opposite directions. On the one hand, there is the younger Lévi-Strauss's frustration and despair when, faced with the object of his ethnographic desire, he cannot know or understand it. His relationship with the exotic other is reduced to the superficiality of the senses, a purely *aesthetic* relationship of touch and reflection. From the older narrator's point of view – and complicitly, that of his reader – this personal tragedy is also, in a way, ironic: the sin of precipitation, the haste to penetrate the mental world of the other, is punished by the impossibility of contact. This limit-case, as we have called it, exposes the weakness of an 'extensive' rather than 'intensive' ethnography, the precariousness of the kind of 'busman's holiday' (*école buissonnière*) that characterises Lévi-Strauss's stay with the Mundé.[13]

On the other hand, in spite of this seemingly pessimistic conclusion, the younger Lévi-Strauss's failure is only a relative one, or rather that failure is in a sense recuperated by the older Lévi-Strauss, the narrator of *Tristes Tropiques*. Because preceding this confession of linguistic impotence, of the haste or lack of foresight which condemns the ethnographer to the prison of his own language, there is the affirmation of the possibility of understanding the other *in spite of* the separation of languages. Faced with the linguistic opacity of the Mundé, the younger Lévi-Strauss does what he has always, and will always do: he improvises, focusing on social and cultural features that ostensibly do not require dialogue between observer and observed. What is striking for the reader, and especially for the reader who is a linguist, is that even without knowing the Mundé language, and even without an interpreter, the ethnographer nevertheless feels capable of grasping (*pénétrer*: literally, to penetrate, or gain access/insight to) 'certain aspects of the Mundé way of thinking and social organization'. It is important to note exactly which aspects of Mundé culture are, according to the narrator, open to such investigation. As it turns out, most of these aspects relate to names, naming and classification. According to Lévi-Strauss, kinship terms, terms denoting parts of the body, colours and shapes occupy an intermediary position in languages, between vocabulary and grammar. It is not clear which area of linguistic theory Lévi-Strauss is drawing on here, nor what it might mean exactly for terms to be 'between' the two categories of language he mentions, the grammatical and the lexical. If one accepts this line of argument, however, it is the intermediate status of such terms which frees them from the specificity of one language, and endows them, so to speak, with an *inter*linguistic quality. This would then make it possible to construct 'hypotheses' of the systems of relations they represent, which would vary in accordance with the divisions of particular languages.

It is difficult for the critical reader to be entirely convinced by this explanation, which is in effect an attempted *theorisation* of the problem of linguistic separation. In the final analysis, it does nothing to resolve the problem of the communication between cultures, and at the most displaces that problem by reformulating it in the terms of a structuralist universalism.[14] If, like the protagonist of *Tristes Tropiques*, the reader is left with a certain 'feeling of emptiness', it is because the narrator's description of this episode continues to elicit the simple and intractable question: how can one delineate the categories of the 'savage' mind without having access to the language in which they are expressed?

If I have insisted on exploring the autobiographical side, so to speak, of structuralist theory, then it is because in a way Lévi-Strauss's structuralism could be read as the sublation of the problem of linguistic alterity, a problem which becomes most urgent in the properly existential situation of fieldwork.

In such a situation, as with the Mundé, the immediate presence of the other is contradicted and frustrated by the infinite distance of non-communication, of the other who does not speak *my* language. From this point of view, the solution of structuralism could be interpreted as a strategy of repression and displacement, in that it forgets and turns away from the linguistic infinite – the infinity of discipline, the infinity of translation, which those of us who deal with languages know would be necessary for a true comprehension of the 'exotic' other. For structuralism, this is the infinity of the state of Babel which exists (or rather, increasingly and tragically, existed) in the New World, and which it is necessary, technically, to overcome. The cognitivism of structural anthropology, its subscription to a pre- or super-linguistic domain of human cognition, would therefore take us back to a state or stratum of human thought that exists *before* Babel.

NOTES

1. For a more detailed discussion of this aspect of *Race and History*, see Johnson 2003: 109–20.
2. For a more extensive explanation of the theories of Sapir and Whorf, see Chapters 1 and 2 of Lucy 1992.
3. The term 'architecture' figures in the French version of this passage: '*la culture . . . possède une architecture similaire à celle du langage*' (1958a: 78).
4. Again, I am paraphrasing the French rather than the English version of the text here.
5. 'The problems of religious anthropology require an intellectualist psychology' (1958a: 227–8; my translation). This sentence does not figure in the English version of the article.
6. See, for instance, Roy Harris's criticisms (2003: 109–32).
7. Several chapters of *Structural Anthropology*, including the chapters on linguistics and anthropology and the structural analysis of myth, were first written in English, and then translated into French for the publication of *Anthropologie structurale* in 1958. The result, Lévi-Strauss confesses, is a sometimes rather uneven text (1958a: i–ii), while the necessarily hybrid character of the English 'translations' that we are using here adds a further level of complication. See Johnson 2003: 8–11.
8. It is difficult for the informed reader not to think here of Marcel Mauss, the putative father of French anthropology, who apart from modern and classical languages, also knew Sanskrit, Hebrew and a number of other ancient languages.
9. 'Here is Rhodes, jump here!' Lévi-Strauss is most probably quoting from *The Eighteenth Brumaire of Louis Bonaparte*, where Marx refers to the point of no return reached by the proletariat in the revolutionary process (McLellan 1977: 303). What is ironic about this quotation is that it seems to replicate the abysmal process of distortion that according to Lévi-Strauss governs the transmission of myth: Marx himself is quoting – inaccurately – a text of Hegel (*Philosophy of Right*), who in his turn is quoting – again inaccurately – one of Aesop's fables (*The Braggart*). Strictly speaking, the Latin *salta* ('dance') in Marx's citation of Hegel should be *saltus* ('jump').

10. On the so-called 'interlingua' approach to machine translation, an approach originally formulated by Harold Somers in the late 1940s, see Somers 2001: 143–9 and Arnold and Balkan *et al.* 1994: 80–4.

11. On the history of the cognitive sciences, see Gardner 1987 and Dupuy 1994 (trans. 2000).

12. See the entries 'Langage (Traitement du)'–'Linguistique' (Language Processing-Linguistics) and 'Langage de la pensée' (Language of Thought), in Houdé 1998.

13. On the difference between 'extensive' and 'intensive' fieldwork, and the question of linguistic competence, see Mauss 1967: 13.

14. This difficult passage actually makes more sense if one juxtaposes it with the structuralist profession of faith that opens one of the book's earlier chapters (1955a: 205; 1992: 178).

REFERENCES

Arnold, D. and L. Balkan, *et al.* 1994. *Machine Translation: An Introductory Guide.* Manchester and Oxford: NCC Blackwell.

Derrida, Jacques 1967. 'La Structure, le signe et le jeu dans le discours des sciences humaines', in *L'Écriture et la différence*. Paris: Seuil.

1978. 'Structure, Sign and Play in the Discourse of the Human Sciences', in *Writing and Difference*. Translated by Alan Bass. London: Routledge.

Dupuy, Jean-Pierre 1994. *Aux Origines des sciences cognitives*. Paris: La Découverte.

2000. *The Mechanization of the Mind: On the Origins of Cognitive Science.* Translated by M. B. DeBevoise. Princeton and Oxford: Princeton University Press.

Gardner, Howard 1987. *The Mind's New Science: A History of the Cognitive Revolution.* New York: Basic Books.

Gumperz, John N. and Stephen C. Levinson (eds.) 1996. *Rethinking Linguistic Relativity.* Cambridge: Cambridge University Press.

Harris, Roy 2003. *Saussure and his Interpreters* (second edition). Edinburgh: Edinburgh University Press.

Houdé, Olivier, *et al.* 1998. *Vocabulaire des sciences cognitives.* Paris: Presses Universitaires de France.

Johnson, Christopher 2003. *Claude Lévi-Strauss: The Formative Years.* Cambridge: Cambridge University Press.

Lucy, John A. 1992. *Language Diversity and Thought: A Reformulation of the Linguistic Relativity Hypothesis.* Cambridge: Cambridge University Press.

Mauss, Marcel 1967. *Manuel d'ethnographie.* Paris: Payot.

McLellan, David (ed.) 1977. *Karl Marx: Selected Writings.* Oxford: Oxford University Press.

Somers, Harold 2001. 'Machine Translation: Methodology', in Mona Baker (ed.), *Routledge Encyclopedia of Translation Studies.* London: Routledge, pp. 143–9.

Saussure, Ferdinand de 1983. *Course in General Linguistics.* Translated by Roy Harris. London: Duckworth.

1986. *Cours de linguistique générale.* Paris: Payot.

Wiener, Norbert 1961. *Cybernetics or Control and Communication in the Animal and the Machine* (second edition). Cambridge, MA: MIT Press.

Part IV

Literature and aesthetics

13   Structuralism, poetry, music: Lévi-Strauss between Mallarmé and Wagner

Jeffrey Mehlman

Lévi-Strauss was characteristically sceptical about the prospects for a 'structuralist' analysis of literature. His sense, voiced in an interview in 1965, was that what passed for as much was frequently little more than a 'play of mirrors', in which the detection of invariant forms tended to give way to a fascination with recurrent contents, and the merely contingent was apt to trump the structurally 'necessary' (Lévi-Strauss 1973a: 323). In that critique of the specular, the reader recognises a tendency surfacing as early in Lévi-Strauss's work – and life – as his dismantling of Georges Dumas's delight, in the opening pages of *Tristes Tropiques* (1973c), at misconstruing a decayed and displaced vestige of his own French roots as an exotic essence of Brazil.[1] Or perhaps the reticence vis-à-vis a structuralist analysis of literature should be understood in terms of the fundamental structuralist postulate of the arbitrary nature of the sign. If literature's deepest aspiration is to effect a fusion of sound and sense, a perfect adequation of one to the other, then there would be a fundamental dissonance between the structuralist and literary projects. As though structuralism might analyse literature in a manner congruent to Lévi-Strauss's 'analysis' of totemism – in order to dispel an ideologically charged mirage.[2]

In his interview, Lévi-Strauss (1973c: 324) proposes as a guide to future thought on the subject the work of the art historian Erwin Panofsky, said to be a 'great structuralist', and to be so precisely to the extent that he was simultaneously a 'great historian'. The gesture may surprise on the part of an author frequently labelled an unrelenting polemicist against the pretensions of history, but it is in many ways characteristic. The unmediated move of the analyst towards his object (literature) is interrupted by a lateral displacement – to the visual arts and to history. In its structure the gesture is congruent with the Saussurean interception of the vertical move from signifier to signified by a horizontal – and well-nigh constitutive – play between signifiers, which is why it will guide us in these pages. Others have claimed that literary criticism, to the extent that it is a kind of *bricolage*, a disassembling and reassembling of 'primary' texts, is a structuralist activity par excellence (Genette 1965: 37–9). Yet, the fit, as Lévi-Strauss all but surmises, may be too neat, too convenient. And that facility issues in a characteristic configuration: 'reciprocal fascination', 'pseudo-dialogue', all too 'skillful ventriloquism' (Lévi-Strauss 1973c: 325).

Were we to indulge in the arch-structuralist gesture of *reculer pour mieux sauter*, taking a distance from the more immediate aim of this chapter – determining structuralism's relation to literature – in order to better grasp the larger economy in which that aim takes on meaning and urgency, we might profitably begin with the discussion in *Myth and Meaning* of myth's affinities with music. After evoking the similarities between the two, which had been the inspiration of the celebrated 'Overture' to *Le Cru et le cuit*, the author suggests a second relation based on contiguity. Precisely when myth, at about the time of the Renaissance, was yielding to the lures of the novel, it is proposed, the emotive and intellectual functions of myth were taken over by the newly emergent – and 'great' – styles of music (Lévi-Strauss 1995a: 46). 'It could be shown also that there are myths, or groups of myths, which are constructed like a sonata, or a symphony, or a rondo, or a toccata, or any of all the musical forms which music did not really invent but borrowed unconsciously from the structure of . . . myth' (Lévi-Strauss 1995a: 51). And if doubts be entertained on the subject, Lévi-Strauss serves up anecdotal confirmation. Frustrated at not finding a musical equivalent of one of his mythical structures, he informed the composer René Liebowitz, who proceeded to re-enact what one hesitates to call the original 'crime'. He composed a work of music based on the myth in question. The structural study of myth, in sum, would appear to be a reclaiming from music of what was originally mythology's own. And it is here that the analysis seems to ring with a literary resonance. For it was Valéry (1924: 250) who once characterised the literary movement that was French *symbolisme* as nothing so much as an effort to reclaim from music what was originally a property of poetry itself.[3]

Now in this effort to take back from music what was originally one's own, the crucial figure, for both symbolist poetry and the structuralist analysis of myth, was Wagner. Consider first the case of Lévi-Strauss. In *Le Regard éloigné* (1983a: 301), he claimed to have found 'the most profound definition ever given of myth' in Gurnemanz's words to Parsifal in the first act of Wagner's last music drama: 'Du siehst, mein Sohn, zum Raum wird hier die Zeit.'[4] In that reabsorption of the temporal by the spatial, the undermining of (sequential) diachrony by (the simultaneity of) synchrony, the reader recognises a principal – and ultimately anti-Bergsonian – inspiration of the entire structuralist project. In *De près et de loin*, Lévi-Strauss speaks of having unwittingly 'incubated' Wagner for decades, before he re-emerged as a principal inspiration (or '*père irrécusable*') of the structural analysis of myth (1964b: 23; 1988a: 243). And when the composer did so emerge it was in a phrase borrowed from Mallarmé's sonnet of 'hommage' to Wagner: the anthropologist claimed to have been offering tribute, ever since childhood, at the altar of 'le dieu Richard Wagner' (1964b: 23). The *Mythologiques*, to be sure, form a tetralogy, and they were completed, with *L'Homme nu* in 1971, on the centenary of Wagner's own tetralogy. Towards the close of *Mythologiques*, Wagner resurfaces in a context, however, marked by a reservation. It may have been through Wagner, we are told, that music became aware of an evolution leading it to 'assume the structures of myth', but it was from that moment on that the development appeared to have 'stalled and run out of breath (*piétine et s'essouffle*)', while waiting for Debussy to provide a renewal music seemed to be yearning for (1971a: 584).

Lévi-Strauss's attitude to Wagner – the awe; the desire to accomplish something analogous, but *on his own terms*; the occasional reservations; and more generally, the will to reclaim from music, by way of Wagner, what was mythology's own – is strikingly congruent with Mallarmé's own attitude. The crucial *symboliste* text here is Mallarmé's *Richard Wagner: Rêverie d'un poète francais*, written with enormous difficulty, according to the author, for the *Revue wagnerienne*, co-founded in 1885 by Edouard Dujardin (whom Joyce would eventually credit with inventing 'stream of consciousness') and Houston Chamberlain (whom Hitler would eventually credit as a principal source of his racial doctrine). Perhaps the best way to characterise Mallarmé's take on Wagner is in terms of his distinction between what he calls 'Legend', marked by an 'anecdote énorme et fruste' and 'Fable', which would be 'vierge de tout, lieu, temps, et personne sus' (Mallarmé 1945: 544). Wagner, although he had unleashed the non-figural potential of music within myth, had ultimately retained the anecdotal dimension of Legend, or what might be called archetype, in what turned out to be a 'harmonious compromise' between the archaically anecdotal and the radically non-figural. The challenge for Mallarmé would be to *fully* unleash the potential of music within myth, thereby supplanting Legend (or archetype) with Fable (or what might be called, in its virtuality, structure). On the one hand, the semantic richness of the archetype; on the other, the syntactical complexity (and semantic void or near-void) of structure. Such would be the opposition between the prodigious maximalism of Wagner, who would combine all arts in his *Gesamtkunstwerk*, and the immense minimalism of Mallarmé, who would allow the non-figural acids of music, as he understood it, to corrode the figural pretensions of every other art. Remarkably, Mallarmé, in his critique of Wagner, resorts to a phrase that might well be translated as the structural analysis of myth: could it be, he asks, that France and the century, 'qui ont dissous par la pensée les Mythes', might regress towards the legendary register into which Wagner had lapsed (Mallarmé 1945: 545)? There is a weak reading of Mallarmé's text, I would suggest, that sees the dissolving of myth by thought in purely positivist terms as a debunking. But surely, given the quasi-Cartesian terms in which Mallarmé situates the debate (the French mind being qualified as 'strictement imaginatif et abstrait, donc poétique'), and above all given the structure of Mallarmé's aesthetic project, the 'dissolution' of myth by thought appears to be anticipatory of structural analysis itself (Mallarmé 1945: 544).

Consider in this context the structural reading undertaken by Lévi-Strauss of the *Ring of the Nibelung* in *Le Regard éloigné*. The central problem of the tetralogy, Lévi-Strauss suggests, is that of 'exchange and its law', the notion that it is forbidden to 'receive without giving' (1983a: 322, 321). Thus, at the outset the dwarf Alberich contracts to pay a price in love to keep the Rhine gold even as the god Wotan agrees to give up Freia, goddess of sensual love, in exchange for the newly built symbol of his power, Valhalla. Lévi-Strauss is interested in how the leitmotif of the 'renunciation of love' on occasion surfaces precisely when the Wagnerian hero (Siegmund, then Siegfried) appears to be *acquiring* the symbol of his love. The anthropologist's point is that the music bespeaks a destitution which is, according to the principle of exchange, the ineluctable counterpart of every acquisition. Simultaneously, the contradiction of scenic event by musical motif seems a gesture in the direction of the non-figural, touchstone of the Mallarméan 'fable' in its opposition to the Wagnerian 'legend'. By the end of his brief analysis, Lévi-Strauss will summarise the longest and most mythically charged sequence in the history of opera as follows: 'Le trésor arraché à l'eau retournera à l'eau, celui arraché au feu retournera au feu . . . Au total rien ne se sera passé' (1983a: 323). Transposed into the idiom of Mallarmé, this yields: 'rien n'aura eu lieu que le lieu'.

Now to the extent that the principle of exchange lay at the heart of the *Ring*, its deepest subject, the author of *Structures élémentaires de la parenté* tells us, is the incest taboo, and here he is confronted with a problem. For, on the one hand, the brother and sister who have made exogamy their vocation in *Die Götterdämmerung*, Gunther and Gutrune, are incarnations of mediocrity and practitioners of deception. And, on the other, from the brother–sister love of Siegmund and Sieglinde to the idealised couple of Siegfried and Brunnhilde, the heroic ideal is fundamentally incestuous. Whence Lévi-Strauss's insistence on the multiple confusions of the last opera, confusions that could only be resolved by bringing the entire edifice down in a moment of 'cosmic collapse' (1983a: 323). Lévi-Strauss is not the first to have noted the anomaly of the ending of the *Ring*. Wagner himself attributed it to his discovery of Schopenhauer and conversion of Wotan to a metaphysic of renunciation. George Bernard Shaw, who cast Siegfried as the anarchist Bakunin, thought the ending reflected the sinister turn of European history in an age dominated by Bismarck. But there has been general agreement that Siegfried's heroic 'humour' was a function of his tonic contempt for the rule of law, dismissed as so many 'obsolescent makeshifts', devices to 'secure the survival of the unfittest', by Shaw in an alternately Nietzschean and Darwinian passage of his examination of the *Ring* (Shaw 1967: 59, 60). Much like Mallarmé, Lévi-Strauss, on the other hand, gives us Wagner as a failed classicist. For it is as though he had intuited the domain of exchange and the incest taboo, the core of Lévi-Strauss's first major work, but proved unable to bring it to completion. Whence the serial 'confusions' and consequent 'collapse' of the fourth night of the *Ring*. To be sure, the anthropologist was able to wrest a Mallarméan–minimalist reading ('rien ne se sera passé') from what is normally received as an apocalyptic work (Shaw: 'an attempt to revive the barricades of Dresden in the Temple of the Grail' (Shaw 1967: xviii)). But the final verdict comes with a reservation that might well have been borrowed from Mallarmé: in its failure to bring its intuition of the law of exchange and its relation to the incest taboo to completion, Wagner, for all his genius, remained, in the poet's words, 'à mi-côte de la montagne sainte' (Mallarmé 1945: 546). A second tetralogy, a century later, would be needed.

[∗ ∗ ∗]

Among Wagner's music dramas, the work on which Lévi-Strauss has written at greatest length is *Parsifal*. The work that consecrated Nietzsche's legendary break with the composer appears, in fact, to have been a favourite of the anthropologist's. Although prepared to agree with Michel Leiris that there are moments of religious sentimentality – '*bondieuserie*' – that make *Parsifal* difficult to swallow, the final verdict is purely musical and entirely positive: 'Pour ma part, quand je suis envahi par la musique de *Parsifal*, je cesse de me poser des questions' (Lévi-Strauss 1993a: 116). Now Lévi-Strauss's essay on *Parsifal*, tellingly titled 'De Chrétien de Troie à Richard Wagner', is first of all interestingly about reclaiming from the arch-Teutonic Wagner a primitive Gallic core. Even in Wolfram von Eschenbach's *Parsifal*, Wagner's putative source, the knights of the Grail are assimilated to the French order of Templars. As for the name Parsifal, the composer may have fallen for a bogus Arabic derivation (*fal, parsi*), we are told, but Parsifal is originally Perceval, he who 'pierces' the secret of the 'valley' (Lévi-Strauss 1983a: 308). Surely, in the context of our remarks about Mallarmé's 'revery of a French poet', this regallicisation of a German work has its pertinence.

The centre of Lévi-Strauss's reading of the music drama consists in casting its plot, with its insistence on a question not asked, as a kind of anti-Oedipus. Amfortas, it will be recalled, was originally the fisher king who remains infirm (and whose land is laid 'waste') because the innocent fool Parsifal fails to ask him the question of the origin of his debilitating wound. Whereas Oedipus was all too quick to answer the Sphynx's riddle and claim his incestuous reward, his opposite number Parsifal, in his chastity, does not even pose the crucial question. Between Perceval or the unasked question, a case of failed communication, and Oedipus or the precipitous supply of an answer, a case of excessive communication, the relations are 'symmetrical' and 'inverse' (1983a: 314). Wagner's innovation, according to Lévi-Strauss, was to incorporate the analysis just presented, with its effective superimposition of two myths (Perceval, Oedipus), one the reverse return of the other, into the musical drama *Parsifal* itself. For Oedipus is present in the music drama in the person of incestuous Kundry. With her propensity to cast herself in the role of Parsifal's mother, she is, the anthropologist tells us, a version of Jocasta, the representative of the Oedipus myth within the music drama. Wagner thus effectively invents structural analysis, in one of its most characteristic moves, within his final music drama. Characteristic? Let the piercing etymology of Perceval's name serve as a transition to another bravura exercise of structural analysis, the anthropologist's excursus, in a text devoted to Max Ernst, on Lautréamont's famous image of the fortuitous encounter, on a dissecting table, of an umbrella and a sewing machine. Lévi-Strauss's tour de force will consist in inventing a kind of necessity to command the apparent randomness of the encounter. For each of the two objects

is endowed with a point, one which, in the case of the umbrella, is protective or surmounts, like an ornament, a gently curved dome that is soft or elastic to the touch; and which, in the case of the sewing machine, is a sharp aggressive point placed at the lower extremity of an angular arm, just where it bends downward. A sewing machine presents itself as an ordered arrangement of solid parts whose hardest one, the needle, has the function of piercing a fabric; an umbrella, quite to the contrary, is graced with a fabric whose function is not to allow itself to be pierced by random liquid particles: rain. (1983a: 329)[5]

Thus, just like Perceval and Oedipus – or within the opera: Parsifal and Kundry – umbrella and sewing machine end up being inverted metaphors of each other.

There is a peculiar atmosphere in Wagner's *Parsifal*, we are told, and Lévi-Strauss characterises it as 'half Christian, half Oriental' (1983a: 310). That observation precedes directly the revelation that Wagner chose to transform the wildly incestuous Kundry from a simple messenger of the Grail into a reincarnation of Hérodias. To say as much, however, is to revive the Mallarméan connection since Hérodiade, the 'half Christian, half Oriental' child of what Mallarmé called his '*nuit d'Idumée*', was, of course, the forbidden obsession around which the poet chose (or failed) to build his entire oeuvre.[6] In fact, with a Kundry perched between Jocasta and Herodias, the result of many an ingenious superimposition, we appear to be broaching a turning point in the history of Mallarmé criticism. For it was by way of a technique of textual superimposition that Charles Mauron generated his reading of Hérodiade as a figure of Oedipal obsession.[7]

Might we then have staged the encounter of Lévi-Strauss and Mallarmé, if not on a dissecting table, on the altar of 'le dieu Richard Wagner'? If so, it may be suggested, the encounter has taken on a certain necessity in the course of our speculation. *Parsifal*, in Lévi-Strauss's reading, is in search of a saving middle 'distance' between the incestuously virulent 'excessive communication' of Kundry and the 'inertia and sterility' of the 'communication trop lente' mythically incarnated by Perceval (1983a: 317). That depressing 'slowness' bears the name in Mallarmé's poetry of '*amer repos*'. Indeed, it would be possible to demonstrate that the entirety of his oeuvre is structured, almost kaleidoscopically (to use a structuralist metaphor), around a homologously unsatisfying alternative: the unbearable boredom of *amer repos* (corresponding, in Lévi-Strauss's Wagnerianised terms, to Parsifal) and the intolerable intensity (seven times more exhausting, as the poet puts it) of the passion embodied by Hérodiade (or Kundry). In between lies the infinitesimal line or barrier within which the poem aspires to find its site and which is no mean emblem for the split in the subject figuring the unconscious.[8]

The unconscious designated as an infinitesimal – and semantically vacant – line? The figure crops up in the crucial chapter of *Tristes Tropiques* entitled 'Comment on devient ethnographe'. Of the three intellectual 'mistresses' invoked by Lévi-Strauss, geology, which follows Freud and Marx, is characterised in terms of its affinities with psychoanalysis: 'Quand je connus les théories de Freud, elles m'apparurent tout naturellement comme l'application à l'homme individuel d'une méthode dont la géologie représentait le canon' (1955a: 59). And geology is on three occasions characterised in terms of the special elation and intelligibility attaching to the unexpected discovery of a mere line of articulation – 'ligne de contact entre deux couches géologiques', 'ligne pâle et brouillée', 'secrète fêlure' – in an otherwise chaotic landscape (1955a: 58, 59). Transpose that line from geology to its 'sister' discipline psychoanalysis, and one finds the demarcation of the unconscious per se, but also the configuration of the Mallarméan poem at its purest.[9]

Geology has a second sister discipline in Lévi-Strauss. Consider the following reminiscence from *Myth and Meaning*:

When I was a child, for a while my main interest was geology. The problem in geology is also to try to understand what is invariant in the tremendous diversity of landscapes, that is, to be able to reduce a landscape to a finite number of operations. Later as an adolescent, I spent a great part of my leisure time drawing costumes and sets for opera. The problem there is exactly the same – to try to express in one language, that is, the language of graphic arts and painting, something which also exists in music and in the libretto; that is, to try to reach the invariant property of a very complex set of codes. (1995a: 8–9)

From geology one thus moves to either Freud (and, I have argued, Mallarmé) or to opera (of whom the prototype for Lévi-Strauss remains Wagner).

The Mallarmé connection, which has for us always been a Mallarmé-via-Wagner connection, once again reveals its pertinence.

In the history of Mallarmé criticism that line, figure of an irreducible metaphoricity, finds its most refined formulation in Jacques Derrida's essay 'La Double Séance' (Derrida 1972: 199–317). The philosopher's gambit in that work is to 'deconstruct' metaphysics by releasing a brief Mallarméan text, 'Mimique', into a Platonic dialogue and observing the perturbations – within the edifice of 'logocentric' metaphysics – that it effects. The line in this case is called 'hymen', both the term for the membrane impeding consummation of desire (i.e. protecting virginity) and the designation, in classical French, for that consummation itself. Its intrinsic ambiguity affords Derrida the leverage that Heidegger had tapped in the bi-valence of a phrase quoted from Ernst Jünger – *über die Linie*, meaning both *de linea* and *trans lineam* – in the essay in which he coined the word 'deconstruction' (or *Abbau*).[10] 'Mimique' is the programme note for a pantomime performed by Mallarmé's young relative, the mime Paul Margueritte, and subsequently published by Paul Margueritte and his brother Victor Margueritte in a jointly written volume titled *Nos tréteaux*.[11] The Mallarmé piece alludes to the plot: Pierrot commits the perfect crime, tickling his wife to death, thereby leaving no trace of violence, with the mime playing both husband *and* wife.[12] It is, in many respects, a rehearsal of all that is at stake in the poet's masterpiece of evanescence, 'L'Après-midi d'un faune'.

Now Derrida's vexed relation with Lévi-Strauss, as mediated by the 'deconstruction' of a key chapter of *Tristes Tropiques*, 'Leçon d'écriture', is a foundational moment in the history of what has been called 'post-structuralism'.[13] But there is a second connection between Derrida and *Tristes Tropiques* that has received scant attention and that takes on its full value in the present context. Consider that one of the few authors whom the anthropologist refers to, not without a measure of irony, as his '*maître*' in *Tristes Tropiques* is none other than the very Victor Margueritte who published with his brother mime (in *Nos tréteaux*) the text of the proceedings culminating in 'Mimique', the very piece that provided Derrida with the lever with which he pretended, via Mallarmé, to overturn (or *displace*) metaphysics. From *Tristes Tropiques*:

Il m'est impossible de passer sur cette période sans arrêter un regard amical sur un autre monde que je dois à Victor Margueritte (mon introducteur à l'ambassade du Brésil) de m'avoir fait entrevoir; il m'avait conservé son amitié, après un bref passage à son service comme secrétaire durant mes années d'étudiant. Mon rôle avait été d'assurer la sortie d'un de ses livres . . . en rendant visite à une centaine de personnalités parisiennes, pour présenter l'exemplaire que le Maître – il tenait à cette appelation – leur avait dédicacé. (1955a: 50)

There was something extraordinarily touching, the anthropologist writes, in the way Margueritte seemed aristocratically to embody French literature itself

(1955a: 51). Years later, Derrida, in search of the wherewithal in French literature to unsettle 'logocentrism', could find no better text than 'Mimique', the brief page in whose production Lévi-Strauss's eccentric 'embodiment' of French letters played so telling a role.

A glance at *Nos tréteaux*, the joint volume by the brothers Margueritte, further complicates the scenario. The brothers' performances were a family ritual, pursued over many years, in a variety of venues, and eventually integrating their own children. But their initial improvised 'theatre', we are told, flourished, in the tutelary presence of their relative Mallarmé, in the town of Valvins, where the poet maintained a country home. What Derrida would eventually offer up as a kind of 'primal scene' (in a virtually Freudian sense) of Western philosophy, effectively 'deconstructing' Plato, was, in a less exalted sense, a 'primal scene' for the brothers: the first of their *tréteaux*. Its original star was Geneviève Mallarmé, the poet's daughter and, in the poem already referred to, the original model of the 'child of an Idumean night'. As such, she was a prototype of Hérodiade herself (Margueritte 1910: 11). Now on the improvised stage in Valvins, Victor performed 'charades' and Paul 'pantomimes'. The first of Victor's charades was a version of Bluebeard, in which the villain is thwarted in his plan to slaughter the last of his wives by the precipitate arrival of his brother. In what appears to be a homology of that plot, the first of brother Paul's pantomimes is also about the killing of a wife, but in the latter case, which will be elaborated by Mallarmé in 'Mimique' and Derrida in 'La Double Séance', it is, at least in conception, a 'perfect' – because bloodless – crime. From one perspective, nothing, with Colombine tickled to death on the soles of her feet, 'will have taken place'. Or shall we say that Paul's pantomime (of bloodless uxoricide) is to Victor's gory charade (of a comparable act) as Mallarméan 'fable' is to Wagnerian 'legend'? It is precisely that tradition, in the person of Lévi-Strauss's '*maître*', Victor Margueritte, that surfaces at an important juncture of *Tristes Tropiques*.

Mallarmé criticism, to be sure, has not been altogether kind to Derrida's argument. In his discussion of Mallarmé's 'Rêverie d'un poète français', Bertrand Marchal, France's premier Mallarméiste (and the editor of the new Pléiade edition of the poet's work), has insisted that the word 'hymen' in that text does not designate a deconstructive instance, but rather 'la formule bâtarde de l'addition', the all too Wagnerian will to settle on a 'harmonious compromise' between 'personal drama' and 'ideal music' (Marchal 1988: 176). Marchal's is a curious Mallarmé indeed: a crypto-disciple of the historian of religion Max Müller and a poet whose project was ultimately to undo the hold which Christianity held over France and steer the French language – and its speakers – back to an awareness of the forgotten solar cult which remains its vital source.[14] Look closely at the tertiary instance in

Mallarmé – say, the window pane – separating the unbearable tedium of the poet's '*amer repos*' (*côté* Parsifal) from the intolerable intensity of the forbidden object (*coté* Kundry) and you will find the reflection of a sunset . . . But therein we again discover the pertinence of *Tristes Tropiques*. Consider first the bravura description of a sunset at sea, surely Lévi-Strauss's least structuralist text and to that extent his most successful stab at phenomenology. The 'pyramides boursouflées', 'bouillonnements figés', 'diaprures blondes', 'sinuosités nonchalantes' and 'bombements blanchâtres' are the stuff of a kind of aesthetic idolatry which in this case all but fuses with the setting sun itself (1955a: 69, 70, 72, 73). But the interesting moment comes subsequently in the book when the anthropologist hazards a first timid sketch of the notion of 'structure'. The pretext is a discussion of the regularity with which cities appear to have their fashionable neighbourhoods to the west and their areas of gross poverty to the east. 'Voilà longtemps que nous n'adorons plus le soleil et que nous avons cessé d'associer les points cardinaux à des qualités magiques', the anthropologist tells us (1955a: 136). And yet it is as though there were a collective and unconscious residual awareness of that ancient cult which ends up endowing space itself with its variegated affective charge. Before long we are told that the *symboliste* 'quest for correspondences' is but a reflection of this residue. Baudelaire and Rimbaud, that is, rather than Mallarmé, but, one is inclined to judge, close enough . . . In brief, in moving from Derrida to Marchal, we have entered an altogether different interpretative universe. Indeed, it may even be a considerably less interesting one: after all, if Mallarmé is at bottom a verbally brilliant disciple, unwitting or not, of a long since (and understandably) forgotten mythographer, so much the less he! What is striking for us is that our moves – from Mauron (via Oedipus–Hérodias) to Derrida (via 'Mimique' and the brothers Margueritte) to Marchal (and the residue of a solar cult) – within the history of the reading of Mallarmé have remained within the confines of the oeuvre of Lévi-Strauss.

[∗ ∗ ∗]

In *Regarder, écouter, lire*, Lévi-Strauss returns interestingly to Wagner, declaring, against Leiris, his utter devotion to *Parsifal*. He then poses a fundamental question: 'Qu'est-ce donc pour moi qu'un opéra?' (1993a: 116–17). The answer is not long in coming and is, in its metaphor, quintessentially Baudelairean: 'J'embarque sur un navire dont, en guise de mâts, de voiles, de cordages, le gréement rassemble tous les moyens instrumentaux et vocaux requis pour le compositeur.' Through music, he finds himself transported 'dans un monde de sons à mille lieues de choses terrestres, comme on l'est en plein océan' (1993a: 116–17). But Baudelaire, it turns out, was but preparation for a development that is fundamentally Mallarméan: 'Aussi je ne vais plus à l'opéra, pressentant que le vaisseau sombrera sous le poids intolérable d'une mise en scène et de décors qui insultent à la fois le poème et la musique' (1993a: 117). The insistence on the sheer materiality of the theatrical setting and the way in which it violates musical ideality is of a piece with Mallarmé's underscoring of all that was '*grossier*' in the archaic '*théatre caduc*' with which Wagner had not fully broken (Mallarmé 1945: 542). Lévi-Strauss pursues his argument, but finds himself taking his distance from Wagner and promoting the thought of an obscure eighteenth-century composer and music-ologist, Michel-Paul-Guy de Chabanon. Chabanon had been saluted earlier in the volume as the man who had done for music what Saussure had done for language, only two centuries earlier.[15] He figures, in fact, as a kind of patron saint of structuralism. In the context of Wagner, however, he is presented as the anticipator of Lévi-Strauss's intuition, at the end of *L'Homme nu*, that music had taken over a territory freshly abandoned by myth: 'J'aperçois quelque analogie entre la conception que Chabanon se fait du passage de la tragédie déclamée à la tragédie chantée, et la façon dont, entre le mythe et la musique, j'ai moi-même tenté d'établir une continuité; et cela, presque dans les mêmes termes' (1993a: 121). We thus find ourselves at this juncture more or less where we started: Lévi-Strauss taking back from music what was alleged to be myth's own, even as Mallarmé laid claim to recuperating from music what was initially poetry's own. Then, as if to clinch our point, Lévi-Strauss quotes Chabanon on a deeply comic mode of music – or opera – of the future, the creation of a 'génie entièrement neuf': 'N'est-ce pas exactement ce programme que Mozart mettait à exécution dans *L'Enlèvement au sérail*, *Cosi* (Despina), *La Flûte*? Plus tard Rossini, puis Offenbach, avant que Ravel, dans *L'Heure espagnole*, ne porte le genre à son plus haut point de perfection?' (1993a: 123). Having begun with Wagner and *Parsifal*, Lévi-Strauss dreams a Gallic coun-tergenre and ends up with the most French of composers, Maurice Ravel, as paragon.[16] It is as Mallarméan a gesture as might be imagined and a final instance in the homology these remarks have attempted to construct.

[* * *]

Having discovered in *Parsifal* as profound a definition of myth as he had encountered (in which space absorbs time), having elaborated out of its libretto a quintessentially structuralist equilibrium, between an excess (Kundry–Jocasta) and an insufficiency (Parsifal) of communication, Lévi-Strauss, in the face of Leiris's misgivings, seems prepared to jettison that libretto, claiming that it is Wagner's music alone that matters to him. Whereupon he gives us a very brief list of the only operas whose libretto matters to him. The list begins with *Carmen* . . . (1993a: 116). For the intellectual historian, that relinquishing – of *Parsifal* for *Carmen* – bears a curious resonance. For such was the musico-philosophical move of Nietzsche at the end of his life. The champion of Wagner in *The Birth of Tragedy* had come to the conclusion that in *Parsifal* the composer had regressed to a Christianity of a particularly decadent variety. The sole remedy, he decided, was the gloriously Mediterranean music of Bizet's 'perfect' masterpiece, said to constitute a salutary 'antithesis' to Wagner (Liébert 1995: 256–7). Like Lévi-Strauss, in sum, Nietzsche, in old age, came to appreciate the operatic 'perfection' of a very French *heure espagnole*. These concluding remarks, which will bring us back from music to literature, are offered as a commentary on what is at stake in that homology.

But once again, as in the question of 'structuralism' and 'literature' with which we began, an oblique strategy will be in order. During the heyday of structuralist interest in literature, it was less Mallarmé than his disciple Valéry who was most frequently mentioned. And even more than Valéry, no doubt, his latter-day adept, Jorge Luis Borges. The work of Michel Foucault greeted – and, in the case of Sartre, ferociously attacked – as quintessentially 'structuralist' began, it will be recalled, by a Borgesian taxonomy. And the final quotation in Gérard Genette's influential essay 'Structuralism and Literary Criticism' is from Borges, on the way in which one might *deduce* the literature of a specific period from the way in which a reader of that time reads a text from a prior period.[17] There was, however, a signature Borges tale that achieved particular prominence during the structuralist heyday, and it will be of interest to us here because of its relation to a fantasy of Lévi-Strauss. The story is 'Pierre Menard, Author of *Don Quixote*', and it turns on the very different interpretation of certain paragraphs of the Cervantes novel one arrives at once one indulges the fantasy that they had been written by a French *symboliste* from Nîmes at the beginning of the twentieth century.[18] Now, it happens that Lévi-Strauss indulges a parallel fantasy, relating to music, at a key juncture of *Tristes Tropiques*. Standing before his 'savages' with a desperation and sense of *temps perdu* redolent of Proust's Swann at the end of his love affair with Odette, the anthropologist finds himself mysteriously haunted by a melody from a Chopin étude and then realises that what haunts him is his ability to hear implicit in the Chopin piece musical developments that Debussy would wrest from the same matrix many years later. It is as though he could hear Debussy *already* in Chopin the way Borges's narrator could hear the thoughts of, say, William James in the words of Cervantes . . . Let that homology between a signature Borges tale and what turns out to be a turning point in Lévi-Strauss's memoir serve as grounds for the excursus on Borges with which we shall conclude.

The musical genre on which Borges wrote most memorably was tango, and his principal piece on the subject is a 'History of the Tango' first published in its entirety in the 1955 edition of *Evaristo Carriego*. Now, as improbable as it may sound, Borges's 'History of the Tango', I submit, is a direct offshoot of Nietzsche's Wagnerian text on the Greeks, *The Birth of Tragedy*. But one has to be something of a structuralist to realise it. Consider the terms of the homology: under the tutelage of Schopenhauer, Nietzsche undertakes a delineation of the degeneration of the genre from the ecstatic heroics, but also the fundamentally Dionysian lewdness, of Aeschylus to the psychological realism, with all its attendant pettiness, of Euripides. A universe of religious mysticism (Aeschylus) has been displaced, in Euripides, by one of distressed and vindictive affect – think of Medea or Phaedra – or *ressentiment*. Now every word of that summary might be transposed *mutatis mutandis* to Borges's history of tango. Under the tutelage of Schopenhauer (who 'has no peers', in Nietzsche's words)...(1967: 123). At a key juncture Borges invokes *The World as Will and Representation*, reminding us that music has no need of the world to exist. A world of Dionysian lewdness...Borges invokes the phallic street corner revels of the old tangos, still alive in such titles as 'El Choclo' (the corn cob) and 'El Fierrazo' (the iron rod). The dancing men in lewd embrace, the 'devilish orgy' of tango at its earliest, but also the dismemberment, the 'properly Dionysian suffering', all make their appearance as aspects of tango at its inception (Nietzsche 1967: 73). Dismemberment? It surfaces, in the history of tango, in an evocation of the tale of one Manco Wenceslao, who loses his hand in a knife fight. But the motif of the knife fight turns out to be central to Borges's genealogy of the genre. Indeed, the specificity of Borges's 'origin' is to complicate the motif of Dionysian lewdness with that of virile combat, the affirmative joy of the clash – as though the original wisdom of the genre lay in its intuition, in Borges's words, that 'a fight can be a celebration'.[19] But this is precisely the Nietzschean point. The issue of the 'spasms' of the 'Dionysian demon' is the intensification of what Nietzsche calls the 'manly desire to fight'.[20] For what Nietzsche's tragic myth mediates is above all 'a glorification of the fighting hero' (Nietzsche 1967: 140). Translate that formulation into Borges on tango and one gets: 'the old tango, as music, immediately transmits the joy of combat which Greek and German poets, long ago, tried to express in words' (Borges 1999: 397). Note the bizarre conflation of Greek and German, the guiding – Wagnerian – thread of *The Birth of Tragedy*, in Borges's genealogy of tango. It is a sure sign that Schopenhauer, who might have been dismissed as a stock accoutrement of Borgesian ornament, is here in his specifically Nietzschean role. This is evidenced, moreover, by the quintessentially Nietzschean dig at Hegel, which just happens to surface in this history of tango. Nietzsche, for the philosopher Gilles Deleuze, is above all a strategy for demolishing Hegel and the claims of dialectic (Deleuze 2003). Tango, for Borges, may be defined in terms of its anarchical energy, its fundamental allergy to the Hegelian aphorism that the 'State is the reality of the moral idea', which is dismissed as a 'sinister joke' (Borges 1999: 398).

But that whole heroic aggressive world of tango, in its Graeco-Germanic essence, its incompatibility with Hegel, was lost, we are told, by the genre's

degeneration into a vast venting of *ressentiment*. The heroic-ecstatic tango
gives way to a 'later tango' that is 'resentful, deplores with sentimental excess
one's miseries, and celebrates shamelessly the misfortunes of others' (Borges
1999: 400). We are left with a gentrified tango, the 'tango of family gather-
ings and respectable tearooms' – in sum, an exercise in 'trivial vulgarity'
utterly inconceivable to the 'tango of the knife and the brothel' from which it
descended' (Borges 1999: 400). Recrimination and self-accusation, the pillars
of reactive *ressentiment*, are amply there in the lyrics of modern tango, which
for Borges becomes the very melody of nihilism.

Our structure – joining Borges and Nietzsche, between Wagner and Bizet –
takes on a new complexity with the realisation that Borges's 'History of the
Tango' is in fact the *second* history of the genre he wrote. The first, entitled
'Ascendencias del tango' initially appeared in 1928 in *El idioma de los
argentinos* and is considerably less ambitious. Drawing on Vicente Rossi's
Cosas de negros (1926), Borges finds himself entertaining the proposition
that the tango may well be not at all Graeco-German, as in the later text, but
Afro-Montevidean and specifically the 'grandchild of the *habanera*' (Borges
1994: 95). Whereupon he stages a fit of mock chauvinism and proposes an
analogy intended to demonstrate the preposterousness of that proposition.
One might just as well claim, on grounds of Columbus's birth, that America
was discovered by the Genoese (rather than the Spanish) as claim that tango is
Afro-Montevidean (rather than *porteño*). Moreover, a humorous aside asks, in
mock confusion, what indeed might the Genoese have to do with anything
since the Boca del Riachuelo, a tango neighbourhood rich in Genoese, had
not yet been discovered (Borges 1994: 96). Somewhere between metaphor
and empirical analysis, we are left, in sum, with an odd nexus between tango
and Genoa . . .

Switch to Nietzsche. On 27 November 1881, at about the time Borges
assigns to the birth of tango, Nietzsche believes he has at last put Wagner,
whose 'slow and abject' return to Christianity in *Parsifal* offended him,
behind him. The antidote is to be the joyously amoral opera *Carmen*, which
Nietzsche had just seen for the first time at the Paganini Theatre in Genoa. 'I
am not far from thinking it is the best opera extant', he wrote to Peter Gast
(D'Iorio 2001: 51). 'Ach wie das Herz klopft!' he would write in the margins
of the score (D'Iorio 2001: 54). But nowhere was he as enthusiastic as in his
annotations on the celebrated *Habanera*: 'Eros as the ancients intuited it:
seductive, playful, nasty, demoniacal, and naïve . . . I know nothing comparable to this song' (D'Iorio 2001: 54). And then, later on in the score, the
supreme compliment on the opera's Mediterranean sensibility: 'Ist Genuesen
Blut darin' ('It's got Genoese blood in it', D'Iorio 2001: 54). Unless, of
course, as the philosopher wrote in *The Case of Wagner*, where he clinched
the case for Bizet as antidote to Wagner, the opera's 'cheerfulness' was

'African'.[21] Thus, Nietzsche, starting with Wagner, arrived, enthralled, at an opera centred on a *habanera* alternately described as 'African' and 'Genoese', even as Borges, ending up with a Graeco-German tango that appears to owe everything to the Wagnerian Nietzsche, began with an essay on tango derived from a *habanera* said to be alternately Afro-Montevidean and (metaphorically) Genoese. 'Luxuria tristona' was Borges's phrase for what he heard in 1928. 'Lascivious melancholy', which translates it fairly exactly, was Nietzsche's.

Where then have we arrived? From Lévi-Strauss's praise and analysis of the *text* of *Parsifal*, we moved to an apparent retreat – with Wagner's *music* overriding any reservations – and endorsement of the libretto of *Carmen*. On that manoeuvre we grafted a major philosophical development: the abjuring of *Parsifal* that marks the transition in Nietzsche from *The Birth of Tragedy* to *The Case of Wagner*. (This in turn raises the question of the articulation of the thought of Lévi-Strauss and Nietzsche, specifically with relation to *Parsifal*. Consider that, on the one hand, what Nietzsche objected to in the music drama was a decadent mix of Christianity and, by way of Schopenhauer, Buddhism. On the other, in the final chapter of *Tristes Tropiques*, Lévi-Strauss laments the fact that Islam had intervened to prevent Christianity's 'slow osmosis with Buddhism, which would have further Christianized us' (1955a: 490). In addition, the magician Klingsor, the villain of *Parsifal*, was said to have affinities, in Wagner's Spain, with the world of Islam. There were grounds, that is, for viewing Lévi-Strauss and Nietzsche as having symmetrical and inverse investments in Wagner's final work.[22]) Onto the transition in Nietzsche, however, we were able to graft a development in Borges, the contemporary author most profoundly attuned to the structuralist project, which was the precise obverse of the development in Nietzsche: his writings on the history of tango went from the Afro-Genoese *habanera* (1928) to the Graeco-German or Wagnerian (1955). Our Borges repeats and reverses Nietzsche even as Lévi-Strauss had originally staked out a position on *Parsifal* symmetrical and obverse to the philosopher's. In the near perfect congruence between Lévi-Strauss and Borges, the Nietzsche–Wagner inter-text, without which that congruence could not have been established, has all but vanished. 'Rien ne se sera passé', to quote the anthropologist on Wagner once again. Or, still again, the *metteur en scène* of our entire sequence of encounters, Mallarmé: 'Rien n'aura eu lieu que le lieu.'[23]

NOTES

1. Concerning Lévi-Strauss's studies with the psychologist Georges Dumas (1866–1946), see *Tristes Tropiques*:

   Dans cette espèce de coup de foudre qui allait se produire entre lui et la société brésilienne s'est certainement manifesté un phénomène mystérieux, quand deux fragments d'une Europe vieille de quatre cents ans – dont certains éléments essentials étaient conservés, d'une part dans une famille protestante méridionale, de l'autre, dans une bourgeoisie très raffinée et un peu décadente, vivant au ralenti sous les tropiques – se sont rencontrés, reconnus et presque ressoudés. (1955a: 13)

2. See Mehlman 1974: 54–5. For Lévi-Strauss, totemism is an 'artificial entity existent solely in the mind of the anthropologist', and to which nothing specific corresponds in external reality (Lévi-Strauss 1962a: 14).

3. For another perspective on Lévi-Strauss's debt to French *symbolisme*, see Boon 1972.

4. In *Le Cru et le cuit* (1964a: 24) Lévi-Strauss suggests that it is as though music and mythology 'had need of time only in order to subject it to a refutation'. All translations from *Le Regard éloigné* are this author's own.

5. For further resonances of this passage, see Mehlman 2000: 190–4.

6. Part of the strangeness of Mallarmé's text is that Salome (Hérodiade) has virtually taken on the name of her mother (Hérodias).

7. On the seminal role of Mauron in Mallarmé criticism, see Mehlman 1999.

8. For a reading of Mallarmé in terms of transformations of that line, see Mehlman 1999: 168–86.

9. Some examples of the 'line' in Mallarmé's poems: the melodic line of the flute in 'L'Après-midi d'un faune'; the line portraying a lake on a Chinese tea cup in 'Las de l'amer repos'; the glass pane of the window in 'Les fenêtres'. . .

10. See Mehlman 1999: 174–5.

11. See Steinmetz 1998: 214–15.

12. As summarised by the brothers Margueritte, the crime of 'Pierrot Assassin de sa Femme' ends up being somewhat less than perfect. Pierrot himself will end up dying in (and of) a fit of uncontrollable laughter at the sight of his deceased wife's portrait (Margueritte 1910: 105).

13. In an influential chapter of *De la grammatologie*, Derrida argued that since the Nambikwara were alienated, according to Lévi-Strauss, by the very structure that gave them their names or identities, there was something inherently awry in the anthropologist's speculation on the corrupting or alienating effects of 'writing' in relation to a presumably pristine pre-literate identity. In the *Cahiers pour l'analyse*, no. 8, 1969, Lévi-Strauss dismissed Derrida's 'deconstruction' of him as particularly futile. 'I thus find it hard to fend off the impression that in dissecting my cloud-like impressions, M. Derrida manipulates the excluded middle with the delicacy of a bear' (1967f: 52; my translation).

14. To this extent, the central work in the Mallarméan corpus, from Marchal's perspective, is the poet's translation/adaptation of George William Cox's *A Manual of Mythology in the Form of Question and Answer* (1867), a popularisation of Müller's theories. Mallarmé's version appeared under the title *Les Dieux antiques* (1879). The centrality accorded by Marchal to that all but forgotten work is a measure of the originality (but also the eccentricity) of his impressive achievement.

15. Double paradoxe. En France, en plein XVIIIe siècle, les principes sur lesquels Saussure fondera la linguistique structurale sont clairement énoncés, mais à propos de la musique, par un auteur qui s'en fait une idée analogue à celle que nous devons aujourd'hui à la phonologie; et cela, bien qu'il tienne le langage articulé et la musique pour des modes d'expression totalement étrangers l'un à l'autre. (1993a: 95)

16. *L'Heure espagnole* will resurface at the very end of Lévi-Strauss's 'tetralogy', in the course of the extended analysis of Ravel's *Bolero*: 'A proprement parler, ce ne sont pas deux tonalités qui s'opposent: un mouvement de pendule "régulier et périodique", comme on dit dans *L'Heure espagnole*, écarte la mélodie d'une tonalité franche et stable où l'y ramène, reconstituant ainsi une sorte d'équivalent de l'opposition rythmique entre binaire et ternaire, et de l'opposition à la fois rythmique et melodique entre symétrie et asymétrie' (Lévi-Strauss 1971a: 594). Lévi-Strauss's construing of the *Bolero* (1971a: 596) as a fugue in which 'the real, the symbolic, and the imaginary' enter into counterpoint is as Lacanian a formulation as one finds in his oeuvre.
17. Mehlman 1999: 296.
18. For a reading of the Borges tale, see Mehlman 1995: 67–81.
19. Borges 1999: 396.
20. Nietzsche 1967: 124.
21. *The Case of Wagner*, in Nietzsche 1967: 158.
22. The circumstance resonates interestingly with Lévi-Strauss's interest, in *Tristes Tropiques*, in a remarkable 'sociological species': 'the Germanized Muslim and the Islamicized German' (1967d: 483).
23. With the possible exception of the entire twentieth century. See the futurist 'circulating' letter of Filippo Tommaso Marinetti, 'Abbasso il tango e Parsifal!' (11 January 1912).

REFERENCES

Boon, James 1972. *From Structuralism to Symbolism: Lévi-Strauss in a Literary Tradition*. New York: Harper & Row.

Borges, Jorge-Luis 1994. 'Ascendencias del tango', in *El idioma de los argentinos*. Buenos Aires: Seix Barral.
    1999. 'A History of the Tango', in Eliot Weinberger (ed.), *Selected Non-Fictions*. New York: Viking.

Deleuze, Gilles 2003. *Nietzsche et la philosophie*. Paris: Presses Universitaires de France.

Derrida, Jacques 1972. 'La Double Séance', in *La Dissémination*. Paris: Seuil, pp. 199–317.

D'Iorio, Paolo 2001. 'En marge de Carmen', in Nietzsche, special issue of *Magazine littéraire*. Paris.

Genette, Gérard 1965. 'Structuralisme et critique littéraire', *L'Arc* 26: 37–9.

Liébert, Georges 1995. *Nietzsche et la musique*. Paris: Presses Universitaires de France.

Mallarmé, Stéphane 1945. *Œuvres complètes*. Paris: Gallimard.

Marchal, Bertrand 1988. *La Religion de Mallarmé*. Paris: José Corti.

Margueritte, Paul 1910. *Nos tréteaux*. Paris: Dorbon Ainé.

Mehlman, Jeffrey 1974. *A Structural Study of Anthropology*. Ithaca: Cornell University Press.
    1995. ' "Pierre Menard, Author of Don Quixote" Again', in *Genealogies of the Text*. Cambridge: Cambridge University Press.

1999. 'Ad centrum?', in Denis Hollier and Jeffrey Mehlman (eds.), *Literary Debate: Texts and Contexts*. New York: The New Press.

2000. *Émigré New York: French Intellectuals in Wartime Manhattan, 1940–1944*. Baltimore: Johns Hopkins University Press.

Nietzsche, Friedrich 1967. *The Birth of Tragedy*. Translated by Walter Kaufman. New York: Vintage.

Shaw, George Bernard 1967. *The Perfect Wagnerite*. New York: Dover.

Steinmetz, Jean-Luc 1998. *Stéphane Mallarmé: l'absolu au jour le jour*. Paris: Fayard.

Valéry, Paul 1924. 'Situation de Baudelaire', in *Variété I*. Paris: Gallimard.

14   Morphology and structural aesthetics: from Goethe to Lévi-Strauss

Jean Petitot

In a 1999 article written as a tribute to Claude Lévi-Strauss for a special issue of the French journal *Critique*,[1] I surveyed Lévi-Strauss's references to Goethe, and this led me to refine the thesis that – as I had already argued in the mid-seventies with regard to René Thom's morphodynamic structuralism – there exists an authentic morphological genealogy of structuralism in the history of ideas.

This is the thesis that I will develop in the present essay, taking as an example a pictorial analysis from Lévi-Strauss's *Look, Listen, Read* (1997). This will enable me to revisit the teachings of a thinker who has left an indelible mark on my intellectual life.

The morphological genealogy of structuralism in Claude Lévi-Strauss

In his presentation of the aims of this Cambridge Companion, Boris Wiseman recalls Claude Lévi-Strauss's assertion that there were only three structuralists in France: Dumézil, Benvéniste and himself (by the way, for Roman Jakobson there were only five structuralists in the world: Saussure, Prince Troubetskoi, Lévi-Strauss, Thom and himself), and he interprets this as a warning against the temptation to dissolve Lévi-Strauss's thinking in the homogeneous cloud 'structuralism'.[2]

Boris Wiseman's remark is well founded. Lévi-Strauss often quite rightly set himself apart from the school of thought which Parisian intellectuals called 'structuralism' before they moved on to 'post-structuralism'. For instance, in his conversation with Didier Eribon (1991b), he drily criticises the 'ridiculous' excesses of the structuralist 'vogue' among the intelligentsia, upbraiding several of his colleagues. Even if he does not do so with the same vigour with which he backed Merleau-Ponty and Aron against Sartre, he proclaims his refusal to be lumped together with Foucault, Lacan and Barthes: 'That still bothers me, as there are no grounds for that combination ... I feel I belong to another intellectual family, the one represented by Benvéniste, Dumézil' (1991b: 72).

Some day it ought to be explained how and why structuralism, which is the pursuit in phonetics, syntax, semantics and in anthropology of one of the most venerable, profound, technical and difficult of scientific concerns – the problem of the coherent or 'organic' (self)-organised composition and structuring of parts into wholes – could ever have become in France a journalistic fad associated with authors who never tackled this problem. Hence, the need to go back quite precisely to the scientific and philosophical genealogy of structuralism.

In the conversation with Eribon (1991b), once again, in the eleventh chapter ('Sensible Qualities') of the second part ('The Laws of the Mind'), Claude Lévi-Strauss makes a series of very illuminating remarks about the way he conceives the epistemology of structuralism and how he locates the latter in the history of ideas. Thus, to a question from Didier Eribon concerning the origin of the central notion of transformation: 'Where did you find it, in logic?' Lévi-Strauss answers:

Neither in logic nor linguistics. I found it in a work that played a decisive role for me ... *On Growth and Form* ... by D'Arcy Wentworth Thompson ... The author ... interpreted the visible differences between species or between animal or vegetable organs within the same genera, as transformations. This was an illumination for me, particularly since I was soon to notice that this way of seeing was part of a long tradition: behind Thompson was Goethe's botany, and behind Goethe, Albrecht Dürer and his *Treatise on the Proportions of the Human Body*. (1991b: 113)

This testimony is crucial not only for the particular history of structural anthropology or the structural study of myth, but also for an intimate understanding of the theoretical genealogy of structuralism in general. According to conventional wisdom, structuralism is of formalist, logicist and linguistic descent and should be understood as the application to certain human sciences of a static, algebraic and combinatory concept of structure which, on the most favourable view, harks back to the great founders of mathematical 'structuralism' Hilbert and Bourbaki. There exists, however, an alternative, essentially different way of situating it – 'another itinerary', as Lévi-Strauss puts it – naturalist rather than formalist, where structures are treated as dynamic forms in development ('growth and form'), as morphodynamically (self-)organised and (self-)regulating wholes, the term 'morphodynamics' referring here to dynamic theories of natural forms. This 'other' tradition is much older and deeper than the formalist perspective, and it is fascinating to see how Claude Lévi-Strauss links up with it.[3]

To be sure, Lévi-Straussian structuralism is mentalist and cognitivist and even, as Philippe Descola reminds us,[4] open to a neural Darwinism. So, even if, formally speaking, it is based on combinations of discrete features and not on continuist primitives,[5] that does not keep it from being deeply rooted in a certain type of naturalism in which, by his own account, Lévi-Strauss has always been very interested:

> The traditional natural sciences – zoology, botany, geology – have always fascinated me, like some sort of promised land I will never have the privilege of entering ... From the time I began to write *Totemism* and *The Savage Mind* up to the end of the Mythology series, I lived surrounded by books on botany and zoology ... my curiosity about such matters dates back to my childhood. (1991b: 111–12)

This naturalist reference goes hand in hand with a critique of the formalist paradigm. After dissociating himself from the latter – 'the nature and importance of my borrowings from linguistics have been misunderstood' (1991b: 112) – he goes on to evaluate the theoretical role of the concept of transformation:

> the notion of transformation is inherent in structural analysis. I would even say that all the errors, all the abuses committed through the notion of structure are a result of the fact that their authors have not understood that it is impossible to conceive of structure separate from the notion of transformation. Structure is not reducible to a system: a group composed of elements and the relations that unite them. In order to be able to speak of structure, it is necessary for there to be invariant relationships between elements and relations among several sets, so that one can move from one set to another by means of a transformation. (1991b: 113)

It is essentially on this point that Lévi-Strauss is in harmony with the morphological tradition from Goethe to D'Arcy Thompson. As he explains in his 960 Inaugural Lesson at the Collège de France:

> Today, no science can consider the structure with which it has to deal as being no more than a haphazard arrangement of just any parts. An arrangement is structured which meets but two conditions: that it be a system ruled by an internal cohesiveness and that this cohesiveness, inaccessible to observation in an isolated system, be revealed in the study of transformations through which similar properties are recognized in apparently different systems. As Goethe wrote, 'All forms are similar, and none is like the others. So that their chorus points the way to a hidden law'. (1978b: 18)

Lévi-Strauss thus returns to Goethe's central thesis: 'Gestaltungslehre ist Verwandlungslehre', the theory of forms is the theory of transformations.

The concomitance of the concept of structure and the concept of natural form runs through all of Lévi-Strauss's writings, from epistemology to aesthetics. He aims for a 'science of the concrete' that calls into question 'the opposition, now classic in western philosophy, between the order of the sensible and that of the intelligible' (1978b: 155). What is more, natural forms likewise represent one of the pinnacles of aesthetics: 'In my view, man must persuade himself that he occupies an infinitesimal place in creation, that the latter's richness far outstrips him, and that none of his aesthetic inventions will ever rival those contained in a mineral, an insect or a flower' (1978b: 241).

In this chapter we will provide a reading of Lévi-Strauss's structural aesthetics on the basis of his analysis of Poussin, and show how close it is to Goethean conceptions. The specific aesthetic problem that will concern us is a structural approach of the specificity of a purely pictorial language: how painting (and also sculpture) 'signifies', in and of itself. But let us begin with some general theoretical remarks.

The morphodynamic-structural triangle

Lévi-Strauss's 'revelation' regarding D'Arcy Thompson and Goethe was in turn a revelation to me. Goethe had in fact been one of the first philosophers of Morphology to whom I had been led in my efforts to reconstruct the philosophical genealogy of Morphodynamics developed by René Thom. Moreover, the applications of the morphodynamic approach to which I was paying especial attention at that time concerned the structuralism developed by Claude Lévi-Strauss, Roman Jakobson and Algirdas Julien Greimas. I had made use of singularities in differential geometry and of bifurcations of attractors in non-linear dynamics in order to model phonological systems, elementary semantic structures and the 'double twist' of the canonical formula of myth proposed by Lévi-Strauss.[6] This had led me to a twofold correlation between Goethe and Thom on the one hand and Thom and Lévi-Strauss on the other.

The fact that, in reconstructing his own theoretical genealogy, Lévi-Strauss went back to Goethe's botany by way of *On Growth and Form* – D'Arcy Thompson having likewise been one of the greatest sources of inspiration for René Thom – showed that there existed a very precise and strongly established *double* genealogical link between the Goethean theory of forms and modern morphodynamic structuralism. We may therefore outline a Goethe/Thom/Lévi-Strauss trinity attesting to the unity of structuralism and morphology.

Goethe, Lévi-Strauss and Propp

In his preface to the French edition of Goethe's writings on art, Tzvetan Todorov emphasises this line of descent running from Goethe to Lévi-Strauss. He recalls that, in *Structural Anthropology*, Claude Lévi-Strauss assents to the view of those who seek 'to trace structuralism back to one of the remote sources of Gestalt thinking – the natural philosophy of Goethe' (1963a: 325). For Lévi-Strauss, the transformation of prototypes is the key to structuralism.

But Todorov also insists upon the lesser-known fact that the famous debate between Claude Lévi-Strauss and Vladimir Propp about the complementarity of the paradigmatic axis (concerning semantic features such as uncooked/cooked) and syntagmatic axis (concerning the characters' roles such as hero, traitor, etc.) in narrativity was played out against the backdrop of a double fidelity to Goethe. Propp held that Lévi-Strauss had misinterpreted his work because the English translation did not include any of the epigraphs, which were all borrowed from Goethe's *Morphology*, as was the very title of Propp's 1928 *Morphology of the Folktale*. In his 1966 reply to Lévi-Strauss, Propp underscores Goethe's naturalism:

Behind this term [morphology], we discover in Goethe a new breakthrough in the study of the laws that permeate nature ... We may cordially recommend these works to structuralists ... There do not exist two Goethes, the poet and the scholar; the Goethe of *Faust,* who aspired to knowledge, and the naturalist Goethe, who attained it, are one and the same person (Propp 1976: 135–6; my translation).

Well versed in Russian traditions, Todorov recalls that a Goethean morphological school linked to formalism flourished in Russia in the 1920s. The culturalist transposition of Goethe's *Naturphilosophie* was a logical reaction against the Diltheyan division between *Naturwissenschaften* and *Geisteswissenschaften* and his morphological concepts are at the origin of the conceptions of the Prague Circle and of the Jakobsonian analyses where form turns into structure in the strict sense, as soon as the parts of the whole assume a function. Russian formalism constitutes a fundamental link between Goethe and Jakobson, and therefore Lévi-Strauss.

The Morphology–Structure and Nature–Culture unity

Claude Lévi-Strauss's oeuvre displays many affinities with that of Goethe. We have just seen that this is true with respect to natural morphologies and *Gestalten*. But it is also true with respect to the relations between nature and culture. In his contribution, Philippe Descola explains that, even if Lévi-Strauss treated the nature/culture opposition as an antinomy insofar as it operates as such in the societies he studies, he nonetheless aims, for his own part, at a monist naturalist conception capable of overcoming the antinomy.[7] In his tribute, Philippe Descola also emphasises this nature/culture monism: 'nature conditions the intellectual operations by which culture receives an empirical content' and 'the roots of culture are to be found in nature, in the organic foundations of the working of the mind'.[8] Françoise Héritier also underscores this key point that Claude Lévi-Strauss always criticised mentalist and rationalist (Cartesian) dualism and emphasised 'structural features which are already there in Nature' (Héritier 2004: 409).

Now, exactly the same thing may be said for Goethe where the same theory of organised structure is the basis for thinking about the work of art and natural forms. His aesthetics is therefore inseparable from his morphology and metamorphosis. He saw structural problems as forming a unity. As Danièle Cohn expresses it so well in her authoritative work *La Lyre d'Orphée* devoted to Goethean aesthetics: 'Goethe, who invented morphology in the natural sciences, thus makes it possible to conceive of an aesthetic morphology ... and a morphological theory of culture' (Cohn 1999a: 11). For him, 'the natural sciences and aesthetics go hand in hand, the process of nature is, like that of the arts, a fashioning, a construction of form' (Cohn 1999a: 37).

Goethe criticised the mechanist physical sciences of his time for divorcing objective knowledge from the organisational complexity of nature. This results in the transcendental opposition between nature (objectivity) and freedom (will), characteristic of modernity, which was thematised by Kant, taken up again by Romantics such as Schiller, and then canonised by Dilthey and the early hermeneuts with the opposition between *Naturwissenschaften* and *Geisteswissenschaften*, between explanation and understanding. Nature conceived as phenomenon and object has been opposed to man conceived as noumenon and subject. The elimination of any organisational interiority of nature in a narrow mechanistic conception has been balanced by a hypertrophic conception of freedom as an unconditioned will. Goethe opposed this scission in two ways:

(1) He broadened the concept of nature to encompass the world of organisation and of the forms which, through semiotising cognitive processes, open onto the sphere of meaning.
(2) But, concomitantly, he restricted the concept of freedom by claiming to reconcile man 'ecologically' with nature.

Goethe understood that there exists a sphere of reality, that of organisation and complexity, of morphology and structure, which is *common* to nature and culture. Lévi-Strauss is undeniably a part of this genealogy, and that no doubt accounts for a certain number of the criticisms he received.

The birth of structuralism

I have shown elsewhere (Petitot 2003) that Goethe can be considered the inventor of modern structural aesthetics and that his *Laokoon* (published in 1798 in the arts journal the *Propyläen*, which he edited with Schiller and Heinrich Meyer) constitutes a sort of birth announcement of structuralism. This is not the place to rehearse all the arguments for this thesis, but the reader will nevertheless allow me to recall a few key points.

Morphologies and transformations

In Goethe's *Morphology*, the concept of phenomenal form (*Gestalt*) is inseparable from that of formation (*Bildung*), of formational force (*bildende Kraft*) and of structure in the sense of the relations between a whole and its parts (what are known as mereological relations). It raises a problem that is genetic, morphological (morphogenetic) and structural.

The heart of the problem is to understand the principle of the spatial connection of parts in an organic whole, especially in biology and, more precisely, as Lévi-Strauss emphasised it, in botany. Goethe introduced (in relation with Kant's treatment of biological organisation in the second part of the *Critique of Judgement*) the hypothesis that there exists a scheme for the idea of organised structure, a scheme open to infinite concrete variations, each transformable into the next.

The scheme is a generic type which can be realised through an infinity of cases, variants, occurrences or different tokens. It is the original identity of a genus or species and as such is the generative principle of an infinite, eventually virtual, variability. It entails laws of organisation and is a generative principle, a mode of construction, a model (*Modell*). As Goethe explains in a letter to Herder dated 17 May 1787, with this model

one may continue to invent an infinity of plants which would necessarily be consequent ... which, even if they do not exist, nevertheless could exist, and which are not merely shadows and pictorial or poetic appearances, but which possess an internal necessity and truth.[9]

The Goethean *Metamorphosis* thus unites the regular and the singular, the generic and the specific, the collective and the individual, unity and diversity. And if a type may have an open-ended diversity of variants, that is because these variants are connected to each other through transformations. The Goethean morphology is inseparable from the Metamorphosis as a theory of morphological transformations. This is the point which was to count the most for Lévi-Strauss in his defence of a transformational conception of structures.

Structure and composition in Aesthetics

This conception of structure was transferred by Goethe to aesthetics especially in his analysis of the Laocoön published in 1798 in the *Propyläen*. At that time, the Laocoön was at the centre of the renaissance of the classic arts and of the problematic of the autonomisation of the plastic arts. It was an absolute masterpiece, a 'miracle of art', and the topic of a spectacular debate between Winckelmann and Lessing. In 1766, as a reply to Winckelmann's

1755 *Gedanken über die Nachahmung der griechischen Werke in der Malerei und Bildhauerkunst* (Reflections on the imitation of Greek works in painting and in sculpture), Gotthold Ephraim Lessing, a great writer and art critic of the Berlin Enlightenment, published his sensational *Laokoon, oder über die Grenzen der Malerei und der Poesie* (see Petitot 2003).

This essay, which introduced the revolutionary thesis of an immanent meaning and a *sui generis* legitimacy of the sensible world, had an enormous impact because, for the first time, the plastic arts (painting and sculpture) were considered to be autonomous, in themselves and for what they truly are, namely arts of spatially extended forms and sensible qualities, and not mere illustrations of literary arts such as poetry, rhetoric, grammar, narrativity or mythology. Lessing separated the visual and the literary and launched into a twofold criticism of the descriptive genre (visual poetry and 'talking painting') and allegory (literary painting and 'silent poetry'). Painting does not have to exemplify and idealise 'the splendor of nature'. It does not have to illustrate the great narratives (previously considered the only ones worthy of great historical painting). It does not have to be pedagogical and to instruct. It does not have to subordinate itself to religion. Visual beauty is in itself a metaphysical value.

By its very nature, painting cannot 'express general ideas'. Owing to this essential limitation of the medium, the parts of any plastic composition must be spatially correlated and the aesthetic properties of the work must derive from the agreement between the parts spatially bound together to form a whole. The Kantian opposition between, on the one hand, the intuitive properties of space, time and movement and, on the other hand, the conceptual, discursive and logical properties of judgement is already present in Lessing, as is the mereological problematic of organisation.

In *Dichtung und Wahrheit* (I, 8), Goethe recalls the impact of Lessing's book:

> One has to be young to measure the influence of Lessing's *Laocoön*, which wrested us from the passivity of contemplation and opened us up to unbounded fields of thought. The *ut pictura poesis*, so long misunderstood, was swept away with a single stroke, and the difference between the plastic and the verbal arts was illuminated; they appeared to us quite distinct at their pinnacles despite the proximity of their foundations.[10]

As to Wilhelm Dilthey, he explains in his essay on Lessing[11] that '[Lessing] thus became the second legislator of the arts ... after Aristotle.' For Lessing demolished 'the rhetoric of the *ut pictura poesis*, which claimed to see in poetry a sort of talking painting and in painting a kind of silent poetry' (Damisch 1990: 8). As H. Damisch emphasises, for Lessing it was a matter of 'going back to what makes up the condition of possibility of the different arts' (Damisch 1990: 9). One may speak in this respect of 'the critical and, in the Kantian sense of the word, foundational operation effected by the Laoc-oön' (Damisch 1990: 9).

The fundamental problem raised by Lessing was that of an immanent theory of the meaning of plastic creations, one able to constitute meaning on the basis of the very constraints imposed by a transcendental spatio-temporal aesthetics. How can a meaning arise and emerge without the expressivity of a meaning transcending the plasticity of the creation and without resorting to allegorical convention? How is it possible to make the leap from empirical forms to aesthetic forms? What accounts for the supplement which the aesthetic adds to what is perceived? Of course, an emotion is present (the sentiment of pleasure and pain, as Kant would put it). But this emotion is itself the consequence of certain properties of form. Taking up and significantly refining some of Lessing's intuitions, Goethe became the first to resolve this problem and, in the process, he quite simply invented structuralism: the immanent meaning emerges from functional correlations between the whole and the parts of a work. There is a schematism of the composition which explains the emergence of properly aesthetic meanings.

Goethe's so-called 'classicism', his turning away from the irrationalist excesses of Romanticism, does not result from an aesthetic 'taste' but rather from a deep theoretical enquiry into the processes of the self-organisation of forms. To employ Danièle Cohn's apt expression, one may speak in this respect of a morphological monism in which Nature and Aesthetics unite in 'a formal shaping of form where the rule is given within the freedom of an achieved creation' (Cohn 1999b: 27). Like Kant, Goethe established a profound identity between the living being (*Naturwerk*) and the work of art (*Kunstwerk*). In a letter to Zelter[12] dated 29 January 1830, he wrote:

Kant did an enormous favour to the world, and, I might add, to myself as well, when, in his *Critique of Judgement*, he placed art and nature side by side and granted both of them the right to act without finality [*Zwecklos*] in virtue of great principles ... Nature and art are far too great to pursue ends, and they have no need to do so, for there are correlations [*Bezüge*] everywhere, *and correlations are life*.[13]

Goethe considered the Laocoön to be a 'perfect masterpiece' (1983: 165), a 'crowning achievement of the plastic arts', an exemplary and universal *type* containing the 'totality' of art 'in its entirety'. It constituted in his eyes an extraordinary solution to the fundamental problem of the balance between unity and diversity.

He treats the Rhodian group as 'a highly organized living structure' (1983: 166). As Richard Brilliant puts it, 'Goethe saw the sculptural ensemble as a quintessential natural sign' (2000: 59). Goethe's conception is 'organic', i.e. systemic and mereological. It is the relations of the parts within the whole – the famous correlations – which define their function, that is to say, their meaning. For the first time in the history of aesthetic thought, we are in the presence of an immanent and systemic analysis founded uniquely on relevant mereological relations. These relations are perfectly identified by Goethe: differences, oppositions, contrasts, symmetries, gradations.

Goethe places great emphasis on the laws of structure: the symmetries that undergird intelligibility, the oppositions that draw on 'fine discrepancies' to make manifest 'strong contrasts' (morphological principle of instability), etc. Such laws are only intelligible when the work is considered to be 'autonomous and closed upon itself' (1983: 168). Without a principle of autonomy and closure, it becomes impossible to bring out the relations of symmetry and opposition, and the non-conceptual perceptive meanings vanish. Here we recognise the basic structuralist principle of the primacy of differential cues which makes it possible for a work to possess a structure and therefore to be autonomous, in other words, to contain within itself the principles and the rules of its own interpretation (principle of immanence).

But that is not all. Of course, to have invented the structuralist principle of the constitutive semiotic function of differences already amounts to nothing short of a revolution. Yet, that would not be enough, far from it, for the following reason. Paintings and sculptures are by definition continuous forms, while (in the structuralist conception) semic units are discrete. Therefore, we still need to know how to go from the continuous to the discrete. This is easier said than done. Percept and concept oppose one another. The signs found in the plastic arts being natural signs, they vary in continuous fashion. In the conceptual domain, it is categorisation which resolves the problem of the passage from the continuous to the discrete: we categorise semantic continua by introducing qualitative discontinuities, and then we take the typical values central to the domains (categories) thus delimited by these boundaries. But categorisation is a conceptual mode of abstraction, and conceptual abstraction is not compatible with the essence of the plastic arts, for each work presents an irreducible spatial individuality. How then are we to inject discreteness into those irreducibly singular continuous compositions that are works of art? The problem is to succeed in extracting a form of discrete expression from a form of continuous intuition.

This is where an absolutely crucial geometric concept must be introduced, that of genericity and non-genericity. This notion was used intuitively by Goethe, but it goes back at least to the geometric painters of the Renaissance. Intuitively, a situation is generic when its properties do not change under small perturbations. On the contrary, it is non-generic if infinitesimal perturbations can change some of its properties. For example, in a plane the property for two straight lines to be parallel or orthogonal is a non-generic property because the modification of the inclination of one of the lines by as little as you want would result in them no longer being respectively 'orthogonal' or 'parallel'. Likewise, it is a non-generic property for two segments to be exactly aligned or for a triangle to be equilateral.

This very intuitive concept was not adequately theorised until the middle of the twentieth century, by such mathematicians as Whitney and Thom, on the basis of initial definitions coming from Italian algebraic geometers of the late nineteenth century. Let us take a form F that can be deformed through the action of parameters w. A state F_w of F will be said to be generic if its qualitative type does not change when w varies a little, in other words, when it resists small deformations. A typical example is that where w varies in a space of vantage points (for example, the vantage point chosen by any painter for a painting) and where F_w is the apparent contour of a 3-D object seen from the perspective w.

Non-genericity has remarkable perceptive effects. For example, it is well known that a 2-D diagram displaying the form which is the apparent contour of a cube is spontaneously interpreted by the visual system as a 3-D object when it is seen in perspective from almost all vantage points. These are the 'generic' vantage points. When the viewer moves from one generic vantage point to a neighbouring one, there is no significant modification to the perceived cube. However, there is a set of exceptional vantage points from which the apparent contour of the cube appears as a hexagonal maximally symmetrical apparent contour. In that case, the third dimension disappears and the diagram is interpreted as a planar hexagon. These are the non-generic vantage points onto the cube (see Figures 1 (a) and (b)).

The visual system being a probabilistic (Bayesian, in all likelihood) neural machine that learns to extract statistical regularities from the environment, it is very good at detecting rare events, and it treats them as intrinsically significant because they are rare. Since the probability of non-genericity is null it is perceptively salient. It provides a purely perceptive immanent criterion of meaningful relevance. What is more, insofar as normal perceptive scenes are, for their part, generic, non-genericity provides an immanent criterion for the difference between perceptive structure and artistic composition.

Since (at least) the Renaissance, great painters have been geniuses of non-genericity. In their works, the disposition of bodies and the vantage point are chosen so that, for example, a finger points exactly in the direction of a symbolically important site, a head is at a tangent to such and such an architectural element, two arms are parallel or orthogonal. These painters had matchless experience with non-genericity as the basis of composition: the art of composition involves arranging the figures and objects depicted on the canvas in such a way that they make up non-generic forms and scenes. The same may be said for sculptors, with one qualification: a sculpture being a 3-D object which the spectator may circumambulate, the non-genericity

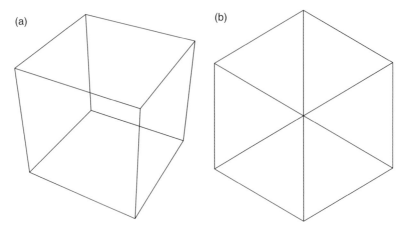

Figure 1 (a) The 2-D apparent contour of a cube in a generic position is perceived as that of a 3-D cube. (b) If the position is non-generic, the visual system interprets the apparent contour as a 2-D form, a planar hexagon, and does not reconstruct the 3-D form.

depending on a particular vantage point disappears, but the non-genericity of mereological relations remains.

Goethe perfectly understood this crucial point which makes it possible to establish a non-conceptual origin of aesthetic meaning on a purely immanent basis (i.e. with sole reference to the forms composed by the artist). Indeed, if we radicalise his response, we arrive at the following fundamental idea:

spatial relations are significant and relevant when they are non-generic, that is, unstable with regard to small continuous variations.

Plucked from the backdrop of an infinite (continuous) variability of possibilities, a symmetry, a contrast, a parallelism, etc. are non-generic. They *select* among all possible relations some that are exceptional and which, for that very reason, are laden with information. Non-genericity is the fundamental process of production of morphological information in a continuous composition, and this purely immanent information constitutes the basis of interpretative meaning.

So, in the plastic arts, non-genericity guarantees significance and provides a specifically morphological criterion of meaning.

What holds true for space holds equally true for time. The artist must 'discover the culminating moment' of a scene (Goethe 1982: 166), choose a unique 'transitory moment' that must be represented for the composition to contain the maximum amount of information and to make manifest a productive dynamic. The scene is a temporal section of a story, and the greatest possible temporal interval must be compressed into a fleeting instant. The represented present is a snapshot. Goethe speaks arrestingly of 'immobilized lightning' and 'petrified wave'. But it is not an arbitrary snapshot. The chosen moment must also be highly non-generic. As Goethe says: 'A little earlier no part of the whole must be found in this posture, a little later each part must be forced to abandon it' (1982: 169). This non-genericity guarantees not only the intelligibility but the pathos as well: 'The loftiest pathetic expression which they [the plastic arts] may represent is located in the transition from one state to another' (Goethe 1982: 169). In summary:

To be significant and capable of mediately expressing more abstract meanings, spatial relations in the plastic arts must be non-generic and unstable. This is the fundamental principle of the emergence of non-conceptual semiotic meanings.

Lévi-Strauss on Poussin: double articulation and composition

In *Look, Listen, Read* (1997), Claude Lévi-Strauss analyses in particular certain paintings by Poussin and, in doing so, he calls several times upon the structural principle of non-genericity.

We will focus here on his analysis of the masterpiece *Eliezer and Rebecca at the Well* (1648, Louvre Museum, Paris).[14] Lévi-Strauss recalls first the debates which the painting ('a pinnacle' among the 'sublime' works of Poussin) provoked at the Royal Academy of Painting in January 1668 and, in particular, the commentaries of Philippe de Champaigne reported by Félibien. An important part of the discussion turned on the fact that, according to Philippe de Champaigne, Poussin did not represent Eliezer's ten camels which play a fundamental role in the biblical text (Genesis XXIV): 'it seemed to him that M. Poussin did not treat the subject of his painting with a sufficient historical faithfulness' (Champaigne 1668). Indeed, God's Angel announced to Eliezer that he would recognise the right virgin he was searching for by the fact that she would water his camels after having supplied him with drink. Watering the camels was therefore the identifying sign. Poussin was supported by Le Brun, who explained that the deformity of the camels would have ruined this tribute to beauty.

In fact, the answer to Philippe de Champaigne is simply that Poussin represented in this painting not Rebecca's recognition but the next moment, when Eliezer gives her the golden ring and the two bracelets. Poussin was perfectly aware of the narrative since in two other versions of *Rebecca at the Well* (the first in 1629 and the second in the early 1660s) he depicted the inaugural moment of the recognition and represented camels. Daniel Arasse emphasised that, in the Louvre 1648 painting, the chosen moment is that of Rebecca's election and 'foreshadows Mary's Annunciation as a synthesis between God's blessing and human *caritas*' (Arasse 1992: 35; see also Glen

1979). This parallel is strengthened by the colours of Rebecca's clothes, blue and red being the distinctive colours of the Blessed Virgin. And Arasse concludes that: 'The camels, which can seem today rather secondary, have been the object of extensive reflections from Poussin, and the three paintings present as a system of transformations whose analysis enables us to reconstruct Poussin's artistic meditation' (Arasse 1992: 35).

Let us return to Lévi-Strauss's commentary. He emphasises the organic character of the composition and the fact that it operates at 'three levels of organization, one nested in the other, each raised to the same degree of perfection' (1991b: 24):[15] first the figures, each one being 'as profoundly thought out as the whole' (1991b: 34), then the groups of figures and finally the picture in its entirety (Figure 2).

This compositional hierarchy leading from internally structured 'first-order' units to higher-order structures is fundamental for Lévi-Strauss, who sees at work in it the universal structural principle of duality of patterning ('double articulation')[16] characteristic of all constructions imbued with meaning: 'Poussin illustrates above all the procedure of double articulation' (1991b: 13). 'In a painting by Poussin no part is unequal to the whole. Each is a masterpiece of the same stature which, considered on its own, is as worthy of attention as the rest. The picture thus appears as a second-order organization of forms of organization already present in the smallest details' (1991b: 34).

Lévi-Strauss starts out from the structure made up of groups of figures:

(1) in the foreground, the couple formed by Eliezer and Rebecca;
(2) to the left, a 'compact and lively' (1991b: 25) group of nine women (structured as $(5 + 1) + 1 + 2$);
(3) to the right, a group of three more hieratic women.

And he makes the fundamental observation that one figure is selected by the fact that it is prolonged by a pillar. He formulates the matter most precisely, speaking 'of the pillar of masonry ... surmounted by a sphere, against which the woman is silhouetted and to which she almost seems attached' (1991b: 26).

I would like to underscore the fact that this selection is achieved by a typical procedure of non-genericity. The perspective is chosen in such a way that the elbow of the right arm leaning above the edge of the well (the distinctive position of the figure) is exactly tangent to the edge of the pillar, and tangency would not survive the smallest perturbation of the vantage point. This effect of non-genericity is further reinforced by the fact that the side of the pillar seen in perspective appears as a narrow band that is exactly prolonged by the neck and the base of the jug; moreover, this alignment precisely divides the elbow from the body of the figure (see frames 3a and 3b of Figure 2).

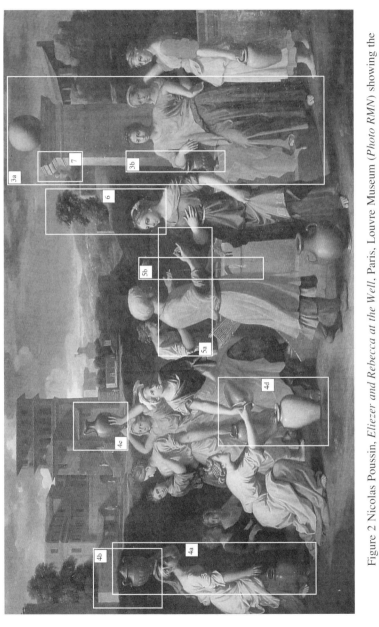

Figure 2 Nicolas Poussin, *Eliezer and Rebecca at the Well*, Paris, Louvre Museum (*Photo RMN*) showing the frames and details on which we will comment.

This non-generic construction selects a figure and imposes, in a structural and immanent manner independent of any external meaning, the identification 'leaning woman = pillar'. And, recalling that Philippe de Champaigne had criticised this figure for being too much 'at variance with the style of antiquity' (1991b: 26), Lévi-Strauss states: 'It is true that this sculptural figure is in sharp contrast with the others. I believe this calculated difference holds the key to the painting' (1991b 24). Indeed, once one has recognised this first identification, one immediately notices that there exists a vertical correspondence between the three groups of figures and the architectural or landscape components of the scenery:

Figures	Left-hand group	Central couple	Right-hand group
Scenery	Palatial buildings	Distant landscape	Pillar and manufactory

Lévi-Strauss returns here to the biblical episode of Genesis XXIV: having arrived in the promised land of Canaan, Abraham does not want his son Isaac to marry an autochthonous daughter of the soil but 'a daughter of his blood' and dispatches Eliezer, his oldest servant, to his home country (Ur in Chaldea) to bring back a wife. Rebecca is the daughter of Bethuel, the son of Abraham's brother Nachor, and the sister of Laban. As an anthropologist, Lévi-Strauss asserts that this episode stages the conflict between blood and soil or, more precisely, 'the contradiction between what the jurists of the Old Regime called race and land' (1991b: 25). If we identify the women with 'race' and the buildings with 'land', then the painting immediately acquires, through its very composition and organisation and the immanent properties of its structure, an intrinsic meaning apart from any extrinsic hermeneutic projection.

With regard to Poussin's compositional genius, Lévi-Strauss makes the following startling remark: 'In one precise point in the picture, Poussin furnishes, formulated in plastic terms, the solution to the problem' (1991b: 26). First of all, the form and tone of the selected figure make it appear to be more a statue than a character, so that it 'realizes the synthesis of an effigy which is still human (and thus of a piece with "race") and a pillar of masonry (already "land")' (1991b: 26). But the most startling facet of this assertion is the idea that a conceptual problem can have a plastic solution. Yet, that is precisely what composition accomplishes: by introducing singular spatial relations between terms naturally invested with meanings (here, the 'race' and the 'land'), it spatialises relations and tells a philosophical tale through the composition itself. In this sense, what the great painters do is not to represent. Instead, they usually are great theorists who produce pictorial solutions to philosophical, theological, moral, political, metaphysical or like problems.

Lévi-Strauss makes several other observations about this painting by Poussin.

(1) The left-hand group is lively; the right-hand group, immobile and the buildings immutable; thus, 'seen as a whole, the picture plays on an opposition between stable and unstable, mobile and immobile' (1991b: 25).

(2) This opposition is amplified by the parallel between the woman on the left (Rebecca's double) carrying an unstable jug on her head and the pillar-woman on the right whose column-body supports a stable sphere.

(3) Finally, concerning the configuration of the jugs, Lévi-Strauss notes the existence of 'a triangle formed by the jug that she [the woman on the left] is carrying on her head (unstable), the jug beneath her (or that of Rebecca) resting on the ground (stable), and the jug upon which the statuesque figure is leaning, located at an intermediate height' (1991b: 26).

One might add some further observations:

(1) The extraordinary interplay of the nine jugs (joined by the tenth which is the sphere) relative to the nine women:

(a) at the far left a figure is associated, by an opposition between her arms, to two vertically superimposed jugs, one on the head (unstable) – exactly tangent to the horizontal borderline between the upper part of the immediate background and the bottom of the wall in the distant background – and the other on the ground (stable);

(b) the leftmost of the group of two figures sitting in the shade is leaning on a jug;

(c) next, in the group of five figures (really only four, since the two holding each other's shoulders make up a single split figure), the central figure, the only one facing the viewer, is carrying on her head a jug exactly framed by one of the facades of the building, while the three other jugs are interlaced near the ground in an extraordinary trinity;

(d) Rebecca's jug is resting on the ground between Eliezer and Rebecca;

(e) the pillar-woman's jug echoes the sphere;

(f) and, finally, the duo at the far right connected by an arm around the shoulder corresponds to a jug held at arm's length (which embodies a stable position symmetrical to the unstable one of a jug carried on the head) (see frames 4a–d of Figure 2).

(2) The no less extraordinary interplay of positions, especially of the arms. One will notice in particular the left arm of the woman standing behind and to the left of Eliezer. The hand, which precisely prolongs her right forearm and is seen behind Eliezer's body to his right, is automatically placed in correspondence with Eliezer's right hand, which points towards Rebecca. These two hands are parallel and their positions are very similar. That of the woman is holding the rope of the well, which

is precisely prolonged by the braid on the hilt of Eliezer's sword (see Figure 2: frames 5a and b). The fingers' positions are also particularly interesting. With his right hand Eliezer at once points towards Rebecca with his index and gives her the golden ring he holds between his thumb and his middle finger. With his left hand he gives Rebecca the two bracelets. With her left hand, the woman behind him at once points towards the golden ring with her index and holds the rope with her other fingers.

(3) The essentially horizontal and vertical organisation of the picture. The fourteen figures ($9 + 1 + 1 + 3$ from left to right) are distributed in a very open triangle pointing towards the viewer (positions of the feet), and there are an ascending series of horizontal lines along which the jugs are arrayed like notes on a musical scale.

(4) Standing above Rebecca there is a tree which must be placed in relation with the other trees, the complementarity stone/tree being an essential feature of the scenery (see frame 6 of Figure 2).

(5) Other elements of the scenery such as the church, in the middle, off in the distance, and above all the second pillar, also in the distance, which the chosen perspective has made exactly tangent to the capital of the first pillar, an example of maximal non-genericity (see frame 7 of Figure 2).

With regard to Poussin's method of composition, Lévi-Strauss recalls that the painter constructed 3-D mock-ups of his pictures so as to be able to move about 'wax figurines' on 'small boards', clothing them in wet paper and taffeta, and that he enclosed these scenes in boxes pierced with holes, allowing him to project light upon the scenes and to analyse the shadows (1991b: 15). Lévi-Strauss considers this to be a 'method of composition so perfectly assimilated that it nearly ends up being a mode of thinking' (1991b: 15).

This method was criticised by, among others, Delacroix, who chided Poussin for the fact that 'his figures are set down one next to the other as if they were statues' (quoted in 1991b: 14). But I would like to stress the fact that varying projections of a 3-D scene onto the 2-D plane of the canvas is the technique par excellence for obtaining non-generic dispositions.

Conclusion

In this chapter, we have sought to show that Lévi-Strauss's structuralism belongs to a specific scientific problematic, that of the morphodynamic organisation of complex systems, whether biological, semio-linguistic or social. The genealogy of this problematic took us back to Goethe, who was himself already the heir to the Kant of the *Critique of Judgement*' and to the great naturalists like Buffon, Geoffroy Saint-Hilaire or Cuvier. From Goethe, we returned to Lévi-Strauss's structuralism by two routes, on the one hand, that of biological morphogenesis leading to René Thom, and, on the other, that of the rediscovery of Goethean morphology by Russian formalism, leading in turn to the Prague Circle and to Roman Jakobson.

We then demonstrated, using the example of Lévi-Strauss's analysis of a painting by Poussin, the continuity that exists between the Goethean principles of composition and correlation and structuralist principles, in particular with respect to the selection of singular elements in a work by means of a criterion of non-generic positioning.

Many scientific trends testify to the contemporary relevance of these approaches. First of all, the models of morphogenesis have been significantly refined and developed. In addition, everything having to do with perceptive *Gestalten* and with structures in the structuralist sense of the term is right at the forefront of current research in cognitive neuroscience, thus confirming the soundness of the intuition behind Lévi-Strauss's naturalist mentalism and neural materialism. Finally, the role of non-genericity in works of art is beginning to be studied within the framework of what is called 'neuro-aesthetics'. It has already been proven experimentally that the visual exploration of a painting involves a different pattern of eye movements from an ordinary perceptive scene, precisely because the framing and composition generate non-generic singularities which 'guide' the gaze. Such experiments confirm the expertise of the artists.

In sum, contrary to what is too often said, structuralism, and first and foremost that of Claude Lévi-Strauss, is assured of an enduring and wide-open future.

Translated by Mark Anspach.

NOTES

1. Petitot 1999.
2. See the 'Introduction' to this volume.
3. I am grateful to Lucien Scubla for pointing out to me that the reference to D'Arcy Thompson is early and recurrent in Lévi-Strauss. It appears in *Structural Anthropology* (1963a: 328), in *From Honey to Ashes* (1973b: footnote, p. 90) and in the 'Finale' of *The Naked Man* (1981: 676–8). The biological structuralism of Goethe and Cuvier is also cited in the 'Leçon Inaugurale' at the Collège de France reprinted in *Structural Anthropology II*, 'The Scope of Anthropology' (1978b: 3–32).
4. This volume.
5. This is not the place to discuss the theoretical problem of the relations between the discrete and the continuous in symbolic systems. The interested reader may consult *Physique du Sens* (Petitot 1992) as well as my morphodynamic modelling of Lévi-Strauss's canonical formula (Petitot 2001).

6. See Petitot 2001.

7. This volume.

8. Ibid.

9. This idea of the virtual plant has now been perfectly realised by artificial life software that constructs virtual reality organisms. Letter available in German online at www.wissen-im-netz.info/literatur/goethe/ital/09/226.htm.

10. Quoted in Lessing 1990 [1766]. The *ut pictura poesis* formula comes from Horace's *Ars poetica*, 361–5.

11. Reprinted in Dilthey 1929: 17–174.

12. Karl Friedrich Zelter, a Berlin architect and musician nine years his junior, was a great friend of Goethe's.

13. Quoted by J. Lacoste 1997: 219.

14. In the same book, Lévi-Strauss also analyses another celebrated Poussin painting: *Et in Arcadia ego*. See Scubla 2004.

15. Lévi-Strauss 1988a.

16. In linguistics, 'double articulation' means that at the phonetic level words are decomposed ('articulated') into phonemes while at the syntactic level sentences are decomposed into words.

REFERENCES

Arasse, D. 1992. *Le Détail*. Paris: Flammarion.

Bouligand, Y. and L. Lepescheux 1997. 'La Théorie des transformations', *L'Origine des formes, La Recherche*, 305: 31–3.

Brilliant, R. 2000. *My Laocoön*. Berkeley: University of California Press.

Champaigne, P. de 1883 [1668]. 'Lecture of January 7 1668', in H. Jouin (ed.), *Conférences inédites de L'Académie royale de peinture et de sculpture, recueillies, anotées et précédées d'une étude sur les artistes écrivains*. Paris: A. Quantin.

Cohn, D. 1999a. *La Lyre d'Orphée: Goethe et l'Esthétique*. Paris: Flammarion.

    1999b. 'La Forme-Goethe', *Problèmes de la Kunstwissenschaft, La part de l'œil*: 15–16, 27–37.

Damisch, H. 1990. *Preface to Lessing's* Laocoön. Paris: Hermann.

Descola, P. 2004. 'Les Deux natures de Lévi-Strauss', in M. Izard (ed.) *Claude Lévi-Strauss*. Paris: Cahier de l'Herne, pp. 296–305.

Dilthey, W. 1929. *Das Erlebnis und die Dichtung: Lessing, Goethe, Novalis, Hölderlin*. Leipzig: Teubner.

Glen, T. L. 1979. 'A Note on Nicolas Poussin's *Rebecca and Eliezer at the Well* of 1648', *The Art Bulletin* 57, 2: 221–4.

Goethe, J. W. von. 1975 [1780–1830]. *La Métamorphose des plantes*. Translated by H. Bideau. Paris: Triades.

    1982. *Werke*, Hamburg edition, vols. 1–14, edited by Erich Trunz. Munich: Deutscher Taschenbuch Verlag.

    1983 [1798]. 'Sur Laocoön', in *Écrits sur l'Art*. Paris: Klincksieck, pp. 164–78.

Héritier, F. 2004. 'Un avenir pour le structuralisme', in Izard 2004, pp. 409–16.

Lacoste, J. 1997. *Goethe, science et philosophie*. Paris: Presses Universitaires de France.

Lessing, G. E. 1990 [1766]. *Laocoön*. Translated by Courtin (1866). Paris: Hermann.

Marin, L. 1995. *Sublime Poussin*. Paris: Le Seuil.

Petitot, J. 1986. 'Structure', *Encyclopedic Dictionary of Semiotics*, ed. T. Sebeok, volume II, 991–1022. Berlin: Mouton de Gruyter.

1992. *Physique du Sens*. Paris: Éditions du Centre National de la Recherche Scientifique.

1999. 'La Généalogie morphologique du structuralisme', special issue on Claude Lévi-Strauss (ed. M. Augé), *Critique* 620–1: 97–122.

2001. 'A Morphodynamical Schematization of the Canonical Formula for Myths', in P. Maranda (ed.), *The Double Twist: From Ethnography to Morphodynamics*. Toronto: University of Toronto Press, pp. 267–311.

2003. *Morphologie et esthétique*. Paris: Maisonneuve et Larose.

Pornschlegel, C. 2000. 'Goethe et la critique du monde techno-scientifique', *Cahiers Art et Science*, Université de Bordeaux I, 6: 51–3.

Propp, V. 1976. *Folklor i dejstivel' nost'*. Moscow: Nauka.

Scubla, L. 1998. *Lire Lévi-Strauss: le déploiement d'une intuition*. Paris: Éditions Odile Jacob.

2004. 'Structure, transformation et morphogenèse ou le structuralisme illustré par Pascal et Poussin', in Izard 2004, pp. 207–20.

Settis, S. 1999. *Laocoönte. Fama e stile*. Rome: Donzelli.

Thom, R. 1972. *Stabilité structurelle et morphogenèse*. New York: Benjamin/Paris: Édiscience.

1980. *Modèles mathématiques de la morphogenèse*. Paris: Christian Bourgois.

Thompson, D'Arcy Wentworth. 1917. *On Growth and Form*. Cambridge: Cambridge University Press.

Todorov, T. 1983. 'Préface' in J. W. von Goethe, *Écrits sur l'art*. Paris: Klincksieck.

Trevelyan, H. 1941. *Goethe and the Greeks*. Cambridge: Cambridge University Press.

Winckelmann, J.-J. 1755. *Gedanken über die Nachahmung der griechischen Werke in der Malerei und Bildhauerkunst*. French edition: *Réflexions sur l'imitation des œuvres grecques en peinture et en sculpture*. Translated by L. Mis. Paris: Aubier, 1954/1990.

15 Structure and sensation

Boris Wiseman

In the 1670s, a famous quarrel occurred at the Académie royale de peinture et de sculpture about whether line or colour is more important in painting. It opposed the Poussinistes, lead by Le Brun, the then director of the Académie and Premier Peintre du Roi, to the Rubenistes. The former defended a rationally inspired pictorial classicism; the latter, the expressive force of colour. One of the key arguments put forward by the former camp, which was ultimately victorious, was that line was superior to colour because it appealed to the intellect, whereas colour only appealed to the senses. Viewed as a purely aesthetic debate, it appears today largely spurious. Its significance lies elsewhere, in what it tells us about seventeenth-century mentalities, and the conceptions that shaped them. It also provides a good analogy for certain aspects of the debate that accompanied the dissemination of structuralist ideas, a kind of modern philosophical version of the quarrel between Poussinistes and Rubenistes.

Lévi-Strauss's detractors have often reproached him for his intellectualism and accused him, as it were, of favouring line – i.e. 'pure' structures – over colour – i.e. the materials or substances from which these structures have been 'extracted'. The first few pages of Derrida's 'Force and Signification', the opening essay of *Writing and Difference*, articulate just such a vision of structuralism. The structuralist method, Derrida argues, attains its goal at the cost of splitting the creative force of a work of literature from the structures in which force inheres. In the process, it relinquishes any attempt to understand force from the inside. Its inspiration, he continues, is essentially 'panorographic'. He derives the term from a little-known instrument, invented in 1824, the panorograph, which projects the perspectival view of a landscape onto a 2-D surface. Like the panorograph, Derrida is in substance saying, structuralism converts the objects it tries to understand into a system of lines, a map. It reduces them to schemata, deserted by the creative forces that once animated them. Or so it is claimed. Derrida compares the result of such analyses to a town that, following some natural catastrophe, stands empty, a mere skeleton, haunted by its former inhabitants. Admittedly, Derrida's essay is aimed specifically at structuralist literary criticism and the later essay in the same volume that he devotes explicitly to Lévi-Strauss, 'Structure, Sign and Play in the Discourse of the Human Sciences', articulates a very different vision. Nevertheless, the opening essay of the volume, which deplores the 'structuralist invasion' of the 1960s (Lévi-Strauss would no doubt agree), has fixed a certain conception of structuralism that informs popular opinion. The reproach of formalism has stuck, and Derrida's denunciation of a certain 'schématisme proliférant' sums up a common – although, I believe, mistaken – view of structuralism. The post-structuralist critique pertained more broadly to the theory of meaning that this 'schematism' implied. Structuralism was deemed to overlook the materiality of the signifying systems (e.g. works of literature, social institutions) that it studied, of ignoring the play of signifiers in which meaning is endlessly deferred, in favour of a movement of transcendence towards some ideal plane of meaning. Critics highlighted the gesture of exclusion by which meaning is located exclusively in a drawing or template which is thought to provide unmediated access to the system of ideas behind the systems of signs. They drew attention, instead, to an immanent meaning, for which the theories of evocation of the colourists provide a parallel of sorts. The argument was that the system of ideas allegedly expressed in the work of literature or the social institution does not exist prior to its expression or 'inscription', i.e. to its material – sensible – embodiment. It does not exist prior to, or outside of, what Derrida called, in an extended sense, 'writing' (i.e. the entrusting of meaning to a trace).

My intention, here, is not to revisit the debate between Derrida and Lévi-Strauss which, in any case, was a non-event, since Lévi-Strauss chose not to answer Derrida, no doubt because he deemed that the important issues, from his point of view, lay elsewhere. If I refer to Derrida's seminal critique of structuralism, which is more complicated than a simple rejection of structuralist thinking, it is because it has obscured, through its popular reiterations at least, an important part of structural anthropology. For Lévi-Strauss does not favour line and the intellect over the senses (despite his love of Poussin). On the contrary he is very much concerned with sensation, its place in a history of humanity, its importance for a theory of cultural creation and for an understanding of cognitive processes. Lévi-Strauss does not relegate the testimony of the senses to the domain of 'error', as does much of Western philosophy after Plato. He attempts to reinstate its powers of explanation. The reputation that he has acquired of being one of the quintessential logocentric thinkers belies the complexity of his theory of sensation and its importance for an understanding of his anthropological project. Lévi-Strauss, as I will try to show, is very much a thinker concerned with the relation of the mind to the perceptible environment, i.e. with embodied thinking. Without trying to turn Lévi-Strauss into a post-structuralist, one may at least try to redeem the value of some of his insights about sensation. However, doing so requires that one gets beyond some of the simplifying labels that have been applied to his thought.

Sensation and difference

Much of structural anthropology – its theory of totemism, of classification and of primitive myth, for example – boils down to the somewhat enigmatic proposition that plants are not only 'good to eat' but also 'good to think with' (Lévi-Strauss 1964b: 89). In many ways, once one has understood what Lévi-Strauss means by this, one has understood the project at the core of structural anthropology. Let us illustrate with regard to totemism, or rather 'totemic thought', for it is not so much the institution of totemism as such which interests Lévi-Strauss as what it tells us about the functioning of the human mind.

Totemism may be defined as the custom of naming certain clans or social groups, sometimes thought to work as exogamous groups (the point is controversial), after various plant or animal species. Totemism became an object of intense theoretical speculation at the turn of the nineteenth century. A series of essays by anthropologist John F. McLennan were published on the topic in 1869, followed, in 1910 by Frazer's four-volume *Totemism and Exogamy*, on which Freud drew for his own *Totem and Taboo*, published in 1913. McLennan and Frazer both saw totemism as an elementary and archaic form of social organisation which preceded and gave rise to exogamy. Other beliefs and customs, including taboos relating to the eating of the totemic species, were subsequently added to these traits to create what was later denounced as a false institution. Totemism, as it was then theorised, was a convenient way of differentiating the civilised from the uncivilised, of rejecting into the realm of the exotic a set of beliefs which were incompatible with the Christian need to establish a fundamental discontinuity between the realm of the human and that of nature.

Closer to the structural interpretation, Meyer Fortes (1906–83), whom Lévi-Strauss cites sympathetically in *Totemism*, saw totems as metaphors. If the Tallensi (northern Ghana), for example, associate ancestors with alligators and other dangerous animals, it is because, like them, they are unpredictable – seemingly docile one moment; dangerous and aggressive the next. Fortes – anticipating Lévi-Strauss – understood, crucially, that the choice of the totemic animal was not arbitrary or based on a sense of mystical 'participation' with the animal. It was based on certain perceptible qualities that it possessed. Construed as a metaphor, the totemic symbol links the sensorium to the domain of language and thought, traversing the field of experience from 'thing' to 'word', thereby unifying it. This, in many ways, Fortes, Radcliffe-Brown (see his 1951 lecture 'The Comparative Method in Social Anthropology') and others (Firth, for example) already understood. But Lévi-Strauss took this insight several steps further. In the latter's view, his predecessors missed the full complexity of the symbol–sensorium connection. It is insufficient, he argued, to root it in an immediately perceived resemblance (ancestors = alligators). Rather, it implies an entire 'argument' that it is the anthropologist's role to reconstruct. And one of the recurring forms this 'argument' takes is that of a comparison between two sets of differences (A : B : : C : D). Lévi-Strauss argued that it was not isolated species that were being endowed with symbolic meaning, but the relationship between these species. Thus, if one clan was named after the Eaglehawk, and the other after the Crow, it was a way of saying that the relationship between these clans was analogous to that between the Eaglehawk and the Crow – both are carnivores, but the former is a predator and the latter a scavenger. The relationship, in other words, is one of simultaneous resemblance and difference. The totemic nomenclature enunciates something similar, Lévi-Strauss argued, about the two clans they designate, namely that they are at once allies and opponents. In other words, totemic symbols express a key aspect of the way in which a social group sees itself as a group.

A metaphor is an equation between two conceptual fields. Here, what connects the conceptual fields is a whole chain of reasoning (not unlike the condensed chains of association that generate images in dream-work). For the purposes of the present argument, the key insight is that differences apprehended in the sensible world, for example between one kind of bird and another, are used to 'think' differences of another kind: religious, ideological, social, etc. The stronger, more radical claim Lévi-Strauss makes is that our ability to apprehend differences in nature, say between one species and another, is the basis of the earliest recognition of the difference between human and non-human, and subsequently between self and other. In other words, it is the foundation of difference *as such* and the key to the passage from nature to culture. Analogy, here, is what gives rise to the earliest elaborations of a social realm: 'man ... came to acquire the capacity to distinguish *himself* as he distinguished *them*, i.e. to use the diversity of species as conceptual support for social differentiation' (Lévi-Strauss 1964b: 101).

In the analysis of totemism contained in *The Savage Mind*, Lévi-Strauss reveals another somewhat different way in which elements taken from the sensorium are used to construct symbolic systems. Any species, such as the Royal Eagle used as a totem by some North American populations, may be envisaged from two alternative points of view: either, extensively (in the sense that logicians give to this term), as a collection of individuals (all Royal Eagles) or, comprehensively (again, as understood in logic), as a system of features or definitions – i.e. as an organism, an animal made up of claws, wings, a beak, etc.[1] In the first case, the species may be used to signify the members of a social group by comparing them to the individuals that make up a given species. In the second, the species may be used, in the manner of the metaphor of the 'body politic', to signify the group as a whole, comparing the individuals of which it is comprised to the parts of the organism that make up the species: claws, wings, etc. (1962b: 165–6; 1966b: 136–7). In short: 'The notion of species ... is the operator which allows (and even makes obligatory) the passage from the unity of a multiplicity to the diversity of a unity' (1962b: 166; 1966b: 136). The totemic animal enables the detotalisation and retotalisation of any complex entity by allowing a passage between a conception of the species as a collection of individuals (point of view of extension) and a conception of the species as a unique system of qualities (point of view of comprehension) distinguishing it from other species. The totem is a logical schema extracted directly from images of the sensible world. It is used, in this instance, as a means of creating social cohesion, as an instrument of stability, but one may imagine other applications that are not necessarily sociological. The general point is that the mind extracts from its immediate, perceptible environment, the logical tools with which it creates.

Adherent logic

Much of Lévi-Strauss's theory of sensation is an elaboration of insights borrowed from Rousseau, whose *Discourse on the Origin of Inequality* (1754–5) contains the project of structural anthropology in germinal form. The most frequently quoted remarks by Lévi-Strauss on Rousseau are to be found in his inaugural lecture at the Collège de France (published in *Structural Anthropology II* (1973a)) and in *Tristes Tropiques* (1955a). These famously make of Rousseau one of the founders of the anthropological method. Lévi-Strauss cites Rousseau's comment that to study men one must look close to oneself, but to study man, one must look afar, for it is by observing differences that one grasps similarities. This formula encapsulates the essence of the comparative method in anthropology. But these frequently cited passages miss a key aspect of the filiation between Lévi-Strauss and Rousseau. *Totemism Today* (1962a; 1963d) is more instructive, in this respect, than *Structural Anthropology II* or *Tristes Tropiques*. In it, Lévi-Strauss cites a famous passage from Part II of the *Discourse on the Origin of Inequality*. It comes from Rousseau's speculative reconstruction of the stages by which a state of society gradually emerged from nature, a motif that would later become central to structural anthropology. In this passage Rousseau imagines an early form of human being, not yet in possession of language, living in a state of pure sensation, yet driven by necessity and demographic change to look for new sources of subsistence and thus compelled to explore a multiplicity of new environments. Rousseau evokes the discoveries made by this prototype of a 'civilised' human being and comments as follows on the effects of his exploration of new habitats:

This repeated interaction of the various beings with himself as well as with one another must naturally have engendered in man's mind perceptions of certain relations. The relations which we express by the words great, small, strong, weak, fast, slow, fearful, bold, and other such ideas, compared as need required and almost without thinking about it, finally produced in him some sort of reflection, or rather a mechanical prudence that suggested to him the precautions most necessary for his safety. (Rousseau 1997: 162; cited in Lévi-Strauss 1964b: 100)

This passage already grasps, more than 200 years prior to *The Savage Mind* (Lévi-Strauss 1966b) the basis for a 'concrete logic' (1966b) or 'logic of sensible qualities' (1966b) and, by extension, that of an anthropology construed, in Lévi-Strauss's words, as a 'general theory of relationships' (1966b) – relationships apprehended not in language but in the perceptible world. The delving into new qualitative worlds that accompanied the early quest for subsistence brought about *a systematic and repetitive process of comparison of 'secondary' qualities* ('cette application réitérée des êtres divers à lui même, et des uns aux autres') which in turn enabled the development of a rudimentary logic. Rousseau had already understood, in his own way, that 'plants are good to think with'. Rousseau does not express himself in the same terms as Lévi-Strauss, of course, but what he refers to as 'some sort of reflection' clearly anticipates the logico-sensible schemas – part percept, part concept – whose functioning structural anthropology will later try to grasp. Of particular interest here, is the anchoring of a form of rationality in the perception of the environment.

It is, no doubt, philosopher Claude Imbert who brought to light, with the greatest acuity, the importance of the conceptions elaborated by Lévi-Strauss in the wake of Rousseau, his patient excavation of an 'adherent' logic, as she calls it, an 'alternative' logic that underpins and predicates our other ties to the world, one that reunites the qualitative and quantitative at the very root of what makes us human and producers of symbolic systems. In her words: 'The first moments of objectivity and consciousness, the adherent but no less shared mode of symbolisation that all other modes of symbolisation presuppose, are qualitative ... the first geometries are qualities of forms' (Imbert 2000: 234; my translation). Similarly, Lévi-Strauss remarks how certain ideas and relations emerge from the inherent qualities of totemic species. These come to light on the basis of empirical observation alone and are subsequently taken up by speculative thought (Lévi-Strauss 1964b: 89). Another passage from Rousseau, this time from *Émile, ou de l'éducation* (1762), evokes the process of comparison of secondary qualities mentioned above, a key turning point in the education of humankind: 'Since man's first natural movements are, therefore, to measure himself against everything surrounding him and to experience in each object he perceives all the qualities which can be sensed and relate to him, his first study is a sort of experimental physics relative to his own preservation' (Rousseau 1979: 125). This act of 'measurement' is already a logic of sorts and Rousseau's 'experimental physics' (divested of the idea of self-preservation), a precursor to Lévi-Strauss's 'primitive science', a speculative science entirely based in an 'aesthetic sense' (1966b: 12).[2] To those who object that it is not a science at all, Lévi-Strauss would answer that the ordering of the sensorium at the level of its secondary qualities is the means of a rudimentary discovery procedure. It is the basis of a 'droit de suite' or 'right of inference' (1966b: 16) which allows the observer to speculate about the properties of things on the basis of their perceptible appearance – for example, that bitterness signifies toxicity (almonds, for example, do indeed contain cyanide). Such a science has no way of demonstrating the necessity of the connections it makes. Indeed, it does not understand these connections from the inside, in the way that modern science does. Nevertheless, in practice, it often works.

This view of a primitive science rooted in sensory intuition is part of a broader historical narrative that underpins the whole of *The Savage Mind*. It may be summed up as follows. Up to and including the Neolithic, human societies developed on the basis of a mode of thought rooted entirely in a logic of sensory properties. This 'logic' was the basis for a 'science of the concrete', whose relationship to the perceptible world was immediate. With the Greeks and the birth of reason (i.e. abstract or 'domesticated' thought) there occurred a fundamental bifurcation in human thinking whereby human-ity discovered another way of accessing the necessary relations previously grasped at the level of sensory experience alone.[3] From this point onwards, two paths were open to human thought, the older path travelled by the Neolithic scientist and his/her ancestors in the Mesolithic and Palaeolithic, and the new path opened by the Greek philosophers when they invented a purely conceptual (theoretical/reflexive) mode of thought that cut its ties with sensation. In the course of its development towards a fully scientific status, this split-off part of 'concrete logic' grew increasingly distant from the modes of thought out of which it emerged and that contained it in germinal form. The earlier modes of thought, however, continued to flourish, in areas that remain relatively free from the influence of domesticated thought, among them popular culture and art. For the path of concrete logic is not only that which eventually leads to modern science, but also to aesthetic creation.

For both Lévi-Strauss and Rousseau, historical speculation about the pas-sage from nature to culture is a means of trying to grasp the connection between sensation and the operations of the intellect. Diachronic consider-ations are treated essentially as a way of better understanding the relationship in synchronic terms, i.e it is a convenient modelling tool. Lévi-Strauss is in agreement with Rousseau in as much as he sees the sensible world as the support for thinking the differences that give rise to 'culture'. However, for Rousseau, this operation of the intellect emerges out of an earlier state of empathetic identification of humans with all other sentient beings. Prior to logical differentiation, there is the recognition of sameness, which is an affective reaction joined to a form of reflexive understanding. For Rousseau: 'the total apprehension of men and animals as sentient beings, in which identification consists, both governs and precedes the consciousness of the oppositions between, firstly, logical properties ... and then ... between human and non-human' (Lévi-Strauss 1964b: 101–2). For Lévi-Strauss, it is the other way round. The key transition occurs when certain concepts emerge as 'attributes of things' (see the 'Overture' to *The Raw and the Cooked* (1969d)), on a par with other secondary qualities. This prepares the ground for the earliest forms of symbolism. Having criticised Durkheim for his erroneous views about totemism, Lévi-Strauss goes on to cite a passage in which the founder of *L'Année sociologique* admits, somewhat in contradiction with himself, that the category of 'class' and the notion of 'opposition' are '*immediate* data of the understanding, which are utilised by the social order in its formation' (Lévi-Strauss 1964b: 97; my emphasis). Later, Lévi-Strauss spells out more explicitly still: 'The advent of culture thus coincides with the birth of the intellect' (Lévi-Strauss 1964b: 100). In other words, for Rousseau, primacy is given to affect (pity) which, when it becomes self-conscious and gives rise to compassion, lights the spark of culture. This enables the formation of a network of relations between individuals otherwise living in a state of isolation. For Lévi-Strauss, primacy is given to the logical schema whereby a system of similarities and differences apprehended in nature becomes the support for thinking the relationship between humans and non-humans and, by extension, that between self and human other, and in the wake of these distinctions, the myriad differences that make social life possible. The intellect, in other words, has primacy; it prepares the stage on which affect emerges. It is worth emphasising that structural anthropology nevertheless does not divorce rationality from sensation; it does not require of the intellect a Platonic-style turning away from perceptible reality. Rather, the operations of the intellect emerge as a kind of extension of the operation of the senses. The mind thus discovers in the world structures that are already written into its own make-up. There is a discontinuity between nature and culture but it is bridged by a kind of mirroring of mental and material structures.

Whichever realm is given primacy, both thinkers sought to understand the conditions under which the intelligible and the sensible are meshed together. The aim of structural analysis is not to separate structures from the sensible, or to impose pre-existing structures (mathematical, linguistic) on it, but to *discover* them immanent in the material world. As Lévi-Strauss points out: 'in a structural analysis it is impossible to dissociate form from content. The form is not outside but inside' (Lévi-Strauss 1964b: 91).[4] Lévi-Strauss's analyses do not follow a transcendental movement, away from embodied thought; they are not an elevation of rationality, but an attempt to discover the latter's conditions of possibility in the material world and to situate the thinking subject in his/her physical environment. Nothing says this better than the very concept of *pensée sauvage* (the English translation 'savage mind' is misleading) which, it is worth recalling, is based on a pun. A *'pensée'* in French is at once a thought and a pansy, a *wild* pansy (the *Viola tricolor*). Human thought, in other words, is a kind of organism, a species among species, and subject to the same laws that govern all life. Structuralism is often presented as an idealism that bypasses the multiform complexity of life. It is thought to sublimate reality into pure intellectual structures. On the contrary, what underpins structural anthropology is a theory of the imbrication of the sensuous-imaginative and the abstract-conceptual. What Lévi-Strauss calls 'concrete logic' or 'logic of sensible qualities' – the mainspring of so-called 'wild' modes of thought – is essentially a theory about how human beings living in different times and places have discovered, in their immediate environment, the conceptual tools with which to solve the various problems that confront them on a daily basis, problems that are social, economic, religious, practical, etc. Nature is more than simply a 'dictionary', as has sometimes been suggested, in which non-literate societies find the signifiers with which they create symbolic systems, activating, as it were, some oppositions within the sensorium, marking them as pertinent, and neglecting others. It is also the source of an elementary 'grammar' of thought.

The environment, therefore, is not simply a backdrop for thought. Structural anthropology points towards a theory of cultural creation that focuses on the dynamic interaction of mind and world. The mind is constantly engaging with the sensorium, delving into it to find new resources and develop cognitive schemas. (Lévi-Strauss comments in the opening chapter of *The Savage Mind*, in the context of his comparison between works of art and scale models, that the child's doll is more than an adversary or even an interlocutor: in it and through it the child becomes a subject (1966b: 23).) This is no doubt in part why there can be such variation in what people perceive – and do not perceive – in their immediate environment. The large number of words that the Eskimo have to designate snow has become legendary. Our amusement and non-comprehension is simply a marker of the limits of our respective sensory worlds, which are shaped by a myriad of cultural factors, including the technologies we use to engage with the environment and our professional and other specialised interests. Nineteenth-century workers in the famous Paris Gobelin dye factory differentiated no less than sixty shades of blue (Balfour-Paul 1998: 181). Japanese dye artists can identify how many times a piece of fabric has been dipped in indigo solution, and give them different names accordingly. We do not inhabit a unitary sensory environment but a kind of honeycomb in which we each carve out our own sensory niches. The sensorium is not an external reality, a unified landscape or horizon, but itself a kind of artefact, produced at the intersection of the subjective and objective dimensions of experience, which is where concrete logic – and arguably culture itself – has its roots.[5]

Symbolist echoes

Lévi-Strauss's works develop around an exploration of our relationship to the perceptible world. One might have followed other strands of thought, but the gradual excavation of an 'adherent' logic is clearly one of his major guiding threads. And it is arguably not until the *Mythologiques* (1964a–1971a), to which I will turn in the conclusion to this essay, that he really gets to grips with this 'logic'. But before turning to mythical thought, I would like to consider an earlier work, *Tristes Tropiques* (1955a), which usefully brings to light some crucial literary influences on Lévi-Strauss's anthropological thinking about the senses.

Tristes Tropiques (1955a), which is partially autobiographical, was written prior to *The Savage Mind* (1962b) and *Totemism* (1962a) and prior to the articulation of such key concepts as *pensée sauvage* and concrete logic. Nevertheless, these ideas are already present in this book in other forms. *Tristes Tropiques* (1955a) is a profoundly Proustian book. Not only because its opening chapters are organised according to a series of mnemonic associations – the 'flying carpet', which transports him from one place to the next, with total disregard for geographical or spatial boundaries – but also because it is centrally concerned with the myriad sensory shocks provided by his travels. The experience of the 'exotic', and of alterity, denounced as an illusion in key philosophical passages (see the sections devoted to the Tupí-Kawahib), is in many ways redeemed as a sensory experience, in the physical descriptions of the New World. This is a book of sensory estrangement. And perhaps one of the lessons of *Tristes Tropiques* is that the exotic is no more than a sensory experience? A kind of temporary dizziness of the central nervous system as it readjusts to a new set of perceptual configurations. Nevertheless, in this brief moment of dizziness, Lévi-Strauss glimpses a whole new system of production of meaning, one that escapes classical linguistic interpretations. Here, Proust is of more help than Jakobson or Saussure (Baudelaire and Segalen are not far away either). It is revealing that Lévi-Strauss highlights the fact that his first contact with the New World was olfactory. Like Proust, Lévi-Strauss challenges the ocularcentrism of Western culture; he reintegrates other sensory modes, and their interconnections (synaesthesia), into processes of production of meaning. It is worth citing at length the passage that describes Lévi-Strauss's first contact with the Americas, as it is one of the first steps on the road to the discovery of the existence of a logic of perceptible qualities:

From the day before, we had been conscious of the New World although it was not visibly present; the coast was too far away ... Nor was it the huge sea birds ... that told us we were at our journey's end, since these birds venture a long way from land. The traveller approaching the New World is first conscious of it as a scent very different from the one suggested back in Paris by the connotations of the word Brazil, and difficult to describe to anyone who has not experienced it. At first, it seemed that the sea smells of the preceding weeks had ceased to circulate so freely; they had come up against an invisible wall: thus immobilised, they no longer claimed the traveller's attention, which was now drawn towards smells that were of a quite different nature and that nothing in his past experience enabled him to define: they were like a forest breeze alternating with hot-house scents, the quintessence of the vegetable kingdom, and held a peculiar freshness so concentrated as to be transmuted into a kind of olfactory intoxication, the last note of a powerful chord, sounded separately as if to isolate and fuse the successive intervals of diversely fruity fragrances. This can only be appreciated by someone who has buried his face in a freshly cut tropical red pepper, after having previously, in some *botequim* of the Brazilian *sertão*, inhaled the aroma of the black honeyed coils of the *fumo de rôlo*, made from tobacco leaves, fermented and rolled into lengths several yards long. In the blend of these closely allied scents, he can recognise an America which, for thousands of years, was alone in its possession of their secrets. (1973c: 78)

At one level, what Lévi-Strauss is evoking here is an experience that one may readily recognise. An exotic location becomes summed up, in one's memory of it (Lévi-Strauss is writing some fifteen years after the event), by a set of distinctive sensory impressions. Mexico City, in my own memory, is inseparable from the smell and sound of frying corn tortillas. But what he evokes is also more complicated, closer to the operations of involuntary memory described by Proust, in as much as sensory impressions intertwine with linguistic associations. These linguistic associations derive from the 'verbal assonances' (see the original French passage) in the word 'Brazil'. Indeed, as Lévi-Strauss explains elsewhere, prior to his trip, this word had always evoked a certain burnt odour, probably because it shares its final vowel sound with '*grésiller*' ('to sizzle'). This association, made possible by a rhyme, is in conflict with the sweeter honey-like smell of the real Brazil, which is evocative of the scent of the inside of a red pepper and of a fermented tobacco coil. 'Reality' is never entirely independent from language. If Lévi-Strauss leaves *fumo de rôlo*, *botequim* and *sertão* untranslated, it is to preserve the incantatory power of their own phonetic texture. For language confronts one with another sensorium, that of its sound systems, with its own networks of autonomous semantic charges and non-referential systems of production of meaning (arguably the basis of poetry).

One is reminded, here, of Proust's meditations on the names of towns and countries, which is also a form of fantasising about the exotic. In the chapter entitled 'Place-Names: The Name' in *Swann's Way*, Proust evokes Parma:

> The name of Parma, one of the towns that I most longed to visit after reading the *Chartreuse*, seeming to me compact, smooth, violet-tinted and soft, if anyone were to speak of such or such a house in Parma in which I should be lodged, he would give me the pleasure of thinking that I was to inhabit a dwelling that was compact, smooth, violet-tinted and soft, that bore no relation to the houses in any other town in Italy, since I could imagine it only by the aid of that heavy first syllable of the name of Parma, in which no air stirs, and of all that I had made it assume of Stendhalian sweetness and the reflected hue of violets. (2002: 467)

For Lévi-Strauss, as for Proust, the sensorium, whether encountered in language or in the 'real' world, provides him with a series of opportunities to escape the present. Sensible reality reveals itself to be porous; it allows the passage to other times and places, past and future. In the boat journey recalled in the above quote, the scents transport Lévi-Strauss towards the unknown continent he is approaching, but also towards the experiences of the first travellers to the New World – Jean de Léry, André Thévet, Columbus and others. As he takes in the smells of the Americas, he is reminded of the written accounts of their journeys, which preserve the trace of a much fantasised about, pristine, first encounter. The world recreated for Lévi-Strauss in the microcosm of a scent is also a literary construct, like Parma was for Proust (it is *Stendhal's* Parma that Proust imagines). The above parallel with Proust highlights the need to view Lévi-Strauss's thinking about sensation in its connections to Symbolist poetics.[6] The traces of Symbolist ideas are visible throughout *Tristes Tropiques* (see, for example, the musical metaphor contained in the above description of Lévi-Strauss's first contact with the Americas). The key passage in *Tristes Tropiques* that ties together Symbolism, Lévi-Strauss's early field experiences and his later anthropological investigations is the following one. It is among the most revealing for an understanding of the project underling structural anthropology:

> What useless irritation we could spare ourselves if we agreed to accept the true conditions of our human experience and realize that we are not in a position to free ourselves completely from its patterns and rhythm! Space has its own values, just as sounds and perfumes have colours, and feelings weight. The search for such correspondences is not a poetic game or a practical joke (as some critic has had the audacity to say it is, in connection with Rimbaud's 'sonnet des voyelles', which is now a classic text for linguists who know the basis, not of the colour of phonemes – which is variable depending on the individual – but of the relationship between them, which admits of only a limited scale of possibilities); it offers absolutely virgin territory for research where significant discoveries are still to be made. If, like the aesthete, fish divide perfumes into light and dark, and bees classify luminosity in terms

of weight – darkness being heavy and brightness light – the work of the painter, the poet or the musician, like the myths and symbols of the savage, ought to be seen by us, if not as a superior form of knowledge, at least as the most fundamental and the only really common to us all; scientific thought is merely the sharp point … and its effectiveness is to be explained by its power to pierce sufficiently deeply for the main body of the tool to follow the head. (1973c: 123–4)

This passage fixes a goal for the scholar, identifies a route which, with hindsight, we can see is the one that will eventually lead to the excavation of a 'logic of sensations'. To my knowledge, no other passage by Lévi-Strauss reveals more clearly the literary sources of his theory of cultural creation and indeed those of his entire project.[7] Structural anthropology, it suggests, is a sociological elaboration of Baudelaire's poetic theory of *correspondences*. Lévi-Strauss is a post-Symbolist writer turned ethnographer, whose antecedents include Mallarmé, Valéry, Rimbaud and Baudelaire (all alluded to in the above quotation). Understanding this genealogy is crucial to how one reads Lévi-Strauss, including anthropologically.

Mythical thought

The journey that leads from the sensory shocks evoked in *Tristes Tropiques* to the formulation of a logic of sensations, in *The Savage Mind*, and the further elaboration of this logic in the *Mythologiques*, was a long one. At the time of writing *Totemism Today* (1962a), Lévi-Strauss seems to construe this immanent logic primarily in terms of a system of simultaneous oppositions and correlations. Symbolically and sociologically, the Hawk and the Crow illustrate the unity of opposites. There is, perhaps, something limiting here. With the move, in the late 1950s and 1960s, to the terrain of myth, and the initiation of a project that transcends the boundaries of ordinary science, that of the *Mythologiques*, Lévi-Strauss started to put into place a much more complex theory of sensation, grasped in terms of its place in mythical creation. In doing so, he reinvented his role as analyst and mythographer. His exploration of Amerindian mythology was also an undeclared return to the field experiences of the 1930s, to the sensory shocks evoked in the autobiographical sections of *Tristes Tropiques* (1955a) but left essentially untheorised.

The four volumes of the *Mythologiques* (1964a–71a), written over a period of some ten years, dissect 2,000 or more myths, explore their intricate transformational connections, and extract from the images they contain the wisdom of a continent. To present this series properly, it would be necessary to follow, in detail, the adventures of a bird-nester, trapped on the face of a cliff and saved by vultures; those of a rolling head and of a wife, whose torso becomes affixed to her husband's back; and many more. It would be necessary to explain, for example, how myths came to pair off honey and tobacco smoke, the one wet, the other dry, and show how these oppositions were used by Amerindian populations to articulate a code of sexual behaviour that opposes the temptations of nature (honey is found ready to be consumed, unmediated by society) to the spirituality of culture, designated by the vertically ascending smoke produced by men. What matters here is the systematic tracking of systems of belief – in short, ideology – to their multiple sensory supports. And what is revealed through this painstaking analysis of how cultural schemas map onto mythical images is not *a* logic of the sensible, but, in fact, three distinct logics: a logic of sensible qualities proper, based on such oppositions as raw/cooked, fresh/rotten, dry/humid (*The Raw and the Cooked* (1969d)); a logic of forms, based on such oppositions as empty/full, container/contained, internal/external (*From Honey to Ashes* (1973b) – see, in particular, the numerous references to cooking utensils); and a logic of temporal intervals, based on such oppositions as long/short (= daily/seasonal), cyclical/serial (*The Origin of Table Manners* (1978c)).

Let us look more closely at the third tier of this grammar of cultural creation, this logic of temporal intervals. It is rooted, in part, in the so-called 'astronomical code' analysed in volume three of the *Mythologiques*. This code is based, in part, on the observation of differences in the patterns of recurrence of various astronomical phenomena. Constellations, for example, are associated with long-term periodic intervals, in as much as they appear and disappear on an annual basis. Other phenomena, such as the moon and the sun, are associated with both long- and short-term periodicities. The moon and sun alternate on a daily basis, producing day and night which, at the equator, are of equal length. In addition to this short cycle, the moon may also be used to denote monthly periodicities, and the sun, which is low and pale in the winter and high and bright in the summer, an annual one. One of Lévi-Strauss's points is that the longer-term cycles, such as the stellar cycles, are inherently more meaningful for the populations that use them, because they are connected with events of major importance for the organisation of daily life, such as the phases of the hunting calendar. They have a positive connotation. The 'serial' conception of temporality associated with the shorter cycles is linked by Lévi-Strauss to a loss of meaning and a historical transition, in Amerindian societies, towards a different conception of temporality, closer to our own modern conceptions. The transition from a stellar to a lunar code (i.e one based on the alternation of night and day) signifies a kind of speeding up of time.

An anthropological project that started, in the 1940s, as an interrogation about the origins of society and about the patterns of kinship exchange thus eventually leads to a reflection on time. The *Mythologiques* show how Amerindian populations use various sensory supports to 'think' what Bergson called *durée* – the raw, undifferentiated subjective experience of time – and convert it into something else: a mathematical notion or a spatial metaphor. What is perhaps most interesting here are the implications of Lévi-Strauss's approach to myth for our own society, which is only post-mythical in appearance. The question here is what sensory supports do we use to articulate our own conceptions of time? Various answers have been put forward by commentators. They have turned their attention, among other things, to the computer technologies that mediate communication in contemporary life. The Amerindian schema, which I have just evoked, aims to symbolically control or regulate change by inscribing various events in circular temporal patterns. The extension of our sensible world by multiple virtual environments poses a different set of problems. Computer technologies, at the same time as reducing the thickness of our sensory ties to the world, replacing it with a screen, collapse temporal and spatial gaps in communication, thereby allowing a kind of unlimited passage, or free circulation between different moments in time. These are all placed side by side on the same virtual plane. The problem is no longer how to master serial change by inscribing it in a circle. It is how to assemble various moments in time – literally, connecting time zones – into a series of parallel tracks. Broadcasting media – at least of the non-mobile variety – allow something analogous, namely the illusion of a synchronous experience (the intense emotions provoked by the live broadcasting of major sporting events is in part due to this illusion). The subjectivity of the viewer is dissolved by the connections that link him/her, via a global network of television sets all tuned to the same channel, to a multitude of other subjectivities, allegedly going through the same experience at the same time.

More importantly, for my argument, the 'method' of analysis that reveals how myths work proceeds in a manner analogous to the myths themselves, namely by displacing structures from one sensible support to another. The schemas found to be at work in myth are assimilated to musical structures (the rondo, the sonata, etc.) to rhetorical figures and to mathematical patterns. But Lévi-Strauss never arrives at a final meaning or 'signified'. His conviction is that, as with music, meaning can never be finally extracted from the forms that express it, but only transferred from one form, or sensible support, to another. Far from splitting force from structure, his analyses arise out of an experience of force, made visible in the endless proliferation of mythical transformations which Lévi-Strauss himself takes up and continues. Lévi-Strauss is carried along, indeed swept away by the endless generativity of mythical structures.

Thus, with the *Mythologiques*, it is not simply a question of understanding how Lévi-Strauss *theorises* the sensible. He appropriates the logico-sensible schemas found in myths and uses them as the basis for an original creation, his own mytho-poem. The *Mythologiques* series – the textual equivalent of a collage (the metaphor is Lévi-Strauss's) – is the product of a much discussed method but also a poetics or poïetics, one that remains to be explored. The analysis of mythical transformations is the outcome of Lévi-Strauss's own processes of transformation, whose precise location – inside or outside the mythographer's mind? – is difficult to determine. The logico-sensible schemas analysed in the *Mythologiques* occupy a space at the junction of several discourses, at once other and familiar. Who can say whether these schemas originate inside or outside of myth? The ambiguity is part of the value of this work. The *Mythologiques* are, at heart, about how images borrowed from the perceptible world enter into dialogue with one another, and, in the process, engender new images. The dialogue takes place in many different heads. Amerindian heads, Lévi-Strauss's head, his reader's head. The enigma posed by the *Mythologiques* is how an act of personal creation and invention of this kind (or several) may also be a form of science.

If metaphors connect the sensorium (lived experience; observations about physical processes) to the domain of language, then the whole of the *Mythologiques* may be seen as an extended experiment in metaphorical thinking. This is true at the level of the analysis of mythical contents, as we have just seen, but also that of Lévi-Strauss's understanding of the *Mythologiques* series itself. It is as if the *Mythologiques* series can only come into existence through its metaphorical representation and indeed through a proliferation of metaphorical analogues (the perceptible supports of conceptual thought). I am thinking not only of the much discussed musical analogy that makes of this work the analogue of a symphony (its first chapter is an 'Overture' and its last a 'Finale'), but the comparison of the structural 'method' of analysis to an anaclastics (the part of optics that deals with the refraction of light); and of the analyst's progress to a journey through a universe in miniature. The last of these metaphors is worth dwelling upon, by way of a conclusion, as it provides an important clue to the status of the *Mythologiques* as a text and, by extension, to the relation of this text to the sensorium. In many ways, it may be seen to belong, beyond its anthropological affiliations, to an important genre of writing concerned with memory.

Proust's *Recherche* has often been written about from the point of view of its treatment of reminiscence, its exploration of an 'involuntary memory', triggered by sensations which preserve intact a world in miniature. In this connection, Proust's novel has been related to Romantic poetry and to the Rousseau of the *Confessions* and the *Reveries of the Solitary Walker*. In his recent, illuminating lectures given at the Collège de France (broadcast on France Culture) Antoine Compagnon has shown that one may also relate Proust's treatment of memory to an older rhetorical tradition whose origins go back to classical antiquity. One of the concerns of rhetoricians has been how to remember complex arguments. In trying to solve this problem, they developed a theory of the relationship of the mind to images that is part and parcel of our classical inheritance and has permeated many aspects of Western culture. The *Mythologiques* may usefully be seen as part of this tradition.

One of the techniques advocated by rhetoricians in, for example, the influential anonymous Roman treatise known as the *Rhetoric at Herenius*, involved the construction of so-called 'memory palaces'. The technique consisted in associating ideas or arguments with vivid or 'active' images (*imagines agentes*) and placing them in the rooms of some imagined edifice. The delivery of the speech was construed as a kind of mental journey through this edifice in which each image, and the arguments associated with it, were retrieved in turn. The narrator of *La Recherche*, Compagnon suggests, constructs a similar kind of 'memory palace'. Compagnon cites, for example, the famous opening pages of *Swann's Way*, in which, having just woken up, the narrator imagines himself in each of the rooms he has occupied throughout his life, rotating them, as it were, around him, in his mind's eye. The rhetorician's mnemonic art, his construction of an 'artificial' memory, Compagnon adds, also provides a key to the memory of literature itself, its intertextuality. Literature remembers its past as a network of places which are visited and revisited, in the manner of Aristotle's topoï or 'common places'. One of Compagnon's conclusions is that literature is perhaps closer to geography than to history, as is commonly thought to be the case. It creates a space that may be inhabited. Hence, the recurring metaphor – to be found in Proust, Montaigne, Descartes and others – which assimilates reading to a kind of walk. The key point, here, is the spatialisation of literature as it becomes incorporated into our memory. Reading converts a diachronic sequence into something that can be apprehended synchronically. Literature, as Compagnon describes it, is a landscape and literary criticism a topography.

The *Mythologiques* is also a 'memory palace' of sorts, one that Lévi-Strauss may not, perhaps, himself construct, but he is a traveller in a mnemonic edifice created by others, which he gradually comes to inhabit and make his own. Memory is not purely personal memory, as it is for Proust's narrator, but rather a collective memory. Nevertheless, as in the earlier versions of the memory palace, reading involves a journey through a series of locations. The journey here is from the tip of South America to the Northwest Coast of Canada. For Lévi-Strauss *follows* the connections between the myth's own *imagines agentes*, patiently piecing together the lost intertext. In the process, the mythical transformations he analyses, which occurred in time (history), are converted into a network that is deployed in space, a series of bisecting paths of transformation. It is no coincidence that when Lévi-Strauss encountered a series of particularly difficult transformations, he felt compelled to construct three-dimensional models of them, which he hung in his office, like mobiles. These mobiles are the logical outcome of an analytic process that cannot be contained by the sequential linearity of prose. The analysis of myths opens up a vista. In the course of this journey from one end of a continent to another, he comes to realise that the world of mythology is round, and that, should he have chosen to travel from North to South instead of the opposite, the outcome of his studies would have been the same.

In what precedes, I have tried to reintegrate the sensory into an understanding of Lévi-Strauss's thought. My aim was to show that to understand Lévi-Strauss's thinking one must reject the false dichotomy that opposes the sensible to the intelligible and view structural anthropology as a long and complex meditation on our relationship to the perceptible world. The *Mythologiques* may be viewed, at its simplest, as a collection of images which, by virtue of the transformational principle that engendered them, provide us with a series of sensible forms to which we can entrust our own dilemmas, thoughts and emotions. In this respect, the significance of the *Mythologiques* lies in front of us, not behind us. The above parallel with Compagnon's reading of Proust further suggests that this unique work fulfils at least one possible definition of literature. One may characterise the *Mythologiques*, using a phrase from Act I of Wagner's opera *Parsifal*, a phrase that Lévi-Strauss borrows himself, in *The View from Afar*, where he quotes it as 'probably the most profound definition that anyone has ever offered for myth' (1983a: 301; 1987b: 219). It is Gurnemanz who is speaking to Parcifal, and who says: 'See, my son, to space here time doth change.'

NOTES

1. The comprehension of a concept is a set of attributes that belong to the class of things designated by that concept, i.e. its qualities. The extension of a concept is the set of things, real or ideal, to which it applies or which it designates. In the sequence 'John', 'European', 'man', 'animal' and 'being', it is apparent that each successive concept encompasses a greater number of individuals, it has a greater extension, but also possesses fewer particularities, it has a lesser comprehension.
2. Lévi-Strauss is playing here on the two senses of the term aesthetic. This semantic ambiguity goes to the heart of Lévi-Strauss's concept of *pensée sauvage*.
3. Cf. Rousseau's *Émile:* 'Man's first reason is a reason of the senses; this sensual reason serves as the basis of intellectual reason' (1979: 125).
4. The same may be said about painting, hence the futility of separating an external meaning given to the work by the intellect, entrusted to line, from the sensory impressions conveyed by colour.
5. The different ways of engaging with the sensorium across cultures, i.e. of creating sensory worlds (which are also political worlds, ethical worlds, aesthetic worlds, etc.) are central to the sensory anthropology/sociology that has been developing in the latter half of the twentieth century (see, for example, Howes 1991).
6. See James A. Boon 1972 and chapter 4 of my own book, 2007.

7. As Claude Imbert notes in this volume, with characteristic clairvoyance: '[*Tristes Tropiques*] opened a philosophical and anthropological programme, which was badly missing in the French philosophical world since the Enlightenment.'

REFERENCES

Balfour-Paul, J. 1998. *Indigo*. London: British Museum Press.

Boon, J. 1972. *From Symbolism to Structuralism: Lévi-Strauss in a Literary Tradition*. Oxford: Basil Blackwell.

Derrida, J. 2005. *Writing and Difference*. Translated by Alan Bass. London: Routledge Classics.

Howes, D. (ed.) 1991. *The Varieties of Sensory Experience*. Toronto: University of Toronto Press.

Imbert, C. 2000. 'Philosophie, anthropologie: la fin d'un malentendu', in A. Abensour (ed.), *Le XXe Siècle en France: art, politique, philosophie*. Paris: Berger-Levrault, pp. 223–37.

    2003. 'Warburg, de Kant à Boas', *L'Homme* 135: 11–40.

    2004. 'Qualia', in Michel Izard (ed.), *Claude Lévi-Straus*. Paris: Cahiers de l'Herne, pp. 432–41.

    2005. *Maurice Merleau-Ponty*. Paris: Association pour la diffusion de la pensée française.

Proust, M. 2002. *Swann's Way*. Translated by C. K. Scott Moncrieff, Terence Kilmartin and D. J. Enright. London: Vintage.

Rousseau, J.-J. 1979 [1762]. *Émile or On Education*. Translated by Allan Bloom. London: Penguin Books.

    1997 [1754–1755]. *The Discourses and Other Early Political Writings*. Edited and translated by Victor Gourevitch. Cambridge: Cambridge University Press.

Wiseman, B. 2007. *Lévi-Strauss, Anthropology and Aesthetics*. Cambridge: Cambridge University Press.

Bibliography of works by Claude Lévi-Strauss

1930. 'Picasso et le cubisme', *Documents* 2: 139–40. (Ghosted for Georges Monnet.)

1933. 'Louis-Ferdinand Céline: *Voyage au bout de la nuit*', *L'Étudiant socialiste* 4: 13–14. (Reprinted in 2004a.)

1942a. 'Indian Cosmetics', *VVV* 1: 33–5.

1942b. 'Guerra e comércio entre os índios da América do Sul', in Egon Schaden (ed.), *Leituras de etnologia Brasileira*. São Paulo: Companhia Editora Nacional, pp. 325–39.

1943a. 'The Social Use of Kinship Terms among Brazilian Indians', *American Anthropologist* 45: 398–409.

1943b. 'The Art of the Northwest Coast at the American Museum of Natural History', *Gazette des Beaux-Arts* 24: 175–82.

1944. 'Reciprocity and Hierarchy', *American Anthropologist* 46: 266–8.

1945a. 'French Sociology', in George Gurvitch and Wilbert E. Moore (eds.), *Sociology in the Twentieth Century*. New York: The Philosophical Library, pp. 503–37.

1945b. 'Le Dédoublement de la représentation dans les arts de l'Asie et de l'Amérique', *Renaissance. Revue trimestrielle publiée par l'école libre des hautes études 2* and 3: 168–86.

1945c. 'L'Analyse structurale en linguistique et anthropologie', *Word* 1: 33–53. (Reprinted in translation in 1963a, pp. 31–54.)

1947 [1945a] 'Sociologie française', *La Sociologie au XXe siècle, II*. Paris: Presses Universitaires de France, pp. 513–45.

1948. 'La Vie familiale et sociale des Indiens Nambikwara', *Journal de la Société des Américanistes* 37 (n.s.): 1–131.

1949a. *Les Structures élémentaires de la parenté*. Paris: Presses Universitaires de France.

1949b. 'L'Efficacité symbolique', *Revue d'histoire des religions* 135 (1): 5–27. (Reprinted in translation in 1963a, pp. 186–206.)

1949c. 'Le Sorcier et sa magie', *Les Temps modernes* 4 (41) (March): 3–28. (Reprinted in translation in 1963a, pp. 167–85.)

1950a. 'Introduction à l'oeuvre de Marcel Mauss', in *Sociologie et Anthropologie*. Paris: Presses Universitaires de France, pp. ix–lii.

1950b. 'Marcel Mauss', *Cahiers internationaux de sociologie* 8: 72–112.

1952a. *Race et histoire*. Paris: UNESCO.

1952b. *Race and History*. Paris: UNESCO.

1952c. 'Le Père Noël supplicié', *Les Temps modernes* 77: 1,572–90.

1953. 'Social Structure', in Alfred Kroeber (ed.), *Anthropology Today*. Chicago: University of Chicago Press, pp. 524–53.

1955a. *Tristes Tropiques*. Paris: Plon (Presses Pocket).

1955b. 'Les Mathématiques de l'homme', *Bulletin international des sciences sociales* 6: 643–51.

1955c. 'Diogène couché', *Les Temps modernes* 110: 1–34.

1955d. 'Des Indiens et leur ethnographe', *Les Temps modernes* 116: 1–50.

1955e. 'The Structural Study of Myth', *Journal of American Folklore* 68: 428–44. (Reprinted in 1967c, pp. 202–28.)

1956a. 'Les Trois Humanismes', *Demain* 35: 16. (Reprinted in 1973a, pp. 319–22.)

1956b. 'Sur les rapports entre la mythologie et le rituel', *Bulletin de la Société Française de Philosophie* 50: 99–125.

1958a. *Anthropologie structurale*. Paris: Plon.

1958b. 'L'Analyse structurale en linguistique et anthropologie', in 1958a, pp. 37–62.

1958c. 'La Geste d'Asdiwal', in *Annuaire 1958–1959*. Paris: École Pratique des Hautes Études, Section des Sciences Religieuses, pp. 3–43.

1960a. 'Les Trois Sources de la réflexion ethnologique', *Revue de l'enseignement supérieur* 1: 43–50.

1960b. 'Le Problème de l'invariance en anthropologie', *Diogène* 31: 23–33.

1960c [1967e] 'The Story of Asdiwal'. (Reprinted in Edmund Leach (ed.) 1967. *The Structural Study of Myth and Totemism*. London: Tavistock, pp. 1–48.)

1961a (with Georges Charbonnier). *Entretiens avec Claude Lévi-Strauss*. Paris: Plon–Juillard.

1961b. *Race and History: The Race Question in Modern Science*. New York: Columbia University Press.

1961c. *Race and History: The Race Question in Modern Science*. Paris: UNESCO.

1961d. *A World on the Wane*. New York: Criterion Books.

1962a. *Le Totémisme aujourd'hui*. Paris: Presses Universitaires de France.

1962b. *La Pensée sauvage*. Paris: Plon (Presses Pocket).

1962c. 'Les Limites de la notion de structure en ethnologie', in R. Bastide (ed.), *Sens et usage du terme structure dans les sciences de l'homme*. La Haye: Mouton, pp. 40–5.

1962d (with Roman Jakobson). 'Les "Chats" de Charles Baudelaire', *L'Homme. Revue française d'anthropologie* 2: 5–21.

1963a [1958a] *Structural Anthropology I*. Translated by Claire Jacobson and Brooke Grundfest Schoepf. New York: Basic Books.

1963b. *Tristes Tropiques*. Translated by J. Russell. New York: Athenaeum.

1963c. 'Réponses à quelques questions', *Groupe philosophique d'ESPRIT* 11: 628–53.

1963d. *Totemism Today*. Translated by Rodney Needham. Boston, MA: Beacon Press.

1963e. 'Split Representation in the Art of Asia and America', in *Structural Anthropology*. New York: Basic Books, pp. 245–68.

1964a. *Mythologiques, I. Le Cru et le cuit*. Paris: Plon.

1964b. *Totemism*. Translated by Rodney Needham. London: Merlin.

1965a. 'Le Triangle culinaire', *L'Arc* 26: 19–29.

1965b. 'Entretien avec M. Delahaye et Jacques Rivette', *Les Cahiers du cinéma* 26: 19–29.

1965c. 'Witnesses of our Time', *Le Figaro Littéraire*, 25 November.

1966a. *Mythologiques, II. Du miel aux cendres*. Paris: Plon.

1966b. *The Savage Mind*. London: Weidenfeld and Nicolson.

1966c. *The Savage Mind*. Chicago: University of Chicago Press.

1966d. 'The Future of Kinship Studies', in *Proceedings of the Royal Anthropological Institute of Great Britain and Ireland for 1965*. London, pp. 13–22.

1967a [1949a] *Les Structures élémentaires de la parenté* (second edition, revised and corrected). Paris and La Haye: Mouton.

1967b (with Raymond Bellour). 'Entretien avec Claude Lévi-Strauss', *Les Lettres françaises* 1,165: 1–7.

1967c. *Structural Anthropology*. Garden City, NY: Anchor.

1967d. *Tristes Tropiques*. Translated by John Russell. New York: Athenaeum.

1967e. [1960c] 'The Story of Asdiwal'. Translated by Nicolas Mann. In Edmund Leach (ed.), *The Structural Study of Myth and Totemism*. ASA Monographs 5. London: Tavistock, pp. 1–48. (Republished, with some changes by translator Monique Layton, in 1978b. *Structural Anthropology II*. London: Penguin, pp. 146–97.)

1967f. 'Une lettre de Claude Lévi-Strauss à propos de "Lévi-Strauss dans le 18ème siècle"', *Cahiers pour l'analyse*, no. 8: *L'Impensé de Jean-Jacques Rousseau* (May–June 1969).

1968. *Mythologiques, III. L'Origine des manières de table*. Paris: Plon.

1969a [1967a]. *The Elementary Structures of Kinship*. Translated by James Harle Bell, John Richard von Sturmer and Rodney Needham. London: Eyre & Spottiswoode.

1969b [1949a]. *The Elementary Structures of Kinship* (revised edition). Edited by Rodney Needham and translated by James Harle Bell, John Richard von Sturmer and Rodney Needham. Boston: Beacon Press.

1969c (with Georges Charbonnier). *Conversations with Claude Lévi-Strauss*. London: Jonathan Cape.

1969d [1964a]. *Introduction to a Science of Mythology*, I. *The Raw and the Cooked*. Translated by John and Doreen Weightman. New York and Evanston: Harper & Row.

1969e. *Totemism*. Translated by Rodney Needham. Harmondsworth: Penguin.

1970 [1964a]. *Introduction to a Science of Mythology*, I. *The Raw and the Cooked*. Translated by John and Doreen Weightman. London: Jonathan Cape.

1971a. *Mythologiques, IV. L'Homme nu*. Paris: Plon.

1971b. 'Race et culture', *Revue internationale des sciences sociales* 23 (4): 647–66.

1971c. 'Le Temps du mythe', *Annales* 26: 533–40.

1972a. *Structural Anthropology I*. Translated by Claire Jacobson and Brooke Grundfest Schoepf. Harmondsworth: Penguin Books.

1972b [1949a]. 'The Effectiveness of Symbols', in *Structural Anthropology*. Translated by Claire Jacobson and Brooke Grundfest Schoepf. Harmondsworth: Penguin Books, pp. 181–201.

1973a. *Anthropologie structurale deux*. Paris: Plon.

1973b. *Introduction to a Science of Mythology*, II. *From Honey to Ashes*. Translated by John and Doreen Weightman. London: Jonathan Cape.

1973c [1955a]. *Tristes Tropiques*. Translated by John and Doreen Weightman. London: Jonathan Cape. (Also translated as 1961. *A World on the Wane*. New York: Criterion Books.)

1973d. *Introduction to a Science of Mythology*, II. *From Honey to* Ashes. New York: Harper & Row.

1975. *La Voie des masques (Les Sentiers de la création)*. 2 vols. Geneva: Éditions Albert Skira.

1976a. *Structural Anthropology II*. Chicago: University of Chicago Press.

1976b. 'Jean-Jacques Rousseau, Founder of the Sciences of Man', in *Structural Anthropology II*. Chicago: University of Chicago Press, pp. 33–43.

1976c. 'Structuralisme et empirisme', *L'Homme XVI* (2–3): 23–38.

1976d. *Structural Anthropology II*. Translated by Monique Layton. New York: Basic Books.

1976e [1942b]. 'Guerra e comércio entre os índios da América do Sul', in Egon Schaden (ed.), *Leituras de Etnologia Brasileira*. São Paulo: Companhia Editora Nacional.

1976f. 'Preface', in Roman Jakobson, *Six Leçons sur le son et le sens*. Paris: Minuit, pp. 7–18.

1977a. 'New York post- et préfiguratif', *Paris–New York*, June–September.

1977b. *L'Identité, séminaire interdisciplinaire dirigé par Claude Lévi-Strauss*. Paris: Grasset.

1977c. *Structural Anthropology II*. London: Allen Lane.

1977d [1958a]. *Structural Anthropology*. Translated by C. Jacobson and B. Grundfest Schoepf. Harmondsworth: Penguin Books.

1978a. *Myth and Meaning: Five Talks for Radio*. Toronto: University of Toronto Press.

1978b. *Structural Anthropology II*. Translated by Monique Layton. Harmondsworth: Penguin (Peregrine Books).

1978c. *Introduction to a Science of Mythology*, III. *The Origin of Table Manners*. Translated by John and Doreen Weightman. London: Jonathan Cape.

1978d. *Introduction to a Science of Mythology*, III. *The Origin of Table Manners*. New York: Harper & Row.

1979a. *La Voie des masques*. Paris: Plon (Presses Pocket).

1979b. 'Entretien avec Claude Lévi-Strauss', in Raymond Bellour and C. Clément (eds.), *Claude Lévi-Strauss: Textes de et sur Claude Lévi-Strauss*. Paris: Gallimard, pp. 157–209.

1981. *Introduction to a Science of Mythology*, IV. *The Naked Man*. Translated by John and Doreen Weightman. London: Jonathan Cape.

1982 [1975] [1979a]. *The Way of the Masks*. Translated by Sylvia Modelski. Seattle, WA: University of Washington Press.

1983a. *Le Regard éloigné*. Paris: Plon.

1983b. 'La Famille', in *Le Regard éloigné*. Paris: Plon, pp. 65–92.

1983c. 'Histoire et ethnologie', *Annales: économies, sociétés, civilisations* 38 (6): 1,217–31.

1984. *Paroles données*. Paris: Plon.

1985a. *The View from Afar*. Translated by Joachim Neugroschel and Phoebe Hoss. Oxford: Blackwell.

1985b. *The View from Afar*. New York: Basic Books.

1985c [1977a]. 'New York in 1941' ('New York post- et préfiguratif'), *Paris–New York*, June–September. (Reproduced in 1985a and 1985b: chap. 20.)

1985d. 'Race and Culture', in 1985a, pp. 3–24.

1985e. *La Potière jalouse*. Paris: Plon.

1987a [1950a]. *Introduction to the Work of Marcel Mauss*. Translated by Felicity Baker. London: Routledge & Kegan Paul.

1987b [1983a]. *The View From Afar*. Translated by Joachim Neugroschel and Phoebe Hoss. Harmondsworth: Penguin (Peregrine Books).

1987c. *Anthropology and Myth. Lectures 1951–1982*. Translated by Roy Willis. Oxford: Basil Blackwell.

1987d. ' Structuralism and Ecology' in 1987b, pp. 101–20.

1988a (with Didier Eribon). *De Près et de loin*. Paris: Plon.

1988b. *The Jealous Potter*. Translated by Bénédicte Chorier. Chicago: University of Chicago Press.

1989a. *Tristes Tropiques*. Translated by John and Doreen Weightman. London: Pan Books.

1989b. *Des Symboles et leurs doubles*. Paris: Plon.

1989c. *The Jealous Potter*. Translated by Bénédicte Chorier. Chicago: University of Chicago Press.

1990a. 'La Place de la culture japonaise dans le monde', *Revue d'esthétique* 18: 9–21.

1990b. *The Naked Man*. Chicago: University of Chicago Press.

1991a. *Histoire de Lynx*. Paris: Plon.

1991b [1988a] (with Didier Eribon). *Conversations with Claude Lévi-Strauss*. Translated by Paula Wissing. London and Chicago: University of Chicago Press.

1992. *Tristes Tropiques*. Translated by John and Doreen Weightman. New York: Penguin Books USA.

1993a. *Regarder, écouter, lire*. Paris: Plon.

1993b. 'Aux gens de Tokyo', *Magazine littéraire* (special issue: 'Claude Lévi Strauss: esthétique et structuralisme') 311: 47–8.

1994a. *Saudades do Brasil*. Paris: Plon.

1994b. 'Sur Jean de Léry', in Jean de Léry, *Histoire d'un voyage faict en la terre du Brésil (1587)*. Paris: Le Livre de Poche, pp. 5–14.

1995a. *Myth and Meaning: Cracking the Code of Culture*. New York: Schocken Books.

1995b. *The Story of Lynx*. Translated by Catherine Tihanyi. Chicago and London: University of Chicago Press.

1995c. *Saudades Do Brasil*. Translated by Sylvia Modelski. Seattle: University of Washington Press.

1995d. 'Myth and Music', in *Myth and Meaning*. New York: Schocken Books, pp. 44–54.

1997. *Look, Listen, Read*. Translated by Brian C. J. Singer. New York: Basic Books.

1998a. 'Retours en arrière', *Les Temps modernes* 598: 66–77.

1998b. 'La sexualité féminine et l'origine de la société', *Les Temps modernes* 598: 78–84.

2000. 'Postface', *L'Homme* 154–5: 713–20.

2001a. *Race et histoire. Race et Culture*. Paris: Albin Michel/UNESCO.

2001b. 'Race, History, and Culture', in *The UNESCO Courier* (December): 6–9.

2003 (with Dominique-Antoine Grisoni). 'Un dictionnaire intime', *Magazine Littéraire* (special issue: 'Lévi-Strauss: l'ethnologie ou la passion des autres') Hors série 5: 16–17.

2004a [1933]. 'Louis-Ferdinand Céline: *Voyage au bout de la nuit*', in Michel Izard (ed.), *Claude Lévi-Strauss*. Paris: Éditions de l'Herne, pp. 23–4.

2004b. 'Pensée mythique et pensée scientifique', in Michel Izard (ed.), *Claude Lévi-Strauss*. Paris: Éditions de l'Herne, pp. 40–2.

2004c (with Marcel Hénaff). 'L'Anthropologie face à la philosophie', *Groupe philosophique d'ESPRIT* (special issue: 'Claude Lévi-Strauss: une anthropologie "bonne à penser" ') 301: 88–109.

2004d. *Groupe philosophique d'ESPRIT* 301. (Special issue: 'Claude Lévi-Strauss: une anthropologie "bonne à penser"'.)

2008 *Œuvres*. Paris: Gallimard, Éditions La Pléiade.

Index